GREAT
AMERICAN
AUTOMOBILES
OF THE

PUBLICATIONS INTERNATIONAL, LTD.

BY RICHARD M. LANGWORTH • JAMES R. FLAMMANG
AND THE AUTO EDITORS OF CONSUMER GUIDE®

Louis Weber, C.E.O.
Publications International, Ltd.
7373 North Cicero Avenue
Lincolnwood, Illinois 60646

Manufactured in the U.S.A.

8 7 6 5 4 3 2 1

ISBN: 1-56173-274-5

Library of Congress Catalog Card Number: 92-80937

Principal authors
James R. Flammang
Richard M. Langworth
Chris Poole

Photography
The editors gratefully acknowledge the cooperation of the following people who have supplied photography to help make this book possible. They are listed below, along with the page number(s) of their photos:

Nicky Wright; 6-7, 14, 15, 17, 32, 33, 41, 44, 45, 54, 58, 59, 94, 119, 131, 135, 136, 137, 154, 155, 172, 173, 174, 175, 182, 183, 186, 189, 190, 192, 218, 219, 231, 251, 262, 267, 302, 303 **Milton Gene Kieft;** 8, 34, 35, 52, 53, 75, 81, 90, 123, 129, 133, 140, 226, 227, 241, 260, 261, 263, 279 **Sam Griffith;** 18, 21, 60, 61, 75, 96, 97, 131, 170, 171, 187, 180, 188, 201, 236, 237, 271, 272, 275 **Doug Mitchel;** 20, 24, 26, 27, 28, 29, 33, 42, 50, 51, 55, 56, 57, 59, 65, 76, 79, 86, 87, 88, 89, 104, 105, 117, 135, 144, 145, 148, 149, 153, 159, 161, 168, 169, 180, 181, 187, 193, 204, 210, 211, 224, 225, 232, 233, 240, 241, 250, 252, 253, 254, 256, 260, 264, 265, 266, 269, 276, 277, 278, 280, 281, 288, 289, 294, 295, 305, 311 **Mark Garcia;** 22, 23 **Vince Manocchi;** 23, 62, 63, 65, 66, 68, 69, 74, 76, 77, 80, 82, 83, 86, 87, 100, 101, 102, 103, 108, 109, 113, 126, 132, 146, 147, 163, 189, 209, 221, 255 **Lisa Orrison, Buick Public Relations;** 30, 32, 34, 36, 37, 38, 40, 43, 44, 45, 47, 48 **Mike Mueller;** 30, 31, 37, 46, 47, 49, 85, 90, 91, 111, 116, 128, 130, 153, 166, 177, 179, 194, 195, 198, 199, 212, 276, 277, 288, 289, 298, 299, 300, 301 **David Gooley;** 35, 312 **Scott Baxter;** 39, 40, 72, 73 **Ken Beebe/Kugler Studio;** 46, 84, 118, 156, 157 **Jerry Heasley;** 49, 60, 164, 165, 205, 290, 291 **Dan Lyons;** 54, 55, 99, 124, 125, 138, 139, 151, 152, 153, 155, 166, 196, 197, 202, 203, 242, 244, 245, 273 **Bud Juneau;** 56, 57, 70, 71, 81, 88, 91, 110, 111, 141, 150, 151, 160, 162, 167, 208, 209, 213, 215, 234, 235, 282, 283, 307, 313 **Larry A. Paule;** 59 **Colin Peck;** 63 **Orazio Aiello;** 64, 78 **Richard Spiegelman;** 67, 178, 179, 184, 185, 304, 308, 309, 314, 315, 316, 317 **Kari St. Antoine, Chevrolet Public Relations;** 79, 92 **Jim Smart;** 84, 227, 230, 243 **Rob Van Schaick;** 22, 93, 132, 191 **Terry**

Boyce; 98, 242, 243, 245 **Bob Tenney**; 106, 107 **David Talbot**; 109, 123 **Chrysler Historical Collection**; 112, 117, 118, 120, 121, 122, 126, 131, 182, 185, 244, 247, 259, 263 **S. Scott Hutchinson**; 114, 115 **Thomas Glatch**; 134, 140, 141, 159, 165, 220, 221, 285, 286, 287 **Alice Preston, Brooks Stevens Automotive Museum, Mequon, Wisconsin**; 142, 143 **Ford Photographic Service**; 149, 161, 171, 190, 194, 209, 214, 216, 300 **Andre VanDePutte**; 176 **John Collier**; 189 **Gary D. Smith**; 200, 201 **Robert Sorgatz**; 206, 207 **Jeff Medves**; 210 **Mitchell Dannenberg**; 216, 217 **Helen J. Early, Oldsmobile History Center**; 222, 223, 224, 227, 228, 229, 231, 238, 239 **Joseph J. Bohovic**; 248, 249, 256, 257 **Alan Hewko**; 257 **Scott Brandt**; 268, 269 **Gene's Studio**; 270 **Abey Studio**; 274 **Mitch Frumkin**; 274 **Rick Asher, Pontiac Photo Archives**; 274, 276, 280, 284, 292, 293 **Alex Gabbard**; 290 **Joseph H. Wherry**; 310, 311 **Zoom Photos**; 312

Owners

Special thanks to the owners of the cars featured in this book for their enthusiastic cooperation. They are listed below, along with the page number(s) on which their cars appear:

Michele King; 6-7 **Frank Wrenick**; 8 **Ken Carmack**; 14 **Ken Havekdst**; 14, 15 **Lee Pontius**; 17 **James and Robert Lojewski**; 18 **Paul Gallo**; 20 **James Lojewski**; 21 **Samuel and Wanda Roth**; 22, 23 **John L. Maciejewski**; 23 **Rick Shick**; 26, 27 **Larry E. Driscoll**; 28, 29 **John Wacha**; 30 **Russel and Shirley Dawson**; 30, 31 **Rex Harris**; 32, 33 **Nick Schafsnitz**; 33 **Les Raye**; 34, 35 **Junior Markin**; 37 **Sue and Horace Mennella**; 39 **Sue and Sally Kuss**; 40 **Ted West**; 41 **Larry Simex**; 42 **Barney Smith**; 44, 45 **Dennis M. Phipps**; 46, 47 **Larry Miller**; 46 **Dan Curry**; 49 **M & W Gutowski**; 49 **James Rudnick**; 50, 51 **Christine and Robert Waldock**; 52, 53 **Ed Oberhaus**; 54, 58, 59 **Dean Stansfield**; 54, 55 **John Gaylord**; 55 **Pete Bose**; 56 **Robert Hallada**; 56, 57 **Sid Slayton**; 59 **Larry A. Paule**; 59 **Bill Woodman**; 60 **Paul S. Bellino**; 60 **Eugene Fattore**; 61 **Alfred L. Olson**; 62, 63 **William Douwsma**; 64 **Terry Lucas**; 65 **John T. Finster**; 66, 86 **Chip Werstein**; 68, 69 **Thomas Crockatt**; 69 **Don Maich**; 70, 71 **Chuck Swafford**; 70, 71 **Jack Gratzianna**; 72, 73 **Douglas and Bev Finch**; 74 **Herbert Zinn**; 75 **David Dawes**;75 **William R. Beutel**; 76 **Les Huckins**; 76 **John and Jeanne Finster**; 77 **Gregory Alan Bruns**; 78 **Howard L. Baker**; 81 **Scott Maze**; 81 **Allen Cummins**; 83 **Bill Kuntz**; 84 **Frank Spittle**; 84, 118, 156, 157 **Mr. and Mrs. Richard D. Miller**; 85 **Burt and Lynda Neuner**; 86 **Earl F. Hansen**; 87 **David A. Ulrich**; 87 **Ernest Gigliotti**; 88 **Ramshead Auto Collection**; 88 **Mike D'Amico**; 88, 89 **Paul McGuire**; 90, 91 **Donald R. Crile**; 90 **Charley Lillard**; 91 **Greg G. Grams, Volo Museum, Volo, IL**; 92, 93, 132, 191 **"T" and Ed DeCamp**; 94 **Kenneth J. Patt, M.D.**; 96, 97 **William Korbel**; 99 **Richard Carpenter**; 100, 101, 102, 103 **Lou Schultz**; 104, 105 **Duane and Carol Silvius**; 105 **Bryan McGilvray**; 106, 107 **Alois Peter Warren II**; 109 **Specialty Sales**; 110, 111 **Larri Stumpf**; 113 **Paul Garlick**; 114, 115 **Patti and J.R. Buxman**; 116 **Larry Rohde**; 117 **Jim Donaldson**; 119 **Scott Brubaker**; 123 **Larry Barnett**; 123 **Ray Banuls**; 124, 125 **Manny Montgomery**; 126, 127 **Tony and Suzanne George**; 128 **William E. Wetherholt**; 129 **Mike Marra**; 130 **Dennis Guest**; 131 **Robert Fraser**; 131 **Eric D. Rosynek**; 132 **Gary R. Thalman**; 133 **Jeffrey Baker**; 134 **Al Fraser**; 135 **Mark Hansen**; 135 **Larry Bell**; 136, 137 **Jack Bart**; 138, 139 **Charlie Wells**; 140 **David Hooten**; 140, 141, 165 **Mike Cowles**; 141 **George Holterman**; 145 **Jack and Holly Stewart**; 146 **Barbara Walker Cadena**; 147 **Claud E. Daniel, Jr.**; 148, 149 **Howard A. Moore**; 150, 151 **Arnie Addison**; 150, 151 **Dick Kainer**; 152 **Kenneth and Linda Coleman**; 153 **Richard Monaco**; 153 **Daniel Mitchell**; 154, 155 **Vic and Cathy Falcone**; 155 **Jerry Butak**; 159 **Christopher M. Krueger**; 159 **Quentin Bacon**; 160 **George Lyons**; 161 **Alice Greunke**; 163 **Ed and Debbie Werder**; 166 **Edward J. Wey**; 166 **Jerry Gibino**; 167 **Robert and Mary Lu Secondi**; 168, 169 **Ed Putz**; 170, 171 **Chris Dawalt**; 172 **Biff and Donna Hitzeman**; 172 **Tom Haase**; 172, 173 **Gary Parttee**; 174, 175 **Glenn Moist**; 176 **Robert Kurtz**; 177 **Jack Shrum**; 178, 179 **Lawrence Pavia**; 180 **Joseph Pieroni**; 180, 181 **Allan S. Murray**; 182, 183 **Blaine Jenkins**; 186 **Col. J.L. Sanders**; 187 **Andy Hotton**; 187 **Frank J. Monhart III**; 187, 188 **Patricia and Rexford Parker**; 189 **Sherman Williams**; 189 **Christine's Classic Continentals, St. Petersburg, FL**; 189 **Vince and Norma Rhodes**; 190 **Donald C. McCallum**; 192 **A. Boyd Anderson**; 193 **Donald F. and Chris Dunn**; 194, 195 **Mark E. Figliozzi**; 196, 197 **Joseph Barrera**; 200, 201 **Bob Sejnost**; 201 **Michael Tesauro, Jr.**; 202, 203 **Bob Bychowski**; 204 **Jim Labertew/ RPM Motors, Scottsdale, AZ**; 206, 207 **Jack Karleskind**; 208, 209, 213, 215 **Joe Burke**; 209 **William Peterson**; 210 **John Cook**; 210 **Ron Voyles**; 211 **Carl J. Beck**; 212 **Hal Kemp**; 216, 217 **George Kling**; 218, 219 **Henry Isaksen**; 220, 221 **Jim Davidson**; 221 **Dennis Urban**; 226, 227 **James and Mary Engle**; 231 **Ken Nelson**; 232, 233 **Michael Morocco**; 234 **Scott Campbell**; 234, 235 **Doug and Judy Badgley**; 236 **Robert Klein**; 237 **David and Norma Wasilewski**; 240, 241 **Jack Driesenga**; 241 **Ron and Kate Hanaway**; 242, 243, 245 **Don McLennan**; 242, 244, 245 **Charles P. Geissler**; 248, 249 **Walter Schenk**; 249 **William W. Kramer**; 252, 253 **Jeff and Trish Holmes**; 254 **Harry and Virginia DeMenge**; 255 **Dave Bartholomew**; 256, 257 **Mary Lee Cipriano**; 257 **Steve Maysonet**; 288, 289 **Bruce Rhoades**; 288, 289 **Rodney Brumbaugh**; 294, 295 **David L. Robb**; 298, 299 **Keith Hazley**; 300, 301 **Stephen Schonegg**; 302, 303 **Rudy and Bonnie Patane**; 304 **Janet Carter Wright**; 304 **M.J. Shelton**; 305 **Bob Patrick**; 307 **Doug Anderson**; 308 **Stephen Gottfried**; 308 **Robert Thorton**; 308, 309 **Doug Movsuik**; 309 **Ronald A. Smith**; 310 **Harold Von Brocken**; 312 **Tom Griffith**; 313 **Don Ross**; 314 **Mel Quirk**; 314, 315 **Mr. and Mrs. Ralph M. Mathiot**; 315 **Mark Ward**; 316 **Brad and Bev Taffs**; 317 **The Beechy Family**; 260, 261 **Mike Baker**; 260 **Tony Legacher**; 262 **Robert Beechy**; 263 **Carl S. Berg**; 264, 265 **Barry and Barb Bales**; 267 **Robert and Karen Christanell**; 268, 269 **Joseph Smiesko**; 269 **Melvin Lewis**; 270 **Wanda Habenicht**; 271 **Michael and Patricia Kelso**; 272 **John W. Siebel**; 273 **Alan N. Basile**; 274 **Jerry Yonker**; 274 **Richard Witek**; 275 **Joe Kelly**; 276, 277 **Autoputer, Inc.**; 276, 277 **Mike and Jim Schaudek**; 278 **Richard and Madeline Martindale**; 279 **Paul Habura**; 280, 281 **Chris Terry**; 282, 283 **Don and Linda Davis**; 282, 283 **David Snodgrass**; 285, 287 **Bill Pearson**; 285 **Si Rogers**; 286

C O N T E N T S

INTRODUCTION

In the annals of automotive history, the Sixties will perhaps best be remembered as a time of ponycars and muscle machines. Yet while these cars undeniably dominate the interest of today's collectors, they represent just a few of the innovative concepts unveiled during this decade of automotive diversity.

Much of the product expansion witnessed in the Sixties was due to the demise of many independent automakers during the previous decade, as well as to a recession that crippled the nation's economy during 1958. Previously, most companies could be categorized as makers of luxury cars, mid-price cars, low-price cars, or economy cars; rarely did they succeed (or try to succeed) in more than one facet of the market. But fewer players meant less competition in many segments, and the economic downturn spurred renewed interest in fuel economy. As a result, the remaining manufacturers rushed to fill the voids; while the luxury makes had learned that it was unwise to "dilute" their hard-earned image by bringing out cheaper products, virtually every other manufacturer had sprouted at least a three-tier product line by mid-decade.

Economy cars were nothing new to American buyers in 1960, but never before had there been so many from which to choose. Most up to that point were cartoonlike European makes with questionable reputations and spotty dealer networks, but that changed with the introduction of the Chevy Corvair, Ford Falcon, and Plymouth Valiant—all of which debuted the same year. Personal-luxury cars had likewise been seen before, but not in such great numbers. The Studebaker Hawk, Chrysler's 300 letter-series, and Ford's Thunderbird all hailed from the Fifties, but the Pontiac Grand Prix and Buick Riviera joined the fray in '62/'63, while the Olds Toronado that debuted in 1966 (followed by the Cadillac Eldorado in '67), "re-introduced" front-wheel drive to America.

But the decade is perhaps best remembered for its muscle cars; mid-size coupes with big-inch engines. Though the award for originating the concept commonly goes to the 1964 Pontiac GTO, automotive historians point to other examples going as far back as the '20s. Nevertheless, the overwhelming success of the GTO spawned a host of rivals, as virtually every manufacturer jumped on the performance bandwagon. Offshoots like the Olds 4-4-2, Ford Torino GT, and Plymouth GTX were expected; oddities such as AMC's SC/Rambler were not.

While the muscle car craze fizzled (or more accurately, was extinguished) in the early Seventies, the other automotive legacy of the '60s—the ponycar—did not. The 1965 Mustang found a previously untapped market niche and touched off what could only be regarded as an automotive revolution. This exciting new upstart inspired many imitators, and although some of the latter have since faded away, the breed survived the turmoil of the succeeding decades and is still with us today.

Despite the fact that many of the independent manufacturers were no longer in the ball game during the '60s, the expanded model lineups fielded by the Big Three, AMC, and Studebaker resulted in a virtual automotive smorgasbord for the American buyer. From ponycars to muscle cars, gas misers to personal luxury yachts, the public faced an array of offerings the likes of which had never before been seen. Many of the most memorable are celebrated within these pages. We hope that *Great American Automobiles of the '60s* captures your imagination, and fosters increased appreciation for the style, spirit, and significance of these classic machines.

The Auto Editors of CONSUMER GUIDE®

1967 Mustang

1960-61
AMC/Rambler Ambassador

Dropping the respected names of Nash and Hudson probably wasn't the smartest thing George Romney ever did, but it wasn't that important, either. The crucial decision—made after AMC president George Mason died in 1954 and Romney took the helm of the newly christened American Motors—was to quit competing across-the-board with the Big Three.

Romney did this by concentrating heavily on the Rambler, which had carved out a niche for itself with economy-minded buyers. For 1956 he had restyled and expanded the Rambler line, and by 1958's unexpected recession he looked like the Wizard of Oz: Sales of big cars bottomed, and Romney was left gloating over his sudden success. It was a case of brilliant timing. All over the country people were getting into Ramblers.

American Motors, which had bumped along at the 100,000-car level for its first three years of life, suddenly found its sales doubled. A year later they doubled again. By 1960, Rambler was number three in the industry, displacing traditional third-place Plymouth. It was the first time an "independent" had scored that high since the 1929 Essex.

The decision to drop the Nash and Hudson brands was made not to kill off two fine old names, but to emphasize AMC's departure from previous practices. Indeed, up until almost the last moment, a large Rambler-based car called the "Ambassador" (the old Nash model name) had been in clay model form bearing Nash and Hudson badges. When this model finally emerged in production as the 1958 "Rambler Ambassador," it was found to be only modestly downsized from the previous big Hudson and Nash. It lost four and one-half inches of wheelbase and a hundred-odd pounds, but it was still powered by the AMC 327 V-8 and had even more horsepower than the '57 big cars. That made it livelier, but without stretching your imagination too much, you could call it a kind of gas-guzzling dinosaur—the type of car Mr. Romney said he wasn't building anymore.

"It was a hedge—a kind of failsafe," remembered former AMC chairman Roy D. Chapin, Jr. "If the small car gambit went bad, we had the Ambassador shell and could expand on it. As it happened, the small cars didn't go bad, so the Ambassador kind of hung around as a sidelight." A valid summation indeed, as in model year 1958, the Ambassador's first year as a Rambler, they managed to sell exactly 1340 examples.

While AMC continued to cut a swathe as America's favorite small car builder, the Ambassador served out its stopgap function. It was too prestigious to drop, too insignificant to publicize much. Sales continued to be modest, topping 23,000 during 1960. This was a good rate for a company as relatively small as American Motors, and justified retaining the Ambassador in the line, but still not a large share of the total.

There were only three body styles, all four-doors: a sedan, hardtop, and hardtop wagon, though some wagons were available in six- or eight-passenger configurations. There were also three trim levels: Deluxe (with cheap trim for fleet use only), Super, and Custom. This all combined to give nine permutations, among which several are exceedingly rare: only 302 Deluxe fleet-sedans, 637 Super eight-passenger wagons, and 435 Custom hardtop wagons. Customs differed from Supers in minor items of body trim and offered a clock, full wheel discs, foam rear seat cushions, padded dash, and padded sun visors as standard equipment. Base prices started at $2395 for the fleet model Deluxe, and rose to about $3200 for the Custom hardtop wagon. Typically equipped, an Ambassador Custom sold for $4000, or about $300 more than a comparable Nash Ambassador back in 1957.

Styling was confined to a facelift, but it came off well on the 1960 model: a full-width eggcrate grille, surmounted by stand-up letters spelling AMBASSADOR. One new feature was a compound windshield, which wrapped around at the top as well as the sides. A full-width bodyside molding, enclosing brushed aluminum on Customs or painted the two-tone color on Supers, added to the impression of length and further distinguished the Ambassador from the much shorter Rambler. Performance, with the 327 delivering 250 or 270 bhp, was decent but not exciting; these were not hot rods that would offer any challenge to the big-block Chevys, Fords, or Plymouths.

American Motors had a banner year in 1960, building nearly half a million cars. It was by far the largest volume on record, and for the first time in AMC history, sales topped $1 billion. But it is important to remember (and AMC did) that the Ambassador was very much a peripheral product, and that prosperity largely depended on the Rambler.

With that in mind, perhaps, a rather different array of models was offered in 1961. The public's fascination with four-door hardtops was waning, so these were given the ax. Sedans and wagons with conventional B-pillars were all that remained. The fleet-series Deluxe stayed on, though it saw just 273 copies (the Ambassador was hardly a fleet-type car). A new entry was the five-passenger Custom 400, a luxury Custom with front bucket seats selling for $200 more than the standard version. The idea was to take advantage of the new fad for bucket seats and stick shifts, but AMC had no floorshift, and its column shift was notoriously clumsy.

The '61 retained the old bodyshell but was radically facelifted, the front fenders extended to a prowlike front end that looked like an old Spanish-American War battleship. The quad headlamps were now placed outboard of a smaller, horizontal-bar grille that peaked in the center, repeating the sharp-nosed theme. Side trim and interiors were shuffled; the drivetrain was unchanged.

It wasn't a sparkling year for anybody—sales were well down from 1960, and AMC's small cars were faced with potent competition from the new Big Three compacts. The Ambassador accounted for less than 19,000 units, and ran up another handful of ultra-rarities: The eight-passenger wagons barely made 1000 sales, and the Custom 400, introduced late in April 1961, found only 831 buyers.

SPECIFICATIONS

Engine:	ohv V-8, 287 cid (4.00 × 3.25), 250/270 bhp
Transmissions:	3-speed manual; overdrive and 3-speed Flash-O-Matic automatic optional
Suspension front:	upper and lower A-arms, coil springs
Suspension rear:	live axle on 4-link trailing arms, coil springs
Brakes:	front/rear drums
Wheelbase (in.):	117
Weight (lbs):	3343-3592
Top speed (mph):	NA
0-60 mph (sec):	NA
Production:	**1960** 23,798 **1961** 18,842

Opposite page, middle: *Top-line Ambassador for 1960 rode a longer wheelbase than "lesser" Ramblers, but styling was quite similar.* Opposite page, top: *Stylized two-tone interior matched the strangely sculptured exterior of the 1961 Ambassador (below and opposite page, bottom), which this year looked markedly different from other Ramblers.*

1963-64
AMC/Rambler
Ambassador & Classic

American Motors reached the pinnacle of prosperity in the early '60s. They had invented something new and different in the stubby, slow, but well built and economical Rambler. However, the handwriting was on the wall for AMC as early as 1960, when the larger manufacturers all fielded their own compacts. As the decade wore on, AMC corralled less and less of total industry sales. In 1963, for example, they built as many cars as they had in 1960, but overall total car sales had increased so much that it gave AMC only sixth place in production; the same output in 1960 had put them third.

In early 1962, George Romney resigned as president and chairman of AMC to run for governor of Michigan. New president Roy Abernethy, whose background included Kaiser and Packard and who had built the great AMC sales effort under Romney, reacted to the mounting sales problem in a logical way: "Let's get rid of this Romney image." But in across-the-board face-offs with the Big Three, AMC was at a disadvantage. It lacked the resources of GM, Ford, and Chrysler, and it hadn't the sales volume to spread out new model expenses and advertising over a million or so cars. An ace in the hole was chief stylist Richard A. Teague, who proved adept at reskinning the dowdy products of his predecessors and inventing new and interesting models like the Marlin, Javelin, and AMX (see entries). The top-of-the-line underwent repeated changes in this period, as management tried to slot it into an area where it would sell better and be a more intrinsic part of the AMC family. In 1962, with a decent share of the compact market still intact, it emerged as a deluxe Rambler, sharing the latter's wheelbase and bodyshell.

For 1963 Teague completely restyled the Rambler, and the Ambassador with it. The earlier body had been around essentially since 1956, and badly needed replacement. Teague's successor was a smooth, streamlined affair on a slightly larger (112 inch) wheelbase, with curved side glass and a clean grille. Gone were the curious angles, semi-tailfins, and tortured sheetmetal of the past. It was an altogether competent styling job, and the following year Teague applied the same design to the smaller Rambler American.

A Mercedes-like three-number model designation was developed, with the Americans occupying 200-400 series, the Rambler Classic 500-700, and the Rambler Ambassador 800-900. To the usual four-door sedan and wagon bodies, a new two-door sedan was added and, in 1964, a two-door hardtop. Unfortunately, the ground-up restyle was a tremendous investment for a smallish company, and AMC had to make do with the timeworn 195-cid six and 327 V-8, which had been around since the

SPECIFICATIONS

Engines:	ohv I-6, 195.6 cid (3.13 × 4.25), 127/138 bhp; ohv V-8, 287 cid (3.75 × 3.25), 198 bhp; 327 cid (4.00 × 3.25), 250/270 bhp
Transmissions:	3-speed manual; overdrive and Flash-O-Matic 3-speed automatic optional
Suspension front:	upper and lower A-arms, coil springs
Suspension rear:	live axle on 4-link trailing arms, coil springs
Brakes:	front/rear drums
Wheelbase (in.):	112.0
Weight (lbs):	3100-3340
Top speed (mph):	NA
0-60 mph (sec):	NA

Production: 1963 Classic Six 194,840 **Classic Eight** 41,186 **Ambassador** 37,811 **1964 Classic Six** 146,813 **Classic Eight** 59,486 **Ambassador** 18,693

Nash and Hudson days. In 1964, a decrease in bore produced a 287 cid version of the V-8, optional on the Rambler Classic.

Baseline Classic 550s were essentially fleet cars, detrimmed and cut to a competitive $2100 base for the sedan models. They accounted for an encouraging 75,000 sales. The bread and butter Rambler was the 660 (135,000 sales), a more posh version with carpets, armrests, Captive Air tires on wagons, and a few minor goodies. The Rambler 770 added as standard a clock, padded dash and visors, full wheel covers, and foam seats.

The Ambassador offered a similar three-level array of trim stages labeled 800 (foam cushions but little else that you'd call a bonus), 880 (armrests, carpets, hood insulation, dome light switch, etc.) and 990 (same extra equipment as Rambler 770).

The feature that chiefly distinguished it from the Rambler, however, was its standard V-8, still at 250 horsepower, with 270 optional. With the Ambassador sharing virtually every other feature with the cheaper Rambler, the V-8 was the only reason to pay the extra money for one (about $300-$400 car for car), since you could not get a V-8 Rambler. The evidence is that AMC had finally hit upon the right Ambassador formula: sales of '63s exceeded 37,000, a record for the model. Also, people definitely wanted luxury: Ambassador 990s outsold 880s nearly 2-to-1, and the baseline 800 hardly registered on the graphs. (Only 43 two-doors were built.)

In 1964, AMC's emphasis was on the redesigned American—as pretty a car as Dick Teague ever crafted. Rambler/Ambassador changes were confined to a facelift, plus one new model, a two-door hardtop. Offered only as an upper-level Rambler 770 or Ambassador, the hardtop offered an enormous glass area, and sales were brisk. Especially attractive was the Rambler Typhoon, a limited edition (2520 units) painted Solar Yellow with black roof and front bucket seats.

Striving again to fine-tune his marketing attack, Roy Abernethy now decreed a move that George Romney would never let him do: put V-8s into Ramblers. To give them some sales room, he pared the Ambassador line to four models, all 990s. The Rambler's 287 was a sprightly engine, probably capable of a lot more power than it produced; but it wasn't the key to riches. People still definitely visualized Ramblers as economy cars, and sixes outsold V-8s by a wide margin. Again the midrange 660 enjoyed most of the sales. The Ambassador, which looked more like a Rambler than ever now, sold at only 50 percent of its 1963 level; even the addition of a "loaded" 990-H model with "everything standard" ($3000) did not rescue the top-of-the-line in 1964.

During calendar year 1964, AMC built fewer than 400,000 cars for the first time since 1961, falling to eighth in the industry. In the next few years it would drop still further behind, ending the decade with annual outputs of about a quarter-million units. The company's problem was twofold: Its traditional best-seller, the Rambler, was no longer in vogue, because prosperity was back and with it a public thirst for horsepower and performance; and because the new models AMC was introducing were not regarded as unique enough to change the buying habits of traditional Big Three customers. It still had many interesting developments ahead, but American Motors as giant-killer had come and gone.

Both pages, bottom: For 1963, Ambassadors rode the same wheelbase as Classics, and styling differed only in minor trim variations. The Ambassador's trump card was its standard V-8, a feature not offered in the Classic that year. In 1964, however, Classic gained a V-8 option (though it was smaller than the Ambassador's), while Ambassador added a top-line two-door hardtop called the 990-H (below).

1965-66
AMC/Rambler
Ambassador & Classic

Ramblers of the mid-'60s offered several contradictions in terms, not the least of which was their advertising slogan. "The Sensible Spectaculars" was certainly an oxymoron if there ever was one. One reason for the company's schizoid image was the fact that it was in a state of transformation, going from a specialty manufacturer of economy cars to a provider of "something for everybody" like General Motors—but on a vastly reduced scale.

Hindsight analyses invariably conclude that AMC was wrong to depart from the unique approach that had previously won it so much prosperity, but the reality is that it had little choice. The concept of compact size combined with luxury and low running costs was certainly original when AMC sprung it on America in the late '50s. But the Big Three had quickly copied that, diluting AMC's market. When public fancy turned back toward the longer/lower/wider idea, the Big Three with their size and resources were able to more rapidly change their model mixes. AMC could only react to a change in public demand by building what the public demanded, but it couldn't react as fast. Yet who could argue that the company was really badly managed? George Romney and his successors had invested $300 million in new plants and equipment during their days of prosperity—they didn't dole it out in lavish union contracts or stockholder dividends, like Studebaker before them. In short, they did everything sensible managers ought to do to ensure survival, but the cards were stacked against them.

Roy Abernethy did his level best. The Ambassador had yielded mixed results as a mere glorified Rambler; Abernethy felt that it had to get bigger and move up-market if it was going to merit a continued role. Dick Teague's tiny design department obliged by stretching its wheelbase to 116 inches (GM, for example, was doing exactly the same thing with its "compacts") and giving it styling that clearly distinguished it from the Classic.

In profile the new Ambassador 880 and 990 resembled the chiseled Lincoln Continentals, their fenderlines highlighted in bright metal. Fronts were distinctive with stacked quad headlamps and a simple bar grille, and the extra four inches of wheelbase made them look like the luxury cars they were. As usual, a V-8 engine (the 287) was standard, with the 327 optional. Ambassadors were luxuriously trimmed in jacquard cloth and vinyl, and offered with unusual standard or optional equipment,

SPECIFICATIONS

Engines:	ohv I-6, 195.6 cid (3.13 × 4.25), 128 bhp; 232 cid (3.75 × 3.25), 145/155 bhp; ohv V-8, 287 cid (3.75 × 3.25), 198 bhp; 327 cid (4.00 × 3.25) 270 bhp
Transmissions:	3-speed manual; 4-speed manual (**1966 Ambassador**) and 3-speed automatic optional
Suspension front:	upper and lower A-arms, coil springs
Suspension rear:	live axle on 4-link trailing arms, coil springs
Brakes:	front/rear drums
Wheelbase (in.):	Classic 112.0 Ambassador 116.0
Weight (lbs):	2860-3432
Top speed (mph):	NA
0-60 mph (sec):	NA

Production: 1965 Classic 204,016 **Ambassador** 64,145
1966 Classic 126,006 **Ambassador** 34,222

Redesigned for '65, the Classic and Ambassador received straight-edged styling, but the Classic featured horizontal headlights and taillights, while those on the Ambassador were, in both cases, vertical. Both models were little changed for '66, with Ambassadors (both pages) still riding a four-inch longer wheelbase.

like mouton carpeting and a "reverb" feature on the radio. With the 327 they were reasonably fast, but also notable for a jerky power brake system that was oversensitive. All Ambassadors carried a base price of less than $3000, and rarely exceeded $4000 with the usual load of optional equipment.

For once, this proved exactly the right tactic. Dealers disposed of nearly 65,000 in model year 1965, far and away the best the Ambassador had ever done and double its next best year. Abernethy, Teague, and the sales department had done their work well.

The most notable Ambassador and Classic model of 1965 was the new convertible, which underlined the winds of change blowing through a company that had once made fun of anything with a pretense of sportiness. The Rambler American had offered a convertible since 1961, but it was a new departure for the Classic and Ambassador, and it looked very slick with Teague's crisp 1965 styling. It was quite popular too, as a total of about 7000 were sold, equally divided between the two models. Convertibles were offered in the top-line 770 and 990 series and represented marvelous value for the money—a Classic 770 could be purchased for about $2700. They were well put together and looked good, though arguably their role was more one of inspiration than of salesmaking. But they did serve to indicate that this wasn't your father's Rambler anymore.

While the company had a decent year in 1965, it was hardly great, yet the same 12 months had produced record production for most of its competition—Chevrolet, for example, produced over 2.5 million vehicles, an all-time blockbusting record. Throughout 1966 there were rumors of a major shake-up in AMC management, but nothing definite would materialize until January 1967.

Not a lot happened in the meantime. The 1966 line was essentially a repeat of 1965, except that for the first time, the company was marketing its top cars, the Ambassador and the Marlin fastback, as "AMCs" rather than Ramblers. This was a desirable change in nomenclature, but it didn't help the sales picture: production of 280,000 cars was the lowest since 1958. The initial impact of the '65 Ambassador and convertibles seemed to diminish rapidly. Ambassador production was down by almost 50 percent from 1965; Classic volume was off almost as much. The addition of a new sporty compact with an old name (Rambler Rebel), bucket seats, a $2500 base price, and optional V-8s wasn't enough. The Rebel sold a respectable 7500 copies, but it was still up against that long-running public reluctance to view a Rambler as something other than an economy car.

The 1966 Classics had a new roofline and front/rear trim shuffle. The 660 was dropped to better distinguish the economy 550 from the deluxe 770. The Ambassador again came as a sedan, wagon, hardtop, or convertible distributed among the 880 and 990 models; there was also a new top-line DPL two-door hardtop. Convertibles were kept in both Classic and Ambassador lineups and sold about the same quantities as in 1965—but they were among the few AMC models that did.

1965-67
AMC/Rambler Marlin

Ford's Mustang fastback was a 2+2 named after a wild horse that did so well that Chevy designed its 1970 Mustang-copy (Camaro) strictly as a fastback. AMC's Marlin was a "3+3" named after a wild fish that bombed thoroughly. In retrospect, they should have called it the "Flounder."

The American public has had recurrent bouts of fascination with fastbacks since the species was invented in the late 1930s. In the late '40s and early '50s it was the GM "torpedos"; in the mid-'60s it was "ponycars" like the Mustang and Plymouth Barracuda. There were even full-size cars with fastback rooflines, like the Dodge Charger. AMC, which was by then reacting to every blip in the Detroit sales picture, chimed in on this one at the Society of Automotive Engineers convention in January 1964 with the Rambler Tarpon.

Off the drawing boards of Dick Teague, this was a fastback version of the Rambler, but on a smaller American (106 inch) wheelbase, 180 inches long and barely more than 50 inches high. It had a deeply angled, compound curved windshield and a backlight that lay almost flat, a sporty dash with a complete bank of round instruments, bucket seats, and snazzy aluminum wheels. Painted gold-flecked vermillion, it looked terrific to the hardened professionals that attended the SAE show (the general public never went but AMC treated Tarpon like a full-scale show car). The Tarpon looked like Dick "meant it," as they say. The Marlin didn't.

Announced as a production Rambler model in 1965 (it officially went under the "AMC" marque in 1966-67), the Marlin was Tarpon-like, but stretched out to fit the standard 112-inch Rambler wheelbase. That made all the difference. "It was too long," Dick Teague remembered. "Its stance was wrong. We should have built the Tarpon." No explanation has been published as to why Roy Abernethy decided on the larger size, and one is puzzled over it. On the smaller American platform, the Marlin would have looked "right," and would have competed directly with the Mustang and Barracuda, which were much more saleable than full-size or intermediate-size fastbacks.

The answer may lie in lead times: when these decisions were being made by AMC, the Mustang had not yet gone on sale and the Barracuda fastback hadn't done particularly well.

A fastback that would seat a family of five might have seemed more sensible. But aesthetically, it was a mistake. One of Teague's stylists, Bob Nixon, told former AMC public relations manager John Conde that designing the Marlin "was like trying to build a Corvette on a Buick sedan body," and dismissed it as an "ugly embarrassment."

Introduced in 1965, the first Marlin was basically a Classic with a fastback roofline. It was little changed for 1966 (above and opposite page, top), when it sold only half as many copies despite a $500-lower base price. For 1967, the Marlin's tail was grafted onto the redesigned Ambassador body (opposite page, middle and bottom), which resulted in the best-looking Marlin of the series—and the lowest sales.

SPECIFICATIONS

Engines:	ohv I-6, 232 cid (3.75 × 3.25), 145/155 bhp; ohv V-8, 287 cid (3.75 × 3.25), 198 bhp; 327 cid (4.00 × 3.25), 270 bhp
Transmissions:	3-speed manual; 4-speed manual and 3-speed automatic optional
Suspension front:	upper and lower A-arms, coil springs
Suspension rear:	live axle on 4-link trailing arms, coil springs
Brakes:	front/rear drums (front discs optional **1967**)
Wheelbase (in.):	112.0 **1967** 118.0
Weight (lbs):	3234-3342
Top speed (mph):	NA
0-60 mph (sec):	NA
Production:	**1965** 10,327 **1966** 4547 **1967** 2545

It did sell about 10,000 copies in its first year, but in America you can sell 10,000 copies of just about anything. The proof of any new model's staying power is arguably its second-year sales, but in 1966 the Marlin accounted for fewer than 5000. The '66 version was little changed, gaining only an extruded aluminum grille, a sway bar added to six-cylinder models, and a black vinyl roof option. The 1965 Marlin had sold for $3100 base, about the price of a Classic hardtop. For 1966, AMC lowered its price $500 by deleting previously standard features like power brakes, and made the aforementioned marque name change from Rambler to AMC. But it didn't help. One could conclude that by 1966 the Marlin had made all the impulse sales it was going to make, and sales to more deliberate customers who compared it with other cars were a lot scarcer. Neither was 1966 a good year for AMC as a whole: total sales were off by 60,000, and 1965's $5 million profit was more than offset by a 1966 loss of $12.6 million. As John Conde wryly noted, "the Romney image was indeed fast disappearing." For unknown reasons, the Marlin was completely revised for 1967; according to Conde, the company had already decided to drop it after that year. Now it rode the Ambassador wheelbase, itself extended to 118 inches in a complete restyle. Apparently, the tooling cost for the fastback roofline on the new Ambassador two-door hardtop wasn't considered excessive. Management probably would have reconsidered its fate had the '67 Marlin done any better, but it enjoyed fewer sales than ever: only 2545 copies. Ironically, it was the best looking Marlin of the lot.

The '67 was announced by a black-out Ambassador grille housing twin rally lights, smooth new sheetmetal below the beltline, and a cleaner deckline that was nicely integrated into the overall lines. "Even with bucket seats," said AMC brochures, "there's still plenty of room for six swingers . . . the flair of a fastback, the luxury of Ambassador." Marlin was offered for under $3000 base price, with options including a four-speed floor shift, tachometer, and power disc brakes. Everyone from Dick Teague to modern day collectors agree that it was the best Marlin built. Its small production, only 15 percent of total Marlins, has made it the most desirable and costly Marlin on today's collector car market.

The Marlin's lackluster 1967 record was only a small part of a general AMC debacle. Sales dropped to only 230,000 and the company lost $75.8 million. The sale of Kelvinator, long a part of AMC-parent Nash, did little to improve the picture. The long-rumored management shake-out now occurred.

Roy D. Chapin, Jr., longtime AMC sales executive and son of one of the founders of Hudson, replaced Richard Cross as chairman, and Bill Luneberg succeeded Roy Abernethy as president. Together, Chapin and Luneberg would lead AMC to one last push for survival, introducing six new models in their first 18 months, and setting the stage for the Hornet, Gremlin, Pacer, Concord, and Eagle, and what proved to be AMC's final attempt to secure a permanent place in the American auto industry.

1967-69
AMC Ambassador

The late Richard A. Teague could do more with less than most any other car designer around—usually because he had to. He'd honed this skill in the mid-'50s during Packard's "last days in the bunker," but would employ it best during the 25-year career he began in 1959 with small but scrappy American Motors.

Teague served 21 of those years as AMC design vice president, a title he credited to his 1964 American, the pretty compact carved from predecessor Ed Anderson's "Uniside" 1963-64 Classic/Ambassador. For 1965, Teague got a substantial budget—at least by AMC standards—to reskin the larger Ramblers, and he came through handsomely with crisp, angular lines. Equally notable, Ambassador again rode its own long wheelbase to become a true full-size car for the first time since 1961. The result of all this was record Ambassador sales of over 64,000.

Expansionist AMC president Roy Abernethy targeted 1967 for even greater change, in line with his longtime aim of matching Big Three models on most every front. This meant a sporty Javelin "ponycar" in the image of Ford's Mustang, plus an all-new Classic and Ambassador. The last emerged as one of the decade's unsung good-lookers.

Some key technical changes helped. Wheelbase, for example, was again pulled out, this time to 118 inches—only one shy of the biggest Chevys, Fords, and Plymouths—which improved ride as much as looks. Overall length rose 2.5 inches to 202.5, and width swelled 3.9 inches to the benefit of interior and trunk space. All-coil suspension was an AMC given since Nash days, but the old torque-tube drive was finally abandoned for a lighter "Hotchkiss" open driveshaft and new one-piece rear axle with four-link trailing-arm location.

Most running gear was new, too, headlined by a pair of optional V-8s replacing the 287 and 327 engines of mid-'50s vintage. Boasting the latest in "thinwall" block castings, the first was a 200-horsepower 290; the second a bored-out 343 in 235-bhp and high-compression 280-bhp tune—the most horses Ambassador had ever offered. Base power remained the equally modern 232-cubic-inch six

SPECIFICATIONS

Engines:	ohv I-6, 232 cid (3.75 × 3.50), 145/155 bhp; ohv V-8, 290 cid (3.75 × 3.28), 200 bhp; ohv V-8, 343 cid (4.08 × 3.28), 235/280 bhp; ohv V-8, 390 cid (4.17 × 3.57), 315 bhp
Transmissions:	3-speed manual w/optional overdrive, 4-speed manual, 3-speed automatic
Suspension front:	upper and lower A-arms, coil springs
Suspension rear:	live axle on 4-link trailing arms, coil springs
Brakes:	front/rear drums; front discs optional
Wheelbase (in.):	118.0 **1969** 122.0
Weight (lbs):	3193-3732
Top speed (mph):	90-115
0-60 mph (sec):	9.0-11.5
Production:	**1967** 62,839 **1968** 54,681 **1969** 76,194

Despite striking new styling for the 1967 Ambassador (opposite page and this page, top), sales dropped off from the previous year. They dropped again for the similar '68 models. Not until the arrival of the '69s (above and below), built on a four-inch longer wheelbase, was Richard Teague's tasteful styling reflected in the sales charts.

introduced for 1964, still packing 145 standard bhp or 155 optional. Transmission choices included three-speed manual, the same with optional overdrive, extra-cost four-on-the-floor manual, and two three-speed automatic options: Borg-Warner "Flash-O-Matic" and Chrysler TorqueFlite marketed as "Shift Command." Optional power front-disc brakes returned from '66. Other technical changes, mostly at Washington's insistence, included a brake-system warning light, four-way hazard flashers, lane-change turn signals, collapsible steering column, and non-injury dash and door surfaces.

But, of course, it was Teague's tasteful new '67 styling that everyone noticed most. No wonder. Smooth and well-proportioned, it was a startling (some said welcome) break with the boxiness of 1965-66. And if a little Fordish in places and GM-like in others, it didn't quite resemble anything else.

Sticking with a three-series lineup for '67, Ambassador offered its usual four-door sedans and wagons in base 880 and spiffier 990 trim, plus an 880 pillared coupe and 990 two-door hardtop sharing a graceful, semi-fastback profile. Topping the line was a DPL model offered in two body styles: convertible and hardtop coupe. The former retained the unusually low top stack from Ambassador's first 1965 convertible, but was reengineered for genuine three-across rear seating.

Oddly, DPLs were quite overdecorated inside, with lush brocade-type upholstery that *Motor Trend* described as something "rich Aunt Harriet might have had on her parlor sofa. Throw pillows are added to complete the atmosphere of Victorian elegance." Sportier types could opt for vinyl front buckets and center shift console.

The '67 Ambassadors should have sold like nickel beer, yet sales dropped over 8800 from '66. Volume fell again for '68, when styling was touched up, and newly required safety and emissions equipment was installed. Offerings thinned to base, DPL, and new SST sedans and hardtops, plus DPL wagon. The base hardtop was dropped for '69, when a major front and rear restyle added four inches to both wheelbase and overall length. An optional 315-bhp 390 V-8 returned from '68, and was really needed to move Ambassadors that were now bigger than full-size Big Three rivals.

Though sales rose for 1969, the Ambassador's popularity waned in later years, and a then-faltering AMC abandoned the marque after 1974. In retrospect, Abernethy's all-fronts marketing strategy was misguided, but not Ambassador's '67 styling. Oddly, Teague never seemed to take much pride in it, though he certainly could have. It may not have been as memorable as his AMX, but it wasn't a Pacer, either.

1968-69
AMC AMX

Richard A. Teague once called himself "a two-seater kind of guy," so it's no wonder that the AMX was his doing. It was born in late 1965 when the American Motors styling director worked up four show cars for company chairman Roy D. Chapin, Jr., who wanted to show the public that AMC was capable of more exciting stuff than the workaday economy Ramblers for which it was noted.

Among these cars, which toured the country as "Project IV," was a slick fastback coupe that Teague dubbed AMX—for "American Motors Experimental." Its most novel feature was Teague's whimsically named "Ramble Seat," an updated version of the old rumble-seat idea, with a rear windscreen and a pair of auxiliary bucket seats that could be flipped down for two *al fresco* passengers. There was also a small, conventional back seat, leading Teague to term the package a "2+2+2." With its taut, eager lines, the AMX met with such overwhelmingly favorable response that AMC had Italy's Vignale build a running model.

Meantime, Teague was working on the Javelin, slated for 1967 as AMC's answer to the Ford Mustang, giving it much of the AMX's flavor. Why not, he thought, slice 12 vertical inches from the 109-inch-wheelbase Javelin to make an AMX-type two-seater that people could actually buy? It could be tooled at relatively low cost, and would provide even more of the image-boosting pizzazz his boss wanted.

The result appeared in February 1968 *sans* "Ramble Seat" but still called AMX. Though a Javelin heritage was obvious, it had a "faster" back, unique grille, and racy rear-fender creases. Engineers stirred in extra spice with their biggest powerplant ever: a 390-cubic-inch version of the "thinwall" V-8 previously offered as a 290 (1966) and 343 (1967), which were respectively standard and optional.

With its two seats and inch-shorter wheelbase, the AMX was often compared in press reports to Chevy's contemporary Corvette, though AMC never called it a sports car. But like early Ford Thunderbirds, the AMX could be a sizzling performer. To prove it, AMC hired Land Speed Record ace Craig Breedlove and his wife Lee to take a couple of AMXs out for a spin around a Texas track. "Spin"

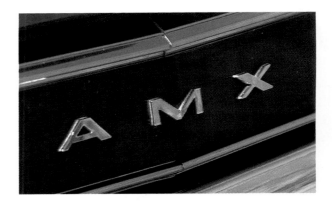

Opposite: *Original AMX show car boasted "2+2+2" seating, having both a small back seat as well as a "Ramble Seat" built into the rear deck. Its popularity on the show circuit spawned the production AMX (below), which debuted for 1968—though with only two seats.*

they did, streaking 24 straight hours to 106 new national and international speed marks while averaging 140.7 mph. They later ran 189 mph in a USAC-sponsored trial at Bonneville. AMXs were soon cleaning up on drag strips (thanks to Lou Downy, Shirley Shahan, and others) and in amateur sports-car competition. In fact, an AMX nearly won the 1969 SCCA national championship (nosed out by a Corvette).

The AMX generated much excitement but few sales: just 6725 for debut '68, something AMC halfway expected. The '69s were predictably little changed apart from a $52 higher base price (still very reasonable at just under $3300), new "Big Bad" colors (a *very* bright blue, orange, and green), and an optional "Go" package of appearance and handling modifications. Volume improved to 8293 units, but that wasn't enough. Accordingly, AMC decided to bail out after the 1970 edition, which featured a restyled nose, "power blister" hood, high-back seats, and a newly standard 360 V-8. Despite the updates, production plunged to half the '69 figure. Teague tried to keep the car alive, mocking up a sectioned AMX version of his new humped-fender '71 Javelin, but to no avail.

Still, he managed a moral victory in two exciting mid-engine exercises, the non-running AMX/2 of 1969 and the fully functional 1970 AMX/3, of which six were built. The latter, developed with help from BMW and Italian sports-car engineering legend Giotto Bizzarrini, boasted all-independent wishbone suspension, big four-wheel disc brakes, a 340-bhp 390 V-8, and tight, muscular lines—arguably Teague's best work and chosen over a surprisingly dull competitive proposal by Giorgetto Giugiaro.

AMX/3 might have seen regular, if necessarily limited production, but AMC was on a long downhill slide by 1970 and had no money for that, let alone a continuation of the Javelin-based AMX. Now AMC itself is gone, and Teague passed away in 1991.

But enthusiasts everywhere can be grateful that Dick Teague was a two-seater guy. In the production AMX he gave us the sort of car he himself loved to drive and lived to design. And that's a wonderful legacy by any measure.

SPECIFICATIONS

Engines:	all ohv V-8; 290 cid (3.75 × 3.28), 225 bhp; 343 cid (4.08 × 3.28), 280 bhp; 390 cid (4.17 × 3.57), 315 bhp
Transmissions:	3/4-speed manual; 3-speed automatic
Suspension front:	upper and lower A-arms, coil springs
Suspension rear:	live axle on semi-elliptic leaf springs
Brakes:	front discs/rear drums
Wheelbase (in.):	97.0
Weight (lbs):	3100
Top speed (mph):	120-130
0-60 mph (sec):	6.7-9.0
Production:	**1968** 6725 **1969** 8293

Opposite: This version of America's only other two-seater is fitted with the popular Red Line tires and carries the most potent powertrain offered for 1968: a 315 bhp 390-cid V-8 mated to a four-speed manual transmission. Interior was quite dressy with perforated-vinyl seats and simulated wood trim. For 1969, AMC offered vibrant new "Big Bad" colors for the otherwise little-changed AMX, available in green, blue, and orange (below).

1968-69
AMC Javelin

On an international scale of values, America had a peculiar automotive industry in the '60s. Although each company was building a car for every market segment, all the cars were surprisingly similar. The only variations from the ancient front-heavy, beam-rear-axle package were the Corvette, Corvair, and Toronado/Eldorado, all of which were more or less "specialty cars"—and one was under fire in the courts and soon to disappear. If it weren't for these exceptions, one could rightfully say that there was little in the way of technological progress in the '60s.

But of course, why change? Boom years were at hand, and within the parameters of the time, we were building some sensational cars. Dick Teague's AMC Javelin was one. Conceived in a hurry as American Motors' "ponycar" answer to the Mustang and Camaro, in style and execution it had the legs of both of them. The Javelin was, first of all, astonishingly beautiful. On a wheelbase only an inch longer than Mustang's, it provided more interior space than any other "ponycar," particularly in the rear compartment, where "ponycars" were notoriously lacking. It was also priced right: at $2482 base, it was less than a Mustang.

But the Javelin was more than a reply to Mustang; it was a frank attempt by American Motors to change its image—drastically. Former AMC president George Romney felt that AMC took a turn for the worse after he left because his successors forsook the Rambler and tried to diversify, and that the company couldn't compete on all fronts with the likes of General Motors. The trouble with being an independent, however, is that no sooner do you develop a good idea than you find yourself, in Rich Taylor's words, "with elephant footprints all over you."

The pioneering, deadly dull Rambler was a success all right—in the '50s and early '60s. But it led every other company, most of them far larger than AMC, to build similar cars. By the mid-'60s, AMC didn't have much choice but to try different products, different avenues. They continued to pick and choose and they certainly did not try to compete across the board—but they were ultimately overwhelmed by the sheer size and diversity of their enormous rivals.

Perhaps the best Javelin from the standpoint of pure design was the first series, built during 1968-69. From every angle it exhibited designer Teague's penchant for clean, flowing edges and corners. There were two models, both hardtops: a standard version, and the more luxurious SST, priced $105 higher.

AMC traditionally suffered from its aging Nash engines, so the Javelin's mechanicals were perhaps not quite up to date. Standard power was the old Nash 232-cid six combined with a three-speed manual transmission—efficient, but not as powerful or up-to-date as the '60s-spawned Slant Six of Chrysler, for example. Still, you could order a good 290 V-8, which was comparable to Mustang's 289, and if that wasn't enough you could get what AMC called the "Go Package": 343 V-8 with 280 horsepower, dual exhausts, E70-14 tires, power front-disc brakes, the "handling" suspension, and special appearance details.

Today the Go-Package SST is more sought-after than the plainer Javelins, but they too have their charm and appeal to some collectors who use them as "daily drivers." They certainly don't look as much like products of 20-plus years ago as the contemporary Mustangs. The 290 was a sweet little engine, not competitive in Trans Am racing (where it gave away a dozen cubes until they stroked it to 304 in 1970), but perfect for the street.

AMC was more than satisfied with their "ponycar's" first-year performance. They had hoped for 45,000 sales; they enjoyed 56,000. This dropped to around 40,000 for the 1969 models, but the "ponycar" rage had peaked, and Javelin's rivals were tailing off, too.

Uncluttered styling and a relatively commodious interior are the big pluses of the Javelin. One magazine in 1968 called it "nattily handsome, sprightly, tidy, altogether appealing." It is still those things today.

Joining the ponycar stampede in 1968 was AMC's Javelin, offered in base and uplevel SST trim (opposite page, top). The '69s were virtually identical, the example shown (this page and opposite page, bottom) being fitted with the Go-Package that included a 343-cid V-8, heavy-duty suspension, and appearance items like body stripes, hood scoops, and special wheels.

SPECIFICATIONS

Engines:	ohv I-6, 232 cid (3.75 × 3.25), 145 bhp; ohv V-8, 290 cid (3.75 × 3.28), 200/225 bhp; 343 cid (4.08 × 3.28), 280 bhp; 390 cid (4.17 × 3.57), 315 bhp
Transmissions:	3/4-speed manual; 3-speed automatic
Suspension front:	upper and lower A-arms, coil springs
Suspension rear:	live axle on semi-elliptic leaf springs
Brakes:	front discs/rear drums
Wheelbase (in.):	109.0
Weight (lbs):	2836
Top speed (mph):	343 V-8: 121
0-60 mph (sec):	343 V-8: 8.6
Production:	1968 55,124 1969 40,675

1965-69
Avanti II

Not many cars get a second chance at life after the original manufacturer expires. When Studebaker left its long-time home at South Bend, Indiana, early in 1964, to make a final stab at success up in Ontario, the futurethink Avanti seemed doomed after a mere two-year existence. After the Canadian venture fizzled in 1966, the Avanti should by all logic have been dead, if not forgotten. Even the greatest cars, after all, cannot survive unless someone chooses to build them.

Leo Newman and Nathan (Nate) Altman, long-time partners in a South Bend Studebaker-Packard dealership, had a great notion—and wound up saving the dramatically different coupe from extinction. Not only did the two buy the rights to the Avanti name and its manufacture, they purchased a portion of an abandoned Studebaker factory, forming a brand-new Avanti Motor Corporation.

Late in 1965, production began at the revitalized plant on Lafayette Avenue, with a goal of building 300 Avanti IIs yearly. That goal never was reached, but the Avanti stayed alive through the 1960s and '70s, and even beyond the 1980s.

Such success is all the more surprising when you consider that the original Avanti wasn't exactly a sizzling seller. Attention it drew, enhancing Studebaker's image; but as other manufacturers also have learned, sales don't necessarily follow achievements on the race course or record-setting 170-mph jaunts.

Had the original Avanti been made of steel instead of fiberglass, its resurrection might have been impossible. Using body panels supplied by the Molded Fiber Glass Body Company and a mini assembly line, the revived Avantis could be built for a reasonable cost. Spread along that line were a host of former Studebaker employees, willing to work for modest wages in exchange for an opportunity to turn out custom-built sport-luxury touring cars.

Not only did Avanti compile an option list that would be the envy of rival automakers, but a customer could dicker for just about anything his or her heart desired. Colors? The rainbow was the limit. Fabrics? Just about anything that could be sewn into seats might be ordered—with stitchwork performed by a former Studebaker craftsman.

Naturally, Avanti had to abandon the original R-series Studebaker engines, turning to readily available Chevrolet drivetrains: specifically, the Corvette 327-cid V-8. Power-shift automatic allowed manual runs through first and second gears, but plenty of buyers opted instead for a fully synchronized Borg-Warner four-speed, often accompanied by a Hurst shifter.

Only a true aficionado could tell the difference between an Avanti II and an original, without searching for a "II" in its nameplate. Profile and detailing changed little, except that the new one sat more level on the ground. The early "rake" (front end lower than the rear) was gone. Otherwise, the revived coupe displayed the same grille-less nose, sharp-edged front fenders, slim bumpers, and "Coke-bottle" profile, with only a slight narrowing of front wheel openings.

Lighter weight gave the car better weight distribution. Front disc brakes provided fade-free stopping power. Road-testers gave it high marks for safety, silence, and a firm but comfortable ride.

While the original Avantis had focused on performance, the new ones qualified as four-seat "personal luxury" machines, partly due to higher prices. Whereas the original had sold for $4445, the Avanti II started at $7200—or as little as $6550 if the buyer agreed to do without a few standard items. Throw in a full load of options, and the sticker could approach 10 grand.

Available equipment included air conditioning, power windows, tinted glass, Eppe driving lights, limited-slip differential, Magnum 500 chromed wheels, and plenty more. Inside, $200 bought an upgrade to textured "Raphael vinyl," while $500 was the price for all leather. As later literature proclaimed, there were "more than 400 ways to 'spoil yourself' inside an Avanti."

This is not to say, however, that the Avanti had become a slouch. Top speed registered at around 125 mph, and a "II" with automatic could accelerate to 60 mph in less than nine seconds. Eugene Hardig, who'd been the last Chief Engineer at Studebaker, was responsible for keeping the engine "legal" as it grew to 350-cid displacement in 1969, and later to 400 cid.

Following the death of Nate Altman in 1976, a succession of owners have manned the Avanti helm. And though the future of the company has at times looked bleak, the car itself has remained true to the styling theme penned over three decades ago—a convincing testament to its timeless design.

SPECIFICATIONS

Engines:	all ohv V-8; **1965-69** 327 cid (4.00 × 3.25), 300 bhp **1969** 350 cid (4.00 × 3.48), 300 bhp
Transmission:	Borg-Warner 4-speed manual or "power-shift" 3-speed automatic
Suspension, front:	upper and lower A-arms, coil springs, stabilizer bar
Suspension, rear:	live axle, leaf springs
Brakes:	front discs, rear drums
Wheelbase (in.):	109.0
Weight (lbs.):	3181-3217
Top speed (mph):	121-125
0-60 mph (sec):	7.5-8.8
Production:	**1965** 21 **1966** 98 **1967** 60 **1968** 89 **1969** 103

Avanti IIs could be custom-built to a buyer's specifications, the factory offering practically any color and material combinations one might desire. Interiors were luxuriously trimmed, and Avanti's "any color you want so long as its available" philosophy resulted in numerous examples being virtually one-of-a-kind automobiles.

1960
Buick Electra

If the 1950s had been a decade of dazzle, the '60s started out by turning down the volume—at least among the GM fold. Big changes had been the rule for the '59 Buicks, with their huge canted "Delta wing" fins and slanted quad headlights. Some considered it the most dramatic Buick of all—and a sharp contrast to the garish '58 with its unexcelled load of chrome doodads.

The new model names and body styles introduced for 1959 continued this year: low-price LeSabre, sporty (more or less) midrange Invicta, luxury Electra, and even bigger Electra 225. That latter nameplate denoted the overall dimensions of the long-deck model, which stretched 4.7 inches beyond an ordinary-size Electra.

Basic appearance was similar to '59, with its then-new long-deck, thin-section roofline, and vast glass area. Changes this year were just extensive enough to soften some of the more frivolous excesses and sharper edges. A more subdued grille was made up of concave vertical bars—quite a change from the bulky pattern of chrome blocks that marked the '59 version—and quad headlights now sat side by side.

Tailfins were comparably canted and integrated into the overall profile, their upper line extending all the way to the windshield. This time around, though, they sat tighter in, helping to highlight rather than conflict with the deeply sculptured bodysides. Hardtop sedans came in two distinct roofline styles: a six-window Riviera with curved rear and triangular rear-quarter panes; or a four-window with flat roof, slim pillars, and huge panoramic wraparound back window.

Traditionalists got something they hadn't seen for several years: VentiPorts. Yes, the row of "portholes" that had first identified Buick fenders in 1949 was back, albeit in modified form.

Beneath Electra and Invicta hoods was the 401-cid V-8 introduced in 1959, dubbed Wildcat 445 (to denote its torque rating) and churning out 325 horsepower. LeSabres carried a 364-cid engine, with 235 to 300 bhp.

Electras came with power brakes and steering, but this year's dual exhaust

SPECIFICATIONS

Engines:	ohv V-8, 401 cid (4.19 × 3.64), 325 bhp
Transmission:	Turbine Drive (twin turbine) automatic
Suspension, front:	upper and lower A-arms, coil springs
Suspension, rear:	live axle, coil springs
Brakes:	front/rear drums
Wheelbase (in.):	126.3
Weight (lbs.):	4453-4653
Top speed (mph):	110-180
0-60 mph (sec):	11.0-12.0

Production: Electra 4d sdn 13,794 2d htp 7416 4d htp 14,488 Electra 225 Riviera 4d htp (6-window) 8029 4d htp (4-window) 5841 cvt 6746

Though tamed down somewhat from flamboyant '59, the 1960 Electra nonetheless exhibited highly stylized lines. "VentiPorts," Buick's trademark front-fender portholes, returned after a two-year absence, while tailfins would be evident for the last time. Underhood sat the 401-cid "Wildcat 445," which got its name from the engine's torque output: a prodigious 445 pounds/feet. Dashboard panel showing speedometer, odometer, and "idiot lights" is actually a mirror reflecting images from horizontal instruments in front of it.

system switched to a single transverse muffler. Limited demand and high cost nixed the Triple Turbine Drive transmission that had been optional since 1958. In its place, a new Turbine Drive transmission featured a variable-pitch fluid-control mechanism that replaced ordinary gears. Buick Transmission Engineer Harold Fischer explained to *Car Life* that "for maximum acceleration . . . you don't shift gears, you shift a constantly flowing stream of oil." Instead of the customary "neck-snapping" downshift when passing, the magazine reported "a smooth surge like a rising wave."

Other magic went inside: namely, a new Mirromagic instrument panel that let the driver read the bar-style speedometer and warning lights through an adjustable tilting mirror. More important to passengers was the lowering of the central tunnel and floor pan, which added leg room. Back doors opened wider than before, doubtless a concession to the age of the typical Electra customer. A smooth ride had long been a Buick trademark, so the company promoted Electra's Torque Tube driveline, full-coil suspension, and solid K-braced frame. Air Poise suspension, formerly optional, was now consigned to the history books.

Electras rode a 126.3-inch wheelbase, 3.3 inches longer than the other Buicks, and carried 8.00 × 15 tires. A convertible came only in the Electra 225 series, priced at $4192. Budget-minded buyers could get a base Electra hardtop sedan for a mere $3818. An impressive option list included Twilight Sentinel that turned headlights on automatically, Guide-Matic to dim them, power windows and six-way seat, air conditioning, and "Wonder Bar" (station-seeking) radio.

Production had risen considerably in 1959, though Buick dropped from fifth to seventh place in industry sales. But fewer cars came off the line for 1960: only 253,807 (including 56,314 Electras), versus 284,248 the previous year. That loss dropped Buick down to the ninth slot, its worst showing in 55 years, while corporate rival Pontiac's fortunes were rising.

Whether the result of poor sales or simply a more conservative styling approach, this revision set the stage for a softening of the look and the quick demise of the slanted fins. Now, Buick was ready to slim down a bit, inject an extra dose of performance, and debut a mini edition to match its full-size luxury tourers.

"When better automobiles are built," trumpeted ads with regularity, "Buick will build them." Whether the 1960 Electra was "better" than the '59 is a matter of taste. With a convertible top down, in particular, either of those huge heavyweights still turns heads today—even if some observers might be taken aback at the sight of all that chrome and bulk.

1961-62
Buick Electra

Looking back from a 1990s perspective, it's popular to decry the tall tailfins and dazzling brightwork that characterized American dreamboats of three decades ago. "What silly fools we were," some say today, "to fall for that sort of nonsense."

Maybe so. But logical or not, that kind of car is precisely what most Americans "fell for" at the time. Bigger, brighter, bolder—those traits equaled "better" in the minds of millions. What a shock it had to be, then, to see that brand of brashness and boldness diminish, and then virtually disappear from the marketplace. Case in point: Buick's full-size lineup for 1961, which on the surface, at least, appeared to share nothing with its most recent ancestors.

That wasn't true, of course. Beneath that exterior lurked a chassis and powertrain that had changed little. Up top, though, was a clean and modern body that appeared to have tossed aside nearly all traces of ostentation and excess. Not only were the fins gone, replaced by squared-off rear quarters with ordinary horizontal taillights, but the entire car had a square, down-to-business look. Buick named this new style "the clean look of action."

Sure, "portholes" rode the front fenders again, having experienced a rebirth in the previous year: three of the reshaped oval accents in a row for the LeSabre and Invicta; four for the luxury Electra and Electra 225 lines. Front fenders ended in pointy contours that matched the projectile shape of the bumper tips below. Bodyside sculpturing wasn't so deep anymore, but still served as an integral part of the design, via a trio of parallel horizontal creases.

This year's quad headlights, however, sat at the edges of a grille that barely compared with the flamboyance that had come to symbolize Buick front ends: just a vertically positioned set of simple horizontal bars with center insignia. Compared to the recent past, here was a Buick that ranked as downright plain.

Gone too was the severely wrapped windshield, replaced by a milder shape that matched the rounded triangular vent wings. Elimination of the "dogleg" added almost five inches of space for entry and exit, across narrower door sills. A new Hide-Away Drive Shaft lowered the tunnel height, giving center passengers extra space. As before, two roofline treatments were available for the hardtop sedan: Riviera-style with triangular rear panes; and the flat-roofed version with wraparound back window.

Wheelbases shrunk only a fraction of an inch, but each Electra model lost a couple of hundred pounds. Mechanical changes were minimal. Power surged again from a 401-cid "Wildcat 445" V-8 that whipped up a rollicking 325 horsepower. Also carried over was Buick's Turbine Drive automatic transmission with its reputation for smoothness without sluggishness. Invictas carried the Electra engine, while LeSabres again came with a 364-cid V-8. Manual transmissions no longer existed for any full-size models, having been installed in only a tiny fraction of recent LeSabres.

Shoppers who craved some sport along with their comforts now had the option of obtaining an Electra engine in a new Wildcat body (see that listing). Traditionalists, on the other hand, could feel secure in the knowledge that "their" kind of Buick would continue to be available, without drastic changes, for many years to come.

Even the pointy front-end elements were gone when the restyled '62 Buick arrived with its revised roofline. VentiPorts were elongated, while back ends adopted simple cut-off quarter panels. Rear pillars were wide and sloping, and grilles grew plainer than ever. The "Advanced Thrust" redesign also moved the engine forward, reducing the transmission hump and creating a floor with a "mere ripple" obstructing the center passenger's feet. Base Electras were gone, as each of the top models took the name "Electra 225."

Perhaps the public wasn't quite as impressed initially by the toned-down Electras as Buick hoped, since production declined by 8391 units in '61—though dropping one Electra 225 model may have contributed to the loss. After everyone accepted the new thinking, 1962 brought a jump to 62,468 Electra 225s, up from 47,923 in '61 and well above the 1960 mark.

Pleasant cars these still-big Buicks may have been when new, but their relatively prosaic profiles just can't attract the kind of avid attention lavished today on the gaudy extravagances that preceded them. What this intermediate generation of Electras did was set the stage for a new breed of formalized Buicks later in the decade.

SPECIFICATIONS

Engines:	ohv V-8, 401 cid (4.19 × 3.64), 325 bhp
Transmission:	Turbine Drive (twin turbine) automatic
Suspension, front:	upper and lower A-arms, coil springs, link-type stabilizer
Suspension, rear:	3-link live axle, coil springs, track bar
Brakes:	front/rear drums
Wheelbase (in.):	126.0
Weight (lbs.):	4235-4441
Top speed (mph):	115
0-60 mph (sec):	10.0-11.0 (est.)

Production: 1961 Electra 4d sdn 13,818 **2d htp** 4250 **4d htp** 8978 **Electra 225 Riviera 4d htp** 13,719 **cvt** 7158 **1962 Electra 225 4d sdn** 13,523 **2d htp** 8922 **4d htp** 16,734 **Riviera 4d htp (6-window)** 15,395 **cvt** 7894

Opposite, top: *Styling of '61 Electra was a radical departure from 1960, abandoning '50s fins for an arrowlike profile. Another restyle appeared for '62 (opposite bottom and this page, top) after sales dropped off the previous year. Production rebounded past 1960 levels. Underneath the skin, these Buicks were little changed, carrying the "Wildcat 445" engine offered since 1959.*

1961-63
Buick Special Skylark

This is à Buick? That's how some folks must have reacted when the compact Special was announced for the 1961 model year. Buick's Special was one of GM's "second wave" compacts, following in the wake of the rear-engined Chevrolet Corvair. Riding a 112-inch wheelbase, this was the smallest Buick in half a century, a close kin to the new Oldsmobile F-85 and Pontiac Tempest.

Were it not for the telltale VentiPorts on the fenders, the car's heritage might be in doubt. Buick described the Special as "revolutionary," a car that "makes no compromise with old concepts" from its "fun-sized dimensions." Compact was its category, but a Special was meant to carry six grownups with some degree of comfort, described by *Motor Trend* as "sensibly sized."

Bodysides presented a sculptured—indeed chiseled—look with their multiple-creased rear quarter panels and rounded-off fender tips up front, highlighted by a full-length chrome trim strip. In his typically colorful manner, Tom McCahill of *Mechanix Illustrated* noted that the body "has more angles than a broken plate glass window."

Something special also went beneath the hood: a lightweight (and economical) all-aluminum 215-cid Fireball V-8 engine, developed by GM Engineering, that produced 155 horsepower. Buick thus became the first major domestic automaker with an aluminum powerplant.

Specials were first offered in four-door sedan and station wagon form, with base or Deluxe trim. A Dual-Path Turbine Drive automatic with planetary gearset was available to replace the standard three-speed stick. Down below, an open driveshaft replaced the traditional torque-tube.

Soon after the Special's debut came a Special Deluxe Skylark pillared coupe, borrowing its name from a 1953-54 limited-production convertible. On sale in spring 1961 at $2395 ($95 more than a Special Deluxe sedan), the Skylark carried

The compact 1961 Specials (below) were the smallest Buicks in 50 years. Sharing a platform with the Olds F-85, Pontiac Tempest, and Chevy Corvair, the Special was perhaps the most conservative of the lot, with a conventional drivetrain layout and lines reminiscent of that year's full-size Buicks. A dressier Skylark coupe was introduced at midyear. Styling was little changed for '62, when the sporty Skylark coupe (above and opposite page) gained a convertible linemate (as did the Special). Smoother lines marked the '63s (this page, bottom), as the output of Skylark's 215-cid aluminum V-8 was increased to an even 200 bhp.

SPECIFICATIONS

Engines:	ohv V-6, **1962-63 Special** 198 cid (3.63 × 3.20), 135 bhp; ohv V-8, **1961-63 Special** 215 cid (3.50 × 2.80), 155 bhp **1961 Skylark** 185 bhp **1962 Skylark** 190 bhp **1963 Skylark** 200 bhp
Transmission:	3-speed manual; 4-speed manual (1962-63) 2-speed Dual-Path Turbine Drive automatic optional
Suspension, front:	upper and lower A-arms, coil springs
Suspension, rear:	4-link live axle, coil springs
Brakes:	front/rear drums
Wheelbase (in.):	112.1
Weight (lbs.):	2579-2896
Top speed (mph):	95-107
0-60 mph (sec):	**V-6** 14.4-15.0 **V-8** 10.2-14.0

Production: 1961 Special 4d sdn 18,339 **Deluxe 4d sdn** 32,986 **2d spt cpe** 4232 **4d wgn (2-seat)** 6101 **4d wgn (3-seat)** 798 **Deluxe 4d wgn** 11,729 **Skylark spt cpe** 12,683 **1962 Special 4d sdn** 23,249 **Deluxe 4d sdn** 31,660 **2d cpe** 19,135 **4d wgn (2-seat)** 7382 **4d wgn (3-seat)** 2814 **Deluxe 4d wgn** 10,380 **cvt** 7918 **Deluxe cvt** 8332 **Skylark htp cpe** 34,060 **Skylark cvt** 8913 **1963 Special 4d sdn** 21,733 **Deluxe 4d sdn** 37,695 **2d cpe** 21,886 **4d wgn (2-seat)** 5867 **4d wgn (3-seat)** 2415 **Deluxe 4d wgn** 8771 **cvt** 8082 **Skylark spt cpe** 32,109 **Skylark cvt** 10,212

bucket seats and a more potent 185-bhp version of the V-8, and could even have a vinyl-coated white fabric top. That engine also became optional in Specials. To eke out 30 extra horsepower, compression rose from the usual 8.8:1 to a tight 10.25:1 and a four-barrel carburetor replaced the usual two-barrel. Trim included long, bright deck and quarter-panel extensions for the wraparound squared taillights. Skylark's temporarily unique grille with thin louvers between a pair of heavy bars (which appeared to "float" between quad headlights), was destined to appear the next year on regular Specials. Slim slots replaced the Special's "portholes," and rear wheel wells were larger on the Skylark. Tufted and buttoned vinyl-and-fabric upholstery mimicked the costly Electra's.

A healthy 12,683 of the sporty new coupes were sold in that partial model year. In 1962, the line expanded to include a convertible, and that (along with the availability of an optional Borg-Warner four-speed gearbox) helped Skylark sales top 42,000. The new convertible came with a power top, and power windows were optional. Otherwise, little changed from the previous year except for the adoption of narrow-band whitewalls. Though not quite dragster caliber just yet, Skylarks already were pretty swift, capable of reaching 60 mph in a touch over 10 seconds.

Base-model Specials were offered with a new 198-cid V-6 starting in mid-1962. Buick earned the *Motor Trend* "Car of the Year" award for this powerplant, billed as "the only V-6 in any American car." Skylark stuck to its aluminum V-8, now rated at 190 bhp. While Skylarks came only in coupe and convertible body styles, the Special lineup also included four-door sedans and station wagons.

Restyling for 1963 turned the sculpted bodysides into a less striking, slab-sided surface. Some of the original Skylark standard equipment, including bucket seats, now cost extra. Output from Skylark's version of the 215-cid V-8 grew to an even 200 bhp.

Popularity of Buick's twin compacts (coupled with rising demand for full-size models) helped put the company back on the success list. Buick's 215-cid aluminum V-8 (which weighed a mere 318 pounds) wouldn't power the next generation of Specials and Skylarks. That doesn't mean it expired. Instead, the V-8 enjoyed a rebirth across the Atlantic, beneath the bonnets of British-built Rover sedans as well as tough four-wheel-drive Land Rovers and Range Rovers. Skylark? Well, Buick had another kind of power—and size—in mind for its smallest performance-driven series.

1962-64
Buick Wildcat

Shoehorning a big engine into a smaller body was nothing new at Buick. That little trick had been learned with the Century, in 1937, and relearned in the mid-1950s when that model made a reappearance. The 1959-61 Invicta, after all, wore a shorter LeSabre body and carried an Electra engine. Tom McCahill, the well-known tester at *Mechanix Illustrated*, managed to send an Invicta from 0-60 mph in as little as eight seconds, and the car could hit 120 mph. In short, Buick already had a Wildcat on tap, even if it didn't answer to that name.

When the Wildcat two-door hardtop emerged as an Invicta subseries during 1962, however, it offered more than just the big 401-cid engine and revised axle ratio. Here was a fresh theme, a new identity, a fulfilled promise of performance. Buick implored prospects to experience the "sure-footed sock of Advanced Thrust" in this "torrid new luxury sports car."

Borrowing the name from that used for the engine itself, Wildcats contained vinyl-upholstered bucket seats and a console-mounted tachometer, wore a black or white vinyl Landau top, and displayed a top-of-the-line $3927 price sticker. Rather than a mere performance image, here was the real thing—but accompanied by the typical Buick comforts.

As *Motor Trend* suggested in its evaluation, Wildcat was a car that "likes to GO in luxury," and whose interior qualified as "a bucket-seat palace." In addition to a boatload of standard equipment, Wildcats came with a big option list that ranged from air conditioning and Twilight Sentinel (for automatic headlight turn-on) to oversize tires and a compass.

So-so sales but impressive potential led Wildcat to ease out from under the Invicta nameplate during 1963, becoming a separate model. The only Invicta left was a station wagon, and that lasted only a year. In 1964, a larger 425-cid "Wildcat 465" engine became optional, with either 340 or 360 horsepower, fed by one or two four-barrel carburetors. Price tag? Just $48 extra for the 340-bhp version, or $188 for the full-bore performer. The same V-8 powered Riviera coupes.

Early Wildcats came with Buick's smooth, Turbine Drive transmission. Because no manual-shift was available, some considered the Wildcat's alleged sportiness to be a tad pretentious. No matter. With so much oomph underhood, Wildcat lived up to its name—as long as the driver stuck to the straightaways and didn't attempt any quick, tight corners. This was a Buick after all, and as the company admitted, a Wildcat might deliver a "sports-car wallop" but it was "designed strictly for American driving." When the time came to slow down, aluminum front brake drums kept their cool longer than cast iron.

Initially offered only as a hardtop sport coupe, the Wildcat line added a four-door hardtop sedan and a convertible in 1963. Brushed panels on front fenders and deck made them easy to spot. So did the special grille with its thick horizontal bars. Bucket seats and a console remained standard, except in four-door hardtops where it cost extra to replace the regular bench. Front passengers benefited from "Advanced Thrust" design, which flattened the floorboard.

Like other full-size Buicks, Wildcats grew a few inches longer in 1964 even though wheelbase did not change, and lost a little weight. A regular pillared four-door sedan also became available. Prices tumbled by more than $500, which helped send Wildcat sales soaring. Nearly twice as many of the hardtop coupes and sedans were built in '64 compared to the previous year. These final first-generation Wildcats displayed a completely different trio of long VentiPort moldings, stacked one above the other on each front fender below the bodyside crease. They also wore distinctively ribbed wide moldings above the rocker panels, and often came with optional chromed "Formula Five" wheels.

A new Super Turbine 400 automatic with three-element torque converter added a dual planetary gear arrangement to Buick's Turbine Drive, trading smooth acceleration for some extra sizzle. By this time, the standard transmission was a three-speed manual, with automatic the optional choice. And contrary to early insistence by Buick that no four-speed manual gearbox would be forthcoming, it showed up this year on the Wildcat option list.

Buick's hefty wild one had gone about as far as it could in its initial incarnation, giving the company sporting machines in two distinct sizes. The performance race was on, and Buick had become a player.

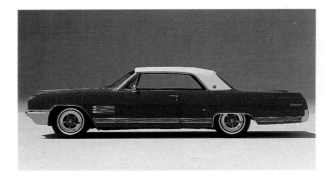

The 1962 Wildcat (opposite page, top) was initially an Invicta subseries with a buckets-and-console interior (this page, top). It scored only 2000 sales its first year, but would do much better in 1963 (opposite page, bottom) when it became a separate model. For 1964 (above) it gained an optional 425-cid "Wildcat 465" V-8 option that produced up to 360 bhp.

SPECIFICATIONS

Engines:	all ohv V-8; **1962-64** 401 cid (4.19 × 3.64), 325 bhp **1964** 425 cid (4.31 × 3.64), 340/360 bhp
Transmissions:	**1962-63** 3-speed Turbine Drive (twin turbine) automatic **1964** 3-speed manual; optional 4-speed manual or Super Turbine 400 automatic
Suspension, front:	upper and lower A-arms, coil springs, link-type stabilizer bar
Suspension, rear:	3-link live axle, coil springs, track bar
Brakes:	front/rear drums
Wheelbase (in.):	123.0
Weight (lbs.):	4003-4228
Top speed (mph):	114-120
0-60 mph (sec):	8.1-10.0

Production: 1962 2000 **1963 htp sdn** 17,519 **htp cpe** 12,185 **cvt** 6021 **1964 sdn** 20,144 **htp sdn** 33,358 **htp cpe** 22,893 **cvt** 7850

Note: 1962 Wildcat production is approximate (total of 12,355 Invicta hardtop coupes, including Wildcats).

1963-65 Buick Riviera

General Motors spent five years watching "Squarebirds" go by before fielding its own personal-luxury contender. But what a contender! Immediately hailed as a design landmark, the Riviera has become precisely what Buick claimed in 1963: "America's Bid For A Great New International Classic Car."

It originated about a year after the four-seat Ford bucked the recessionary 1958 market with vastly higher sales than any two-seat Thunderbird. Initial work produced a full-size mock-up nicknamed the "Double Bubble" or "Buck Rogers" car, but it was too far out for newly installed GM design chief William L. Mitchell. He thought any Thunderbird-fighter should look like the razor-edge Rolls-Royce he'd recently glimpsed on a foggy night in London.

As it happened, Buick chief stylist Ned Nickles had sketched that very thing, only for yet another proposed revival of LaSalle, Cadillac's lower-price companion make of 1927-40. Nickles had designed a "LaSalle II" roadster and hardtop sedan for the 1955 Motorama, and there was still some hope among GM veterans that the romantic nameplate might return. With Mitchell's endorsement, Nickles' work became the genesis of experimental project XP-715.

Convertible, hardtop sedan, and even a phaeton were modeled along with the inevitable hardtop coupe, but only the last would see production, even though Thunderbird also offered a ragtop. Essentially finished by mid-April 1960, it was eventually reassigned to Buick. Cadillac didn't have facilities for a companion product, and though Olds and Pontiac lobbied hard for the new model, both had more important fish to fry.

It was a wise decision, for Buick badly needed a shot in the sales arm. By 1960, Flint had fallen from a strong third and nearly 750,000 units in banner 1955 to ninth in production and a quarter-million sales. Though a recovery was underway by the time of Riviera's late-1962 unveiling, the posh personal-luxury newcomer sparked Buick's image like nothing since the limited-edition Skylark convertible of a decade before.

Individual and elegant, the Riviera was an adroit blend of sharp edges and smooth curves set off by just the right amount of chrome, plus a lowish beltline with a saucy dip. Even the dual dummy air scoops ahead of each rear wheel looked right. So did the eggcrate grille flanked by large, LaSalle-like "sub-grilles" with wraparound parking/directional lamps.

Underneath, the Riviera was decidedly conventional and all Buick. Relatively compact on a unique 117-inch wheelbase, it stood some 14 inches shorter and 200-300 pounds lighter than other big Buicks. The chassis was GM's typical X-member affair (still criticized as vulnerable to side-impact damage) with all-coil suspension, big power-assisted drum brakes, and power steering. The drivetrain, borrowed from Buick's premium Electra, comprised a 325-horsepower 401 V-8 and two-speed Turbine Drive automatic transmission.

Despite a bit of cornering wallow, handling was well up to the performance—which was formidable: 0-60 in around nine seconds, the standing quarter-mile in 16 seconds at 85 mph. With that, Car and Driver rightly raved about the Riv, saying "it stands alone among American cars in providing . . . luxury, performance, and general roadworthiness that approaches Bentley Continental standards at less than half the price"—which was a reasonable $4333 at introduction.

As planned, Buick built exactly 40,000 Rivs for '63. The '64s saw some 2400 fewer copies despite a mere $32 price increase and two significant mechanical changes. First was an optional new 425-cubic-inch engine delivering 340 bhp with four-barrel carb, or a smashing 360 with dual quads. Also newly available was a more efficient three-speed Super Turbine 400 automatic (a.k.a. Turbo Hydra-Matic) for all engines. Styling didn't change much, and didn't need to. Ditto the lush interior with its four bucket seats, full-length center console, and handsome vinyl or optional leather upholstery.

For 1965, the dummy side scoops were erased, taillamps moved down from back panel to bumper, and the horizontal quad headlamps went into the fenders, where they stacked behind sub-grilles made into electrically operated "clamshell" doors. Enthusiasts welcomed a new Gran Sport option with imitation interior wood, 360-bhp engine, limited-slip differential, and firm suspension with "Gyro-Poise" roll control. Handsome five-spoke road wheels were a separate option made just for the potent GS, which could do 0-60 in close to eight seconds and upwards of 115 mph at the top end. Yet for all the improvements, Riviera sales fell again, this time by over 3000 units.

But the point had been made in convincing, memorable fashion. Today, the 1963-65 generation is not only the most revered Riviera, but among the most sought-after of postwar cars. It may have taken five years to come to fruition, but this Buick was obviously time well spent.

Factory shot of the '63 Riviera (this page, top) *shows the car's sculptured, well-balanced profile. Above and opposite page, top: Separate taillights and fixed headlights marked the '63s. Styling was little-changed for 1964, though a larger optional engine and three-speed automatic (rather than the previous two-speed) made performance news. Opposite page, bottom: For 1965, headlights were hidden behind the vertical pods at grille's edge, while taillights were incorporated into the rear bumper.*

SPECIFICATIONS

Engines:	all ohv V-8; **1963-65:** 401 cid (4.19 × 3.64), 325 bhp; **1964-65:** 425 cid (4.31 × 3.64), 340/360 bhp
Transmission:	2/3-speed automatic
Suspension front:	upper and lower A-arms, coil springs
Suspension rear:	live axle on coil springs
Brakes:	front/rear drums
Wheelbase (in.):	117.0
Weight (lbs):	3988-4035
Top speed (mph):	110-115
0-60 mph (sec):	8.1-9.5
Production:	**1963** 40,000 **1964** 37,658 **1965** 34,586

1964-65 Buick
Skylark & Gran Sport

Buick's noble experiment with smallness and distinctive design certainly hadn't failed. Skylarks and the more plebeian Specials of compact dimensions sold quite well in 1961-63. Special production rose from 74,185 in its opening season to 110,870 the next year. Skylark's prospects were particularly promising, considering that 42,000 copies a year were finding customers with only two body styles to choose from.

Nevertheless, the next generation added some inches, competing in the mid-size rather than the compact league. The new A-bodies were larger, stretching nearly a foot farther overall. Yet they were similar in slab-sided appearance to the '63 evolution of the original design, which had already deleted the deep sculpture lines that gave it such a unique look. The same basic body, with its conventional straight-up silhouette atop a 115-inch wheelbase, also went on the new Chevrolet Chevelle.

Two new engines went under Skylark (and Special) hoods: a standard 225-cid Fireball V-6 that cranked out an impressive 155 horsepower; and a new 300-cid V-8 that delivered 210 bhp with a two-barrel carb, 250 with a four-barrel and tight 11:1 compression. That kind of extra power cost only $71 and $93 extra, respectively. Either a four-speed manual shifter or Super Turbine 300 automatic could replace the standard three-speed.

Leather-grained vinyl front bucket seats and console were optional in the sport coupe. Skylarks had bigger brakes with finned cast-iron drums, a new front suspension, and a step-on parking brake like their big brothers. Tires grew to 14-inch size. Skylark's sport coupe went for $2669, while a convertible set a buyer back $2823.

Skylark production approached that of the cheaper Special in 1964, and was destined to whiz into the lead. Therefore, the Skylark series got the nod in 1965

Compact Special/Skylark grew to mid-size dimensions for 1964 (above and below), and engines followed suit. Standard was a 155 bhp 225-cid V-6; optional was a cast-iron V-8 of 300 cid with 210/250 bhp. Opposite page, left column: For 1965, Skylark received a mild facelift, while buckets-and-console interior added to its sporting nature. Adding even more to its sporting nature was the midyear introduction of a Gran Sport package (opposite page, right) that included a 401-cid V-8 pumping out 325 bhp.

SPECIFICATIONS

Engines:	ohv V-6, 225 cid (3.75 × 3.40), 155 bhp; ohv V-8, 300 cid (3.75 × 3.40), 210/250 bhp **1965 Gran Sport** 401 cid (4.19 × 3.64), 325 bhp
Transmissions:	3-speed manual; 4-speed manual and 2-speed Super Turbine 300 automatic optional
Suspension, front:	upper and lower A-arms, coil springs
Suspension, rear:	4-link live axle, coil springs
Brakes:	front/rear drums
Wheelbase (in.):	115.0 **Wagon** 120.0
Weight (lbs.):	3057-3750
Top speed (mph):	99-116
0-60 mph (sec):	GS 7.0-7.8

Production: 1964 spt cpe 42,356 **4d sdn** 19,635 **4d spt wgn** 2709 **4d spt wgn (3-seat)** 2586 **Cust spt wgn** 3913 **cvt** 10,225 **Cust spt wgn** 4446 **1965 cpe** 4195 **2d htp cpe** 4549 **4d sdn** 3385 **V-8 4d sdn** 22,335 **4d wgn** 4226 **4d wgn (3-seat)** 4664 **Cus wgn** 8300 **Cus wgn (3-seat)** 11,166 **cvt** 1181 **Gran Sport cpe** 11,877 **Gran Sport htp cpe** 47,034 **Gran Sport cvt** 10,456

when the time came to take careful aim at the youth market. If excitement was lacking in either the enlarged Special or the marginally sportier Skylark, Buick's Gran Sport set another tone entirely. What came to define the "performance" Buick of the late 1960s started out as an option package for the Skylark, introduced at midyear.

Most prominent element of that package was a monster 401-cid "Nail Head" V-8 (so named for its small vertical valves). Yanked out of the far bigger Wildcat, it enabled the Gran Sport to compete in the muscle car race started by Pontiac's GTO, and soon joined by Oldsmobile's Cutlass-based 4-4-2. By comparison, Buick's big mill delivered an even greater wallop of torque (445 pound/feet) than either GM rival, even if its horsepower fell a trifle short at 325. All that energy could be harnessed to a three-speed or close-ratio four-speed manual gearbox, or Buick's two-speed Super Turbine with a console-mounted selector. Options included a tachometer, limited-slip differential, and chromed steel wheels.

Underneath what Buick modestly described as a "howitzer with windshield wipers" was a reinforced convertible frame carrying heavy-duty suspension and oversized 7.75 × 14 tires. Carefully selected axle ratios, boasted the sales brochure, "lay power on the road with tremendous authority." Low-restriction dual exhausts were standard; vinyl bucket seats a required option.

Red-filled script on the grille, deck, and sail panels (or rear fenders) identified the first Gran Sports, which could be based on the Skylark hardtop coupe, thin-pillar coupe, and convertible that otherwise changed little for 1965 (apart from a loss of some brightwork). Buick General Manager Ed Rollert called the early Gran Sport "a completely engineered performance car." True enough when stomping the gas pedal; not quite so true when trying to wrestle a GS (or any other American muscle car) around a quick corner, even though the Gran Sport carried a stabilizer bar twice as stiff as that installed in an ordinary Skylark.

Two-door Skylark sales proved rather puny in 1965, while the muscular (and spiffier) Gran Sports faced an astounding clamor of eager buyers: 69,367 produced in all, including 10,456 ragtops. As it turned out, this opening year would be the Gran Sport's best; but what a year it was, with those 325 wild horses let loose in a mid-size body that displayed only a few hints of what lurked within. Gran Sport wasn't the first (or last) of the Sixties "sleepers," but it's become one of the most fondly remembered.

1965-69
Buick Electra 225

Neither full-size Buicks nor other American big cars looked like planes about to take off any longer. Down-to-business boxiness was shouldering aside most of the flamboyance and extravagance that had characterized the Fifties. Slicing off the fins in 1961 led to a squared-off profile in '63, which continued in the 1965-69 generation of Buick's biggest and plushest series.

Size was "in," and the mid-Sixties Electras looked the part with their right-angle rear quarter panels. Oddly, after completely abandoning tailfins in '61, this mildly restyled Electra's back fenders protruded past the deck to give just a hint of the old finned look. Coincidence? Or was it a mild harkening back to the bolder past?

Either way, the horizontal look now was *de rigueur*. Electra filled that bill handily, highlighted by a wide ribbed trim strip that extended all the way from the front wheels to the back bumper, crossing the rear fender skirts, to enhance the car's vastly long silhouette. The expected quad headlights stood side-by-side in a straight-up mesh grille. Four wide stylized VentiPorts arranged in a row told viewers this was indeed a Buick.

"It's big, it's sleek, and it rides like a dream," Electra prospects were informed by the 1965 sales catalog. Better yet, it "has the look of solid success," just the thing to let people know "you've arrived." No idle boast, that. An Electra sedan stretched out at the curb really did look like it belonged to someone who'd achieved worldly success, and, like Zero Mostel in *The Producers*, didn't hesitate to flaunt it. At least a little. Stretching 224 inches from stem to stern, an Electra proclaimed one's role in the material world with restrained elegance as opposed to gaudy baubles.

Interiors, to no one's surprise, put plush comfort uppermost, fitted with a selection of fine fabrics and leather-grained vinyls. Customers didn't have to be content with a single engine choice, either. This breed of Electra came with any of three Wildcat V-8s, rated at 325, 340, or 360 bhp, the latter breathing through twin four-barrel carburetors. Variable-pitch Super Turbine automatic was standard, of course; shifting gears in a luxury motor car belonged to the past, or to European upstarts.

Expensive? But of course, though the top Electra convertible at $4440 cost only a tad more than a Riviera. And that was an easy thousand lower than a comparable Cadillac. By this time, Buick was building 50 percent more cars than it had in 1960, rising to fifth in the marketplace (thanks largely, but not entirely, to the Riviera's popularity).

Buick pushed the idea of the "tuned car" for 1966, suggesting that they "tune the entire car from the ground up." Actually, no major change was evident, though Electras wore a new grille and rear-end look. Lowered spring rates and a larger front stabilizer bar played a role in improved handling, while the Super Turbine automatic now contained dual planetary gearsets plus the customary variable-pitch stator. Engine choices this time were the standard 401-cid "Wildcat 445" with its 325 bhp, or optional 425-cid V-8 rated at 340/360.

"Stodgy? Never." That's what Buick said of the restyled 1967 Electras with their new roof curvature and sweeping full-length contour lines. Hardtop coupes had a semi-fastback profile, promoted as "the luxury car built for the man or woman young enough to enjoy a luxury car." Custom models contained woodgrain door moldings. A new 430-cid V-8 was Buick's biggest ever, ready to deliver a "subtle throb of power," though its output was identical to the prior 425 engine.

Restyling for 1968 consisted of a new split grille and front bumper, recessed windshield wipers, a new hood molding, fresh taillights, and revised rear bumper. Front disc brakes were available to replace the usual drums.

All-new upper-series bodies for 1969 had ventless side glass, as front vent wings faded out of the picture. This final Electra of the Sixties had an even squarer, more formal profile than before. Sculptured sweeplines extended the car's full length from front wheel housing to rear bumper in a straight diagonal line. A Turbo Hydra-Matic 400 transmission was standard, substituting for the abandoned Super Turbine. Under the hood? Still the 430-cid V-8 powerplant.

Record-setting sales (past the 665,000 mark) gave Buick its long-sought Number Four spot. Plenty of Americans, it seemed, still appreciated what Buick had to offer in a big, powerful automobile.

Electra for '65 (opposite page) continued with the clean, angular lines of the previous generation, though styling was updated with a slight hump over the rear wheels. The '66s were very similar. For 1967 (this page, top), the hump was exaggerated and joined by a sweeping creaseline, a design that was carried over for '68 (this page, middle). The '69s were redesigned, the creaseline now starting above the front wheelwell (above), and vent windows were eliminated.

SPECIFICATIONS

Engines:	all ohv V-8; **1965-66** 401 cid (4.19 × 3.64), 325 bhp **1965-66** 425 cid (4.31 × 3.64), 340/360 bhp **1967-69** 430 cid (4.19 × 3.90), 360 bhp
Transmission:	3-speed Super Turbine automatic or (**1969**) Turbo Hydra-Matic 400
Suspension, front:	upper and lower A-arms, coil springs, link-type stabilizer
Suspension, rear:	4-link live axle, coil springs
Brakes:	front/rear drums (front discs optional **1968-69**)
Wheelbase (in.):	126.0
Weight (lbs.):	4176-4344
Top speed (mph):	114-118
0-60 mph (sec):	9.0-10.0 (est.)

Production: 1965 htp cpe 15,872 **htp sdn** 42,774 **4d sdn** 19,656 **Cus cvt** 8505 **1966 htp cpe** 15,001 **htp sdn** 44,941 **4d sdn** 21,108 **Cus cvt** 7175 **1967 htp cpe** 19,001 **htp sdn** 53,469 **4d sdn** 20,893 **Cus cvt** 6941 **1968 htp cpe** 27,531 **htp sdn** 66,222 **4d sdn** 23,633 **Cus cvt** 7976 **1969 htp cpe** 40,146 **htp sdn** 81,223 **4d sdn** 28,955 **Cus cvt** 8294

Note: Hardtop coupe/sedan and 4-door sedan totals include both base and Custom models.

1965-69
Buick Wildcat

Mixing impressive performance with plush comforts wasn't hurting Buick sales one bit. Not everyone who wanted to experience a kick of power when hitting the gas was willing to do without American-style conveniences and roominess. Following its early success on a LeSabre-size wheelbase, the second-generation Wildcat borrowed its chassis from the bigger Electra 225, stretching an extra three inches between the axles.

Did the added bulk hurt its potential? Not painfully, since *Mechanix Illustrated*'s Tom McCahill managed to blast to 60 mph in 9.1 seconds, and a Wildcat could hit as high as 125 mph with its most potent Super Wildcat V-8. As Buick boasted in the 1965 sales catalog, "Wildcats come in three strengths: wild (325 bhp), wilder (340 bhp), and wildest (360 bhp)." A year later, McCahill cut that 0-60 time down to a sizzling 7.5 seconds.

No traditional VentiPorts adorned Wildcat fenders, but they did display three horizontal strips at the cowl. A long crease line highlighted the car's profile, just below door-handle level. A nearly fastback coupe roofline and long quarter windows gave the two-door Wildcat a far less formal look than the Electra—precisely what Buick wanted, of course.

Prices were only modestly higher than for the prior year's smaller Wildcats, starting at $3182 for the four-door sedan and peaking at $3727 for a Custom convertible. Wildcat's temptingly lengthy option list included a tachometer, close-ratio four-speed gearbox, three-speed Super Turbine automatic, and chromed steel wheels.

A sharply vee'd grille made up of thin vertical elements highlighted the '66 Wildcat. Rear ends were restyled, and a new instrument panel went inside. Two engines were offered: a 325-bhp edition of the familiar 401, plus a larger (425-cid) version that added 15 horses.

Both the smaller Skylark and "personal-size" Riviera had added Gran Sport packages to lure sporty-minded customers. Could Wildcat do otherwise? Surely

Above and below: While earlier Wildcats were based on the LeSabre platform, in 1965 they moved up to the longer Electra chassis, gaining three inches in wheelbase. Styling, however, was more rounded and flowing than the Electra's. Convertible (below) is fitted with the optional front cornering lamps. Mild front and rear facelifts marked the '66 models (opposite page).

not, so an extra $254.71 bought a new Gran Sport High Performance Group that included the bigger V-8. That wasn't all, by any means. The package added a selection of practical and pretty extras: a chromed air cleaner, cast aluminum rocker covers, dual exhaust, 3.23:1 Positive-Traction differential and heavy-duty suspension, for starters. Keeping all those goodies secret wouldn't do, so a big "Gran Sport" badge on the side of the grille told the world. A few more checks on the option list could bring all sorts of other niceties, from air conditioning at $421 to wire wheel covers ($58) and a $111 vinyl top.

While GS Skylarks helped maintain Buick's new-found performance image into the early 1970s, the Gran Sport package lasted only a single year on Wildcat models.

Wildcats wore an all-new body for 1967, with fresh molding treatment, new grille and back end, and large triangular quarter windows that curved at the base. A sweeping contour line was sculpted into bodyside metal. Taillights consisted of full-width twin horizontal bands. In Buick's words, the revised 'cat was "low, long and sinewy as its namesake," but as always, qualified as a "performance car that looks like a luxury car." *Car Life* branded it "more friendly than fierce."

Changes beneath the surface were no less vital: namely, a new 430-cid V-8 holding 360 horses at bay. Customers were induced to "feel the tickle of 360-hp touch your toes" in a car that "pulses with response and agility on the road." Buick's three-speed Super Turbine automatic was now standard.

A rather rare event for big American dreamboats happened for 1969: the Wildcat's wheelbase was shortened from 126 to 123 inches, just what it had measured during the first generation. This fresh body displayed a longer hood and shorter deck, along with a modified sweepline and new grille. New dual air intakes were contained in the front bumper. As in all upper-series Buicks, side window vents were eliminated this year.

Wildcats switched from Super Turbine automatic to Turbo Hydra-Matic, coupled to the same 430-cid engine of 1967-68 and controlled by a column- or console-mounted selector. Other mechanical boosts included a Directional Stability System, power disc brakes, and Accu-Drive suspension that employed the "reverse-camber" principle to help glide over bumps.

The Wildcat name was destined to last only one more season, but the '70 version was a different breed: riding the restyled LeSabre chassis with a 455-cid engine beneath its bonnet. Muscle cars as a whole were becoming an endangered species, and the notion of a full-size luxury automobile with muscle—already an anomaly to some—wasn't likely to hang on.

SPECIFICATIONS

Engines:	all ohv V-8; **1965-66** 401 cid (4.19 × 3.64), 325 bhp; 425 cid (4.31 × 3.64), 340/360 bhp **1967-69** 430 cid (4.19 × 3.90), 360 bhp
Transmissions:	3-speed manual; optional Super Turbine automatic or (1969) 3-speed Turbo Hydra-Matic 400
Suspension, front:	upper and lower A-arms, coil springs, link-type stabilizer
Suspension, rear:	4-link live axle, coil springs
Brakes:	front/rear drums (1969, front discs)
Wheelbase (in.):	126.0 **1969:** 123.0
Weight (lbs.):	3926-4220
Top speed (mph):	117-125
0-60 mph (sec):	7.5-9.6

Production: 1965 htp cpe 33,544 **htp sdn** 36,280 **4d sdn** 19,949 **cvt** 9014 **1966 htp cpe** 20,574 **htp sdn** 28,141 **4d sdn** 14,389 **cvt** 5480 **1967 htp cpe** 22,456 **htp sdn** 28,657 **4d sdn** 14,579 **cvt** 5189 **1968 htp cpe** 21,984 **htp sdn** 29,212 **4d sdn** 15,201 **Cus cvt** 3572 **1969 htp cpe** 24,552 **htp sdn** 27,401 **4d sdn** 13,126 **Cus cvt** 2374

Note: Production totals include base, Deluxe (1965 only) and Custom models.

New styling graced the '67 Wildcat (above), which was carried over with few changes for '68 (left, and opposite page, top). Hardtop coupes wore fastback rooflines, while all received a sweeping side creaseline like the Electra. Proving that "what goes up must come down," the '69 (opposite page, bottom) reverted to the shorter 123-inch wheelbase (from 126) that it rode in '64. The accompanying restyle brought new front and rear ends and a different side crease design.

1966-69
Buick Riviera

Success is sometimes like candy: too much of it can leave you with weighty problems. Take the second-generation Buick Riviera. When redesigned for 1966, Flint's posh personal-luxury hardtop lost the adroit blend of creases and curves that had made the 1963-65 original so distinctive. It also became longer, wider, and heavier.

But worst of all, at least for some Flint fans, the Riviera was no longer a Buick exclusive. The original's instant high acclaim and strong sales had spurred Oldsmobile and Cadillac to lobby for similar cars, which were duly granted: the all new '66 Toronado and similar '67 Eldorado. The Riv did retain a small distinction in continuing with rear-wheel drive, eschewing the radical front-drive system of its new sisters.

None of this was bad, mind you. GM was a master at tailoring shared platforms for its various makes, and the new Riviera/Eldorado/Toronado E-body was no exception. What's more, Riviera's '66 styling, if not as trend-setting as '63, was at least svelte and elegant in the curvy humped-fender idiom then taking hold at GM and elsewhere. The man largely responsible for it, David R. Holls, then nearing the end of a four-year stint as Buick chief designer (and bound for Chevrolet, where he'd have a hand in the '68 Corvette), later termed it his personal favorite of the various Buicks he worked on.

Buyers liked it too, for the '66 Riv drew over 10,000 more orders than the '65—nearly 45,500—helped by a base price upped only $16 (to $4424). And as events would prove to Buick's undoubted satisfaction, this Riviera would consistently outsell its divisional sisters, though not Ford's Thunderbird, still flying high at around 69,000 units.

Compared to the '65, the '66 Riv rode a two-inch longer wheelbase, stood 3.2 inches longer (211.2), about two inches wider (a girthy 76.6), and a half-inch lower. Curb weight was up about 120 pounds (though appearance suggested more), and there were no great chassis changes. Headlamps remained hidden but rolled down ahead of the grille from a horizontal resting place above, thus avoiding the unsightly trim mismatches of the previous clamshell doors. A sweeping new roofline displayed a virtual fastback profile, yet managed a hint of the original Riv's razor-edge formality.

Inside was a new slim-section dash sloped away from the top instead of out toward the driver, with gimmicky revolving-drum instruments that weren't nearly as legible as the former needle gauges. But that dash and the enlarged bodyshell improved interior space. Indeed, the Riv could now accommodate six instead of merely five, as a three-person front bench seat (with reclining right backrest) was newly standard. Buckets moved to the options list, still split by a console holding a new inverted-U "horseshoe" selector for the standard Hydra-Matic transmission. A significant new comfort feature was flow-through ventilation with dashboard registers, air-extraction louvers in the low-pressure area just below the backlight, and no door ventwings (eliminated as unnecessary).

A burly new 430-cubic-inch V-8 was the big news for '67. Shared with other big Buicks, it belted out the same 360 horsepower as the top version of the superseded 425, meaning the Gran Sport option had no more muscle than standard Rivieras. But the GS still had a performance edge with a 3.42:1 rear axle providing livelier standing-start acceleration than the base 3.07 cog. Also making news were optional front-disc brakes and more cooling fins for the standard 12-inch power drums. As before, the GS package included dual-inlet air cleaner, limited-slip differential, whitewalls, and discreet exterior i.d.

Riviera finished the decade with no other noteworthy changes save those safety and emissions-control measures dictated by Washington starting with 1968 models. Appearance was freshened that year, though the massive new bumper/grille was debatable, adding four inches to overall length. Equally dubious was the vinyl roof covering still optional for any Riviera; it needlessly interrupted the smooth transition from roof to lower body. But happily, the Gran Sport option was still around, too—and a better-than-ever bargain at just $132.

The '69s changed only in detail: new grille insert, revamped center console, and the usual color/trim shuffles. However, they sold better than any previous Riv, breaking the 50,000-mark after several years at the 40,000-45,000 level.

Then again, Buick's high '60s success was built on consistency, and Riviera was nothing if not consistent. Though destined to be ever overshadowed by the peerless original, the second generation has come to be appreciated by collectors for its part in that sweet success—and you can never have too much of that.

SPECIFICATIONS

Engines:	all ohv V-8; **1966** 425 cid (4.31 × 3.64), 340/360 bhp; **1967-69**: 430 cid (4.19 × 3.90), 360 bhp
Transmissions:	3-speed automatic
Suspension front:	upper and lower A-arms, coil springs
Suspension rear:	live axle on coil springs
Brakes:	front/rear drums; optional front discs **1967**
Wheelbase (in.):	119.0
Weight (lbs):	4190
Top speed (mph):	NA
0-60 mph (sec):	NA

Production: 1966 45,348 **1967** 42,799 **1968** 49,284 **1969** 52,872

Restyle for '66 (top) carried through to '69 (above) with few changes besides the usual year-to-year "facials." Opposite page, top: The Gran Sport option package for 1966 (identified by the "GS" logo behind the Riviera Script on the front fender) added special trim bits and a lower-ratio Positraction rear axle. In the annual facelift, taillights on the '68 Riv (opposite page, bottom) were incorporated into the rear bumper, where they remained for '69.

1966-67 Buick Skylark & Gran Sport (GS)

After two years of standing tall, the Skylark's A-body adopted a modest leaning-forward stance not unlike that of the bigger Riviera, formed from all-new sheetmetal. Bumper-to-bumper, the coupes stretched longer (to 204 inches) than before, even though the 115-inch wheelbase was unchanged. Some branded the restyled Skylark (and performance-focused Gran Sport) as less distinctive than the '65 models. Others disagreed—just as latter-day enthusiasts still argue the point.

Foot-to-the-floor fans again benefited from Buick's decision to stuff the hefty 401-cid V-8 beneath the Gran Sport hood, eager to flaunt its 325-horsepower muscularity. This year's roofline reached the broadly sloping sail panels quite a distance past the recessed rear window, creating a smooth, ready-to-leap silhouette.

Subtlety was still the Gran Sport's ace in the hole. Apart from a simple "GS" emblem on the rear flank, matte black rear panel, and "Gran Sport" nameplate decorating the blacked-out grille, there was little to proclaim the pleasures that lurked within the fully fitted coupe, hardtop, or convertible. Oh yes, the hood held a pair of fake airscoops; but they weren't flashy enough to attract much notice.

Gran Sport interiors were all vinyl, with a notchback bench seat standard; but $47 Strato-Buckets were typically one of the first items to be added. Other popular extras included a floor-shift four-speed at $184 (or Super Turbine automatic for $205), and performance axle ratio at $42. Wire wheel covers commanded $63. For the $2956 base price of a GS thin-pillar coupe, customers got dual exhausts, a heavy-duty suspension, three-speed gearbox—and the "Wildcat 445" engine. A convertible cost only $211 more.

During the year, Buick advertised an optional engine with 15 extra horsepower. Car and Driver blasted one of the 340-bhp examples through the quarter-mile trap in less than 15 seconds, reaching a mite past 95 mph. Ads also trumpeted the availability of metallic brake linings and a rear stabilizer.

Sales of the Gran Sport slipped from their lofty opening season, as only 13,816 were built. Skylarks in general were doing well, with 106,217 hitting the showrooms.

Modifications were minor for 1967, but the performance leader shortened its official title to "GS" (full name, GS400) and was considered a separate series. Red "GS" letters adorned the distinctively sculptured, red-banded grille and the rear fenders. "Buick's personal sports car" (that's ad language) wore blacked-out headlight bezels, twin hood scoops, and rally stripes, plus red- or white-striped F70×14 Wide-Oval tires. Simulated air extractors behind the front wheel openings switched from a triple-grid motif to a pair of slanted elements. Taillights were restyled, as they were on other Skylarks. A three-speed Super Turbine automatic or floor-shift four-speed could replace the standard three-speed box.

To the surprise of many, Buick debuted a new 400-cid V-8 for the GS, developed by Cliff Studaker, to replace the 401. The new mill whipped up 340 horses and looked more muscular under the hood with its massive red plastic air cleaner. A total of 13,813 GS400s were built this time, including 2140 convertibles.

Acceleration with the new engine proved to be downright astounding: 0-60 in six flat with automatic, as reported by Car and Driver, and actually slower (6.6 seconds) with a Muncie four-speed. "Tire spinning," the magazine reported, was "available at the touch of a toe."

Anyone who liked the Gran Sport notion but didn't need that many inches had another choice at midyear: a red-trimmed GS340 Sport Coupe, styled like its musclebound brother but carrying a 260-bhp, 340-cid V-8. Painted only in White or Platinum Mist, the GS340 sported flaming red hood scoops and Rally accent stripes low on the bodysides, along with red Rally wheels and a red lower-deck molding. Priced $111 less than the GS400 thin-pillar coupe, a total of 3692 were built. An optional Sport Pac with heavy-duty rear stabilizer, springs, and shocks boosted the 340's handling agility even if it lagged in off-the-line muscle. Front disc brakes were optional.

Corrosion inevitably plagued Skylarks and GS machines in the snowbelt, as it did most American cars of this vintage. Those that survived such an ignominious fate continue to attract attention for their clean lines and subtle promises. "Your father never told you there'd be Buicks like this," ads had proclaimed; and there were more Skylark surprises to come.

SPECIFICATIONS

Engines:	**Skylark** ohv V-6, 225 cid (3.75 × 3.40), 160 bhp; ohv V-8, 300 cid (3.75 × 3.40), 210 bhp **1966 GS** ohv V-8, 401 cid (4.19 × 3.64), 325/340 bhp **1967 GS340** ohv V-8, 340 cid (3.75 × 3.85), 220/260 bhp **1967 GS400** ohv V-8, 400 cid (4.04 × 3.90), 340 bhp
Transmissions:	3-speed manual; 4-speed manual and 2-speed or 3-speed Super Turbine automatic optional
Suspension, front:	upper and lower A-arms, coil springs
Suspension, rear:	live axle, coil springs
Brakes:	front/rear drums **1967** front discs optional
Wheelbase (in.):	115.0 **Wagon** 120.0
Weight (lbs.):	3034-3876
Top speed (mph):	99-122
0-60 mph (sec):	**GS400** 6.0-7.6

Production: 1966 V6 cpe 1454 **V8 cpe** 6427 **V6 htp cpe** 2552 **V8 htp cpe** 33,326 **V6 htp sdn** 1422 **V8 htp sdn** 18,873 **V6 cvt** 608 **V8 cvt** 6129 **V6 4d wgn** 2469 **Cus 4d wgn** 6964 **V6 4d wgn (3-seat)** 2667 **Cus 4d wgn (3-seat)** 9510 **GS cpe** 1835 **GS htp cpe** 9934 **GS cvt** 2047 **1967 V6 cpe** 894 **V8 cpe** 3165 **htp cpe** 41,084 **htp sdn** 13,721 **4d sdn** 9213 **cvt** 6319 **4d wgn** 5440 **4d wgn (3-seat)** 5970 **Cus 4d wgn** 3114 **Cus 4d wgn (3-seat)** 4559 **GS340 htp cpe** 3692 **GS400 cpe** 1014 **GS400 htp cpe** 10,659 **GS400 cvt** 2140

This page, top, and opposite page, top: More rounded, flowing contours marked the redesigned '66 Skylarks, and of course the Gran Sport versions followed suit. Underneath the new skin, however, there were few mechanical changes, though a stronger 401 with 340 bhp (versus the standard 325) was made optional at midyear. For 1967, a tamer GS340 was added to the line (above), and Buick's top hot rod was renamed GS400 in honor of its new 400-cid V-8 with 340 bhp (opposite page, bottom).

1968-69
Buick Skylark & GS

Not everyone fell in love with the new body installed on the smaller Buicks for 1968, whether in ordinary Special/Skylark trim or carrying a full load of GS equipment. Front ends had a clean and pleasing appearance, true, focused on a grille reminiscent of the Riviera. A longer hood and shorter deck weren't the problem. Neither were the concealed windshield wipers. No, what looked out of place to some—then and now—was the new deep-sculptured body sweepline, borrowing its "sweepspear" curvature from the distant past, arcing across the bodyside before it came to a halt ahead of the rear wheel opening. No less jarring was the concave rear end, with new taillights contained in a large rear bumper below pointy back fenders. In this incarnation, two-doors rode a shorter wheelbase: 112 inches versus 116 for the four-doors (121 for Sportwagons).

Evidently, quite a few people did indeed take a liking to the new look, because Skylark sales set a record in '68. By this time, the Special name was close to fading out, outsold by Skylarks by a nearly five-to-one ratio.

For base Skylarks, Chevrolet's familiar inline six-cylinder engine replaced the former V-6. Farther up the scale, a new GS350 model took the role of the previous GS340, powered by a bored-out 350-cid V-8 developing 280 bhp along with a resounding 375 pounds/feet of torque. A less-potent edition of that mill (230-horse) was standard in Skylark Customs, and optional elsewhere.

Topping the performance charts once again was the GS400, with its 400-cid V-8 ready to unleash 340 horses. That was enough to shoot a "400" to 60 mph in a trifling six seconds. The most muscular GS still didn't look all that tough; but as in its prior guise, this kind of zest was treading closely on Corvette territory.

Automakers weren't shy about pushing their muscular products shamelessly in the male direction in those days. Buick was no exception, proclaiming its GS selection to be: "Clean. Fresh. Masculine."

Not every GS ranked as the "real thing" this time. In addition to the honest

Above and below: Redesigned '68 Skylarks gained "heavier" styling with a pronounced side creaseline, evidenced by these GS350s. As indicated by the "350" nomenclature, engine size increased this year from the previous 340 cid, bringing with it 20 extra horsepower (now 280). The '69s were little changed in appearance (opposite page, right), but GS400s could be ordered with the "Stage 1" option, which brought a modified engine (opposite page, left) fitted with a hotter camshaft, larger carburetor, low-restriction exhaust, and ram-air induction.

SPECIFICATIONS

Engines:	**Skylark** ohv I-6, 250 cid (3.88 × 3.53), 155 bhp; ohv V-8, 350 cid (3.80 × 3.85), 230 bhp **1968-69 GS350** ohv V-8, 350 cid, 280 bhp **GS400** ohv V-8, 400 cid (4.04 × 3.90), 340 bhp
Transmissions:	3-speed manual; 4-speed manual (**GS**), Super Turbine automatic or (**1969**) Turbo Hydra-Matic 350 optional
Suspension, front:	upper and lower A-arms, coil springs
Suspension, rear:	4-link live axle, coil springs
Brakes:	front/rear drums (front discs optional)
Wheelbase (in.):	112.0 **4d sdn/wag** 116.0
Weight (lbs.):	3240-3594
Top speed (mph):	GS 105-120
0-60 mph (sec):	**GS350** 8.0-10.0 **GS400** 6.0-7.7

Production: 1968 htp cpe 32,795 **Cus htp cpe** 44,143 **Cus htp sdn** 12,984 **4d sdn** 27,387 **Cus 4d sdn** 8066 **Cus cvt** 8188 **4d Sportwagon** 22,908 **GS350 htp cpe** 8317 **GS400 htp cpe** 10,743 **G400S cvt** 2454 **1969 htp cpe** 38,658 **Cus htp cpe** 35,639 **Cus htp sdn** 9609 **4d sdn** 22,349 **Cus 4d sdn** 6423 **Cus cvt** 6552 **4d Sportwagon** 20,670 **GS350 htp cpe** 4933 **GS400 htp cpe** 6356 **GS400 cvt** 1776

GS340 and GS400, Buick announced a California GS. Sure enough, it wore "GS" badges and carried the GS's styled steel wheels. Underneath, however, this was a sheep in wolf's garb: really a vinyl-roofed Special Deluxe pillared coupe toting the smaller V-8 engine.

The performance-plus GS coupes and convertibles were identical except for their badges to denote engine displacement. Each had a special hood with air intake near the cowl.

For 1969, a new GS hood blister contained an integrated air intake carrying displacement badges. Functional GS400 scoops yanked incoming air into a dual-snorkel air cleaner.

No more bright strips were installed on front fenders. In fact, little brightwork at all decorated the '69s, except for wheelwell moldings and five-spoke chrome wheels. Up front was a new eggcrate grille with large "holes." Dual paint stripes followed the sculptured sweepline down each bodyside. More noticeable yet was the lack of front vent windows.

The California GS made another appearance, wearing telltale front vents just like the Special Deluxe Coupe it actually was. Authentic or not, a California GS stormed to 60 mph in 9.5 seconds at the hands of Tom McCahill, inveterate tester for *Mechanix Illustrated*.

Added to the option selection for 1969 was Turbo Hydra-Matic, replacing the customary Super Turbine transmission. Acceleration freaks took greater note of the new Stage I engine package, which raised a GS400's output from 340 to 345 bhp (at higher rpm). Doesn't sound like much, but it gave the car quite a jolt when the time came to stomp the pedal. The Stage I package included a high-lift cam, special carburetor, dual exhausts, and 3.64:1 Positraction axle. To help keep all those horses flying, a short-throw Hurst shifter was available for the four-speed manual.

Corrosion remained a problem for Skylark/GS, and this wasn't Buick's high point for fit and finish either; but customers liked them anyway. A total of 21,514 GS Buicks were built in 1968 (including 2454 GS400 convertibles), though the total slipped to 13,065 the next year. Even so, Buick ended the decade by regaining its long-lost fourth spot in the industry sales ranking. Yet another "Stage" of performance would soon enter the GS lineup for the early 1970s, as the mighty V-8 grew to 455 cubic inches; after that, Buick settled back into its cushy image and the muscle-car era faded into history.

1960
Cadillac

If "wretched excess" was a reasonable way to describe the Cadillacs of 1959 with their mile-high tailfins, their counterparts of the following year had to rank as rather subdued. Yet had the '59 fins not been so ever-present—so impossible to ignore—their 1960 descendants might indeed hold the record for too much of a good (or a bad) thing. Nevertheless, the narrow red lenses contained within each curvaceous blade give the back end an almost graceful look, at least when compared to the bold and blustery units of the prior year. Even though they actually stood only an inch or so lower than their predecessors, the 1960 fins were intended to display a single flowing line, rather than looking plopped onto the top of the fenders.

Common sense dictated that the only reasonable direction the fins could go was down. That was especially true since GM's innovative design chief, Harley Earl—a fancier of projectile shapes who'd initiated the whole tailfin trend with the 1948 Cadillac—retired in 1958. His replacement, Bill Mitchell, helped usher in a more restrained era highlighted by crisp, chiseled lines rather than staggering shapes. He favored graceful elegance over chrome-laden ostentation—so long as the traditional Cadillac identity remained.

Fins aside, the '60 models were little more than facelifts of the prior year's model lineup, though Cadillac touted its "classic new profile" and "restrained use of adornment." While still laden with a fair share of brightwork, the grille was simpler this year, with a similar pattern of multitudinous chrome "buttons" but lacking the former divider bar. Within the next couple of years, the fins would diminish in both size and significance. By the middle of the decade, they'd virtually disappear (though subtle vestiges remained for years).

All Cadillacs came with standard Hydra-Matic Drive, power steering, and power brakes. Under their hoods sat the same powertrains used in 1959. With a four-barrel carburetor, the 390-cid V-8 engine produced 325 horsepower. Eldorados

Cadillac's top-of-the-line convertible for 1960 was this Eldorado Biarritz, of which only 1285 were built. No doubt the $7401 price contributed to its limited appeal, as this was nearly $2000 more than a Series 62 ragtop. All Eldorados carried fancier trim, a higher level of standard equipment, and 20 more horsepower than "lesser" Cadillacs, the last courtesy of triple two-barrel carburetors in place of the standard four-barrel. Exclusive to the Biarritz was a fiberglass "boot" covering the convertible top.

SPECIFICATIONS

Engine:	ohv V-8, 390 cid (4.00 × 3.88), 325/345 bhp
Transmission:	Dual Range Hydra-Matic
Suspension, front:	upper and lower A-arms, coil springs
Suspension, rear:	4-link live axle, coil springs
Brakes:	front/rear drums
Wheelbase (in.):	130.0 **Series 75** 149.75
Weight (lbs.):	4670-5560
Top speed (mph):	118-125
0-60 mph (sec):	10.0-11.5

Production: Series 62 4d htp sdn (4-window) 9984 **4d htp sdn (6-window)** 26,824 **htp cpe** 19,978 **cvt** 14,000 **DeVille 4d htp sdn (4-window)** 9225 **4d htp sdn (6-window)** 22,579 **htp cpe** 21,585 **60 Special htp sdn** 11,800 **Series 75 9-seat sdn** 718 **9-seat limo** 832 **Eldorado Seville htp cpe** 1075 **Biarritz cvt cpe** 1285

enjoyed 20 extra horses, by virtue of a triple-carb setup. Self-adjusting brakes and an automatically releasing emergency brake were new this year.

Prices were identical to 1959, ranging from $4892 for a Series 62 hardtop coupe, all the way to $9748 for the Series 75 limousine. Once again, two different four-door hardtops were available. The four-window version had a flat-topped Vista roof with a severely wrapped, panoramic back window. Its mate was a more traditional six-window design with less dramatic rear glass, plus long triangular vent panes built into the back doors. As before, the Series 75 nine-passenger sedan and limo rode a 149.8-inch wheelbase, versus 130 inches for all other models.

Cadillac production was almost identical to 1959, with 142,184 built. Yearly sales set a record, however, cementing the company's hold on 10th spot in the industry. Series 62 again was the top seller, but the upmarket DeVille series, introduced in 1959, was rising fast.

Production of the posh Fleetwood Sixty Special sedan slipped a bit, to 11,800. Sixty Specials were easy to spot with their dark red cloisonné crest on front fenders and chrome louvers below the fins, and wore leather-grained fabric on their roofs. Three Eldorados were offered again in 1960: a Seville hardtop coupe, Biarritz convertible, and the custom-built Brougham (see separate listing). A Biarritz "Emerald Edition" with emerald body and complementary green ragtop wore the new profile particularly well, making the Eldo's rather garish rear cove molding appear almost subtle.

Caddies were still big cars in these days, measuring 225 inches from stem to stern (244.8 inches for the Series 75). Self-leveling air suspension was still available (standard on Eldorados), though a number of owners had found the system trouble-prone and it wasn't a hot-selling option. A radio and heater were standard only on Eldorados, which also came with fog lamps and power door locks. Among other extras, Cadillac's option list included air conditioning, cruise control, power seats and windows, Guide-Matic headlight dimming, and E-Z-Eye glass.

Sure, these Caddies look immense—even grotesque—to modern eyes trained on subcompacts. They were also rust-prone. But as the 1960s began, Cadillac still laid a strong claim as "Standard of the World," and few who gazed upon those pointed fins traveling down the street dared to disagree. While the flamboyant '59 Cadillac served as a statement of its times, a virtual icon of that optimistic decade, its more sophisticated 1960 successor heralded a step into a new and different age.

1960 Cadillac Eldorado Brougham

Back in the 1920s and '30s, custom bodies had been the rule among luxury cars. People of means could order a Cadillac, Lincoln, or Duesenberg chassis, then have a one-of-a-kind body created and crafted by a skilled coachbuilder. By the 1950s, most of the American coachbuilders were gone, but in Europe—especially Italy—such artists as Ghia, Zagato, and Pininfarina continued to ply their trade on both sports and luxury motorcars.

When Cadillac wanted an evolutionary replacement for the Brougham that had been marketed in 1957-58, it made sense to turn to the other side of the Atlantic and the Pininfarina studio, in Turin (Torino), Italy. What Farina's artisans created and built wasn't as far removed from the ordinary Cadillac as that earlier Brougham had been. Nevertheless, it was special enough to warrant a $13,075 price tag—a whopping $5674 more than an Eldorado Biarritz convertible.

Unlike the Brougham of 1957-58, which sported such distinctive touches as a brushed stainless steel roof and mouton carpeting, this version retained a closer kinship with everyday Eldorados. In 1959, however, it was the only model that lacked the flamboyantly gigantic fins with their "bullet" taillights. The Brougham wore a grille with comparable brightwork, but devoid of the usual horizontal bar. In fact, that Brougham foretold some of the styling changes that soon would be coming on all Cadillacs.

In its second year, differences between Broughams and basic Caddies seemed subtler yet, as the latter enjoyed a restyling. At a glance, in fact, it's hard to tell a Brougham from its "lesser" 1960 Cadillac four-door hardtop counterparts. A closer look reveals a number of distinctive touches, starting with the unique windshield curvature. Instead of the usual extreme wraparound into a "dogleg" A-pillar containing slim vertical rectangular vent wings, the Brougham's front glass wrapped only slightly down at the bottom. That change permitted installation of much larger, triangular vent panes to complement the three-sided panes at the back. The rear window barely wrapped at all, so C-pillars were a lot narrower. And the roofline itself had a more crisp, formal profile, lacking the roundness of other Cadillacs.

Only a couple of minor changes occurred between the 1959 and '60 models. The original Pininfarina nameplate, for one, was abandoned. Hubcaps were mildly revised, and cloisonné emblems were visible at the ends of the rear fenders. A low crease line was evident in the bodysides at a level just below the top of the front wheel arches. In both years, only Broughams came with standard narrow-band whitewalls.

Broughams included a tempting selection of extras that were optional on other Eldorados, including Guide-Matic automatic headlight dimming, air conditioning, and E-Z-Eye glass. Air suspension was standard, keeping the car at normal height no matter how many people (or how much luggage) went inside.

Cadillac called the 1960 Brougham its "finest expression of the new era of automotive elegance." Here, they insisted, was "a motor car that stands out—even among Cadillacs." To help give their exclusivity a push, Broughams came in their own selection of colors.

Partly because Italian coachbuilders tended to use a sizable quantity of body filler in their creations, Broughams were even more rust-prone than other Cadillacs. And since their body panels were used on no other models, forget about trying to find a replacement today. Buy a Brougham that still carries its original air suspension, and you're likely to face more than a trace of leakage.

In its two years of life, only 200 Broughams were shipped out of Italy (99 in 1959). That was well below the 704 units of the American-made (by Fleetwood) 1957-58 version, which also was better constructed. Thus, the long-established tradition of a custom-built Cadillac quietly faded away after its brief rebirth.

Oh sure, the Brougham name stuck around, and adorns the last rear-drive Cadillacs of the 1990s. Still, the mystique of coachbuilt motorcars, produced in small numbers for a discerning clientele, was becoming part of the distant past. European marques, notably Mercedes-Benz, kept up the tradition. Americans did not.

Instead, the industry turned to high-volume sales and mass-market taste, where the word "custom" meant just one more humdrum model name. Not until the Allante of the late 1980s would Cadillac form another meaningful alliance with a European styling firm—Pininfarina, again—to produce its distinctive two-seater. Luxury sedans and limousines, meanwhile, became the province of "stretch" bodybuilders who focused more on size than on distinction.

Above: *First class accommodations, circa 1960.* Opposite page: *Outrageously expensive Fleetwood Brougham saw but 200 copies in two years of production. Example shown is a 1959 version, which differed from the '60 only in slight trim details. Brougham's squared-off, angular roofline forecast a design destined for Cadillac's 1961 sedans.*

SPECIFICATIONS

Engine:	ohv V-8, 390 cid (4.00 × 3.88), 345 bhp
Transmission:	Dual Range Hydra-Matic
Suspension, front:	upper and lower A-arms, coil springs
Suspension, rear:	4-link live axle, coil springs
Brakes:	front/rear drums
Wheelbase (in.):	130.0
Weight (lbs.):	5200
Top speed (mph):	120
0-60 mph (sec):	10.5
Production:	**1960** 101

1961-62
Cadillac

Against the garish excesses of 1959-60, the cleaner, somewhat leaner 1961 Cadillacs seem a triumph of good taste. Yet they hardly get a mention except in the most exhaustive historical works. Reason: Lincoln showed even better taste in an all-new '61 Continental that was hailed for styling excellence by no less than the prestigious Industrial Design Institute.

But credit the '61 Caddys for reversing the division's slide toward substandard styling—and for putting it back on an ascending sales track. Lincoln notwithstanding, Cadillac had been America's overwhelming luxury favorite for a good two decades in 1961, and it wouldn't be challenged in either image or sales supremacy for another 20 years (and then only from abroad).

Carrying another new GM C-body, the '61s were the first Cadillacs influenced by William L. Mitchell, installed as GM design chief in 1958. He didn't influence them very much, however, as they'd been largely developed during the twilight years of his renowned predecessor, Harley Earl, with some inspiration from the Pininfarina-built 1959-60 Eldorado Brougham. The '61 Cadillacs, along with their divisional sisters, thus mark a transition between two historic eras in GM design.

The 1960 models had literally backed down from the absurd heights of Cadillac's '59 fins. The '61s backed down even further, though their trimmer fins now had company: chrome-lined "bottom fins" or "skegs" flaring outward from sheetmetal creases above the rocker panels. This was one sign of Earl's hand, a direct lift from his '59 Cadillac Cyclone show car, and also seen on designer Drew Hare's late-1959 "Double Bubble" mock-up that contributed to the '61 Oldsmobile. The latter also donated the new "French-curve" A-pillars that gracefully eliminated the old knee-banger "doglegs," while maintaining a modest windshield wrap on all of GM's full-size '61s save Caddy's big Series 75s. Those cars would retain 1959 architecture and unique 149.8-inch wheelbase all the way through 1965.

Other '61 Caddys rode an unchanged 129.5-inch chassis. Width remained just shy of 80 inches, but overall length was trimmed three inches from 1960 and curb weights lightened up an average of 120 pounds—more welcome evidence that design sanity had returned at last. Underneath was the familiar X-member chassis with all-coil suspension, recirculating-ball steering, and big, finned all-drum brakes, the last two power-assisted, of course. Air suspension was scratched from the option list after five years of service headaches and slow sales. But the '61 roster was more than compensated with new hot-air rear-window defogger, limited-slip differential, and a crankcase venting system that was mandatory on cars bound for smoggy California.

There was only one drivetrain: the new-for-'59 390 V-8 in 325-horsepower four-barrel form, teamed with evergreen Dual-Range Hydra-Matic. The 345-bhp Eldorado engine with its twin four-barrel carbs was gone. So was the Seville hardtop coupe and the custom-built Brougham, leaving the Biarritz convertible as the sole Eldorado—and still not all that special next to the "everyday" Series 62 model.

Besides that ragtop, Cadillac's "entry-level" line continued with four- and six-window hardtop sedans plus the obligatory pillarless coupe. All but the convertible repeated with slightly upmarket trim as Series 63 DeVilles, while the 60 Special remained a premium six-window hardtop sedan and flagship of the standard-body fleet. The year also brought one Series 62 newcomer: a six-window four-door hardtop trimmed seven inches in the tail. Like the single "low-power" V-8, this "Short Deck Sedan" was a belated nod to a market made economy-conscious by the recessionary shock of 1958. It was a poor seller, however, as fewer than 3800 were built for the model year.

Cadillac's total '61 sales were 139,000, the lowest since '58. The new Continental undoubtedly stole some customers, but only a few. Cadillac was still far ahead of both Lincoln and Chrysler's Imperial in the luxury sweepstakes.

With Mitchell settled in, the '62s were basically toned-down '61s. Highlights included still-lower fins, tidier grille, backup/turn/stop lights combined behind a single white lens, and standard dual-circuit "safety" brake system. Four-window sedans lost the radically wrapped backlight of 1959-61 for conventional flat glass and squarish C-pillars. Front-fender cornering lamps were a new across-the-board option. Also new was a pair of "shorties": Series 62 Town Sedan (replacing the six-window '61) and DeVille Park Avenue. Again, though, this idea had scant appeal, sales totaling just 2600 apiece.

But Cadillac as a whole decisively turned the corner for 1962, with record production of nearly 161,000. And this was only the beginning. For Cadillac more than most other makes, the years just ahead truly would be "The Soaring '60s."

Above and opposite page, bottom: *The "extruded" look with lowered tailfins marked Cadillac's 1961 styling, and interior design featured clean, restrained elegance. Fins were trimmed further for 1962 (opposite page, top), when Cadillac set an all-time sales record of over 160,000 units.*

SPECIFICATIONS

Engine:	ohv V-8, 390 cid (4.00 × 3.88) 325 bhp
Transmission:	4-speed automatic
Suspension front:	upper and lower A-arms, coil springs
Suspension rear:	live axle on coil springs
Brakes:	front/rear drums
Wheelbase (in.):	149.8 Series 75, 129.5 others
Weight (lbs):	4560-5420
Top speed (mph):	approx. 117
0-60 mph (sec):	11.2

Production: 1961 Series 62 htp sdn 6W 26,216 **htp cpe** 16,005 **htp sdn 4W** 4,700 **Town Sedan htp 6W** 3,756 **cvt** 15,500 **chassis** 5 **DeVille htp sdn 6W** 26,415 **htp cpe** 20,156 **htp sdn 4W** 4,847 **Eldorado Biarritz cvt** 1,450 **Series 60 Special htp sdn** 15,500 **Series 75 4d sdn 9P** 699 **limo 9P** 926 **chassis** 2,204 **1962 Series 62 htp sdn 6W** 16,730 **htp sdn 4W** 17,314 **htp cpe** 16,833 **cvt** 16,800 **Town Sedan htp 4W** 2,600 **DeVille htp sdn 6W** 16,230 **htp sdn 4W** 27,378 **htp cpe** 25,675 **Park Avenue htp sdn 4W** 2,600 **Eldorado Biarritz cvt** 1,450 **Series 60 Special htp sdn 6W** 13,350 **Series 75 4d sdn 9P** 696 **limo 9P** 904 **chassis** 2,280

1963-64
Cadillac

To those who harbor the opinion that car companies build only what they want to—regardless of buyer sentiment—a look at Cadillac in the '60s must surely test their resolve. From decade's dawn, Cadillac (and others) responded to the public's rejection of '50s flash, fakery, and fuelishness with more tasteful styling, more efficient powertrains, and genuinely useful new features. Add the broadest model line in the luxury field, and it's no wonder that Cadillac set new sales records almost every year during the '60s. It was as though the cleaner and more rational Cadillacs became, the more people bought them.

That was certainly true for 1963, when Cadillac production reached just over 163,000, the best ever. Styling, if not the best ever too, was definitely right for the market: bolder than 1961-62, yet simpler. Tailfins were newly "tailored to present a lower profile," as *Motor Trend* put it, while A-pillars were straightened to eliminate any vestige of the wrapped windshield. Bodysides bulged discreetly, a longer vee-contoured hood capped a more formal grille, and rooflines were more crisp. Even back panels were tidied up with large vertical lamp housings, and a low middle section made the cars look wider, even though they weren't. The '63s also weren't changed in wheelbase, though they stretched two inches longer overall. Yet, despite the increase in length, weight was actually down a bit.

One reason was a major redesign for Cadillac's overhead-valve V-8, the first in its 14-year history. Bore and stroke were unchanged from '62, as were valves, rocker arms, heads, connecting rods, and compression (still 10.5:1). But everything else was new: lighter, stronger crankshaft; a stiffer block weighing 50 pounds less than the previous one; ancillaries relocated to improve service access; and first-time use of lightweight aluminum for accessory drives. While all this did little for performance, the revised 390 was smoother and quieter by far. Enhancing its refinement was an industry first: CV joints at the rear axle and driveshaft centerpoint. The new 390 was also more compact than its predecessor (Cadillac's original 1949 V-8 stretched to its displacement limit), measuring an inch lower, four inches narrower, and 1.5 inches shorter.

Cadillacs had long been surprising performers. The '63s were more so—typically able to do 115 mph, 0-60 mph in about 9.5 seconds, the standing

Chrome, leather, woodgrain trim, and rich carpeting highlighted Eldorado interiors for 1963 (above), while exteriors (opposite page) were somewhat more ornate than "standard" Cadillacs. Note the Eldo's "roulette wheel" hubcaps. Series 62 convertible (below) shows off the '63 Cadillac's slab-sided styling and still-lower fins. At $5590, the Series 62 convertible cost over $1000 less than the Eldo ragtop, which may explain why it sold nearly 10 times as many copies.

SPECIFICATIONS

Engines:	all ohv V-8; **1963:** 390 cid (4.00 × 3.88) 325 bhp; **1964:** 429 cid (4.13 × 4.00), 340 bhp
Transmissions:	**1963:** 4-speed automatic; **1964:** 3-speed automatic
Suspension front:	upper drag links and lower A-arms, coil springs
Suspension rear:	live axle on coil springs
Brakes:	front/rear drums
Wheelbase (in.):	149.8 Series 75, 129.5 others
Weight (lbs):	4505-5300
Top speed (mph):	115-120
0-60 mph (sec):	8.5-9.7

Production: 1963 Series 62 htp sdn 6W 12,929 **htp cpe** 16,786 **htp sdn 4W** 16,980 **cvt** 17,600 **chassis** 3 **DeVille htp sdn 6W** 15,146 **htp cpe** 31,749 **htp sdn 4W** 30,579 **Park Avenue htp sdn** 1,575 **Eldorado Biarritz cvt** 1,825 **Series 60 Special htp sdn** 14,000 **Series 75 4d sdn 9P** 680 **limo 9P** 795 **chassis** 2,527 **1964 Series 62 htp sdn 6W** 9,243 **htp sdn 4W** 13,670 **htp cpe** 12,166 **cvt** 17,900 **DeVille htp sdn 6W** 14,627 **htp sdn 4W** 39,674 **htp cpe** 38,195 **Eldorado Biarritz cvt** 1,870 **Series 60 Special htp sdn** 14,550 **Series 75 4d sdn 9P** 617 **limo 9P** 808 **chassis** 2,639

quarter-mile in about 17. Even economy was decent for the day at 12-14 miles per gallon overall. Near-silent high-speed running continued to be Cadillac's forte, and here, too, the '63s were the best yet. In this, many held Cadillac superior to even vaunted Rolls-Royce.

Cadillac was arguably a better dollar value, too, and there was no question that it offered more model choices. The '63 slate repeated 1962's minus the short-deck Series 62 Town Sedan, which disappeared for want of sales. The companion DeVille Park Avenue continued, but found even fewer takers than the year before—just 1575. Predictably, it wouldn't return for '64.

Despite all its '63 improvements, Cadillac raised prices only a few dollars above '62 levels. A Series 62 cost as little as $5026, and even the fancy Eldo Biarritz convertible was a fair value at $6608. Standard equipment, generous as always, ran to Hydra-Matic, power steering, self-adjusting power brakes, heater, backup lights, and left remote-control door mirror. A six-way power seat became standard on Eldorado, and power windows were included on all models except closed 62s. Of course, Cadillac was king of comfort and convenience, and its new '63 options included power vent windows, six-position tilt steering wheel, and AM/FM radio. Also new were extra-cost vinyl roof coverings. *Motor Trend* noted that Cadillac cataloged a record 143 interior treatments including wool, leather, and nylon upholstery plus bench or bucket front seats. There was also a new dash sporting woodgrain trim, which also adorned the doors and seatbacks.

Design revisions for '64 were minor. Tailfins were lowered even more to create nearly straight-through fenderlines that further accentuated length; grilles got a body-color horizontal bar; and taillamp housings were reshaped. A new "Comfort Control" heating/air-conditioning system maintained a set temperature automatically (via thermostat) regardless of conditions. This was also the first year for "Twilight Sentinel," combining a headlamps-off timer with a photoelectric cell that switched on the beams at dusk.

More significant was yet another revised engine: the 390 bored and stroked to 429 cid, delivering 340 bhp. And because it teamed with a more efficient new three-speed Turbo-Hydra-Matic with full torque converter, performance improved accordingly. In fact, some road tests reported 0-60 in as little as 8.5 seconds and quarter-mile times in the mid-16s—lively if not thrilling, something we tend to forget about '60s Cadillacs.

Buyers simply loved the '64s, snapping up nearly 166,000 to give Cadillac another new model-year production record. But even better Cadillacs—and better Cadillac sales—were just around the corner.

1965-69 Cadillac

It's hard to think of more pleasing standard Cadillacs than the 1965-69 models. The '65 was especially good: stronger, quieter, and arguably the handsomest thing from Clark Avenue since the first, trend-setting tailfinned Caddys of 1948-49.

Motor Trend's assessment was typical: ". . . [T]he whole car is laid out with an architect's precision, and every inch . . . is Cadillac in character." Yet the '65 actually had more in common with lesser GM cars than any previous Cadillac, though this was long before General Motors abandoned make "philosophies" and "character" to economize with divisional look-alikes.

Another new C-body gave Cadillac's '65 standards a tauter, trimmer look. But what was this? No fins? Well, rear fenders *were* rule-straight, but new vertical taillamp clusters jutting out from the back panel had notched tops that suggested fins. Headlamp pairs went from horizontal to vertical, permitting an even wider grille. Curved side glass appeared, and pillared sedans returned for the first time since 1958, ousting six-window hardtop sedans.

Beneath Caddy's knockout '65 styling was a more rigid new box-section perimeter frame (replacing the old X-member type) with body mounts revised for less noise, vibration, and harshness. Also featured was a modernized all-coil suspension with four-link rear-end geometry incorporating anti-squat control. Front suspension (still by lower A-arms and upper drag links) was modified to reduce nosedive.

Though they looked smaller, the standard '65s were slightly longer than the '64s: a majestic 224 or 227.5 inches overall. The latter applied to the premium Sixty Special, which regained its exclusive 133-inch wheelbase, another return to '58. Other models, save the big Series 75s, retained a 129.5-inch wheelbase. Curb weights hardly changed at all.

Model choices still numbered 11, but the Series 62, a fixture since 1940, was renamed Calais. It shared two- and four-door hardtops plus the revived pillared sedan with DeVille, which also offered a convertible. The last was the basis for the ragtop Eldorado Biarritz, which added some additional trim—for an $1100 premium. The Sixty Special was now a pillared (not hardtop) four-door, and carried the Fleetwood designation like the Eldo and Series 75s. Added trimmings included wreath-and-crest badges, broad lower-body brightwork, and rectangular-pattern rear appliqués. A new Fleetwood Brougham package added a vinyl roof with rear-quarter "Brougham" script. Automatic rear self-leveling was another new option exclusive to the Sixty Special.

SPECIFICATIONS

Engines:	all ohv V-8; **1965-67:** 429 cid (4.13 × 4.00), 340 bhp; **1968-69:** 472 cid (4.30 × 4.06), 375 bhp
Transmission:	3-speed automatic
Suspension front:	upper drag links and lower A-arms, coil springs
Suspension rear:	live axle, coil springs
Brakes:	front/rear drums; optional front discs **1967-68**
Wheelbase (in.):	129.5 (Calais/DeVille), 133.0 (60 Special), 149.8 (Series 75)
Weight (lbs):	4390-5555
Top speed (mph):	120-125
0-60 mph (sec):	8.5-10.0

Production: 1965 Calais htp sdn 13,975 htp cpe 12,515 4d sdn 7,721 **DeVille** htp sdn 45,535 htp cpe 43,345 cvt 19,200 4d sdn 15,000 **Eldorado Biarritz** cvt 2,125 **Sixty Special** 4d sdn 18,100 **Series 75** 4d sdn 9P 455 limo 9P 795 chassis 2,669 **1966 Calais** htp sdn 13,025 htp cpe 11,080 4d sdn 4,575 **DeVille** htp sdn 60,550 htp cpe 50,580 cvt 19,200 4d sdn 11,860 **Eldorado Biarritz** cvt 2,250 **Sixty Special** 4d sdn 5,455 **Fleetwood Brougham** 4d sdn 13,630 **Series 75** 4d sdn 9P 980 limo 9P 1,037 chassis 2,463 **1967 Calais** htp cpe 9,085 htp sdn 9,880 4d sdn 2,865 **DeVille** htp cpe 52,905 htp sdn 59,902 cvt 18,202 4d sdn 8,800 **Sixty Special** 4d sdn 3,550 **Fleetwood Brougham** 4d sdn 12,750 **Series 75** 4d sdn 9P 835 limo 9P 965 chassis 2,333 **1968 Calais** htp cpe 8,165 htp sdn 10,025 **DeVille** htp cpe 63,935 htp sdn 72,662 cvt 18,025 4d sdn 9,850 **Sixty Special** 4d sdn 3,300 **Fleetwood Brougham** 4d sdn 15,300 **Series 75** 4d sdn 9P 805 limo 9P 995 chassis 2,413 **1969 Calais** htp cpe 5,600 htp sdn 6,825 **DeVille** htp cpe 65,755 htp sdn 72,958 cvt 16,445 4d sdn 7,890 **Sixty Special** 4d sdn 2,545 **Fleetwood Brougham** 4d sdn 17,300 **Series 75** 4d sdn 9P 880 limo 9P 1,156 chassis 2,550

Opposite page: *Cadillac's 1965 restyle brought straight-through fenderlines and squared-off rear end with vertical taillights. Little changed for '66 (above), but the '67s gained forward-canted headlights and a "hump" over the rear wheelwells (below). A restyle for 1969 brought horizontal headlights (this page, bottom) while deleting the front window vent wings.*

Drivetrains were unchanged save for a "sonically balanced" exhaust system, but the 429 V-8 still enabled a '65 Caddy to hustle right along. One Japanese report had a Sixty Special doing 0-60 in just 8.5 seconds, the standing quarter-mile in 16.4, and 121 mph all out—amazing for a big, opulent cruiser.

Equally amazing, prices weren't far above what they'd been in '61. No wonder Cadillac produced a record of nearly 182,000 cars—16,000 more than in '64.

Calendar-year volume broke 200,000 units in 1966, and 14,250 more Cadillacs were built for the model year. A mild facelift brought a new front bumper and grille, plus better-integrated taillights. Series 75s switched to the perimeter frame and were fully rebodied for the first time since 1959. Among new '66 options was variable-ratio power steering, which "speeded up" as the wheel was turned from center. The Brougham became a separate model, still more luxuriously trimmed than the plain-roof Sixty Special and priced about $320 higher.

Cadillac's big news for '67 was the smashing front-wheel-drive Fleetwood Eldorado coupe (see entry), which replaced the open Biarritz. But other standards received a major restyle, with larger grille eggcrates, front fenders thrust forward at the top, and rear fenders raised via a jaunty "kickup" to again suggest fins. Helped by the new Eldo, Cadillac built 200,000 cars for the model year, another record.

The '68 spotlight was on motive power: an all-new 472-cubic-inch V-8 with 375 horsepower. Designed for that first year of government emission standards, it was lab-tested the equivalent of 500,000 miles. Though not as fuel-efficient as the superseded 429, the 472 could push a Coupe DeVille from zero to 100 mph in under half a minute. Outside were new federally required side marker lights, a hood extended at the rear to conceal the wipers, a revised grille, and a trunklid reshaped for increased cargo space.

Cadillac built a record 266,798 cars for calendar 1969, breezing past Chrysler and American Motors to claim ninth in industry production. It was still 11th for the model year, though, at just over 223,000. Standards were fully rebodied, gaining squarer rooflines but losing front-door ventwings to a new flow-through interior ventilation system. Headlamps reverted to horizontal, and parking lights wrapped around from a higher grille, still prominently vee'd. More Washington edicts brought standard front-seat headrests, energy-absorbing steering column, pushbutton seatbelt buckles, ignition-key warning buzzer, and anti-theft ignition lock. Prices, which had been creeping up, ran from just over $5400 for a Calais to well over $10,000 for the 75 limousine.

No question about it: Cadillac made all the right moves during the '60s. Sadly, the division would soon lose its way and not get solidly back on track for another 20 years.

1967-69
Cadillac Eldorado

For Cadillac, the front-wheel-drive Eldorado was a revolutionary development, as important as the 1915 V-8, the 1930 Sixteen, the 1938 Sixty Special, and the 1949 V-8. It was the first Cadillac with FWD; moreover, it was an entirely new approach to the Eldorado's marketplace.

Its technology wasn't new. Oldsmobile, traditionally the "experimental division" of General Motors, had launched the Toronado the year before. But the Eldos' styling was quite different from the Toronado's. This followed a dictum laid down by chief of design Bill Mitchell (and too often ignored by GM since) that there must be specific "images" for the products of each GM division, regardless of how much technology they might share under the skin. It was the first time Mitchell had applied his five-seat "personal car" theme to a Cadillac (his major past works in this field were the Buick Rivieras of 1963-on). The result was certainly one of the great shapes of the '60s, completely lacking in rough spots, good looking from every angle, yet sufficiently "formal" to be consistent with Cadillac's current styling.

The name packed appropriate tradition: Cadillac had launched its first Eldorado, a limited production "personal" car, in 1953. Interim Eldos were somewhat less special, their goal being profit more than just pizzazz, yet the Eldorado nameplate always retained exclusivity. Briefly during development, management in the grips of nostalgia had considered calling the new car "LaSalle"; but then someone pointed out Jeff Godshall's LaSalle chapter in the Cadillac marque history, dubbing that make "Cadillac's only failure." That, according to Cadillac insiders, made them unanimous for "Eldorado." The one thing lacking was a convertible version—GM didn't have one yet—but it would come along in the next design generation.

In addition to its superb, razor-edge styling, the new Eldorado was blessed with fine engineering. What Cadillac had specified was a big, luxurious car with all the traditional virtues allied to outstanding roadability—a combination it arguably never offered before. Cadillac teamed its 429 V-8 with a "split" transmission: the torque converter and gearbox were separate from each other, linked by a chain drive and sprocket. The key was the chain, developed by Hydra-Matic Division and Borg-Warner: unbreakable, flexible, light, and not too expensive to produce. The split transmission made the drivetrain quite compact, although the car itself was huge: 221 inches from stem to stern, on a 120-inch wheelbase. Despite those dimensions, there wasn't all that much room in the back seat, but few seemed to care.

Front-wheel drive gave the Eldo almost neutral handling characteristics, which was quite novel for Cadillac, traditionally known for its final and irrevocable understeer. *Automobile Quarterly* editor Don Vorderman wrote that in cornering, the car displayed "mounting understeer when under full power," but this was "easily neutralized by backing off the accelerator, at which time the tail will move out in the classic FWD tradition." Vorderman admitted that it was doubtful whether "one owner in a thousand will drive the car this way, but it does speak volumes on how thoroughly Cadillac engineers have done their job."

The Eldorado was not greatly changed during its first three-year design generation. A handsome eggcrate grille adorned the 1967 and '68 models, the latter of which can be distinguished by parking lights that were repositioned from the bumper to the fenders. Briefly, too, in 1968-69, Cadillac adopted a 472-cid V-8 engine.

Although the "unbreakable" chain drive did fail on occasion, and the U-joints packed up regularly, for such a complicated car the early Eldorado was remarkably reliable. Collectors consider the '67 the superior model because it was the first of the series, but the 472 is a better engine, and prices of nice examples haven't diverged much to date. Remarkably enough, you can still find one of these big beasts in show condition for under $10,000. That's a lot of Cadillac for the money.

Eldorado debuted in 1967 (opposite page), and while based on the Olds Toronado introduced a year earlier, the Eldo had distinct styling and was powered by Cadillac's 429-cid engine. Styling was carried over for 1968 (below), though the front parking lights were moved to the fender edges and the engine bay now carried a 472-cid V-8. For 1969 (this page, bottom), headlights were no longer concealed within the grille, but other changes were minimal.

SPECIFICATIONS

Engines: all ohv V-8; **1967** 429 cid (4.13 × 4.00), 340 bhp; **1968-69** 472 cid (4.30 × 4.06), 375 bhp

Transmission:	3-speed Turbo Hydra-Matic
Suspension, front:	upper and lower A-arms, torsion bars, stabilizer bar
Suspension, rear:	live axle, leaf springs
Brakes:	**1967** front/rear drums (front discs optional) **1968-69** front discs/rear drums
Wheelbase (in.):	120.0
Weight (lbs.):	4500-4580
Top speed (mph):	NA
0-60 mph (sec):	NA
Production:	**1967** 17,930 **1968** 24,528 **1969** 23,333

1960-69
Checker

Morris Markin, a Russian immigrant who founded Checker Motors in 1922, had one trait in common with Henry Ford: a distaste for change. Once you get the right design, Markin figured, it made sense to stick with it. Apart from the Model T Ford, then, few automobiles have exhibited less year-to-year revision than the Checker.

Checkers were built tough and driven tough. When Markin entered the business in Chicago, competition from rival John Hertz's Yellow Taxi was anything but genteel. Drivers who were handy with their fists were far more useful than those who merely knew the city streets. Through all those years, Checker cabs rolled regularly out of the plant at Kalamazoo, Michigan.

But wait: what are taxicabs doing in a book on Great Cars? They're here because Checker decided to give the general public an opportunity to drive one of the tough and dependable (if unfashionable) super-square sedans themselves. So for the 1960 model year, Checker took its A8 taxi series introduced four years earlier, spiffed up the interior, and placed it on sale as the Superba with a $2542 price tag. A heavier four-door station wagon also went on the market. Except for their interiors and lack of commercial markings, they were virtually identical to the taxis that prowled the streets of nearly every American city. Those who thought the basic model a tad too austere could choose a Special; but even that wasn't quite plush inside.

Customers didn't exactly wait in frenzied lines, checkbooks in hand, for a chance to take home a Checker. Still, a few hundred practical souls yearly saw the merits of a tested, down-to-earth, no-frills design, billed as "the common-sense car America asked for." If Checker taxis could hold up under the rigors of day-and-night operation, buyers reasoned, surely their non-commercial counterparts would also experience impressive longevity.

Contributing to that dependability was the 226-cid Continental six-cylinder engine, offered in either L-head (80 horsepower) or overhead-valve (122 bhp) form. Sizable torque peaked at only 1400 or 1800 rpm, permitting smooth acceleration without constant downshifts.

Longer in wheelbase than the typical American sedan, Checkers were shorter overall, measuring just 199.5 inches. As many as eight passengers could ride in reasonable comfort inside a Superba, through use of optional twin jump seats in the back, enjoying a hump-free floor. Wide doors made it easy to climb in and out.

For 1961, a new Marathon sedan replaced the initial Superba Special, and all sedans switched from 15-inch to 14-inch tires. Wagons adopted the ohv engine as standard. Prices ranged from $2542 for a Superba sedan to $3004 for a Marathon wagon. Checker customers had a growing option list, including air conditioning, power steering, and an automatic transmission. By the end of the 1960s, the choices included bucket seats, a vinyl roof, two-tone paint, and Powr-Lok rear axle.

Sedans reverted to 15-inch tires in 1962. New that year was a Town Custom Limousine on a 129-inch wheelbase (nine inches longer than normal), carrying a hefty $7500 price tag along with its vinyl top and glassed-in driver's compartment. Overhead-valve engine output got a boost for 1963, to 141 horsepower. In 1964 the Superba name was dropped, so all standard-size Checkers were called Marathons.

Probably the most significant change was a switch from Continental to Chevrolet engines for 1965. The initial list included a 230-cid six (140 bhp), a 283-cid V-8 (195 bhp) for $110 extra, and 327 V-8 (250 bhp). Either an automatic transmission or overdrive was available, at $248 and $108 (respectively). "No other car looks like . . . is built like . . . rides like . . . The Checker Marathon," trumpeted the mid-1960s sales literature.

A Marathon Deluxe sedan came in 1966, as well as a lower-priced ($4541) limousine. Both dropped out the following year, but soon returned. A 307-cid V-8 became available in 1968, and a 350-cid in '69. By that time, the basic Marathon was selling for $3290, a long-wheelbase Deluxe for $3983, and the limo went for $4957. At the end of 1968, a 327 V-8 cost an extra $108, and the 350 V-8 brought $194. Perkins diesel power also was available, at an eye-opening $1279.

Checker production slumped in the 1970s when Morris Markin died and his son David took over. By mid-1982, the final Checker rolled off the assembly line. The fact that so many Checkers remain on the street, both in taxi and privately owned form, attests to the practical design and rugged build quality of this unyielding and unusual automobile.

Opposite page, top: "Taxi-cab tough" was no idle boast to Checker, for what the cars lacked in luxury they made up for in ruggedness. Interior of this '65 (above) is quite spartan for the period—and it's a "dressed-up" civilian version! Station wagons were offered throughout the decade, this '65 version (opposite page, bottom) being priced at $3140; about $150 more than a contemporary Chevy Impala wagon.

SPECIFICATIONS

Engines:	**1960-64** L-head I-6, 226 cid (3.31 × 4.38), 80 bhp; **1960-62** ohv I-6, 226 cid, 122 bhp **1963-64** ohv I-6, 141 bhp **1965-68** ohv I-6, 230 cid (3.88 × 3.25), 140 bhp **1969** ohv I-6, 250 cid (3.88 × 3.53), 155 bhp; **1965-66** ohv V-8, 283 cid (3.88 × 3.00), 195 bhp **1965-67** ohv V-8, 327 cid (4.00 × 3.25), 250 bhp **1968** 275 bhp **1969** 235 bhp **1968** ohv V-8, 307 cid (3.88 × 3.25), 200 bhp **1969** 350 cid (4.00 × 3.48), 300 bhp
Transmission:	3-speed manual; optional Dual-Range automatic
Suspension, front:	upper and lower A-arms, coil springs, stabilizer bar
Suspension, rear:	live axle, leaf springs
Brakes:	front/rear drums
Wheelbase (in.):	120.0 **Town Custom/DeLuxe** 129.0
Weight (lbs.):	3320-5000
Top speed (mph):	90-112
0-60 mph (sec):	**V-8** 10.8

Production: 1960 6980 **1961** 5683 **1962** 8173 **1963** 7050 **1964** 6310 **1965** 6136 **1966** 5761 (1056 non-taxi) **1967** 5822 (935 non-taxi) **1968** 5477 (992 non-taxi) **1969** 5417 (760 non-taxi)

Note: A few Checkers were built in 1964 with Chrysler engines.

1960
Chevrolet Impala

Space—Spirit—Splendor. Those were the key words used by Chevrolet to promote its relatively restrained line of full-size models for 1960. (Restrained by standards of the Fifties, that is.) The soaring "batwing" back end that caused many a customer to sour on the 1959 Chevrolets didn't exactly disappear—though it would the following year. But at least the soaring horizontal fins were toned down in this season's otherwise-modest restyling.

Although still sharp-edged and omnipresent, the fins no longer overpowered the entire rear view. Not only did their tips no longer give the impression of grasping past the bodyside, they had a more angular, tapered look with thin edge moldings, integrating smoothly into the quarter panels. Also helping to lessen their formerly frightful impact was the substitution of a trio of small round taillights for the huge teardrop-shaped lens that lurked beneath each '59 fin. Up front, the former nostrillike air intakes were gone, giving the car a calmer look.

Impalas appeared first in 1958 as a "limited edition," but would become the most popular car in the U.S. during the Sixties, outstripping the midrange Bel Air and bottom-rung Biscayne. Impalas differed from Bel Airs mainly in their greater abundance of chrome: specifically, the distinctive side moldings that occupied much of the quarter-panel space above the rear wheels. A bright rear-end panel contained thin vertical blacked-out areas, as opposed to the Bel Air's plainer tail. Impalas wore such extras as air-intake scoops (nonfunctional) in lower rear window moldings, and on rear fenders, Impala script stood alongside a crossed-flags insignia. Body styles included the four-door hardtop Sport Sedan with its panoramic back window that stretched in a massive curve to meet slim rear pillars, as well as a pillarless Sport Coupe, four-door sedan, and the expected convertible.

Mechanical changes were minor, but powertrain choices dwindled. Chevrolet

SPECIFICATIONS

Engines:	ohv I-6, 235.5 cid (3.56 × 3.94), 135 bhp; ohv V-8, 283 cid (3.88 × 3.00), 170/230 bhp; ohv V-8, 348 cid (4.13 × 3.25), 250/280/320/335 bhp
Transmissions:	3/4-speed manual; 2-speed Powerglide and 3-speed Powerglide automatic optional
Suspension, front:	upper and lower A-arms, coil springs
Suspension, rear:	live axle, coil springs
Brakes:	front/rear drums
Wheelbase (in.):	119.0
Weight (lbs.):	3530-3635
Top speed (mph):	90-135 (est.)
0-60 mph (sec):	9.0-18.6
Production:	about 411,000 (plus 79,903 convertibles)

offered a pair of V-8 engines (283 and 348 cid) with seven levels of output ranging from 170 to 335 horsepower, plus the long-lived Blue Flame six with 135 bhp. That compared with a dozen horsepower "steps" offered in 1959 from the same three engines. No matter. Before long, Chevrolet would be expanding its engine selections with an even more tempting palate of power.

Topping the charts this year was the 348-cid Super Turbo-Thrust Special V-8, employing a trio of two-barrel carburetors plus tight 11.25:1 compression and dual exhausts to whip out its 335 horsepower. The era of slumping compression ratios was still a decade away, after all, and premium gas was cheap. Four less-potent versions of the 348 V-8 also were available, producing 250, 280, 305, or 320 bhp. Back again was the carbureted Turbo-Fire 283-cid V-8, with either 170 or 230 bhp at the ready. Not making a return appearance: fuel-injected variants of the 283. Transmission options included overdrive and a floor-shift four-speed, as well as either two-speed Powerglide or "triple turbine" Turboglide automatic.

For 1960, top-line Impala body styles included two-door Sport Coupe (above), four-door Sport Sedan (below), convertible (opposite page), and pillared four-door sedan (not shown). Impalas could be quickly told from "lesser" full-size Chevys by their bright rear panel holding three taillights on each side, and a white band running lengthwise through the rear fender. Top power option for 1960 was a 348 V-8 with 335 bhp.

Full-size Chevys of this period were truly large by today's standards, the public's thirst for economy being satisfied by the new rear-engine Corvair and the soon-to-appear Chevelles and Chevy IIs. The big cars rode a 119-inch wheelbase, just four inches shorter than that of a Buick LeSabre. Thumbing through the option list let the buyer add many of the extras ordinarily found only on luxury automobiles, from air conditioning to a six-way power seat—a selection of American-style comforts that would grow larger yet as the decade progressed.

Styling for the regular passenger-car lineup would change dramatically for 1961, which may have been the death knell for the low-volume El Camino sport pickup. Built on the full-size passenger-car platform, it was offered for only two years ('59 and '60), though the name would later grace a similar vehicle based on the mid-size Chevelle.

Looking back, many enthusiasts admit with more than a twinge of guilt that the dangerous-looking fins of '59 and even their softened counterparts of 1960 add sparkle to an old Chevrolet's appeal. Later models have their undeniable virtues, as will be seen. Still, were those "batwings" really that terrible?

1960-64
Chevrolet Corvair
Monza

It is often said that the Corvair Monza started the sporty car boom in America. Many would argue that it began long before the Monza was even a gleam in Chevrolet's eye, giving the honor instead to early Corvettes, Thunderbirds, and Studebaker Hawks. While certainly a valid argument, these were comparatively expensive vehicles, and the modern interpretation is that a "sporty car" leans toward the more affordable end of the price spectrum. But whether a pioneer of the concept or simply a follower, it *can* be accurately said the Monza saved the Corvair—and incidentally introduced the marketing ploy of sticking vinyl buckets and a floor-mounted shifter into a compact and calling it a sports car.

Ironically, the Monza is perhaps more noted for what it led to (the Mustang) than what it did for the Corvair. As it turned out, GM's unique rear-engine compact proved one of the corporation's major albatrosses; it was the subject of endless litigation, and played the lead villain in the book that launched Ralph Nader. (That book, *Unsafe at Any Speed*, conclusively proved that the inattentive should not drive early Corvairs.)

Though the 1960-61 Corvairs could indeed be a bit tricky to handle, later models were much improved, and by 1965 the Corvair sported a superb suspension that made it one of the most imaginative, efficient, and progressive cars of the decade.

The first Monza arrived late in the 1960 model year as a "spring special" to shore up the Corvair's disappointing sales. Against the plug-ordinary Falcon and Rambler, and the unique-looking but technically mundane Plymouth Valiant, the Corvair was doing much poorer than expected. Indeed, the Monza was barely on the market when GM Styling was hard at work on what would become the 1962 Chevy II, later the Chevy Nova—a conventional compact that would, finally, outgun the Falcon. But

The Corvair debuted in 1960 as the first of GM's new line of compacts. Monza variant didn't appear until late in the model year, but by 1961 (below), production of the sporty newcomer was in full swing and selling like hotcakes. A station wagon version (this page, bottom) was introduced in 1962, but lasted only one year. A four-door sedan also joined the line in 1962, though this 1964 version (opposite page) was outsold even by the convertible that year.

SPECIFICATIONS

Engines:	**1960** flat 6, 140 cid (3.38 × 2.60), 80/95 bhp; **1961-63** 145 cid (3.44 × 2.60), 102 bhp; **1964** 164 cid (3.44 × 2.94), 95/110 bhp
Transmissions:	3/4-speed manual; 2-speed automatic optional
Suspension front:	upper and lower A-arms, coil springs
Suspension rear:	**1960-63** semi-trailing swing axles, coil springs **1964** semi-trailing swing axles, transverse compensating spring
Brakes:	front/rear drums
Wheelbase (in.):	108.0
Weight (lbs):	2280-2569
Top speed (mph):	NA
0-60 mph (sec):	NA

Production: 1960 11,926 **1961 cpe** 109,945 **sdn** 33,745 **1962 cpe** 144,844 **wgn** 2362 **cvt** 13,995 **sdn** 48,059 **1963 cpe** 117,917 **cvt** 36,693 **sdn** 31,120 **1964 cpe** 88,440 **cvt** 31,045 **sdn** 21,926

then an unknown product planner got the idea of dolling up a Corvair coupe with a colorful vinyl interior, carpets, and other luxurious widgets, and Chevy dealers finally had something to cheer about.

Here at last was a Corvair that would sell. There was nothing wrong with the coupe's styling: it looked European, not too unlike the little German NSU, but longer, more balanced. It lacked a conventional grille (stylists gave it a fake one in 1962), but it was pleasant enough otherwise. Sales took off fast, and though there was only time to build about 12,000 Monzas for 1960, Chevy soared into volume production with the '61s. When the dust settled, that model year had accounted for 110,000 Monza coupes plus another 34,000 of the new Monza four-door sedans—more than all the cheaper Corvair models put together. In 1962 they added a handsome convertible, and Monza sales went to over 200,000, which was the best ever. By the end of the first Corvair design generation in 1964, there were only two non-Monzas in the lineup, and the Monza was *still* racking up six-figure sales totals—which was something, considering all the competition that had developed by then.

Largely the work of longtime Chevy engineer and later GM president Edward N. Cole, the Corvair was an enthusiast's car, radical and innovative. Its flat-six engine developed 80 or 95 bhp and was complicated: two cylinder heads, six separate cylinder barrels, and a divided crankcase. Unfortunately, it weighed nearly 400 pounds, which was 100 pounds more than Cole had hoped. The initial suspension comprised wishbones and coil springs up front, semi-trailing swing axles at the back. Enter the lawsuits, filed by people who wrecked their Corvairs mainly because they disregarded the manual's instructions and inflated the tires equally—a potentially expensive mistake on Corvairs. In 1962, an option of stiffer springs, shorter rear axle limit straps, and a front sway bar was made available; the '64s were improved again when a transverse camber compensating spring was adopted.

Meanwhile, horsepower edged up to 110 and a decent four-speed gearbox was brought out as an option. There was even a Monza station wagon in 1962, but it wasn't in keeping with the sporty car's image, and only 2362 were built before it was dropped. Today it is the most desirable Monza next to the convertibles, which are far more numerous but offer unlimited head room. People who think Ralph Nader was right about the Corvair ought to try a 110 bhp four-speed '64. Few cars of the era handle better, and fewer still offer more fun for the money.

1960
Chevrolet Corvette

America's only true sports car had come a long way in its seven seasons. Starting off in 1953 with a "Blue Flame" six-cylinder engine coupled to smooth if sluggish Powerglide automatic, the pretty-as-a-picture two-seater turned to V-8 power for 1955. Even greater potency came as the V-8 grew to 283 cid and added fuel injection—rare in the Fifties—which enabled this engine to scream out the fabled one horsepower per cubic inch of displacement. Reworking for 1958 added 10 inches of length and quad headlamps. By 1959, the 283 could churn out a whopping 315 horsepower. In sum, the fiberglass-bodied roadster was changing all the time, being continually tweaked and tuned to enhance its already-inspiring brand of driving fun.

As the new decade opened, avid sports-car fans could expect their latest 'Vettes to handle better than ever, not just tear off at the touch of the gas pedal and look handsome when idle. This one not only carried a tougher front anti-roll bar, but added another one out back—the first such installation on an American car. Those revisions were made to deliver more neutral handling, along with a smoother ride, taking advantage of an extra inch of rear-wheel rebound.

Inside was a new 7000-rpm tachometer, plus deeper bucket seats and better-fitted carpeting. Flat-faced gauges were easier to read. A locking compartment between the seats added some needed interior storage space.

Apart from a few new Magic-Mirror colors, appearance differed little from the 1958-59 editions. Two-tones could be ordered, with Sateen Silver or Ermine White in the sculptured side cove panels. Wheelbase was the same 102 inches as before.

Weight saving was a perpetual goal for Corvette engineers, who turned to aluminum to shave off a few pounds. Clutch housings were made of aluminum, as was the radiator on cars with the most potent engines. So were cylinder heads on fuel-injected engines, which slimmed down by 53 pounds. Unfortunately, that latter choice soon turned to trouble as the lightened heads failed, inclined to warp

SPECIFICATIONS

Engines:	ohv V-8, 283 cid (3.88 × 3.00), 230/245/270 bhp (carbureted), 275/315 bhp (fuel injected)
Transmissions:	3-speed manual; 4-speed manual and 2-speed Powerglide automatic optional
Suspension, front:	unequal-length A-arms, coil springs, anti-roll bar
Suspension, rear:	live axle, semi-elliptic leaf springs
Brakes:	front/rear drums
Wheelbase (in.):	102.0
Weight (lbs.):	2840
Top speed (mph):	105-130 (est.)
0-60 mph (sec):	8.4
Production:	10,261

when overheated or suffer the pains of internal flaws. Casting wasn't an easy matter, and the aluminum heads soon evaporated from Corvette's equipment list. The time wasn't yet right.

Five variants of the familiar 283-cid engine were available, ranging from 230 horsepower with a single four-barrel carburetor to 315 bhp (at 6200 rpm) with Ramjet fuel injection. That latter mill got a boost from 290 horses by way of a compression hike to 11.0:1. In between: 245- and 270-bhp editions with dual four-barrel carbs, and a 275-bhp variant of the fuelie that reached its peak at a less-shrill 5200 rpm. Both the 270-bhp and 315-hp V-8s had solid valve lifters.

Throw in the choice of three transmissions (close-ratio three- or four-speed manual, or two-speed Powerglide) and an impressive selection of axle ratios, and it was possible to tailor each Corvette for any purpose. Want one for touring? For all-out racing? Somewhere between? The correct check marks on the option list brought the precise mix of components to deliver exactly what was needed.

Sticker prices for all this excitement started at $3872, which was over $900 more than an Impala convertible. Spending too much time on that option chart, of course, could easily add another grand to the final figure. Less than one-third of the 'Vettes came with the basic three-speed gearbox. A removable fiberglass hardtop was another popular extra. Both heavy-duty brakes and sintered-metallic linings made the list. New extras included a thermostatically controlled fan and a 24-gallon gas tank. The all-out 315-bhp engine cost an extra $484.20, while a four-speed added $188.30. Mounting a set of 6.70 × 15 tires to replace the usual 5.50 × 15 rubber ran $15.75.

On the racing scene, Briggs Cunningham entered three Corvettes into the LeMans events, one of which finished eighth. Also in 1960, a Corvette appeared as a major player in the new TV series, *Route 66*, transporting Martin Milner and George Maharis across the country in search of adventure.

More and more sports-car fans were turning their attention to this uniquely American product which, in the words of the sales catalog, "captures hearts and laurels for sheer good looks and pure performance . . . elegant on the boulevard, eager on the road." Production set a record at 10,261 Corvettes, up from 9670 the year before. In fact, Chevrolet was headed on an upward sales trend that would backtrack only once through the balance of the decade.

Corvettes wearing "Fuel Injection" badges on their front fenders (opposite page) gained instant respect—and for good reason. The top fuel-injected 283-cid engine for 1960 (above) squeezed out 315 bhp, up from 290 the year before. Base Corvettes were rather plain-looking, but could be considerably dressed up with whitewall tires, sporty wheel covers, and silver or white-colored side coves (below).

1961-62
Chevrolet Corvette

"No matter what the occasion—black tie or tennis shoes—Corvette is appropriate." So said the sales brochure for Chevrolet's sports car, which boasted a new look for 1961. Many considered this to be the best 'Vette since the "classic" 1957 model, enhanced refinement placing it in greater demand than the 1958-60 versions, both then and now.

Rumors had surfaced that the new Corvette would stem from the Stingray racer "privately" run by GM's design chief Bill Mitchell. Not quite. Instead, considerable chrome was sliced off the two-seat body in its 1961 restyling. Even more noticeable was the new flowing "ducktail" rear end, seen earlier on both that Stingray and the XP-700 show car, which added luggage space along with an attractive profile.

Blending smartly into the new tail, a pair of small round taillights sat just above each of the slim bumperettes that reached outward from the license plate recess, while a trunklid creaseline slithered through the round Corvette medallion. Dual exhausts now exited separately, instead of through the body or bumper guards. Corvette's cleanup also extended to the front end, which featured body-colored headlight bezels and a horizontal-mesh grille insert.

Standard equipment was still somewhat sparse, with even a heater optional at $102, though windshield washers, sunvisors, and a parking-brake alarm were now included in the $3934 base price. Almost two out of three customers paid $188.30 for a four-speed gearbox, now cased in aluminum. Under the hood, radiators were all made of aluminum. Engines were the same as 1960: the tried-and-true 283-cid V-8 rated at 230, 245, 270, 275, and 315 bhp. Even with the mildest 283 and automatic, a '61 could scamper to 60 mph in 7.7 seconds. With a fuel-injected four-speed model, times were one second quicker.

Inside, both driver and passenger gained leg and foot room due to a narrower transmission tunnel and repositioned seat track. Even without the independent rear suspension that would arrive in the next generation, the latest Corvette was a dream to handle, and was improving steadily in workmanship.

Cleanup work continued with the 1962 model, which, though not universally realized at the time, was destined to end the two-seater's early history. Some of the styling details hadn't changed much at all over the years, such as the wraparound windshield. This would be the last one with exposed headlights and an ordinary trunk, accessible from outside.

Appearance changes were comparatively minor, if meaningful. Chrome outlines around the bodyside coves were abandoned, which meant no more contrasting colors in that area. Not everyone applauded, but like it or not, single hues gave the car a more unified, serious demeanor. Triple chrome accent spears within the reverse scoop were dropped in favor of more subtle black ribbed-aluminum gridwork. The grille mesh and its flanking cutouts were black, not chromed. Rocker panels, meanwhile, added ribbed anodized-aluminum moldings. For the first time, a heater was standard, with factory air and power brakes optional. Naturally, extra gear helped jack the base price past the $4000 barrier. Optional whitewall tires now wore narrow bands, as wide whites became history. A detachable hardtop was available, as usual, at $236.75; and scads of customers continued to request one.

Biggest news for '62, though, lay under the hood, since the old favorite 283-cid V-8 had been bored and stroked to 327 cubic inches. As usual, the mill came in a broad range of strengths: 250, 300, and 340 bhp when fed by carburetor; 360 bhp with fuel injection. All but the least-potent engine had a longer-duration camshaft, larger ports, and tougher bearings. The two top engines had solid lifters and 11.25:1 compression, whereas their less-athletic mates made do with a mere 10.5:1. Twin four-barrel carburetors atop the manifold were a feature of the past, usurped by single big Carters.

Only the two mildest engines could have Powerglide, now aluminum-cased to cut weight. The 300-bhp version with Powerglide could hit 60 in 8.3 seconds. Stiff springs returned as an option, helping Doctor Richard Thompson to take the Sports Car Club of America A-Production honors. Sales took a big jump, with 14,531 built for the model year.

Though no less charming than the 'Vette that had emerged nearly a decade earlier, this one was faster, nimbler, better looking, and more civilized. The new 327 V-8 would hang around; but coming soon was a entirely different breed of Corvette.

This page, top: *Corvettes of this period featured "twin cove" instrument panels. V-8 was enlarged to 327 cid for 1962, with outputs ranging from 250 bhp (above) to 360 bhp. Opposite page, top: A new "duck tail" rear end graced the '61 Corvette. Exteriors were a bit more subdued for '62 (below), as the chrome cove trim was deleted along with the optional cove colors.*

SPECIFICATIONS

Engines:	all ohv V-8; **1961** 283 cid (3.88 × 3.00), 230/245/270 (carbureted); 275/315 bhp (fuel injected) **1962** 327 cid (4.00 × 3.25), 250/300/340 bhp (carbureted); 360 bhp (fuel injected)
Transmissions:	3-speed manual; 4-speed manual and 2-speed Powerglide automatic optional
Suspension, front:	unequal-length A-arms, coil springs, anti-roll bar
Suspension, rear:	live axle, semi-elliptic leaf springs
Brakes:	front/rear drums
Wheelbase (in.):	102.0
Weight (lbs.):	2840
Top speed (mph):	109-132
0-60 mph (sec):	5.9-8.3
Production:	**1961** 10,939 **1962** 14,531

1961-64 Chevrolet Impala Super Sport

Yearning for a certain automobile wasn't a new phenomenon among American teens when the Beach Boys released their hit single "409" in 1962. But focusing on a specific engine—now that was something different. Few V-8s have been immortalized at all, much less recalled so fondly as the 409-cid motor that growled within big Chevys of the early Sixties.

Up to that time, the sporty full-size car was a virtual oxymoron: two concepts that just didn't work together. With its Super Sport edition of the restyled '61 model, Chevrolet was out to change that perception.

Toning down the Impala/Bel Air/Biscayne trio had begun in 1960 by subduing their broad tailfins. This year's body finished the job. Three rooflines were created, led by a Sport Coupe with gently sloping front pillars and plenty of glass. Though still on the gaudy side with its creased bodysides, tapered trim strip, jutting fender tops, and rear-deck sculpturing, the Impala's lines were undeniably cleaner—ready to usher in a new era.

One paragraph of the '61 sales catalog summarized the Super Sport as the "highly personalized version" of any Impala body style. Priced as low as $53.80, the option package included special trim, simulated knock-off spinner wheel covers, power brakes and steering, heavy-duty springs/shocks, metallic brake linings, a 7000-rpm tachometer alongside the steering column, and narrow-band 8.00 × 14 whitewalls. Inside was a front-passenger assist bar (as on Corvettes), but ordinary bench seats.

This initial Super Sport came with a choice of 348-cid engines (305, 340, or 350 bhp) and a four-speed manual gearbox; or the 305-bhp could get Powerglide. Farther down the Impala lineup, the top engine choice delivered only 280 bhp.

Target market: "customers who like sports car flair and go, teamed with big car elegance." That was just the start of what would become the "SS" phenomenon,

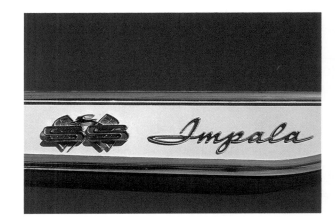

Below and opposite page, bottom: *Super Sport was initially an option package available on any Impala body style, but most were probably two-door Sport Coupes. Interiors wore special trim, a 7000-rpm tach, and a front-passenger grab bar (opposite page, top). The package also included a 305-bhp 348 V-8 with either a four-speed manual or Powerglide automatic. Optional 348s with up to 350 bhp were offered (but only with a four-speed), and at midyear, the mighty 409 debuted.*

SPECIFICATIONS

Engines:	ohv I-6 **1962** 235.5 cid (3.56 × 3.94), 135 bhp **1963-64** 230 cid (3.88 × 3.25), 140 bhp; ohv V-8, 283 cid (3.88 × 3.00), 170/195 bhp; **1961 only** 348 cid (4.13 × 3.25), 305/340/350 bhp; **1962-64** 327 cid (4.00 × 3.25), 250/300 bhp; 409 cid (4.31 × 3.50) **1961** 360 bhp **1962** 380/409 bhp **1963-64** 340/400/425 bhp
Transmissions:	3-speed manual; overdrive, 4-speed manual, and Powerglide 2-speed automatic optional
Suspension, front:	upper and lower A-arms, coil springs, stabilizer
Suspension, rear:	live axle, coil springs
Brakes:	front/rear drums
Wheelbase (in.):	119.0
Weight (lbs.):	3265-3565
Top speed (mph):	103-140
0-60 mph (sec):	**V-8** 6.3-12.8

Production: 1961 453 **1962** 99,311 **1963** 153,271 **1964** 185,325

for at the same time, Chevrolet was preparing a massive 409-cid engine. What better place to introduce it than beneath the hood of a Super Sport?

Essentially a bore/stroke job on the 348-cid V-8, the 409 wielded 360 bhp (at 5800 rpm) along with an energetic 409 pounds/feet of torque. It looked the part, too, painted red with silver rocker covers, topped by a dual-snorkel air cleaner.

The first 409-equipped Super Sports hit the showrooms in mid-1961. Most of the 453 examples built that year were Sport Coupes, with a handful of convertibles, though the package was theoretically offered on any Impala body. Only about 142 carried the big engine.

"Without trying hard," declared *Motor Trend* in its trial of the 409, "the SS will shoot away from practically anything else on the road." Testers achieved 0-60 times as quick as 7.0 seconds with a 4.56:1 axle. An ordinary Impala with 250-bhp 348 required more than 10 seconds.

More 409s became available for 1962; but curiously, the Super Sport turned into a $156 trim package offered with any Impala engine, even the 135-bhp six. However, SS body styles were strictly limited to the Sport Coupe (hardtop) and convertible. Styling grew cleaner yet, with a more squared-off profile and trailing body creaseline.

SS interiors now sported front bucket seats with anodized aluminum edging. "Swirl-pattern" anodized aluminum inserts adorned bodyside moldings, versus painted trim in regular Impalas.

Chevrolet's familiar 283-cid V-8 was bored and stroked to 327 cid to replace the 348. Top dog of the 409s gulped through a pair of four-barrel carburetors to yield 409 bhp. This year, *Motor Trend* roared its 409 test car to 60 in 6.3 seconds, blasting through the quarter-mile in 14.9 seconds. A 380-bhp edition took an extra second to hit 60 in the hands of *Car Life*. Sales virtually doubled those of the rival Ford Galaxie 500XL.

Impala's body was boxier yet for '63, as a 427-cid V-8 arrived, intended for professional drag racers. Most customers had to be content with a 425-bhp enhancement of the 409. A new "police option" 409 was rated 340 bhp. All SS Impalas had floor shifters this year. As usual, the $161 option could be ordered with any engine, down to the new 230-cid six. Inside, the grab bar was gone.

Super Sports were considered a distinct model in 1964. By this time, the SS owner could tune in to the Beatles on an AM/FM radio, and grasp a rarely seen twin-spoke walnut-grained steering wheel. "Any of three big 409 V-8's," said the '64 catalog, "is especially saucy in highway passing situations." Impala fans couldn't agree more, and the Super Sport phenomenon was well underway.

New sheetmetal graced the '62 Impalas (below), and the Super Sport option became a trim package available with any engine, including the lowly 235-cid six. The '63s (opposite page, top) wore a mild facelift, and though a 427-cid V-8 was offered, quantities were very limited and most customers had to "make do" with a new 425-bhp version of the 409. Styling was updated for 1964 with squarer corners, and the Super Sport (opposite page, bottom) became a separate model rather than an option package.

1962-64
Chevrolet Corvair
Monza Spyder

One of the characteristics plaguing the Corvair's development into more of a sporting (rather than economy) car was go-power. The 80 bhp engine couldn't compete with an Austin-Healey Sprite, and the 95-102 bhp units, though reasonably lively, were hardly powerhouses. Conventional hot-rodding techniques used on ordinary in-line or V-8 engines was inappropriate for the flat six, so General Motors ventured down another avenue: turbocharging.

The turbo-supercharger was invented by Sanford Moss in the 1920s, where it was used initially in aviation. The principle is simple: exhaust gasses spin an impeller, whose power is transferred by a shaft running to a compressor, which in turn pressurizes the fuel/air mixture on its way to the carburetors. As the exhaust flow increases and its temperature rises, the turbine spins faster, thus adding positive manifold pressure or "boost."

By the time the Spyder came along, turbochargers were widely used on Diesel trucks, and today, of course, they are commonplace on performance cars. For a car in the 1960s, however, it was a fairly novel idea, but it offered obvious advantages over conventional superchargers as fitted to Corvairs by Judson and Paxton. The turbo required no mechanical drive, made no noise or vibration, was efficient in the use of space, functioned only on demand, cost little in fuel economy, was cheap to build, and, of course, greatly increased power.

The Spyder's was made by the Thompson Valve Division of Thompson-Ramo-Wooldridge Inc., and hooked to a fairly ordinary Carter YH sidedraft carburetor (the same one as used on the early Corvettes and Nash-Healeys). Because of the heat generated by the system, super-strength materials were specified for many internal applications: chrome steel for the crankshaft, for example. The entire induction and exhaust system was tailored to the engine. By using a special reverse-flow muffler, a tuned air cleaner, and a tailpipe exactly nine inches long, Chevrolet not only

successfully kept maximum pressure down to a safe limit, but also obtained a throaty exhaust note. Impeller speed remained constant after 4600 rpm, but if the muffler was removed the low restriction and increased output could exceed the engine's strength.

The result of all this work was 150 horsepower at 4400 rpm or better than one bhp per cubic inch—nearly 50 percent better than the concurrent 102 bhp "stage two" Corvair engine. Torque shot up 64 percent to 210 pounds/feet at 3200-3400 rpm. "Chevy boosted the size of its air-cooled engine from 145 to 220 cid (the equivalent if naturally aspirated), yet the extra weight involved is only 30 lb!," said *Road & Track*. Chevrolet claimed that "usable" power was up 90 percent over the 102 hp version, which was at least partly true around 3000 rpm; past that point, torque fell off.

Though the Monza Spyder was announced in coupe and convertible form in February 1962, production actually began in April. Despite all that went into it, the Spyder package (RPO 690) cost only $317.45. Orders soon exceeded capacity—this was just not a car that could be built quickly. Of some 150,000 1962 Monza coupes, only 6894 emerged as Spyders, and there were only 2574 Monza Spyder convertibles out of over 16,000 Corvair ragtops built.

Though there wasn't much about the outside of the Spyder that made it recognizable (script, turbo emblems, a hunky tailpipe were the main points), the engine compartment abounded in chrome-trimmed components. Inside, there was no mistaking it: in place of Corvair's standard and sparse instrumentation was a round 6000 rpm tachometer and matching speedometer, with gauges for fuel, boost, and temperature. All were set into a brushed aluminum panel and matched by a similar panel over the glove box on the right. The radio also had a brushed aluminum plate, and a turbo emblem was on the horn button.

In 1963, Spyder production was up by over 100 percent despite a strong decline in total Corvair sales: 19,000 were built, of which about 7500 were convertibles. Volume fell in 1964 to 11,000 (4761 convertibles), but by then Corvair sales in general were well down. However, the technology lived on in the 1965 Corvair Corsa (see entry).

The survival rate for Monza Spyders is relatively high because people knew at an early date that these were singular cars, remarkably limited in numbers for a company like Chevrolet. Though the "standard-size" behemoth was still the quintessential Detroit car in the '60s, the Spyder proved that one company at least was willing to design an efficient, high-performance sporting machine for the enthusiastic driver. As a contemporary ad read, "the Spyder's thrust is not so much hot air."

SPECIFICATIONS

Engines:	**1962-63** flat 6, 145 cid (3.44 × 2.60), 150 bhp; **1964** 164 cid (3.44 × 2.94), 150 bhp
Transmission:	4-speed manual
Suspension front:	upper and lower A-arms, coil springs
Suspension rear:	**1962-63** semi-trailing swing axles, coil springs **1964** semi-trailing swing axles, transverse compensating spring
Brakes:	front/rear drums
Wheelbase (in.):	108.0
Weight (lbs):	2440-2650
Top speed (mph):	NA
0-60 mph (sec):	NA

Production: 1962 cpe 6894 **cvt** 2574 **1963 cpe** 11,627 **cvt** 7472 **1964 cpe** 6480 **cvt** 4761

Below: *Spyder variant of the Corvair debuted in 1962, its turbocharged engine* (opposite page, top) *producing 150 bhp— nearly 50 percent more than the hottest non-turbo version. The '63 coupe* (opposite page, bottom) *was the most popular of all Spyders, with nearly 12,000 built. Production was down for 1964, when the convertible* (opposite page, middle) *accounted for over 40 percent of Spyder sales.*

1963-67 Chevrolet Chevy II Nova SS

Ford's compact Falcon had Chevrolet worried. The rear-engined Corvair, though technically innovative, lagged in universal appeal. Chevrolet needed something new—but not so different—to compete in the growing compact category. So, the boxy little Chevy II dashed into the 1962 lineup to fill the void.

At first, it didn't look like much: just basic ho-hum transportation to rival the Falcon and Valiant, as well as the rising number of imports. Chevrolet billed its unibody senior compact as "the thrift car," though insisting that its "no-nonsense styling . . . will catch glances years away from the showroom." Sedans and wagons came in basic 100 and midrange 300 series. The luxury Nova 400 line added a sport coupe (hardtop) and convertible.

Either a 153-cid Super-Thrift four-cylinder engine or 194-cid six provided the power. Single-leaf rear springs were claimed to eliminate the "inherent harshness found in multi-leaf springs." Giving a hint of things to come, front bucket seats were available on the Nova 400 two-door.

Chevy's first four-cylinder powerplant since 1928 isn't what cemented Chevy II's spot in the automotive annals. Neither did the practical six. No, what did the trick was the Super Sport option introduced for 1963—plus the potential for V-8 power.

Installation of V-8s was underway during 1962, but only at individual dealerships, using over-the-counter parts. When an early 360-bhp conversion by Bill Thomas dashed to 60 mph in a stunning 5.2 seconds, more than a few performance fans took note.

Mild restyling with a bolder aluminum grille for 1963 was accompanied by the availability of a $161 Super Sport package, claimed to deliver "Nova 400 glamor with a sports car flourish" when installed on sport coupes and convertibles. It required larger (14-inch) tires and included a four-gauge instrument cluster, front bucket seats, silver-striped body moldings—but the ordinary six-cylinder engine. Ford dropped a V-8 into its Falcon this year. Could Chevrolet not follow suit?

SPECIFICATIONS

Engines:	ohv I-6 **1963-67** 194 cid (3.56 × 3.25), 120 bhp **1966** 230 cid (3.88 × 3.25), 140/155 bhp **1967** 250 cid (3.88 × 3.53), 155 bhp; **1964-67** ohv V-8, 283 cid (3.88 × 3.00), 195/220 bhp; 327 cid (4.00 × 3.25) **1965** 250/300 bhp **1966-67** 275/350 bhp
Transmissions:	3-speed manual; 4-speed manual and 2-speed Powerglide automatic optional
Suspension, front:	strut-supported lower A-arms, coil springs, anti-roll bar
Suspension, rear:	live axle, single leaf springs
Brakes:	front/rear drums (front discs optional in 1967)
Wheelbase (in.):	110.0
Weight (lbs.):	2410-2880
Top speed (mph):	Six 94 V-8 100-112
0-60 mph (sec):	V-8 7.2-11.3

Production: 1963 SS package 42,432 (total of 87,415 Nova sport coupes and 24,823 Nova convertibles built) **1964 Nova SS spt cpe** 10,576 **1965 Nova SS spt cpe** 9100 **1966 Chevy II Nova SS htp cpe** approx. 23,000 (6700 six and 16,300 V-8) **1967 Chevy II Nova SS htp cpe** 10,100 (1900 six and 8200 V-8)

First-generation Chevy II, which debuted in 1962, gained a Super Sport option package the next year, but buyers had to be content with a six-cylinder engine. A 195-bhp 283-cid V-8 was added in '64, but in 1965, the Super Sport (opposite page) gained some real teeth with a newly optional 300-bhp 327. The little Chevy's first major restyling came for 1966, when an even more-potent 350-bhp 327 was offered for the SS (above). Few changes occurred for '67 (this page, top), though the top 327 option was cut to "just" 275 bhp.

At last, for 1964, a V-8 became official: the 195-bhp Turbo-Fire 283, priced at $108. Amazingly, the sport coupe and convertible (and Super Sport options) were dropped. Protests brought the Super Sport back in hardtop coupe form by midyear, but the ragtop was gone for good. Thin body-peak moldings went on SS coupes, and the rear cove was silver-colored. Inside were front bucket seats and a console-mounted gearshift, for either the Powerglide automatic or—yes, there it was—a four-speed for the V-8. More than one-third of this year's sport coupes had the SS option.

"Despite its new vigor," ads declared, "it's still a nice, quiet, sturdy, sensible, unpretentious car. With sharper teeth." Full-throat screamers these were not, even with V-8 power. *Motor Trend* managed only an 11.3-second time to 60 mph with the 195-bhp engine. Additional vigor could be ordered for 1965 in the form of a 327-cid V-8, churning up 250 or 300 horsepower. A mild facelift produced a cleaner front end with bumper-mounted signal lamps. A more potent version of the 283 arrived at midyear, with dual exhaust pipes helping to whip up 220 horsepower. Even so, Super Sport production slipped to 9100.

Extensive restyling for 1966 gave the series a sharp-edged, masculine look appropriate with the changing times, accented by a semi-fastback roofline taper and angular rear end. Strato-bucket front seats were part of the $159 SS package, which included console shift. A tachometer was optional; other gauges were not.

As before, the SS package came with any powertrain, except the four-cylinder. Two tougher versions of the 327 emerged: one cranking out 275 bhp, the other tweaked to 350. A close-ratio four-speed gearbox was available with that top powerplant, but not Powerglide automatic.

In five years, the Chevy II had grown from a mild-mannered utility vehicle to one of the hottest street performers, capable of traveling to 60 in 7.2 seconds—provided that the assertive 327 was installed. Even the milder 327 with Powerglide did the trick in 8.6 seconds. All this potential must have struck a chord with the public, as Super Sport sales more than doubled.

Elation had to be short-lived, as SS production for '67 slumped back to 10,100. A black-out grille and visored headlights weren't enough to lure customers—some of whom were moving upward to Chevelle's SS and its 396-cid potential. Loss of the 350-bhp 327 didn't help. Super Sports would continue as the Nova line gained a massive revamping for 1968; but the SS mystique edged over to the bigger Chevrolets for its final years.

1963-67
Chevrolet Corvette
Sting Ray

Popular as America's sports car had grown since its 1953 debut, it was time for a change. Even the most superlative design grows whiskers after a decade. Chevrolet chief Bill Mitchell and stylist Larry Shinoda faced a tough task: to improve a living legend. Not only did they succeed, but their creation turned into a modern classic—the most collectible Corvette of them all—and sent sales soaring to record levels.

Seeds were planted by the Stingray Special racer and experimental XP-720, which displayed a smooth fastback profile and split back window. These and other styling details—pivoting hidden headlights, doors cut into the roof, a beltline dip—wound up in the production Sting Ray.

Quad headlights aligned with the pointy front end when shut, rotating open when needed. Luggage space grew, though lack of a trunklid earned few plaudits. Less fiberglass but nearly twice as much steel went into the sculptured-tail body, which rode a shorter (98-inch) wheelbase.

For several years, a removable hardtop had been optional. This generation went further, producing both the expected roadster and a full-fledged (doubly dramatic) hardtop coupe.

What drew the eye most in the coupe's shape was that split window, an idea from Mitchell that was not universally adored. It served as part of a full-length dorsal "spine" that began on the hood, continuing as a creaseline across the roof and down to the tip of the "boattail" canopy. One of the naysayers was renowned

Corvette got a new look for '63 (below), added the Sting Ray suffix to its name, and gained a coupe body style to complement the traditional convertible. Interiors and suspensions were also redesigned. Only minor trim variations marked the '64s (opposite page, top), though the top fuel-injected 327 now made 375 bhp, up from 360. The '65s (opposite page, bottom) were likewise changed only in detail, the vertical (rather than horizontal) "gills" behind the front wheels being the most noticeable, while a big-block 396 joined the option list.

Corvette engineer Zora Arkus-Duntov, who praised the performance but faulted the coupe's rearward visibility.

Public reaction was far more favorable, but critics prevailed, so a single pane was used the next year. Thus, the split-window Sting Ray later became the most coveted 'Vette in history, both for its distinctive silhouette and its comparative rarity.

Because many mechanical components were carried over from 1962, including the then-new 327-cid engine, the Sting Ray wasn't quite so revolutionary as it appeared. Underneath, a ladder-type frame replaced the old X-braced chassis. Far more noticeable was the new independent rear suspension: a three-link setup with double-jointed drive shafts on each side, and a single transverse leaf spring.

Power steering became available for the first time, except on the most potent engines. Only 12 percent of Corvettes had it. Even fewer customers opted for air conditioning or leather seats. Corvette fans, it seemed, still scoffed at frills. Four-speed gearboxes were far more popular, installed in more than four out of five cars.

Output of the carbureted 327-cid V-8 ranged from 250 to 340 bhp, while the $430 fuel-injected version reached 360 bhp. Could it move? You bet! A fuelie could hit 60 in 5.6 seconds, blasting through the quarter-mile in as little as 14.5 seconds (at 102 mph). As for handling, *Road & Track* reported that the "new Sting Ray sticks [with] great gripping gobs of traction."

The Sting Ray's debut was nearly as startling as that of the E-Type Jaguar a couple of years earlier, and the public yelled "yes" to the design. Production leaped by 50 percent over record-setting 1962, totaling 10,919 convertibles and 10,594 coupes, priced at $4037 and $4252, respectively.

Except for the loss of the backbone window and fake hood air intakes, 1964 brought minimal change. Simulated vents on the coupe's pillar became functional and instrument bezels turned black. Variable-rate springs helped smooth the ride and flatten the cornering. The solid-lifter V-8 got a higher-lift cam for 365 horsepower, while the fuelie added 15 bhp.

Extra inches arrived during 1965: namely, the Mark IV "porcupine" V-8 (named for its valve configuration), with 396 cubic inches eking out 425 horsepower. To keep all that energy under control, four-wheel disc brakes became available. Anyone craving more attention could order side-mounted exhaust pipes. A 427-cid enlargement followed the next year, adding no horsepower but developing more torque, as an eggcrate-patterned grille replaced the horizontal-bar form.

Final Sting Rays had the cleanest look of all, with every surface smoothed out. Top 427s whipped up 400 or 435 horsepower, using triple two-barrel carburetors and the option of $369 aluminum heads. Regular folks could only fantasize about the ultimate competition mill, with 12.5:1 compression and 560 horses champing at the bit—plus a thirst for 103-octane fuel. An "ordinary" 427-cid Sting Ray, able to run the quarter-mile in 13.6 seconds at 105 mph, surely was enough to satisfy any reasonable person. At least until the next 'Vette generation arrived.

SPECIFICATIONS

Engines:	ohv V-8, 327 cid (4.00 × 3.25)
	1963 250/300/340/360 bhp
	1964-65 250/300/350/365/375 bhp
	1966-67 300/350 bhp; 396 cid (4.09 × 3.75)
	1965 425 bhp; 427 cid (4.25 × 3.75)
	1966 390/425 bhp **1967** 390/400/435 bhp
Transmissions:	3-speed manual; 4-speed manual, 2-speed Powerglide automatic optional
Suspension, front:	upper and lower A-arms, coil springs
Suspension, rear:	independent w/halfshafts, lateral struts, radius rods, transverse leaf spring
Brakes:	front/rear drums **1965** front/rear discs
Wheelbase (in.):	98.0
Weight (lbs.):	2859-3020
Top speed (mph):	118-152
0-60 mph (sec):	4.7-8.0

Production: 1963 cpe 10,594 **cvt** 10,919 **1964 cpe** 8304 **cvt** 13,925 **1965 cpe** 8186 **cvt** 15,376 **1966 cpe** 9958 **cvt** 17,762 **1967 cpe** 8504 **cvt** 14,436

The '66s looked much like the '65s, but the big-block option grew from 396 to 427 cid. Front fender badges and domed hood (below) served fair warning that a Turbo-Jet 427 lay within. Five (rather than three) front-fender gills, a backup light over the rear license plate, and new power-dome hood on 427 models marked the '67s (opposite page).

1964-67 Chevrolet Chevelle Malibu SS

As American car buyers took a fancy to the mid-size phenomenon of the mid-Sixties, Chevrolet was left with a gap in its lineup. Bel Airs and Impalas were too big for some; Chevy II and Corvair too tiny. The answer came in the form of the A-body Chevelle, traditional in both engineering and upright styling—actually harking back in size and shape to the "classic" 1955-57 models.

Apart from curved side glass, little was extraordinary about these first Chevelles, which rode a perimeter-type frame with 115-inch wheelbase. Base engine was a 120-bhp Hi-Thrift 194-cid six; optional was a larger (230-cid) six developing 155 bhp. Ah, but either of those sixes left a promising expanse of space under the hood, space that could easily accommodate a V-8—which it did: Chevrolet's long-familiar 283-cid V-8, to be exact, with a moderate 195 horses at the ready. Add dual exhausts and a four-barrel carburetor, and the rating rose to 220 bhp. Just as interesting was the availability of a four-speed gearbox in place of the usual three-speed, overdrive, or Powerglide.

That wasn't all. "Everyone has a bit of swashbuckler in him," warned the sales catalog, a trait that could be indulged by purchasing a Super Sport. Offered on the top-rung Malibu Sport Coupe (hardtop) and convertible, the $162 SS package was similar to Impala's, including a black or white vinyl interior, front bucket seats, quartet of gauges, console, and radial-pattern wheel covers. Deletion of the Malibu's wide beltline trim strip gave SS two-doors a cleaner, even less cluttered appearance, though it meant greater vulnerability to damage. A fist-size ball atop the four-speed's gearshift suggested the car's intended audience, though a tachometer cost extra. A heavy-duty suspension added less than five dollars.

Close to half of the Malibu coupes and convertibles built for 1964 had Super Sport equipment. Performance with the 283, if not exactly overwhelming, qualified

as respectable. *Motor Trend* sent a 220-bhp edition with four-speed to 60 mph in 9.7 seconds, completing the quarter-mile in 17.5 seconds.

More was soon to come. A 327-cid V-8 was approved during Chevelle's first model year, ready to deliver 250 or 300 bhp. The calm family mover was showing signs of turning into a threatening machine, rivaling the new Pontiac GTO and Oldsmobile 4-4-2.

A modest facelift gave the '65s a few extra inches and a lower profile, led by a vee-shaped grille and extended hood. Super Sports wore less chrome, and were again available with any powertrain. Flat black SS grille accents actually started a trend toward black-out front ends. During the year, textured vinyl front bucket seats replaced the earlier corduroy pattern. A more potent 350-bhp Turbo-Fire 327 with high-lift cam and chromed dress-up items saw only a handful of installations.

As a hint of things to come, Chevrolet's 396-cid "porcupine" V-8 with 375 bhp saw early duty in 201 Chevelles this year. At $1501, this Z16 styling/chassis package wasn't for everyone. Chevrolet head Pete Estes favored the idea, so the 396 soon became an official choice.

Major restyling for 1966 brought an adjustment. This time, only Chevelles with the 396 V-8 earned the right to wear the Super Sport designation, known as SS 396. In fact, the big V-8 wasn't available in "lesser" models. The SS 396 had stronger springs, recalibrated shocks, and thicker front stabilizer bar. Sport Coupes displayed a fresh roofline with deeply inset "tunneled" rear window, and could have a black or beige vinyl top. Some items included with prior SS packages were optional, such as bucket seats. Styling included dual simulated hood air intakes, color-accented sills, and a black-filled rear cove panel. Body-colored wheels wore plain hubcaps unless covers were ordered.

The 396 V-8 put out 325 bhp in standard trim, or 360 with a hotter camshaft. Fewer than 100 solid-lifter examples rated at 375 bhp were installed, all on special order. Lesser Chevelles added a 350-bhp 327-cid V-8, but few found buyers.

Little changed for 1967, as the 375-bhp engine faded away and Turbo Hydra-Matic joined the familiar Powerglide as an option. By this time, Super Sports cost $285 more than a regular Malibu, with the 325-bhp engine as part of the package. "If you have a taste for action," declared the catalog, "here's the satisfier." More and more customers were wholly satisfied with their SS Chevelles, but the next generation was waiting in the wings.

SPECIFICATIONS

Engines:	1964-65 ohv I-6, 194 cid (3.56 × 3.25), 120 bhp; 230 cid (3.88 × 3.25), 140/155 bhp; ohv V-8, 283 cid (3.88 × 3.00), 195/220 bhp; 327 cid (4.00 × 3.25), 250/300/350 bhp; 396 cid (4.09 × 3.76) **1965** 375 bhp **1966-67** 396 cid only, 325/350/360/375 bhp
Transmissions:	3-speed manual; 4-speed manual, 2-speed Powerglide and (1967) 3-speed Turbo Hydra-Matic optional
Suspension, front:	upper and lower A-arms, coil springs, stabilizer bar
Suspension, rear:	live axle, coil springs
Brakes:	front/rear drums (front discs optional in 1967)
Wheelbase (in.):	115.0
Weight (lbs.):	2875-3485
Top speed (mph):	**V8-283** 109-110 **SS 396** 115-135
0-60 mph (sec):	**V8-283** 8.5-9.7 **SS 396** 6.0-7.5

Production: 1964 76,860 **1965** 101,577 (201 w/396 V8) **1966** 72,272 **1967** 63,006

Opposite page, top: *Biggest engine offered for the Chevelle SS in '64 was the 327 V-8 (opposite page, middle) with 250 or 300 bhp. In '65, a few Super Sports were equipped with a Z16 package that included a 375-bhp 396 (opposite page, bottom). Chevelles were redesigned for '66, and a 396 was made standard in Super Sports, which carried over to '67 (below) with few changes.*

1965-69
Chevrolet Corvair Corsa & Monza

The Corvair died a tragic death, kept in production only long enough to amortize the die expenses of the second generation (1965) redesign. Contrary to myth, the Corvair was not scrubbed because of Ralph Nader's attacks. Chevrolet documents examined by several writers prove that the word had been passed to start development of a conventional front-engine, rear-drive car in 1964, before the new Corvairs hit the streets. This was likely prompted by the phenomenal success of the Mustang, introduced in the spring of that year, as it was well before Nader's book was published.

Nevertheless, the 1965 Corvair was a stunning automobile—one of the few that look good from virtually any angle. "It is simply not possible to photograph this car from an angle that makes it look ugly," said one veteran automotive photographer. "I don't know any other mass-production car from its period that you could say that about."

A tribute to Bill Mitchell's brilliant staff at GM Styling, the new Corvair looked like the work of one of the leading Italian houses. It was nicely shaped, but not overdone, with just the right amount of trim. It was new under the skin, too, with a turbocharged model, the Corsa, producing an unprecedented 180 bhp, and a new non-turbo with 140 bhp. Important too was its new rear suspension, a virtual copy of the Corvette Sting Ray's: upper and lower control arms, the uppers doubling as axle half-shafts, the lowers being unequal length non-parallel bars. These four arms controlled all lateral wheel motion. The sole difference from the Corvette was the use of coil springs, whereas the 'Vette had a transverse leaf spring.

No longer was there any question about tricky handling on hard corners. The Corvair's handling was now virtually neutral, with mild final oversteer at very high speeds. Attention was also paid to the front suspension, which was tuned to complement the new rear design and to provide roll stiffness.

Chevy came close to retaining "Monza Spyder" for the turbocharged Corsa, but switched at the last moment. The Corsa retained the handsome brushed aluminum dash and full complement of instruments of the Monza Spyder, though it could be had without the turbocharger: the 140 bhp engine with its four carburetors was standard on Corsas. The 180 gave the Corsa performance amounting almost to drag strip stuff for a six-cylinder car: 0-60 in 11 seconds, the standing-start quarter-mile in 18 seconds at 80 mph. Top speed was 115, given enough straightaway; yet gas mileage still averaged around 20 mpg. Corsas could be told at a glance from their brushed aluminum rear deck panel. A convertible and two-door hardtop were offered, and production was triple that of the previous Monza Spyders, though hardly anything to enthuse about given Mustang's stupendous half-million-plus.

The Monza continued to be Corvair's bread-and-butter model, available in four-door hardtop form as well as two-door coupe and convertible. Monzas were slugs with the 95 bhp engine, reasonable with the 110, and exhilarating with the 140, though the latter was rather finicky and difficult to properly tune. At the bottom of the line was the 500 series, a plain-trimmed coupe and sedan base-priced at little over $2000, which seems incredible today. For that paltry sum, they delivered singular styling, good fuel economy, and decent performance. It was rare when a 500 or Monza cost more than $2750.

But Mustang was the hot "ponycar" now, and the Corvair appealed only to what Lee Iacocca called "the enthusiasts, the real nuts." Volume exceeded 200,000 in 1965, mostly on the strength of the new styling; a year later it was down by more than half, and in 1967 the Corsa was dropped. The following year saw the demise of the four-door hardtop and 140 bhp engine, and the Corvair finished life with a three-model line comprised of two coupes and one convertible, all powered by a standard 95 bhp (110 optional) engine increasingly stifled by emission controls. The air pump fitted to the final '69s was notorious for causing severe ping and carburetor flooding. As a consolation to '69 buyers, Chevy offered a coupon entitling them to a discount on their next Chevrolet. Most of them didn't use it, because Chevy was no longer building a car that appealed to their technical interest and enthusiasm.

This page, bottom: Corvair was restyled for 1965, and the turbocharged model, now called Corsa, boasted 180 bhp. Opposite page, top: Four-doors were now hardtops rather than pillared sedans, but by 1966, their popularity was on the wane and they would be cut from the line after '67. Below: Convertibles would remain until the bitter end, but only 2109 of the '67s were sold, a figure that would drop further in '68 and '69. Opposite page, bottom: By the end of 1968, the once-popular Monza coupe had sold but 6807 copies, and the Corvair would be discontinued a year later.

SPECIFICATIONS

Engines:	flat 6, 164 cid (3.44 × 2.94), 95-180 bhp
Transmissions:	3/4-speed manual; 2-speed automatic optional
Suspension front:	upper and lower A-arms, coil springs
Suspension rear:	fully independent with trailing arms and coil springs
Brakes:	front/rear drums
Wheelbase (in.):	108.0
Weight (lbs):	2440-2725
Top speed (mph):	115 (Corsa)
0-60 mph (sec):	11.0 (Corsa)

Production: **1965 Monza cpe** 88,954 **sdn** 37,157 **cvt** 26,466 **Corsa cpe** 20,291 **cvt** 8353 **1966 Monza cpe** 37,605 **sdn** 12,497 **cvt** 10,345 **Corsa cpe** 7330 **cvt** 3142 **1967 Monza cpe** 9771 **sdn** 3157 **cvt** 2109 **1968 cpe** 6807 **cvt** 1386 **1969 Monza cpe** 2717 **cvt** 521

1967-69
Chevrolet Camaro

It's commonly believed that the Camaro was just a me-too response to Ford's Mustang, but it just isn't so. Though quite by accident, Chevrolet's Corvair Monza had uncovered the huge market for sporty compacts that Mustang exploited. What's more, General Motors had contemplated a Mustang-type car better than two years before the Ford's stupendous mid-1964 launch.

Nevertheless, some General Motors executives felt their restyled, second-generation Corvairs would stem the stampede to Mustang-style "ponycars." Yet however handsome, the '65 Monza and its kin retained an air-cooled, rear-engine design that was just too quirky to sell well against the orthodox, $2500 Falcon-based Mustang. And because it remained technically unique within the Chevrolet family, Corvair was a costly bother to build. So, even as the redesigned '65 models were debuting, GM managers were deciding that the Corvair would be allowed to fade away.

Meantime, Chevy rushed to complete a conventional front-engine replacement as a direct Mustang-fighter. Called Camaro, it predictably followed Ford's formula down to an identical wheelbase, under-skin components liberally borrowed from a "family" compact (here, the Chevy II), standard front bucket seats, rakish long-hood/short-deck styling, and numerous options that eventually numbered 81 factory items and 41 dealer-installed accessories.

A key early decision was to combine unit construction with a front subframe that cradled the engine/transmission package on large rubber mounts to minimize noise, vibration, and harshness. Front suspension involved the usual wishbones and coil springs, but with the springs between the arms instead of atop the upper ones, which benefited handling. Unfortunately, the rear suspension had cheap "Mono-Plate" single-leaf springs that allowed severe axle tramp in hard acceleration with the planned V-8 engines. Because this went undiscovered until the 11th hour, V-8 Camaros had rear traction bars for '67, then added staggered shocks, though neither was a genuine cure. Easy rear-end bottoming was another flaw.

Styling, on the other hand, was nearly perfect: chiseled yet flowing, and decisively different from Mustang. Naturally, it was created under the watchful eye of GM

Opposite page, top: *The hottest Camaro in debut '67 was the Super Sport, an option package that included a 295-bhp 350 V-8. Opposite page, middle: By 1968, competition had heated up to the point that Camaro engine offerings expanded to include Chevy's big-block 396 with up to 375 bhp. Above and opposite page, bottom: Camaro was facelifted for '69, gaining modified side sculpturing in addition to new grille and taillight treatments. It would carry on in this form into 1970, being replaced by a completely new design at midyear.*

SPECIFICATIONS

Engines:	ohv I-6, 230 cid (3.88 × 3.25), 140 bhp (**1967-68**); 250 cid (3.88 × 3.53), 155 bhp (**1969**); ohv V-8, 307 cid (3.88 × 3.25), 200 bhp (**1969**); 327 cid (4.00 × 3.25), 210/275 bhp; 350 cid (4.00 × 3.48), 255/295 bhp; 396 cid (4.09 × 3.76), 325/350/375 bhp
Transmission:	3/4-speed manual, 2-speed Powerglide automatic
Suspension front:	upper and lower A-arms, coil springs
Suspension rear:	live axle on semi-elliptic leaf springs
Brakes:	front/rear drums, optional front discs
Wheelbase (in.):	108.0
Weight (lbs):	2770-3295
Top speed (mph):	105-120
0-60 mph (sec):	7.5-11.0

Production: 1967 Six 58,808 **V-8** 162,109 **1968 Six** 50,937 **V-8** 184,178 **1969 Six** 65,008 **V-8** 178,087

design chief Bill Mitchell—who ironically didn't much like the finished product.

Again mimicking the Mustang, Camaro aimed to be all things to all sporty-car buyers. Your choices began with a basic hardtop coupe or convertible with 230-cid six. From there you went to a 250-cid six ($26), 327 V-8 ($106), or 350 V-8. The last, though, was tied to a $211 Super Sport package comprising stiff suspension, D70×14 tires, modified hood with extra sound insulation, and "bumblebee" nose stripes. From midseason, a pair of 396 big-blocks (325 and 350 bhp) was offered through dealers to get around a GM ceiling on "excessive" small-car displacement and horsepower.

Other tempting '67 options included Custom interior, Strato-Back front bench seat (rarely ordered), fold-down rear seat, extra gauges, and console shifters for the optional two-speed Powerglide automatic, Heavy-Duty three-speed manual, and four-speed manual. A $105 Rally Sport package added a hidden-headlight grille among other touches. Additional extras ran to tinted glass, heater, air conditioning, cruise control, and a vinyl roof for hardtops. Functional items included sintered-metallic brake linings, vented power front-disc brakes, quick-ratio manual steering, Positraction limited-slip differential, and a dozen different axle ratios. With all this, delivered prices could easily exceed $5000.

Camaro may have trod Mustang's trail, but was successful on its own. Though Mustang outsold it for 1967, Camaro's 220,000 orders represented fully 10 percent of Chevy's total volume that year. Among them were 100 "Official Pace Car" convertibles from the Indianapolis "500" (not publicly sold) and 602 of the now-legendary Z-28s (see entry).

Sales improved by some 15,000 units for '68 despite few changes and new competition. Washington's mandated side-marker lights provided easy identification, as did a revised grille and one-piece door glass (signaling Chevy's new flow-through "Astro Ventilation"). Options remained substantially the same save for a third 396 (375 bhp) offering.

The '69s saw more extensive revisions—a good thing, as they would sell into early 1970 pending a delayed, all-new second-generation Camaro. A deft lower-body reskin introduced a vee'd eggcrate grille, "speed streaks" above the wheelarches, and a reshaped tail. RS headlamps remained hidden when off, but glass slots allowed some light to shine through should their covers fail to retract. Instruments were revamped, as were some engine choices. Sales eased, but not greatly.

Camaro again paced the Indy "500" in '69, but Chevrolet cashed in this time by selling 3475 "Pacesetter Value Package" convertibles at about $3500 apiece. Of these, only four (perhaps more) were equipped like the three "real" pacers.

1967-69
Chevrolet Camaro Z-28

The first Z-28 was to Chevrolet's Camaro what the Boss 302 was to Ford's Mustang: a factory-engineered race-ready "ponycar" available at your corner showroom. But where Camaro trailed Mustang to market by two years, the Z-28 appeared two years before the Boss.

Announced in early 1967, some six months after the Camaro itself, the Z-28 was conceived by Chevy engineer and product-promotion specialist Vincent W. Piggins. The impetus, as Piggins later explained, was "to develop a performance image for the Camaro that would be superior to Mustang's. Along comes [Sports Car Club of America] in creating the Trans-Am sedan racing class for professional drivers in 1966 . . . I suggested a vehicle that would fit this class and, I believe . . . it gave them the heart to push ahead. . . ."

Initially, the Trans-Am involved Group II production cars with wheelbases of 116 inches or less and engines of no more than 305 cubic inches. Certification required at least 1000 be built per model year. Chevy met this by entering the standard V-8 Camaro as a Group I sports car (over 305 cid) and the Z-28 *option* under Group II.

Rule-bending aside, the Z-28 was a racer's delight: heavy-duty suspension, power front-disc brakes, metallic-lined rear-drum brakes, 15×6 Corvette wheels mounting 7.75×15 tires, special hood with functional air intakes, close- or wide-ratio four-speed gearbox, and a new 302 V-8. The last came from slotting the crankshaft from the older 283 engine into the then-current 327 block, yielding 302.4 cid—just under the limit. Outputs were conservatively stated as 290 horsepower and as many pounds/feet of torque, but actual bhp was nearer 400, thanks to a huge four-barrel Holley carb, oversize intake manifold, big ports and valves, wild 346-degree-duration cam, and cast-iron headers.

Chevy called the Z-28 "the closest thing to a 'Vette, yet," and not without reason. *Car and Driver* clocked one at a blazing 6.7 seconds 0-60 mph, versus 7.8 seconds for the typical four-speed SS350 and slightly under 11 seconds for an automatic 210-bhp 327. Handling was racer-sharp; braking as good as it could be with contemporary technology.

The "civilian" Z-28 package, which also included broad dorsal racing stripes, ostensibly added just $400 to a Camaro's price. But it was closer to $800 because the four-speed, front discs, headers, and special rear brake linings were separate "mandatory options." Of course, you could add all manner of regular Camaro goodies, including Positraction limited-slip differential, rear spoiler, and the Rally Sport appearance group. So delivered, prices could easily exceed $5000—still hardly outrageous.

But wins, not sales, were the Z-28's main goal, and in due time they were convincingly achieved. Mustang claimed the Trans-Am championship in 1966 and again in '67, when Z-28s won only three events. But Camaro dominated the series in 1968 and '69, thanks to the all-star Roger Penske team and ace driver Mark Donohue.

A raft of improvements occurred for '68. The power front discs became standard, four-wheel discs arrived as a late-season "service option" for more stopping power on the track, main bearings were enlarged, five-leaf rear springs replaced the wimpy monoleaf units, and a new $500 twin-four-barrel manifold option arrived. Factory competition equipment proliferated to include plastic bucket seats and purpose-designed airdams, spoilers, and steering components.

Other than a substantial facelift, shared with other Camaros, the most obvious change in the '69 Z was a mean-looking "Cowl Induction" hood with a rear-facing scoop that gulped in air from the high-pressure area just ahead of the windshield. The deep-breathing, high-winding 302 switched to four-bolt main bearings, and rolling stock slimmed to six-inch-wide rims wearing E70-15 high-performance tires.

Paralleling the entire Camaro line, the '69s are the most numerous of the first-generation Z-28s with 19,014 built—quite high for such a specialized machine. That figure also represented a substantial gain on the 7199 of 1968, which in turn was a sizeable increase over the mere 602 for '67. Needless to say, those first-year models are today the most collectible Z-28s, not least for being most like the all-out competition cars Piggins had in mind.

Of course, the Z-28 has since seen far higher volume, but only by becoming more and more like other Camaros—and far less potent. Happily, it's still with us in the '90s, and a lot more exciting than it was in the late '70s. But today's Z will never cast the same spell as the 1967-69 originals. Magical muscle machines all, they were a unique, short-lived breed the likes of which we shall not see again.

Z-28s carried a specially built 302-cid V-8 (this page, top) rated at a conservative 290 bhp. Only 602 were built during Camaro's debut 1967 season (opposite page, top), but production jumped to 7199 for the similar '68s (above), which added stronger rear springs along with optional four-wheel disc brakes and dual-quad manifold. All Camaros received revised styling for '69, and the Z-28 (opposite page, bottom) added a new "Cowl Induction" hood. Production topped 19,000.

SPECIFICATIONS

Engines:	ohv V-8, 302 cid (4.00 × 3.00), 290 bhp (nominal rating; actual estimated horsepower 400)
Transmission:	4-speed manual
Suspension front:	upper and lower A-arms, coil springs
Suspension rear:	live axle, semi-elliptic leaf springs
Brakes:	front discs/rear drums (opt. four-wheel discs **1968-69**)
Wheelbase (in.):	108.0
Weight (lbs):	2950-3150
Top speed (mph):	124-132
0-60 mph (sec):	5.3-6.7
Production:	**1967** 602 **1968** 7,199 **1969** 19,014

1968-69
Chevrolet Chevelle SS 396

When Chevrolet's mid-size adopted an all-new body on a shorter (112-inch) wheelbase for 1968, the SS 396 hardtop coupe and convertible became a separate series. Even before, the Super Sport option had been offered only with the 396-cid V-8, helping to earn plenty of performance accolades for that model. Sales had slipped a bit in 1967, the fourth season of the intermediate design, so a fresh approach made sense. Competition in the muscle-car ranks grew stronger each year, and creative thinking was needed to reel in the customers.

This final Chevelle of the Sixties displayed a more rakish, sculptured look with tapered front fenders, rounded beltline, and semi-fastback flowing hardtop roofline. An upswept curve followed the base of the rear side windows. Like many models of this vintage, Chevelles adopted the long-hood/short-deck profile, with a high rear-quarter kickup. The entire front hood/fender assembly took on an assertive, leaning-forward stance, reaching past the grille and headlights. Hide-A-Way windshield wipers on upper-level Chevelles (including the SS 396 and new luxury Concours) disappeared below hood level when not in use.

Standard in the SS 396 was the 325-bhp edition of the Turbo-Jet 396-cid big-block V-8, hooked to either a standard floor-shift three-speed, four-speed, Powerglide, or Turbo Hydra-Matic. For additional "go," two higher-powered engines with dual exhausts were available: an easy-to-buy 350 bhp or, on special order, the no-holds-barred 375-horsepower screamer. Even the base engine yielded gobs of torque—a muscular 410 pounds/feet.

Tread width grew an inch. Red-stripe wide-oval F70×14 tires were SS standards. Both coupe and convertible were easy to spot with their black-accented grilles and twin-domed hoods. Black accents also decorated the lower body (except on dark-colored cars). At the rear, a black-filled panel linked the taillights. Displacement badges ("396") were incorporated into new side marker lights. Other

The SS 396 became a separate model in 1968 (above) when the entire Chevelle line received new styling. A 375-bhp version of the 396 was the top engine option, though few were built. Changes to the '69s were minor (above and opposite page), and though the limited-production 375-horse 396 engine was dropped, about 500 SS "396s" were fitted with 427-cid V-8s.

SPECIFICATIONS

Engines:	ohv V-8, 396 cid (4.09 × 3.76), 325/350/375 bhp
Transmissions:	3-speed manual; 4-speed manual, 2-speed Powerglide and 3-speed Turbo Hydra-Matic optional
Suspension, front:	upper and lower A-arms, coil springs, stabilizer bar
Suspension, rear:	live axle, coil springs
Brakes:	front/rear drums (front discs optional)
Wheelbase (in.):	112.0
Weight (lbs.):	3550-3570
Top speed (mph):	116-126
0-60 mph (sec):	5.8-7.7
Production:	**1968 htp cpe** 60,499 **cvt** 2286 **1969** 86,300

Chevelles could have everything from a 140-bhp 230-cid six to a 325-bhp 327 V-8. Higher-rate springs and shocks gave SS 396 models a tighter ride than their less-potent Malibu mates.

Two different all-synchro four-speed gearboxes were offered, with first gear's ratio either 2.52:1 or 2.20:1. Bucket seats and a console were on the option list. So was a special SS instrument package that included gauges, a clock, and vertical-scale tachometer. Chromed rocker covers, air cleaner upper plates, and oil filler cap gave the SS engine an appearance no less handsome than its body. Price for all this was $2899 for the hardtop coupe—just $236 more than an ordinary Malibu sport coupe with 307-cid V-8. With the hottest engine, an SS 396 could accelerate to 60 in a snappy 6.6 seconds, winding up the quarter-mile in 14 (and nearing 100 mph).

Oddly, the SS 396 reverted from a model on its own to a $347.60 option package for 1969, available not only on Malibu coupes and convertibles but even on equivalent lower-rung Chevelle 300 coupes. For the first time, in fact, a pillared two-door sedan could be ordered with the SS option. Apart from a restyled black-out grille and taller taillights, not much changed in any of the Chevelles. Like all GM cars, the front windows lost their vent wings, a change that carried the impressive-sounding title of "Astro Ventilation." New SS five-spoke chrome Sport wheels held white-stripe or white-letter F70×14 rubber, and power front-disc brakes were standard.

Only the 325- and 350-bhp editions of the 396-cid V-8 made the lineup. Powerglide did not, making Turbo Hydra-Matic ($222) the only shiftless option. Depending upon the axle and transmission, an SS 396 could still roar off the line with gusto, reaching 60 in as little as 5.8 seconds.

At least 500 Chevelles leapt one step higher on the performance spectrum, coming off the line with 427-cid V-8s installed. Most options were less dramatic, on the order of headlight washer, power door locks, Comfortilt steering, or a vinyl roof.

Shoppers evidently liked the revised SS 396, signing on the dotted line for 62,785 copies in 1968 and an even bigger total of 86,300 the next year. The restyled 1968-69 Chevelle body wasn't finished yet, either, destined to last through 1972 with 396- or 454-cid power. America's muscle-car era had a couple more years to run, and Chevrolet's mid-size still had another trick or two waiting.

1968-69
Chevrolet Corvette

"Classic" status came later for the 1963-67 Sting Ray. After five years in one form, however handsome, it was just one more aging design, ready to be upstaged by a completely different fifth-generation sports car. That successor, dubbed the "Shark," was destined to enjoy considerably greater longevity, remaining on the market with remarkably little change through the 1970s and beyond.

Rumors abounded that the fifth-generation Corvette would be of mid-engine configuration, undoubtedly prompted by such show cars as the CERV II and Astro II, both of which had their engines mounted midships. Yet it was another show car, the famous Mako Shark II, that lent inspiration to the '68 design.

Both a front air dam and rear spoiler were part of the blunt-profiled restyle, directed by David Holls, which wasn't quite so blissfully aerodynamic in notchback coupe form as it appeared. At a glance, little trace remained of the Sting Ray. As a matter of fact, that designation no longer was used (though early catalogs announced the name). Headlights again were concealed, but in simple vacuum-operated pop-up style, no longer pivoting into place. Wipers hid beneath a pop-up panel.

Coupe passengers could enjoy the breezes almost as much as convertible riders, since both the twin roof panels and the rear window were removable. Truth be told, the "Shark" showed more than a passing kinship to the new Camaro, whose Z-28 edition soon would rival Corvette in the performance arena.

International Blue, British Green, and Polar White were among the year's colors. Interiors came in eight textured vinyl shades, while optional leather could be ordered in half a dozen hues. A black vinyl cover option for the removable hardtop drew few requests. Vent wings were a feature of the past.

Turbo Hydra-Matic was the sole choice for automatic shifting, replacing the tame two-speed Powerglide. A three-speed gearbox remained available, though four-speeds attracted the lion's share of customers. Powerplants came in two sizes,

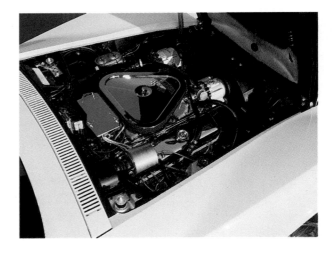

Below: *Restyled 1968 Corvette debuted* sans *Sting Ray moniker, which would reappear in '69 as one word (Stingray). As before, the top engine option was a tri-carb 427 boasting 435 bhp (above). The '69 looked nearly identical to the '68, but could be ordered with bright inserts for the front fender gills (opposite page), which many were.*

similar to 1967: a 327-cid V-8 with 300 or 350 horsepower, and three flavors of 427 (390, 400, or 435 bhp). The hottest two employed a trio of two-barrel carburetors. A high-domed hood was needed to clear the big-block.

All-disc brakes were standard. Wider rims held low-profile F70×15 tires, which gripped the road tighter due to a wider track. Trunk space was skimpier, still lacking outside access. No glove compartment was installed, either. Thieves took a growing interest in Corvettes, prompting installation of an alarm that triggered the horn. Headlight washers were standard.

While some testers praised the new styling, others branded it a step backward: fat and flashy, more boulevard cruiser than race/ride machine. *Road & Track*, for one, claimed it lacked finesse and exemplified the trend "toward Image and Gadget Car," especially with the increased front overhang and added weight. Workmanship slipped, marking a low point in Corvette history. Cooling also became a problem, especially with big-block engines. Quick the 427s were, capable of 0-60 mph times well under six seconds (two seconds faster than a 327); but not trouble-free.

Because sales shot up to a record 28,566—and the basic design would last into 1982—either the critics were mistaken or the public disagreed with their appraisals. Even in 1968, though, *Car and Driver* readers voted Corvette the Best All-Around Car.

Curiously, the Stingray designation (now one word) returned for 1969, written in script on the front fenders. Grille bars went from chrome to black. New this year: a 350-cid base V-8, able to deliver either 300 or 350 bhp. Race drivers had choices unavailable to the general public, including an L88 engine in 1968 that whacked out 560 horsepower and, in 1969, an aluminum-block ZL-1 with a $3000 price tag. The latter appeared in regular catalogs as a 430-bhp off-road selection "that we don't recommend for street use."

Convertibles were most popular at first, but coupes earned well over half of sales the next year. Production of 38,762 'Vettes in 1969 would remain the record for the next half-dozen seasons. "Corvette has a gauge for everything but your blood pressure," claimed the '69 catalog. Maybe they should have installed one, because the two-seaters had a propensity for overstimulating drivers. For countless Americans, including the millions who would never own one, Corvettes symbolized the transition in sports cars from quaint, rough-riding European roadsters to muscular masterworks of technology. Come to think of it, they still do.

SPECIFICATIONS

Engines:	ohv V-8, 327 cid (4.00 × 3.25), 300/350 bhp; 427 cid (4.25 × 3.76), 390/400/435 bhp
Transmissions:	3-speed or 4-speed manual; 3-speed Turbo Hydra-Matic optional
Suspension, front:	upper and lower A-arms, coil springs
Suspension, rear:	independent w/tubular shafts, transverse strut, transverse leaf spring
Brakes:	front/rear discs
Wheelbase (in.):	98.0
Weight (lbs.):	3055-3145
Top speed (mph):	117-160
0-60 mph (sec):	5.7-7.7

Production: 1968 cpe 9936 **cvt** 18,630 **1969 cpe** 22,154 **cvt** 16,608

1960-62
Chrysler 300F/G/H

When Chrysler substituted a wedgehead V-8 for the fabled Hemi on the 1959 300E, enthusiasts of the "Beautiful Brute" were momentarily dumfounded. What was the 300 without the Hemi? But they were soon reassured by the wedgehead's tremendous performance, which, if anything, was better than the old Hemi. Unfortunately, fewer than 700 of the '59 300s were produced.

With 1960 dawned a five year cycle of prosperity for Chrysler, and business immediately picked up, along with 300 production. Topping the technical news was Chrysler's first unit body-chassis; with it came self-activating swivel seats (they pivoted outward when a door was opened) an electro-luminescent instrument panel, and the best styling since 1957. Virgil Exner was still in command of Chrysler design, and still partial to tailfins: the '60s were taller than ever, ending in sharp points above the neatly fitted taillights.

The 1960 300F represented a major comeback for Chrysler's limited production high-performance car. Though it used the same basic bodyshell as other models, its styling was purposely restrained: the rectangular grille was blacked-out, except for a big "300" emblem supported by four thin chrome bars; the sides were decorated as usual with a short bright metal spear aft of the doors, carrying the same emblem. All told, the "F" wore the flamboyant 1960 styling rather better than the more conventional workaday Chryslers.

Thanks to its ram-induction 413-cid wedge and the first four-speed gearbox offered on a postwar Chrysler, the 300F was a hot car indeed. The four-speed was built by Pont-a-Mousson, and was the same unit used in the Facel Vega (for which Chrysler had long been supplying Hemi and wedge V-8 engines). The ram manifolds, optional on Plymouth, Dodge, DeSoto, and junior Chryslers, were standard on the 300F.

Ram induction had been used earlier in racing, and Chrysler had been dabbling with it since 1952. By 1960, they learned how to calculate intake manifold length by experiments using telescoping tubes and a dynamometer, concentrating on midrange engine speeds (2000-3500 rpm). The optimum was 30 inches for each tube, one per

Above: *Interior of the 300F featured new self-activating swivel seats that swung to the side when the door was opened. As in the past, styling of the 1960 300F (both pages) was similar to "lesser" Chryslers, differing primarily in trim such as the black-out grille and chrome side spear, both carrying "300F" emblems. Fake spare-tire design on trunklid (sometimes referred to as a "toilet seat") was also available on other Chryslers.*

port. Placing carburetors on the ends of the tubes rather than in the middle gave a steady power increase all along the torque curve, eliminating pulsations. The carbs were also easier to tune in this configuration, and ran cooler.

Motor Trend tested a 300F with the 375 bhp ram-tuned engine, running the standing quarter-mile in 16 seconds flat at 85 mph. It handled as well as ever, though the editors felt that the 300F had "traded a measure of its 'brute, racy' feeling for that of a 'sporty, personal type' car, like the four seater Thunderbird." Yet the 300F was, in their view, more potent than the preceding 300E.

The Pont-a-Mousson gearbox was fitted to only seven 300Fs, all with the optional 400-bhp engine. It was a tight, notchy gearbox that did not like speed shifts, but it did prove its worth at Daytona, where six four-speeds turned in flying miles between 141.5 and 144.9 mph.

The 300F used four contoured seats with a full-length console, and came in black, red, white, or terra cotta. A fake spare tire outline was added to the F's deck, receiving enough criticism from the enthusiast press to be dropped on the 1961 300G. The latter was a minor update of the F with '61 styling features, the four-speed option replaced by a floor-mounted three-speed. The engine lineup was unchanged, and Chrysler switched back to 15-inch wheels on the 300G. Again at Daytona, 300s set the pace, Greg Ziegler doing 143 mph for the flying mile.

Chrysler sold 1212 300Fs and 1617 300Gs, better than the 300E but still a mere handful by the standard of Detroit measurement. Its image was tremendous, however, and caused Chrysler to produce a whole line of non-letter, mass-volume 300s to replace the Windsor in 1962. Alongside came the 300H, shorn of its fins like other Chryslers, but packing a still more powerful pair of 413 V-8s with 380 and 405 bhp.

In many ways the 300H was the nicest letter car of the 1960s. Retaining the clean front end of the 300G with its canted quad headlamps, its bodyline flowed smoothly back to flat fenders capped with slim taillamps. As before, it came with buckets-and-console, a speedometer calibrated to 150 mph, a tachometer, and Blue Streak racing tires as standard. Colors were again black, red, white, or "caramel." Power windows, seats, brakes, and steering were fitted. The Milestone Car Society has recently recognized the 300H's worth by adding it to their list of "the great postwar cars"; heretofore, MCS recognized letter Chryslers only through the 300G. Today, a show-quality "H" is worth as much, perhaps even more, than the "F" and "G," partly because of its rarity. Chrysler built only 435 "H" hardtops and 123 convertibles, the lowest figure to that date in letter-series history.

SPECIFICATIONS

Engines:	ohv V-8, 413 cid (4.18 × 3.75), 375-405 bhp
Transmissions:	3-speed manual, 4-speed manual, 3-speed automatic
Suspension front:	upper and lower control arms, longitudinal torsion bars
Suspension rear:	live axle, leaf springs
Brakes:	front/rear drums
Wheelbase (in.):	**1960-61** 126.0 **1962** 122.0
Weight (lbs):	4010-4315
Top speed (mph):	140+
0-60 mph (sec):	NA

Production: 1960 cpe 964 **cvt** 248 **1961 cpe** 1280 **cvt** 337 **1962 cpe** 435 **cvt** 123

Opposite page: The 300G of 1961 wore styling similar to the 300F, but the much-criticized "toilet seat" was dropped from the rear deck, and the front end carried Chrysler's new canted-headlight design. Like other 1962 Chryslers, the 300H (below) had its rear fins shaved off, but otherwise continued with the usual letter-series trim. Optional for the 300H was a 413 V-8 with 405 bhp, the most powerful engine that would ever be offered in the letter series.

1963-64
Chrysler 300J/K

The 1963 Chrysler 300J (the letter "I" was skipped to avoid confusion with the number "1") tallied the lowest production total of any letter-series car: a mere 400. It was also the first time since 1956 that a convertible was absent from the line. This was hardly surprising, however, as the previous-year's 300H had done only marginally better (558), leaving some question in the planning stage as to whether the 300J would be offered at all.

In 1963, Chrysler was riding high in the volume market, building a line of handsome, powerful cars and insisting that there would "never be a small Chrysler." That, Chrysler implied, would weaken its heritage, and spokesmen suggested surprise that erstwhile rivals such as Pontiac, Olds, and Mercury would insult their customers with the likes of a Tempest, F85, or Comet. Of course, all Chrysler dealers were dualled with Plymouth, which meant that you could buy a Valiant in the same showroom. Still, there is something to be said for avoiding the dilution of an image by altering its character, and it was a formula that seemed to be working for Chrysler.

In 1963, Chrysler retained its hold on eleventh place in sales, and corporate net earnings were at a record $162 million. The various divisions built more than a million cars, their best performance since 1957; stock split four ways and kept gaining. President Lynn Townsend credited the gains with the nearly 500 new dealerships added during the year, along with the advent of Chrysler's five-year/50,000 mile warranty, the first extended guarantee in the business.

Styling was completely revised this year under Virgil Exner, his last work before leaving the company to be replaced by former Lincoln designer Elwood Engel. Totally altered from before, Chryslers now touted their "crisp, clean, custom look," a hunky design with sharply creased fenders and inverted trapezoidal grilles.

No body styles were changed within the individual models, though the New Yorker now shared the smaller, 122-inch wheelbase that the letter series had adopted

SPECIFICATIONS

Engines:	ohv V-8 413 cid (4.19 × 3.75), 360/390 bhp
Transmissions:	3-speed automatic
Suspension front:	upper and lower control arms, longitudinal torsion bars
Suspension rear:	live axle, leaf springs
Brakes:	front/rear drums
Wheelbase (in.):	122.0
Weight (lbs):	3965-4000
Top speed (mph):	NA
0-60 mph (sec):	NA
Production:	**1963 cpe** 400 **1964 cpe** 3022 **cvt** 625

Opposite page, top: Only 400 of the 1963 300Js were built, and for the first time since 1956, no convertible version was offered. Production rebounded for 1964, though the 300K (below and opposite page, bottom) changed little externally save for rectangular taillights in place of the previous round units. Also in 1964, a convertible returned to the letter-series lineup.

the year before—so size was tending downward after all! The 300J was equipped with the New Yorker 413-cid engine, tuned to produce 360 bhp (20 more than the New Yorker), with 390 bhp optional.

Unfortunately, the 300J looked all too much like a standard Chrysler. This impression was heightened by advertising that dwelled on its comfort, rather than its performance. Even the distinguished red, white, and blue "300" emblem was replaced by a black dot on which the model name and letter "J" were set in thin, unreadable lines. As might have been expected, these changes didn't set well with the small but enthusiastic crowd that made up the traditional letter-series market, but nobody in Highland Park was worrying about them. Policy, not sales, governed the output of 400 "Js," just enough to keep the line going. Things got better in a hurry the following year.

For 1964, the Chrysler facelift amounted to hardly more than a tinsel shift: model lineups, wheelbases, and engine combinations remained the same. Grilles, medallions, wheel covers, and side moldings were altered, and rear windows were bigger. Taillamps were hexagonal and rear panels slightly modified. The letter series, now 300K, continued to use a black mesh grille with bold cross bars, and now featured loud, paint-filled side stripes with textured aluminum inserts.

But Chrysler as a whole did commendably well. The styling was something people took to, there was plenty of power, gas was cheap, and the public had money in its pocket. Chrysler Division produced over 150,000 cars, more than in any previous year for a decade. "We actually feel that we can set a record next year, surpassing Cadillac," said Division general manager P. N. Buckminster. He was right, too: 1965 would see Chrysler in tenth place, 30,000 units ahead of Cadillac.

In this fabulous year, even the declining letter series set a record—3647 cars, including 625 of the reinstated convertible. But the "K" came with the mild, 360-bhp version of the New Yorker engine, which was also available in the non-letter 300 series. The 390-bhp mill was still an exclusive letter-series option, but the final watering down of the flagship line was obvious. For one more year it continued, and the 1965 300L sold well enough; but the 390-bhp engine was gone, and the car looked exactly like every other Chrysler in the showroom. For today's collectors, the letter series stops at "K."

1965 Chrysler 300L

Automakers have come to rely on letters as much as names to denote their various models. Among the most common is "L," which has meant everything from "luxury" to "long-wheelbase" to "low-line." But in 1965, "L" after "300" meant but one thing: the 11th iteration of Chrysler's high-performance limited edition. Sadly, the 300L would be the last of the fabled "letter series" and the least special of the lot.

The reason was as close as the showroom. Since 1962, Chrysler had offered a "non-letter" 300 convertible, hardtop coupe, and hardtop sedan that delivered most of the letter-series' style and performance for hundreds of dollars less. Though just a ploy to bolster sales in the middle of the lineup, it worked beautifully. In its first season the standard 300 line outsold the previous Saratoga series by almost 6000 units; by 1964, sales had gone from 23,000 to over 31,000, versus a relative handful of letter-series cars. With little reason for buyers to prefer a letter-car over a non-letter, it was only a matter of time before Chrysler threw in the monogrammed towel.

Nineteen sixty-five would have been a convenient year to do so, for Chryslers changed stem-to-stern. Most obvious was a new corporate C-body (shared with senior Dodges and Plymouth's reborn full-size Furys) with squarish Elwood Engel styling in the manner of his Lincolnesque '64 Imperial. Wheelbase stretched two inches to 124 inches, and overall length grew three inches—mostly in the rear deck—to a rangy 218.2. Curb weights increased by an average of 200 pounds over the "Crisp, Clean Custom Look" 1963-64s—not surprising given the more expansive new package.

The inclusion of a new letter-series convertible and hardtop coupe *was* surprising, especially since you had to look at least twice to tell they weren't standard 300s. Visual distinctions came down to the customary round emblems on nose and tail, the merciful omission of the non-letter models' fake lower-body vents, and the usual four-place letter-series interior with full-length center console and twin rear bucket seats instead of a bench.

Of course, the L-models carried the most standard power, per letter-series tradition. For 1965 this again came from a four-barrel, 413-cubic-inch V-8 with the same 360 horsepower as in the 1963 J and '64 K. But there was no more twin-four-barrel 390-bhp option, and the 300L engine was optional for non-letter '65s (and even New Yorkers). TorqueFlite automatic was again on hand too, albeit newly controlled by a column lever instead of pushbuttons. Four-on-the-floor manual returned from '64 as a no-cost alternative, but few if any 300Ls were so equipped.

Like other '65 Chryslers, the 300Ls retained unibody construction, a Highland Park hallmark since 1960. This year, however, the front sub-frame was bolted to the main structure instead of welded on, in order to provide better isolation of noise, vibration, and harshness. Also retained was Chrysler's vaunted torsion-bar front suspension—and the superior big-car handling that went with it—plus a well-controlled leaf-sprung rear axle and big all-drum power brakes. The new styling lowered beltlines, raised rooflines, and increased glass area to make interiors feel even more spacious than they already were. Dashboards were restyled with a refreshingly simple design that boasted a pull-out central drawer containing—did Honda note this?—a handy coin holder.

Predictably, the 300L was not the performer its predecessors were. *Motor Trend*, for example, reported 8.8 seconds 0-60 mph and 17.3 seconds at 82 mph in the standing quarter-mile. That compares with *Car and Driver*'s 7.5 and 15.4 at 94 mph for a 390-bhp '63 J. But the L was quick enough, eminently roadable, and arguably the smoothest-riding letter-series yet. Then again, standard 300s with comparable equipment would do as well for $600-$700 less—which makes one suspect that the letter-series was a last-minute addition to the '65 line, given one more chance based on the sharp unexpected rise in 300K sales.

The Ls sold almost as well. In fact, they proved the second most popular letter-series models after the 300K, production totaling 2845, versus 3645 for the K. But non-letter volume was nearly 10 times that, and sporty big cars were becoming peripheral to a performance market increasingly dominated by mid-size muscle.

Thus did the once-great letter-series pass into history after 1965, not with a bang, but with a whimper—a real pity. Considering its glorious past, "The Beautiful Brute" deserved a better send-off.

While the 300L might not rate as highly as its predecessors, it was nonetheless distinctive—though one had to look hard to tell. Only minor trim alterations differentiated it from the standard 300 model, and the L's 360-bhp 413-cid V-8 was optional on both the 300 and New Yorker.

SPECIFICATIONS

Engines:	ohv V-8, 413 cid (4.19 × 3.75), 360 bhp
Transmission:	3-speed TorqueFlite automatic
Suspension front:	upper and lower A-arms, longitudinal torsion bars, anti-roll bar
Suspension rear:	live axle on semi-elliptic leaf springs
Brakes:	front/rear drums
Wheelbase (in.):	124.0
Weight (lbs):	4170-4245
Top speed (mph):	110+
0-60 mph (sec):	8.8-9.0
Production:	htp cpe 2,405 cvt 440

1967-68
Chrysler 300

Like Packard in the '30s, Chrysler Division in the '60s followed a sales strategy based on price, price, and price. Indeed, it's not hard to imagine this fictional conversation taking place in early 1960 between division chief Clare Briggs and company chairman L.L. "Tex" Colbert:

"Jeez, Clare, our sales are lousy," grouses Colbert. "That little Valiant and the new Dodge Dart are doing okay, but our medium-price business stinks! DeSoto's a dead duck, and *what* do we do about Chrysler?"

"We could take some stuff off the Windsor to get it down below $3000," Briggs says. "And we could change the name to Newport, like our old hardtops. I can see the advertising now: 'A full-size Chrysler for just a few dollars a month more than a small car.' They'll eat it up!"

"Good thinking," says Tex, smiling. "But what about your Saratoga? That's pretty dull."

"Well," Briggs replies, "Virg Exner's gonna slice the fins off the '62s. Why not make the Saratoga look like the 300? Heck, we'll even *call* it 300, but without the letter. And it'll be priced lower, too."

"Sensational."

And it was. Helped by an economy improved with increasing military production for an escalating civil war in Southeast Asia, Chrysler zoomed from 77,000 cars for model-year 1960 to a record 206,000-plus for '65. More impressive still, calendar 1965 sales were a resounding 63 percent higher than '64. But most everyone else had also improved, so the division remained fairly low on the industry totem pole, moving from 12th to 10th place among 15 major makes.

Still, the division's strategy was right on. The low-price Newport sold like no Chrysler before, accounting for the bulk of make volume from its 1961 debut until well into the '70s. Though less popular, the non-letter 300 convertible, hardtop coupe, and hardtop sedan made far more money than any letter-series, contributing a goodly share of Chrysler's vastly higher profits—and to the letter-series' demise after 1965's 300L.

Though Chrysler remained 10th for '66, it built over 64,000 more cars. Production eased throughout Detroit in a mild 1967 recession, but not severely in Chrysler's case, ending just short of 219,000 for another 10th-place finish.

Those '67s were structurally new, but retained the wheelbases and general architecture of the hugely popular 1965-66 models, the first Chryslers created by Elwood Engel, Exner's replacement as chief designer. If not better-looking, the '67s were at least different, with more heavily sculptured lines, simpler bumpers, busier grilles and, for hardtop coupes, a semi-fastback roofline with big, vision-blocking triangular C-pillars. The 300s arguably looked best, their hood and traditional "cross-hair" grille prominently bulged (instead of flat-faced), complemented by pointy rear fenders good for 3.5 inches of extra length (223.5 overall) versus other models' square-cut flanks.

Chrysler had introduced a big-bore 440-cubic-inch wedgehead V-8 on '66 New Yorkers and Imperials. For '67, it became the standard 300 engine, with 350 base horsepower or 375 optional. The latter was achieved via wilder camshaft, larger four-barrel carb, and low-restriction exhaust with dual outlets. Chrysler aptly called it the TNT. Even better, 300s could be ordered with a TNT package comprising that engine plus H-D rear axle and either TorqueFlite automatic or a new four-speed manual—the first shift-it-yourself 300 since the 1960 F. Power front-disc brakes were also available, so a '67 300 could be a surprisingly competent road machine—though a letter-series it wasn't.

It also wasn't as popular as the '66, model-year production plummeting by more than half. The reason was the advent of a Newport Custom line priced about $200 upstream of the standard Newports but over $500 below the 300s. Chrysler was obviously trading on Newport's popularity, and the Custom was a hit, with over 50,000 sales to less than 22,000 for the 300.

Chrysler recovered to near 265,000 units for '68. An adept facelift gave all models a more massive look, and 300s acquired hidden headlamps to stand apart from Newport/Customs and New Yorkers. As before, each series had specific front- and rear-end styling, but the sheetmetal revisions made all '68s slightly trimmer at 219 inches long overall. There were no big changes in specifications or prices, but sales results changed markedly. The 300 gained nearly 13,000, while Newport Custom lost about the same amount.

But this was just an aberration. Demand for sporty big cars, like the non-letter 300s, had peaked years before. Chrysler gamely hung onto them longer than most, but finally gave up after 1970.

Though the letter-series was extinct, the standard 300 that carried on was no slouch in either style or performance. Exterior styling of the 300s differed notably from lesser Chryslers, with distinctive grilles and different rear-end treatments. The '68 version (opposite page) carried concealed headlights and a unique taillight/backup light combination, while interiors featured unique trim. Standard power was a 350-bhp 440-cid V-8, but a 375-bhp "TNT" version was optional.

SPECIFICATIONS

Engines:	ohv V-8, 440 cid (4.32 × 3.75), 350/375 bhp
Transmission:	3-speed TorqueFlite automatic
Suspension front:	upper and lower A-arms, longitudinal torsion bars
Suspension rear:	live axle, semi-elliptic leaf springs
Brakes:	front discs/rear drums
Wheelbase (in.):	124.0
Weight (lbs):	3985-4135
Top speed (mph):	120+
0-60 mph (sec):	8.0

Production: 1967 htp cpe 11,556 **cvt** 1,594 **htp sdn** 8,744 **1968 htp cpe** 16,953 **cvt** 2,161 **htp sdn** 15,507

1969
Chrysler Three Hundred

Big news for Chrysler in 1969 was the new "fuselage styled" models, which the Division proudly described in advertising as "Your Next Car." Years before, Virgil Exner had pioneered the idea of combining the bumper and the grille on his XNR show car, in which the bumper surrounded the radiator opening and lights. But unlike the XNR, the bodylines on the new Chryslers were free of creases, wrinkles, tailfins, and asymmetrical humps, making them appear very smooth and sleek. It looked as though 1969 would be a very good year.

At the corporate level, now-chairman Lynn Townsend was laboring to maintain the profit picture. On the production line, quality control became an end in itself for the first time in Chrysler history, and judging by road tests of mid-'60s models, it was truly needed. Production had been setting records (1968 was an all-time high at 263,266), but high volume was often achieved by compromising build quality.

The Chrysler 300 (non-letter) line of coupes, sedans, and convertibles had been introduced in 1962 to replace the Windsor, and capitalize on the sporting image of the "letter series" 300s. In market position, the 300 largely filled the gap left by the DeSoto, which breathed its last in 1961: an upmarket car just short of the New Yorker, square in the middle of the Chrysler range. Since 1965 it had shared the New Yorker's long, 124-inch wheelbase, but it was carefully positioned about $300-$400 short of the New Yorker's price. For this, the buyer got a big engine (the reliable 440 from 1967), luxurious trim, and clean styling that traced its influence to the letter series. The 300 also featured the most expensive convertible in the volume line, since there had not been a New Yorker convertible since 1961.

Model developments in the late '60s reflected what Chrysler saw as the temper of the times. New Yorker wagons were quietly dropped for 1966, after selling scarcely 3000 units the year before; Newport wagons commanded the utility sector, though by 1968 all wagons were confined to a separate Town & Country series with its own wheelbase. The four-door pillared sedan had been in and out of the line during the '60s; for 1969 it was out. That year's Three Hundred, therefore, was offered in only three body styles: the hardtop coupe, hardtop sedan, and convertible coupe. About 32,000 were built, including some 2000 convertibles and an even number of two- and four-door hardtops.

And make no mistake, the name was now *spelled out*. This is a common practice when a manufacturer wants to impart more to a product than the product may really have. The Three Hundred was certainly no letter-series Chrysler, and it was not found on race tracks, but it was a solid, sporty big car that offered good value for the money. Nor was its ancestry forgotten by the promoters. "It can hide its headlights, but not its heritage," went the refrain. "Its 440 V-8 and three-speed automatic transmission supply instant recollection of victories past. The combination of welded fuselage and adjustable torsion-bar suspension, a subtle reminder of rally championships . . . a solid-yet-soaring driving impression."

Up front, that heritage was certainly unmistakable. Headlights were hidden (the only '69 Chrysler with this feature) and the grille was in traditional black, a round "300" emblem supported by the famous cross bars. Invoking other familiar themes, the Three Hundred came standard with individual "pleated-and-pillowed bucket seats" divided by a center cushion and armrest. A center console could be ordered as an option. Instrumentation was comprehensive, but lacked a tachometer. Alongside the standard 350 bhp 440 was the "TNT" 440 with four-barrel carburetor, high-performance camshaft, dual exhausts, and twin-snorkel air cleaner. This 375 bhp engine really *had* to be ordered by the serious 300 nostalgia buff. Useful too were power front-disc brakes and heavy-duty suspension. With all these features, the Three Hundred was as roadable and rapid a big car as the American auto industry produced in 1969. At a time when the federal government and insurance companies were fast putting the dampers on high performance, that in itself was a fair achievement.

Bearing the "fuselage styling" shared by all full-size Chryslers for 1969, the Three Hundred remained the "sporting" entry of the fleet. Though lacking the flair of past letter-series cars, it nonetheless featured bucket seats, hidden headlights, and discreet "300" badges to differentiate it from other '69 Chryslers.

SPECIFICATIONS

Engines:	ohv V-8, 440 cid (4.32 × 3.75), 350/375 bhp
Transmission:	3-speed automatic
Suspension front:	upper and lower control arms, longitudinal torsion bars
Suspension rear:	live axle, leaf springs
Brakes:	front disc/rear drum
Wheelbase (in.):	124.0
Weight (lbs):	3965-4095
Top speed (mph):	120+
0-60 mph (sec):	8.0
Production:	cpe 16,075 sdn 14,464 cvt 1933

107

1960-61
DeSoto

DeSoto died in late 1960 after 33 years as Chrysler Corporation's "in-between" medium-price make. It followed by some 13 months the demise of Ford Motor Company's Edsel, another victim of a medium-price market decimated by the 1958 recession. But DeSoto was in trouble long before that. In fact, one writer termed it "excess baggage" almost from the start.

Introduced for 1929, DeSoto was conceived to bridge the price gap between Plymouth and Dodge in the General Motors-like "stairstep" model hierarchy Chrysler was then evolving. By the late '30s it had become a junior Chrysler, priced slightly above Dodge. Sales were good, if not spectacular, into the postwar period. But by the late Fifties, DeSoto was being squeezed out of its traditional price territory.

This reflected a change in Chrysler marketing after 1954. Previously, the firm maintained three dealer networks: Chrysler-Plymouth, DeSoto-Plymouth, and Dodge-Plymouth. Pairing the low-price make with each medium-price brand had saved Chrysler during the Airflow debacle of the '30s. But when Imperial became a separate make for '55, Chrysler Division started moving downmarket, interfering with the upper end of the DeSoto line. Meanwhile, Dodge headed upmarket with larger, lusher cars that hurt sales of the cheaper DeSotos. Come the '58 recession, and the firm consolidated from five divisions to just Dodge and Chrysler-DeSoto-Plymouth (the latter absorbing an interim Imperial Division). With that and sharply lower sales, rumors of DeSoto's demise began spreading by 1959, which only accelerated the slide.

The statistics were indeed ominous. Though DeSoto's 1959 calendar-year production rose slightly over '58, model-year volume dropped nearly 4000 units, and output in both years was less than half its '57 tally. Rivals Oldsmobile, Buick, and Mercury were hurting just as much, but they'd been generating higher volume and could stand to lose more sales. Moreover, they were readying compacts that promised to offset their reduced big-car sales. While forward planning called for smaller '62 DeSotos, there was no compact—other than the 1960 Valiant, which was logically assigned to bread-and-butter Plymouth.

At first, Chrysler denied DeSoto would be dropped, staging a 30th anniversary party in 1959 when the two-millionth DeSoto was built. The firm also noted that $25 million had been earmarked for future DeSotos, that tooling had been ordered

DeSoto styling for 1960 (below and opposite page, top) obviously mimicked Chrysler's, but powertrain offerings didn't include Chrysler's big 413-cid V-8—or even the most potent 383. The last-gasp '61 DeSoto (opposite page, middle and bottom) featured styling that differed a bit more from its Chrysler counterpart, but the changes were not necessarily for the better.

SPECIFICATIONS

Engines:	all ohv V-8; **1960:** 361 cid (4.13 × 3.38), 295 bhp; 383 cid (4.25 × 3.38), 305 bhp; **1961:** 361 cid (4.13 × 3.38), 265 bhp
Transmissions:	2-speed PowerFlite automatic, 3-speed TorqueFlite automatic
Suspension front:	upper and lower A-arms, longitudinal torsion bars, anti-roll bar
Suspension rear:	live axle on semi-elliptic leaf springs
Brakes:	front/rear drums
Wheelbase (in.):	122.0
Weight (lbs):	3760-3945
Top speed (mph):	NA
0-60 mph (sec):	NA

Production: 1960 Fireflite htp cpe 3,494 **4d sdn** 9,032 **htp sdn** 1,958 **Adventurer htp cpe** 3,092 **4d sdn** 5,746 **htp sdn** 2,759 **1961 htp cpe** 911 **htp sdn** 2,123

for '61, that work toward 1962-63 was underway—and that DeSoto had regularly made a profit.

But the public literally didn't buy any of this. DeSoto sales in the first two months of 1960 were just 4746 units, a mere 0.51 percent of the industry and less than its comparable '59 performance. By Christmas 1960, the planned '62 DeSoto was terminated along with production of the '61 models, announced that October. DeSoto-Plymouth dealers then became Chrysler-Plymouth stores—to the chagrin of existing C-P dealers nearby.

DeSoto's deep distress was evident for 1960, when its two lower-priced series of 1957-59 disappeared, leaving Fireflite and Adventurer four-door sedans, hardtop sedans, and hardtop coupes. Adventurer, no longer a high-performance limited edition, was still priced a few hundred dollars above '59 Fireflites. But Fireflite prices were cut dramatically, dropping down to the $3000 region formerly occupied by Firedome and the Dodge-based Firesweep.

All models shared the 122-inch Dodge/Chrysler wheelbase and the corporation's much-ballyhooed new 1960 unibody construction. Adventurers carried the low-line Chrysler Windsor's 383-cubic-inch V-8 with 305 horsepower, while Fireflites borrowed a 295-bhp 361 from midrange Dodges. Two-speed PowerFlite automatic was standard for Adventurers and optional on Fireflites, and both could be ordered with Chrysler's superb three-speed Torqueflite, also with pushbutton control. Styling was identical to the 1960 Chrysler's save for a busier grille and taillights. Though the package looked serious, performance was not: An Adventurer could keep pace with a Windsor, but not with the more potent 383 Chrysler Saratoga or Dodge Phoenix.

Like Edsel, DeSoto fielded a token last-gasp line, but only a nameless two- and four-door hardtop. Publicists extolled styling "individuality," but the '61s were frankly quite ugly. They shared new diagonal quad headlights with the Chrysler line, but were differentiated by a clumsy rear-end make over and an odd double grille.

After building barely 3000 of these, Chrysler quietly terminated DeSoto, filling outstanding orders mostly with '61 Windsors. It was a sad finale—and actually premature. Less than a year later, an upscale "full-size" Custom 880 had to be hastily added to the Dodge line in order to offset sales losses suffered by that division's shrunken, oddly styled '62 standards. The 880 was basically a '62 Chrysler bodyshell wearing a '61 Dodge front end, and though it looked somewhat contrived, this DeSoto-level entry saved the day for the Dodge Boys. In retrospect, DeSoto died as much from a "loser" image as a difficult medium-price market.

1960-61
Dodge Dart

Though better known today as a compact, the first Dodge Dart was a full-size car. It was also a huge sales success.

The sharp contraction of the medium-price market after 1957 forced Chrysler to pare down from five divisions to just Dodge and Chrysler-DeSoto-Plymouth. This left many Dodge franchises without a companion make for the first time, and they were jealous because the timely new 1960 compact Valiant would be sold only by that "other" division.

But management placated Dodge dealers by granting a greatly expanded 1960 lineup divided between two "senior" series, replacing Royal and Custom Royal, and lower-priced "junior" models to take over for Coronet as full-size Plymouth competitors. This considerably fattened the Dodge catalog, which went from 19 models to no fewer than 35.

Christened Dart, after a finny '57 Chrysler show car, the new junior line was almost a separate make, with three series, a full range of body styles, and 23 individual models. Seneca was the price leader, followed by Pioneer (which offered a hardtop coupe) and the line-leading Phoenix (which duplicated that and added a convertible too). Non-wagons spanned the 118-inch wheelbase Plymouth had used since '57. Wagons rode the 122-inch platform adopted for that year's Dodge and DeSoto (plus Plymouth wagons and the '59 Chrysler Windsor). The latter also served Dodge's 1960 seniors (see entry).

Also common to 1960 Plymouths, Dodges, DeSotos, and Chrysler Windsors were the corporation's famed torsion-bar front suspension and a familiar family of wedgehead V-8s. But chassis were now fully welded to inner body structure—the tighter, more solid *monocoque* construction that Chrysler called unibody. Per Detroit custom, different exterior sheetmetal set the various makes apart. Darts probably fared best among Plymouths and Dodges, with modest fins and a busy but not unattractive face. If not the prettiest cars of 1960, they were certainly better looking than the more exaggerated senior Dodges and the equally overdone Plymouths.

Dart powerteams were basically those of Plymouth's 1960 "standards," plus a few more. All models save the V-8-only Phoenix ragtop came with the larger, 225-cubic-inch version of the Valiant's new 170-cid Slant Six, a modern overhead-valve design with efficient wedge-shape combustion chambers and 145 horsepower. The base Seneca/Pioneer V-8 was a 230-bhp version of the familiar Dodge/Plymouth 318. Phoenix offered a 255-bhp option, standard on the convertible. Next came a 295-bhp 361 for Pioneer and a 383 with 325/330-bhp for Phoenix, all with four-barrel carb, 10:1 compression, and Chrysler's tuned "Ram Induction" intake manifolding.

Transmissions were also familiar: standard three-speed column-shift manual, the same with extra-cost overdrive, and the proven two-speed PowerFlite and three-speed TorqueFlite automatics, also optional. The automatics' famous pushbutton controls were newly matched by a touch-activated climate system in a rather ornate two-tier Dodge dash. Futuristic features were typical of Chrysler in this period, and the Dart had its share. Options included those two '59 Chrysler novelties, swivel front seats and automatic day/night rearview mirror. And Phoenixes sported the corporation's new 1960 oval-square steering wheel, which gave more under-rim thigh clearance but looked quite odd—aggravated by Dodge's stylized hub that one magazine likened to "a man on a torture rack."

Properly equipped, a 1960 Dart could be a hot performer in the great D-500 mold. That, along with attractive prices in the $2300-$3000 range, made Dart amazingly popular, and Dodge happily retailed over 323,000—a whopping 87 percent of 1960 production and more than double its '59 tally. Dodge promptly went from eighth to sixth place in the industry—at the expense of Plymouth, which lost about 10,000 sales despite the Valiant.

Dodge lost far more than that for '61, plunging from nearly 368,000 to just over 269,000 and a ninth-place finish. It should have done better. Dart was back with the same broad lineup, virtually unchanged prices, and even a sizzling new ram-induction 413 V-8 option with 350/375 horses. Furthermore, Dodge gained its own compact, a Valiant clone called Lancer. But Dart styling was now an odd combination of senior-Dodge front end and '61 Plymouth "plucked chicken" rear fenders with canted blade fins stuck on—backwards. Sales plummeted to about 183,500, though this was nothing like the disaster that awaited the '62s—shrunken to near compact size and even uglier.

Which only proves how much styling sold cars in the '60s, as indeed it does today. But though the full-size Dart vanished after '61, the name didn't, destined for new success from 1963 as a compact with far better looks.

Opposite page, top: *Top-of-the-line Dart Phoenix for 1960 featured nice lines and bountiful chrome trim, making it very popular that year. Styling of its 1961 counterpart (above and opposite page, bottom) wasn't as well accepted, and sales took a nose dive, but the newly available 413-cid V-8 could make it a real screamer.*

SPECIFICATIONS

Engines:	ohv I-6, 225 cid (3.40 × 4.13), 145 bhp; ohv V-8, 318 cid (3.91 × 3.31), 230/255 bhp (**1960**), 260 bhp (**1961**); 361 cid (4.12 × 3.38), 295 bhp (**1960**), 305 bhp (**1961**); 383 cid (4.25 × 3.38), 325/330 bhp; ohv V-8, 413 cid (4.19 × 3.75), 350/375 (**1961 only**)
Transmissions:	3-speed manual; 2-speed PowerFlite automatic and optional 3-speed TorqueFlite automatic
Suspension front:	upper and lower A-arms, longitudinal torsion bars, anti-roll bar
Suspension rear:	live axle on semi-elliptic leaf springs
Brakes:	front/rear drums
Wheelbase (in.):	122.0 wagons, 118.0 others
Weight (lbs):	3290-4065
Top speed (mph):	NA
0-60 mph (sec):	NA

Production: 1960 Seneca 6 93,167 **Seneca V-8** 45,737 **Pioneer 6** 36,434 **Pioneer V-8** 74,655 **Phoenix 6** 6,567 **Phoenix V-8** 66,608 **1961 Seneca 6** 60,527 **Seneca V-8** 27,174 **Pioneer 6** 18,214 **Pioneer V-8** 39,054 **Phoenix 6** 4,273 **Phoenix V-8** 34,319

1960-61 Dodge
Polara/Matador

As the "Soaring '60s" dawned, Chrysler Corporation seemed to be its own worst enemy. Design chief Virgil Exner, so masterful with the corporation's '57 styling, had since conjured some truly bizarre things that made one wonder about the executives who approved them. Highland Park had definitely lost the tight, solid workmanship it had evidenced before '57. Chrysler still boasted great engines and the world's best automatic transmission, but these were no help in the 1958 recession that shriveled the medium-price market like a prune, sent buyers dashing from performance to economy, and boosted demand for funny foreign cars like a Redstone rocket. Chrysler did move with the market's swing to compacts, right along with GM and Ford, but its 1960 Valiant didn't sell nearly well enough to reverse a worsening sales situation.

Retrenchment seemed wise, so Chrysler consolidated from five divisions to two, then axed stalwart but slow-selling DeSoto at the end of 1960—the third major American make to disappear in as many years. As related earlier in this book, that culminated a long "squeezing out" process in which Dodge moved steadily upward into DeSoto's price territory even as Chrysler moved downward. A greatly expanded 1960 Dodge line and the low-price '61 Chrysler Newport dealt the final deadly blows.

Dodge actually stomped on DeSoto's grave for model-year 1960, moving from eighth to sixth in industry production with more than double its 1959 volume. The vast majority of this—fully 88 percent—was owed to the new low-price Dart, a three-series line of Plymouth-based cars replacing Coronet. Up in the middle ranks, where Royal and Custom Royal had been, were two senior Dodges, the 1960 Matador and Polara. These shared a slightly larger, 122-inch-wheelbase platform with 1960 DeSotos and Chryslers, all newly engineered with Highland Park's highly touted unibody construction.

Dodge Polara for 1960 (both pages) shared styling cues with the smaller and cheaper Dart, but the front end was busier and the rear end featured an unusual—and not particularly attractive— tailfin treatment. As a result, sales of the full-size Polara and similar Matador (Polara's less-dressy mate) were dismal, totaling less than 15 percent of Dodge's 1960 volume.

D O D G E

Those keeping score will note that Matador/Polara accounted for only 12 percent of 1960 Dodge sales. That's hardly surprising considering their close similarity to the Darts (and Plymouths), plus higher prices in the $3000-$3600 range (vs. Dart's $2300-$3000). Styling was busy, bordering on gimmicky, just like '59; there was even a new rendition of the previous year's four-pod taillights, with "rocket tubes" jutting firmly out from below abbreviated fins (though a tad higher than Dart's).

Inside was an equally jazzy dash holding a wide translucent speedometer and pushbuttons for climate functions as well as automatic transmission. Other wowie-zowie accoutrements included optional swiveling front seats and self-dimming mirror (both continued from '59).

Such "features" tend to obscure the fact that Matador and Polara were basically sound, roadworthy automobiles. Chrysler's "Torsion-Aire" suspension, a fixture since '57, still provided handling unmatched by any full-size car outside the corporate camp. Complementing it was the new unibody design, which made for a tighter, more solid structure than traditional body-on-frame, though it tended to transmit more road noise—and was very rust-prone. Engines comprised three hardy V-8s: a standard 295-horsepower 361 for Matador, and two 383s for Polara (optional on Matador) with 325 or 330 bhp. Three-speed manual transmission was standard, but most of these Dodges were likely sold with optional two-speed PowerFlite or superb three-speed TorqueFlite automatic. Polara offered a novelty in its pillarless wagon, which also came with some genuinely useful features including two we take for granted now: hazard warning flashers and power door locks.

Still, there was no getting around the funky looks, still-suspect workmanship, or the feeling that Chrysler might not be around too long. With their relatively poor 1960 sales, senior Dodges predictably withered to just six Polara models for '61 (leaving AMC to resurrect the Matador name a decade later). Styling changes were good and bad. A new front end with simple concave grille and integral headlamps was nice. But the back was something else, with "reverse fins" peaking above the rear wheels, then tapering down around pod-like taillamps to form an ellipse with a lower-body creaseline. But '61 Darts had all this, too, so Polara's main visual distinctions were just badges and a big starlike grille emblem. Prices stayed basically pat, and you could still get a high-performance D-500 engine—the 325/330-bhp 383 option with tuned "Ram-Induction" manifolding.

Again, though, Dodge didn't have enough of the right stuff, and '61 Polara production ended at a paltry 14,000. Mercury's cheaper, more rational full-size '61s sold somewhat better, while Buick, Olds, and Pontiac had nifty new styling that helped them to still-higher volume.

Not that it mattered, for Dodge was about to take a radically different tack over the next three years. That's a story in itself—or rather two stories, told in the following pages.

SPECIFICATIONS

Engines:	all ohv V-8; 361 cid (4.12 × 3.38), 295 bhp (**1960**), 265/305 bhp (**1961**); 383 cid (4.25 × 3.38), 325/330 bhp
Transmissions:	3-speed manual; 2-speed PowerFlite automatic, 3-speed TorqueFlite automatic
Suspension front:	upper and lower A-arms, longitudinal torsion bars, anti-roll bar
Suspension rear:	live axle on semi-elliptic leaf springs
Brakes:	front/rear drums
Wheelbase (in.):	122.0
Weight (lbs):	3705-4220
Top speed (mph):	NA
0-60 mph (sec):	NA

Production: 1960 Matador 27,908 **Polara** 16,728 **1961 Polara** 14,032

Matador was dropped for 1961, and the Polara (below and opposite page, top) once again wore styling similar to the smaller, cheaper, and more popular Dart, but both models lost sales this year. Top Polara engine offering was a 383 with 325 bhp (opposite page, bottom left) or 330 with ram induction. An unusual option was the Highway Hi Fi 16 ⅔-rpm record player (opposite page, bottom right).

1962-64
Dodge "Standard"

In late 1958, Chrysler styling chief Virgil Exner began groping toward the next "Forward Look": a new design theme to leapfrog the competition and bring profits rolling in like his '57s had done. This "S-series" program envisioned a totally new 1962 corporate fleet styled like the forthcoming compact Valiant and wild "XNR" show car, both 1960 developments. That meant long hoods, bladelike front fenders, sharply slanted windshields, quirky beltline and window shapes, sculptured "chicken wing" rear flanks, and short, sloped, finless tails. Exner also stirred in some of his beloved "Classic" elements: big square grilles, freestanding head/taillamps, and trunklids bulged to simulate spare tires (the infamous "toilet seat").

Final styling models were ready by February 1960, and newly elected Chrysler president Bill Newberg blessed them for '62. But he was soon forced to resign in a scandal, and "Tex" Colbert returned to power. Tex looked at the S-series and had second thoughts. By year's end he'd not only ditched DeSoto, but the S-series Chrysler and Imperial as well (in favor of "definned" '61s). But he couldn't stop the new Plymouth and Dodge.

The result was a sales disaster. Here were "standards" that not only looked like compacts but were almost as small: chopped six inches in wheelbase, up to seven inches in overall length, they lost hundreds of pounds of road-hugging weight. No matter that interior room was hardly affected, or that performance and mileage benefited from the reduced poundage. Buyers wanted full-size cars to *be* full-size—and nothing less. Of course, there *was* a market for the "intermediate car." Indeed, Ford's newly shrunken Fairlane sold quite well in '62.

Plymouth, though, fell to eighth in 1962 model-year production, its lowest rank ever. Dodge managed to remain ninth despite building 39,000 fewer cars than it had in '61, but would have fared worse had it not revived a true full-size model at midyear. Despite a short selling season, this 122-inch-wheelbase hybrid called Custom 880 accounted for over 17,000 sales.

Though compacts were quite popular in the early '60s, the public still wanted full-size cars to be full-size. As a result, sales of Dodge's shrunken 1962 "standards" dropped significantly from '61, though awkward styling certainly didn't help. Even the top-line Polara 500, available in coupe (this page), hardtop sedan, and convertible, sold a total of only 12,268 copies. Opposite page: For 1963, the standard-size Dodges gained three inches in wheelbase and more conservative styling.

D O D G E

Most '62 Dodge standards were called Darts, after the division's successful full-size 1960-61 junior line. These included base two- and four-door sedans and a four-door wagon, the same plus a hardtop coupe in midrange 330 trim, and a 440 four-door sedan, wagon, hardtop coupe and sedan, and convertible. Topping the list were bucket-seat Polara 500 convertible, hardtop coupe and (later in the year) hardtop sedan. Darts could be ordered with a 225-cubic-inch Slant Six, or 318 and 361 V-8s; Polaras came with the 361. All models offered big 413 wedgehead V-8s with up to 420 mighty horsepower, courtesy of Ram Induction manifolding. Funny they may have looked, but the lightest high-power Darts were soon taken very seriously on drag strips, where they trounced bigger, heavier rivals.

The '63s put on some 45 pounds while growing three inches in wheelbase to 119 inches, thus matching full-size Chevys and Fords. Exner, in one his last jobs at Chrysler (he left in '62), applied square, Thunderbird-style rooflines to hardtops and a slightly less bizarre "face" to all models. Dart transferred to Dodge's '63 compact line (replacing Lancer), so standards became 330, 440, Polara, and Polara 500 models without a sub-marque name. The 361 and 413 engines departed. Polara's standard V-8 was a 318; 500s came with a 305-horse 383. But the big news—literally—was a squadron of 426 wedgeheads for the quarter-mile crowd, with up to 425 bhp in twin-four-barrel, ultra-high-compression (13.5:1) "Ram Charger" tune. Dodge leapt to seventh in industry production as model-year volume soared some 194,000, though most of this came from the handsome new compact Dart.

With ex-Lincoln designer Elwood Engel firmly in charge of '64 styling, Dodge standards were fully reskinned, becoming cleaner and more conventional. Styling cues included a slightly lower cowl, the first of Dodge's distinctive "dumbbell" grilles, and a rakish new hardtop roofline with vee'd C-pillars and "bubbled" backlight. Models and engines stood basically pat. Chrysler as a whole now climbed out of its early-'60s financial hole, and Dodge claimed sixth in production with over half a million cars—almost twice its volume of just two model years earlier.

In all, these Dodges emerge as a classic case of sow's ears being made into profitable silk purses. And with yet another restyle, they would sell even better for '65 under the revived Coronet badge, which testifies to their inherent design qualities. Too bad they still get such a bad rap, but that's what poor timing and oddball looks will do.

Dodge's standard-size cars took on some new model names to go along with their new styling for 1963. The line started with a base 330, then moved up to 440 (above), Polara, and top-line Polara 500. Replacing the 413-cid V-8 was a "wedgehead" that produced up to 425 bhp in "Ram Charger" tune. In 1964, drag racers could also get a 426 Hemi engine in a lightweight 330 body (below), making for a very potent package. Opposite page: The '64s received some minor front and rear styling alterations, along with new thin, tapered C-pillars for hardtop coupes.

SPECIFICATIONS

Engines:	ohv I-6, 225 cid (3.40 × 4.13), 145 bhp; 318 cid (3.91 × 3.31), 230/260 bhp; ohv V-8, 361 cid (4.12 × 3.38), 305/310 bhp (**1962 only**); 383 cid (4.25 × 3.38), 305/320/325/330 bhp; 413 cid (4.19 × 3.75), 410/420 bhp (**1962 only**); 426 cid (4.25 × 3.75), 365/370/375/415/425 bhp
Transmissions:	3/4-speed manual; 2-speed PowerFlite and 3-speed TorqueFlite automatic
Suspension front:	upper and lower A-arms, longitudinal torsion bars
Suspension rear:	live axle on semi-elliptic leaf springs
Brakes:	front/rear drums
Wheelbase (in.):	116.0 (**1962**), 119.0 (**1963-64** exc wgns)
Weight (lbs):	2965-3640
Top speed (mph):	NA
0-60 mph (sec):	NA

Production: 1962 Dart Six 43,927 **Dart V-8** 17,981 **Dart 330 Six** 11,606 **Dart 330 V-8** 26,544 **Dart 440 Six** 3,942 **Dart 440 V-8** 42,360 **Polara 500** 12,268 **1963 330 Six** 51,761 **330 V-8** 33,602 **440 Six** 13,146 **440 V-8** 49,591 **Polara Six** 68,262 **Polara V-8** 40,323 **Polara 500 (V-8)** 7,256 **1964 300 Six** 57,957 **330 V-8** 46,438 **440 Six** 15,147 **440 V-8** 68,861 **Polara Six** 3,810 **Polara V-8** 66,988 **Polara 500 (V-8)** 17,787

1962-64 Dodge Custom 880

Downsized big Dodges seemed a good idea when Chrysler design chief Virgil Exner conceived them in the recession-wracked late '50s, but they were literally bad business when introduced to the improved market of 1962. Though medium-price cars still weren't selling like they used to, DeSoto's demise in late 1960 had left the Newport as Chrysler's sole entry in the still-important $3000-$3500 segment. Dodge dealers, suffering poor sales of their newly downsized '62 "standards," screamed for relief.

They got it at mid-model year with a revived big Dodge called Custom 880. This was either the recently canned '61 Dart/Polara with finless "plucked chicken" '62 Chrysler rear, or a '62 Newport with the peaked-fender '61 Dart/Polara front. Actually, either conception is correct. Both '62 Newport and Custom 880 used the 122-inch-wheelbase unibody platform found under all full-size Chryslers and Dodges since 1960.

Of course, that had also served the last DeSotos, which the Custom 880 essentially replaced. It was, after all, the same package offered at similar prices, but in more models with nicer looks.

Speaking of style, the old Dodge front mated remarkably well with the new Chrysler rear, but the combination was not the result of a hasty design decision. According to Virgil Exner, Jr., it had been proposed in an ornamentation drawing as a last-gasp effort for a 1962 DeSoto. Though shelved then, the idea was dusted off when Dodge's shrunken '62 standards met sales resistance, which is how the Custom 880 got to market so quickly.

What Chrysler obviously did was abandon a lackluster nameplate (DeSoto) for a more saleable one (Dodge) without really changing the product. And the ploy worked every bit as well as the hybrid styling. Though the '62 Newport saw over 83,000 sales, the Custom 880 generated a healthy 17,705 despite its six-month selling season—important added business at a time when Dodge desperately needed it.

Marketing aside, there was nothing new about the Custom. The numerals related to nomenclature in the '62 mid-size line, and if an 880 wasn't twice the car a Dart 440 was, it was pushed hard as a full-size machine of the type many buyers craved. "Big" was the operative word: "Big room, big ride, big power!!!!"

SPECIFICATIONS

Engines:	all ohv V-8; 361 cid (4.12 × 3.38), 265 bhp; 383 cid (4.25 × 3.38), 305 bhp (1963-64)
Transmission:	3-speed TorqueFlite automatic
Suspension front:	upper and lower A-arms, longitudinal torsion bars, anti-roll bar
Suspension rear:	live axle on semi-elliptic leaf springs
Brakes:	front/rear drums
Wheelbase (in.):	122.0
Weight (lbs):	3615-4185
Top speed (mph):	105-110+
0-60 mph (sec):	10.8-13.2

Production: 1962 Custom 880 17,505 1963 880 9,831 Custom 880 18,435 1964 880 10,526 Custom 880 21,234

The 880 was born in 1962 out of Dodge's need to restore a full-size car to its "downsized" model line. At first carrying a '61 Dodge front end grafted to a '62 Chrysler body, the 880 got cleaner, more integrated styling for '63 (above), with round taillights and a simple grille design. Opposite page: The next year brought wraparound horizontal taillights and concave (rather than convex) grille bars.

screamed one ad. Another blared, "Overall length almost 18 feet" (more precisely, 215 inches for wagons, 213.5 for other models).

That "big ride" naturally reflected Chrysler's proven "Torsion-Aire" suspension, which also still provided Detroit's best big-car handling. Power was courtesy of a corporate 361 V-8 trumpeted as "high performance" but also "surprisingly economical" (two-barrel carb). There were "no optional performance engines; no need for them," Dodge boasted, though this was probably to keep prices down.

Trim was limited to one level in four-door sedan, hardtop coupe and sedan, convertible, and hardtop wagon models (the last left over from 1960-61). Three-speed manual transmission was standard for all, but most were ordered with optional TorqueFlite automatic as well as power steering (which reduced turns lock-to-lock from a cumbersome 5.5 to 3.5). Big "Total Contact" drum brakes, seven-stage rustproofing, and newly extended 32,000-mile lube intervals were included at prices pegged within a few dollars of Newport's. Performance was naturally close to the Chrysler's as well, and respectable. Workmanship, on the other hand, remained far below Ford/GM levels, and Highland Park products still had a deserved reputation for early rustout.

Nevertheless, the Custom 880 earned its keep, so it returned for '63 with little-changed prices and a minor restyle incorporating round taillamps and a simple flat-face grille composed of fine vertical bars. More importantly, styling was no longer "me-too," as Chryslers were heavily reskinned with the "Clean, crisp, custom look." Models regrouped around three base-trim 880s and five Customs. But despite a full season, sales rose by less than 11,000—still far behind Newport's. The advent of cleaner, slightly longer '63 standard Dodges was the likely reason.

Deliveries improved to near 32,000 for 1964, when the old 1960 bodies received a final facelift marked by wraparound taillamps and an evolutionary concave grille. Model choices stayed put, prices rose a paltry $13, and options expanded to include four-speed manual transmission (rarely ordered) and Comfort-Tilt steering wheel. *Motor Trend* tested a Custom convertible, judging it "a top-rated package," happily reporting that "close inspection . . . didn't turn up any flaws caused by careless workmanship."

With 1965 came totally new full-size Dodges that included 880s, after which the name was retired. Today, the 1962-64s are forgotten by all but the most ardent Dodge devotees, and that's a shame. If not the greatest American cars of the '60s, they had a lot to like. Come to think of it, they still do.

1963-66 Dodge Dart GT

Virgil Exner did some goofy things in his last years as Chrysler styling chief, but the '63 Dodge Dart wasn't one of them. Clean, even Italianate in some ways, it elegantly refutes the notion that Exner's design talents were waning when this car was initiated circa 1960.

That year brought Chrysler's first compact, the Valiant, which was assigned to Plymouth. Dodge did without, but prospered anyway with low-price full-size Darts. The next year, though, Dodge got a Valiant-clone called Lancer. This matched GM's new 1961 Buick Special, Olds F-85, and Pontiac Tempest, but wasn't nearly as popular. Lancer also trailed Valiant in sales despite the 1962 addition of a sporty GT hardtop.

With rebodied compacts scheduled for '63, Dodge sought a more distinctive Lancer to better compete with the B-O-P trio and Mercury's Comet. The result was a larger, prettier compact bearing the familiar Dart name (substituted at the 11th hour). Wheelbase swelled five inches except on wagons, which kept the original 106-inch span, as did the '63 Valiants. Offerings included new convertibles in midrange 270 and bucket-seat GT trim, the latter again offering Dodge's sole compact hardtop. Rounding things out were 270 and base 170 two- and four-door sedans and four-door wagons. Save the last, which measured 190.2 inches overall, Darts stretched 7.1 inches longer than Lancers—much closer to competitors' sizes.

Pricing wasn't so close. Dart GT undercut comparable GM models by a hefty $400-$600, the Comet S-22 by $200-$350. Though Chrysler didn't yet have a V-8 for its compacts, the GT was satisfying except on freeway acceleration lanes. The standard 101-horsepower 170-cubic-inch Slant Six (inherited from Lancer/Valiant) delivered 0-60 in a leisurely 20 seconds or so. The extra-cost 145-bhp 225 engine reduced that to about 15, raised top speed to near 100 mph, and returned 16-17 mpg (the smaller six added 1-2 mpg at most). Transmissions were the expected three-speed manual or optional TorqueFlite automatic, the latter a real competitive advantage.

So too was Chrysler's torsion-bar front suspension, still earning plaudits after six years. *Motor Trend* felt "there's nothing . . . in the Dart's size and price class that can touch it for all-around roadability." As usual, the standard manual steering was manageable but painfully slow (5.3 turns lock-to-lock). The optional power setup was quicker (3.5) but generally judged over-boosted. Well, you can't have everything.

But Dodge suddenly had a lot more compact sales, the '63 Darts generating a spectacular 250 percent more than the '62 Lancers. The GTs accounted for roughly 20 percent, which they would hold through 1966.

Dart did even better for '64, volume sailing from 154,000 to over 193,000. Styling changes were confined to a mild facelift, but the big news for performance fans was the midyear availability of a V-8 option. This was a lively, free-revving 273-cid unit derived from Chrysler's new-generation 318 and boasting the latest in "thinwall" block castings à la Ford's contemporary 260/289. Though only 50 pounds heavier than the Slant Six, the 273 delivered 25 percent more horsepower—180 in all—plus a healthy 260 pounds/feet of torque. It was a natural for the GT, which now lived up to those initials with 0-60 times of 10-12 seconds and a top speed comfortably above the magic "ton." But though it cost only $131 extra, the V-8 went into barely a fourth of that year's near 50,000 GTs.

Styling became more aggressive for '65. So did performance, as an even hotter V-8 option arrived with 235 bhp courtesy of a four-barrel carb and wilder cam. Even better, it could be combined with a new heavy-duty suspension kit and four-on-the-floor manual gearbox. *Car and Driver* loved its test GT with all these goodies. The fortified V-8, said the editors, "is a robust, eager engine that makes all sorts of neat sounds while whisking the Dart around in fairly impressive fashion"—which timed out as 8.2 seconds 0-60, a strong showing even today. Dart sales were stronger than ever, too: over 209,000 in all.

Volume slipped to 176,000 for 1966, though this was due more to market conditions than any Dart deficiencies. The '63 design was restyled one last time, with a squarish front predominating. With the "right stuff," the GT remained, as *Motor Trend* put it, "one of those rare cars that add a certain pleasure to driving, and that's saying something for a machine designed as a compact family vehicle."

Indeed it was, though even hotter Darts were in the offing for 1967 and beyond. Today, the 1963-66 GTs are the very model of inexpensive enthusiast wheels (even the low-volume ragtops don't cost much)—more proof that good things really do come in small(er) packages.

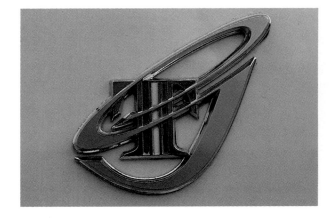

The Dart moniker was applied to Dodge's compact line for 1963, offered in 170, 270, and top-line GT trim. Though only six-cylinder engines were offered that year, the 1964 Dart GT (above) could be ordered with a 180 bhp 273-cid V-8. A stronger 235-bhp version of that engine was available for the 1965 Dart GT (opposite page), when finally it lived up to its name.

SPECIFICATIONS

Engines:	ohv I-6, 170 cid (3.40 × 3.13), 101 bhp; ohv I-6, 225 cid (3.40 × 4.13), 145 bhp; ohv V-8, 273 cid (3.63 × 3.31), 180/235 bhp (1964-66)
Transmissions:	3/4-speed manual, 3-speed TorqueFlite automatic
Suspension front:	upper and lower A-arms, longitudinal torsion bars, anti-roll bar
Suspension rear:	live axle on semi-elliptic leaf springs
Brakes:	front/rear drums
Wheelbase (in.):	111.0
Weight (lbs):	2690-2995
Top speed (mph):	90-110
0-60 mph (sec):	8.2-19.5

Production: 1963 34,227 **1964** 49,830 **1965** 45,118 **1966** 30,041

1965
Dodge Coronet 500

Topping its class in '65, the Coronet 500 served as luxury leader of the mid-size Dodge lineup, which also included base and "440" Coronets. Familiar to car shoppers a decade earlier, the Coronet name hadn't been used by Dodge since 1959. Now it was back and ready to roll, featured on the "500" hardtop coupe and convertible that sales literature described as "The newcomer that's a real goer."

Go it could, too, depending on which of the half-dozen V-8s went under the 500's hood. Lesser Coronets started off with six-cylinder engines, but nothing short of a V-8 could power a Coronet 500. Topping the list was the famous 426 Hemi (named for its hemispherically shaped combustion chambers), conservatively rated at a whopping 425 horsepower but actually capable of considerably more. "Handle this one with care," the sales brochure warned. "It leaves nothing to the imagination." Running on 12:1 compression with twin Carter AFB carburetors, Hemis were intended for competition action, but a fair number wound up beneath the hoods of street-driven machines, including Coronets.

Serving as the base engine was a pleasant but considerably smaller 273-cid V-8, rated at 180 horsepower and backed by a standard three-speed manual transmission. For additional muscle, customers could elect a wide-block 318-cid V-8 (230 bhp); 361- and 383-cid V-8s with 265- and 330-bhp ratings; or a 365-bhp "wedge" V-8 with the same 426-cubic-inch displacement as the Hemi. Only a four-speed gearshift or optional TorqueFlite automatic could handle either of the 426 V-8s.

Advertisements for performance-oriented Coronets referred to "that wild wedge" under the hood and its prowess as an "animal tamer" (a nudge directed at the Mustang, Cougar and other performance cars named after living creatures). A Hemi-powered Coronet 500 offered such temptations as "buckets, padded dash,

Coronet 500 was the top of Dodge's mid-size line for 1965, offering a sporty buckets-and-console interior and engine choices up to the wild 426 Hemi. Most carried more mundane powerplants, but all were V-8s.

SPECIFICATIONS

Engines:	ohv V-8, 273.5 cid (3.63 × 3.31), 180 bhp; 318 cid (3.91 × 3.31), 230 bhp; 361 cid (4.12 × 3.38), 265 bhp; 383 cid (4.25 × 3.38), 330 bhp; 426 cid (4.25 × 3.75), 365/425 bhp
Transmissions:	3-speed manual; 4-speed manual and 3-speed TorqueFlite automatic optional
Suspension, front:	control arms, torsion bars
Suspension, rear:	live axle, leaf springs
Brakes:	front/rear drums
Wheelbase (in.):	117.0
Weight (lbs.):	3255-3340
Top speed (mph):	**V-8** 106-117 **V8-426** 118+
0-60 mph (sec):	**V8-426** 7.7-7.8
Production:	32,745

console and an impatient attitude toward getting you away from it all."

Straight-edge, virtually slab-sided styling with minimal trim was the rule for Coronets, which wore a flat grille and back end. For the most part, the body shaping was similar to 1964 models, albeit with restyled sheetmetal intended to target the burgeoning youth market that was gaining so much attention from automakers. A full-length chrome strip ran across the beltline, with "Coronet 500" script just behind front wheel openings. Deluxe spinner-style wheel covers were standard. Up to 15 body colors were offered, with two-tones optional, sprayed with the new acrylic enamel. Like other Chrysler products of this era, Coronets used torsion-bar front suspension, with ordinary leaf springs bringing up the rear.

Interiors held a console with storage section, sun visors, and air-foam bucket seats, upholstered in "rich, supple saddle grain and tallow calf vinyl" that came in a selection of six colors (including two-tone white/gold). Gearshift levers could go on the floor with the four-speed manual or three-speed TorqueFlite automatic. Instead of the typical Chrysler pod-style dashboard, the Coronet's instrument panel contained a horizontal speedometer in a wide window. Coronets could be customized with everything from a black or white vinyl top to a tachometer, Sure-Grip differential, variable-speed wipers, and power windows. Air conditioning also was available, though not with every engine.

Motor Trend pushed its "wedge" 426 test car with four-speed up to 60 mph in just 7.7 seconds, crossing the quarter-mile line in barely more than twice that time at 89 mph. That was enough to name it "Super Sleeper of the Year," claiming a top speed past 120 mph. *Car Life* tests yielded similar results. Including a Hurst shifter, the performance package added $513.60 to the Coronet's sticker.

A total of 32,745 Coronet 500s were built in 1965, priced at $2894 for the convertible and $2674 for the hardtop coupe. The Coronet 500 badge continued into 1966, decorating a fresh bodyshell.

Hardly as striking as the fastback Charger due to arrive for that year, Dodge's Coronets were nonetheless handsome in their own quiet way. With the right selection of engine and transmission, a Coronet 500 could also eat up the road or the track as avidly as many a flashier carriage, and convey a full load of passengers in praiseworthy style and comfort.

1965-66
Dodge Polara
500/Monaco & Monaco 500

Luxury with more than a touch of sport was the key for Dodge's top-of-the-line full-size models in the mid-'60s. In fact, Dodge described its Polara 500 package for 1965 as just the answer "for special, sports-minded, fun-loving people."

Maybe so, but in the looks department, few would rank these as the most alluring Dodges ever—or even of the decade. Some might even call them stodgy, perhaps ordinary. Yet they were eminently representative of their times, displaying the brand of straight-up, no-nonsense styling that was gaining favor throughout the industry. Body/chassis structures were closely allied to the redesigned Chryslers, whose square shapes were penned by Elwood Engel.

Finally distancing itself from the bonds of its excessively colorful and flamboyant recent past, Dodge could now focus on creating a distinguished— yet youthful—demeanor for its biggest automobiles. Juggling those two seemingly contradictory themes was a trick that each American automaker had to learn in a hurry.

If the goodies weren't tempting enough outside, a peek under the surface might convince skeptics that Dodge could build some interesting full-size excitement. Beneath that hood might lurk anything from the basic Polara 383-cid V-8 with two-barrel carburetor and 270 horsepower, right up to the big 426-cid "wedge" with 365 horses ready to gallop. In between was a four-barrel 383, as well as a 413-cid version of the Chrysler V-8.

Extras in the Polara 500 sports package, offered on hardtops and convertibles only, included all-vinyl front bucket seats with center console, a floor-shifted four-speed or three-speed TorqueFlite automatic, padded dashboard, and deluxe wheel covers. Like other Polaras, the 500 had a torsion-bar front suspension with anti-sway bar, curved side-window glass, and crank-type vent panes. Polaras displayed a slim, full-width "dumbbell" shaped grille made up of thin vertical bars, incorporating quad headlights. Outward-angled, Delta-shaped taillights

Opposite page, top: *Only 400 of the 1963 300Js were built, and for the first time since 1956, no convertible version was offered. Production rebounded for 1964, though the 300K (below and opposite page, bottom) changed little externally save for rectangular taillights in place of the previous round units. Also in 1964, a convertible returned to the letter-series lineup.*

SPECIFICATIONS

Engines:	ohv V-8, 383 cid (4.25 × 3.38), 270/315/325 bhp **1965** 413 cid (4.19 × 3.75), 340 bhp; 426 cid (4.25 × 3.75), 365 bhp **1966** 440 cid (4.32 × 3.75), 350/365 bhp
Transmissions:	3-speed manual; optional 4-speed manual, 3-speed TorqueFlite automatic
Suspension, front:	non-parallel control arms, lateral torsion bars
Suspension, rear:	live axle, leaf springs
Brakes:	front/rear drums
Wheelbase (in.):	121.0
Weight (lbs.):	3765-4315
Top speed (mph):	103-118
0-60 mph (sec):	**V8-413** 8.4

Production: 1965 Polara 12,705 **1965 Monaco** 13,096 **1966 Polara** 107,832 **1966 Monaco** 49,773 **1966 Monaco 500** 10,840

rested at the rear. Fender skirts cost extra.

Monaco for '65 was billed as the "Limited Edition Dodge for the man with unlimited taste." This "one-of-a-kind, best-of-everything Dodge" sold only as a two-ton, two-door hardtop, with a $3355 price tag. Riding the same 121-inch wheelbase as the Polaras, Monaco reached even further in their quest for a mix of luxury and vigor, sophistication and spirit.

Interiors earned special attention. Deep pleated bucket seats came in soft saddle-grain vinyl with a rattan wicker pattern on the backs (and matching door panels); or a combination of Dawson-pattern cloth and vinyl. Full-length consoles could get an optional tachometer, inset in brushed aluminum. Rear passengers enjoyed integrated bucket seats, while the driver faced a three-spoke translucent steering wheel.

Appropriate ticks on the option list brought even more pleasures, from electric windows to an Auto Pilot and air conditioning. Monaco bodies, meanwhile, came in a selection of 15 colors, which could be accented by an optional grained-vinyl roof in black or white.

A healthy helping of torque permitted the *Motor Trend* Monaco with 413-cid engine to blast to 60 in a sizzling 8.4 seconds—less than a second slower than a 426-cid Polara 500 had achieved a year earlier. That's rapid motion indeed for a car with so many pounds to haul along, and a TorqueFlite transmission. Chrysler's four-speed gearbox with the 426 engine would contribute even more prowess. Standard Monaco mill was a four-barrel edition of the 383, rated at 315 bhp.

Tapered taillights grew much wider for 1966, reaching into 'MONACO' block lettering on the rear. Monaco 500 was the top model this time, highlighted by sill moldings and paint striping. Dodge promoted Monaco's "lavish display of luxury on the inside that some people call downright sinful." The standard 383-cid engine with TorqueFlite now wielded 325 bhp. Both the Polara and Monaco 500 could get a 440-cid V-8 this year, rated at 350 bhp (365 with dual exhausts). Front-disc brakes were optional on each full-size Dodge. This year's grille had the same "dumbbell" shape, but with its thin vertical bars in an evenly spaced pattern.

Not the best-remembered of Dodges today, the poshest Polara and Monaco two-doors earned a spot in history for their clever blend of formality and frivolity. They helped bring Dodge to a decade-high production total in 1966, earning fifth spot in the sales rankings. Both names continued into the 1970s, though the cars themselves were overshadowed by the rising popularity of mid-size muscle machines.

1966-67
Dodge Charger

"This is no dream car," explained the Dodge sales catalog. Rather than mere advertising hype, as most such explanations inevitably turn out to be, this statement had reason behind it. The startlingly shaped fastback Charger had indeed evolved from a recent show car, and lost little of its sensuously dramatic appeal on its way to the showroom. Only the original extended rear quarters were hacked off, replaced by a flat rear panel.

By the mid-1960s, Dodge was ready to go the full performance route. They had the engines (led by the revived Hemi V-8, toned down for street use), the tough transmissions, plus an eagerness for taking on the competition. With the striking fastback-roofed Charger, they now had the right car for the job.

As had been true of the Charger II show car that toured the country a year earlier, the production Charger's greatest trait was its sharply defined shape. Here was a really *long* fastback roofline, with as thick a rear pillar as anyone was likely to see. From the side, the view was as distinctive as anything on the market, even though some critics carped that the Charger profile was comparable to that of AMC's Marlin. With windows rolled down, the space left by the large quarter glass gave the hardtop a wild open-air presence.

Headlights hid behind a full-width rectangle of clean-as-a-whistle grille, which also concealed the turn-signal lenses. Switch on the headlights, and the units rolled into position. Rear views were nearly as impressive, focusing on the full-width taillamp with widely spaced CHARGER block lettering. A slightly recessed back window, with thin rails on each side, created a modest "flying buttress" look. All of these styling touches served to conceal the fact that a Charger was basically a Coronet hardtop, which just happened to wear a fastback roofline and hidden headlights.

Having earned its subsequent reputation in the performance arena with a Hemi under the hood, it's easy to forget that the Charger was conceived as a luxury car. Of course, as the sales catalog promised, it was also "nimble enough and quick enough and challenging enough to make you glad you can't afford a chauffeur." At $3122, a Charger cost $417 more than a Coronet 500 hardtop.

Ads reached deeper yet into the performance lexicon, pushing the possibility of a "deep-breathing 426 Street Hemi growling under the hood" of this "big, brawny, powerful fastback" with its "come-hither styling." The Street Hemi package was more than an engine. It included a heavy-duty suspension, Blue Streak tires, and 11-inch brakes (front discs optional). TorqueFlite (if ordered) would be set for full-throttle shifts at 5500 rpm; or the proud owner could get a competition-type four-speed gearbox. Dashboards contained round gauges with a tachometer right next to the speedometer.

Not that a full-boat Hemi was required. Base powertrain was a docile 230-bhp 318, with three-speed column shift. Both 361- and 383-cid V-8s also were optional.

Chargers weren't the choice for large families. Four bucket seats with barriers between meant that was the passenger limit. On the other hand, an owner could drop the back seats down and wind up with a practical 4 × 7 1/2-foot cargo space. Cologne-grain vinyl interiors came in half a dozen colors to accent the futuristic look, laden with brightwork. Standard equipment included a full-length console, three-spoke simulated woodgrain steering wheel, and deep-dish stainless steel wheel covers. Power brakes and steering were optional, as were a Sure-Grip differential and bumper guards. Shortening the console for 1967 allowed Chargers to accommodate that extra fifth passenger.

Just how hard-charging were these Chargers? With a 383-cid V-8 and TorqueFlite, *Car and Driver* dashed to 60 in 7.8 seconds. *Car Life* sent a Hemi to that speed in 6.4 seconds. Chargers also tore up the nation's stock-car tracks, winding up with the NASCAR Grand National Championship. Enough said?

Advertising pounded home the notion of the "Dodge rebellion," with Charger leading the siege. That it did, even though the design was not universally praised at the time. Today, it's difficult to think of many better representatives of their era than a fully equipped Hemi-Charger. Customers liked them well enough at first, buying 37,344 copies (468 with the Hemi); but production slipped to a meager 15,788 the next year. Not to worry. Dodge had another Charger concept in mind for the balance of the decade.

Chargers were basically Coronets with a fastback roofline, but over 35,000 customers felt the difference was worth the $400 premium. Original '66 model (opposite page) came with four bucket seats, the rears able to fold down to create a huge cargo area in back. The '67 was little changed outside (below), but it carried a bench seat in back that increased passenger capacity. Car shown is one of only a handful that were equipped with the 426 Hemi.

SPECIFICATIONS

Engines:	all ohv V-8: **1966** 318 cid (3.91 × 3.31), 230 bhp; 361 cid (4.12 × 3.38), 265 bhp; 383 cid (4.25 × 3.38), 325 bhp; 426 cid (4.25 × 3.75), 425 bhp **1967** 318 cid, 230 bhp; 383 cid, 270/325 bhp; 426 cid, 425 bhp; 440 cid (4.32 × 3.75), 375 bhp
Transmissions:	3-speed manual; optional 4-speed manual and 3-speed TorqueFlite automatic
Suspension, front:	unequal-length A-arms, torsion bars, link stabilizer bar
Suspension, rear:	live axle, leaf springs
Brakes:	front/rear drums (front discs optional)
Wheelbase (in.):	117.0
Weight (lbs.):	3480-3499
Top speed (mph):	106-134
0-60 mph (sec):	5.3-10.9
Production:	**1966** 37,344 **1967** 15,788

1967-69
Dodge Dart GT & GTS

Ever since 1965, Dodge had been issuing a GT edition of its compact Dart. Name aside, these upgraded hardtop coupes and convertibles didn't quite qualify as full-fledged Grand Touring or performance machines—not with a 273-cid V-8 as top engine, and a hard-to-combat image as low-budget, uninspired family movers.

When Darts enjoyed a major restyle for 1967, the GT came along for another trial run, winding up the year with a modest but welcome sales gain. Bigger inside and out, more rounded along the bodysides, the reworked Darts kept the same 111-inch wheelbase as the originals, but delivered, in the words of the sales brochure, "... more room. New pow. More posh." Well, that was the claim. In reality, not much had changed apart from a cleaner fastback-styled silhouette and full-width grille, and a fresh selection of vinyl and cloth/vinyl interiors. Some of that size increase was illusory, in fact, since overall length actually shrank by a fraction of an inch.

Clearly, more than bucket seats and an identifying plaque were needed to turn a plain-Jane Dart into an honest GT. Ordering the optional Rallye suspension package helped, especially when combined with front-disc brakes and D70×14 Red Streak tires. So did the more potent four-barrel variant of the 273-cid V-8, available with either TorqueFlite or a four-speed, and an optional tachometer. Nevertheless, these useful doodads were attached to an otherwise no-frills American compact that had a difficult time eliciting excitement.

Something was missing. A wider front end had given the '67 Darts a broader stance and additional engine room—but nothing new to fill that extra space. That shortcoming was corrected for 1968 with the arrival of the GTSport (GTS, for short) as a member in good standing of the new Dodge "Scat Pack," which also included the Charger and Coronet R/T editions.

Beneath the hood of the freshened Dart sat a zesty new 340-cid V-8 with four-barrel carb and high-lift camshaft, eager to send its 275 horsepower to the ground via a Rallye suspension and E70×14 wide-tread tires. Scoop-style hood louvers, square-tipped dual exhaust pipes, and "bumblebee" stripes out back told the world that this was a new breed of Dart, ready to take on some (if not all) comers. Anyone who didn't care for those flashy rear stripes could nix them.

Restyled '67 Dart GT (below) still came with a 235-bhp 273 V-8 as its top power option, but the sporty GTS that debuted in '68 (opposite page, left column) came with a 275-bhp 340, and could be ordered with a 300-bhp 383. For 1969 (opposite page, right) the 383 was tuned to 330 bhp, though there were few other changes.

SPECIFICATIONS

Engines:	**1967-69 Dart GT** ohv I-6, 170 cid (3.40 × 3.13), 115 bhp; 225 cid (3.40 × 4.13), 145 bhp; ohv V-8, 273.5 cid (3.63 × 3.31) **1967** 180/235 bhp **1968-69** 190 bhp; 318 cid (3.91 × 3.31) **1968-69** 230 bhp **1968-69 Dart GTS** ohv V-8, 340 cid (4.04 × 3.31), 275 bhp; 383 cid (4.25 × 3.38) **1968** 300 bhp **1969** 330 bhp
Transmissions:	3-speed manual; optional 4-speed manual and 3-speed TorqueFlite automatic
Suspension, front:	upper wishbones, lower arms w/struts, torsion bars, stabilizer bar
Suspension, rear:	live axle, leaf springs
Brakes:	front/rear drums (front discs optional)
Wheelbase (in.):	111.0
Weight (lbs.):	2715-3210
Top speed (mph):	GT V-8 108-111 GTS 111-122
0-60 mph (sec):	V8-273 9.0 GTS 6.0-6.3

Production: 1967 GT 38,225 **1968 GT** 26,280 **1968 GTS** 8745 **1969 GT** 20,914 **1969 GTS** 6702

If that wasn't enough to induce "Dodge Fever," then perhaps the optional 383-cid V-8, also four-barrel carbureted but churning up 25 extra horses, could finish the job. With that choice came a vented, bulged hood. TorqueFlite automatic was the standard transmission, shiftable through an optional console, but a four-speed manual gearbox cost no more.

Performance got a boost in the regular GT line as well, with a 318-cid V-8 option joining the 273. Far more Dart GTs than GTSports found customers, helped by the simple fact that they were more than $500 cheaper. The GTS hardtop and convertible drew scads of attention but not as many orders, with only 8745 built.

A modest facelift with fresh horizontal-bar grille and restyled taillights didn't change the Darts dramatically in 1969. Joining the GT and GTS this time was a bargain-basement Swinger, available with the 340-cid V-8 engine but carrying fewer extras.

While Dodge's GTSport never quite ranked with a Hemi-Charger or Super Bee in the public eye for all-out performance, the figures and contemporary comments speak for themselves. With the 340-cid engine and automatic transmission, *Motor Trend* required a measly 6.0 seconds for its GTS to hit 60. Rocketlike acceleration wasn't its only skill, either. *Car and Driver* called Dodge's top Dart a "tough little machine on curves and bends." *Car Life* voted GTS one of the best cars of the year: "more nimble than most" and able to deliver "neck-snapping acceleration," actually topping a Hemi-equipped Charger for "versatility, agility, road-ability" and off-the-line starts.

Because some folks never are satisfied, a few hundred Darts even had 440-Magnum engines installed by outside specialists. Even without such unofficial help, though, Dodge had turned its dowdy compact in sheep's garb into a snarling wolf, eager to snap at the heels of its muscle-car rivals.

GTS production slipped to 6702 for this final season in the Dart lineup, and only the Swinger would hang on into the Seventies.

DODGE

1968-69
Dodge Charger

After an impressive start-up in 1966, sales of the dramatic fastback Charger slipped in its second season. What to do? Unleash a restyled edition, naturally, with an even tougher stance and extra muscle. Many considered the revised Charger to be one of the best-looking mid-size cars around, though the original fastback roofline was replaced by a notchback semi-fastback profile with "flying buttress" sail panels.

To satisfy the muscle-car crowd, Dodge released a Charger R/T (for Road/Track) as part of its "Scat Pack," which also included the Coronet R/T and Dart GTS. Each wore bumblebee stripes around its tail and carried an engine appropriate for its title.

Ads for "The Clean Machine" (Charger R/T) noted that it was "not built for the common car crowd." For many, that's all it took to induce an insatiable craving for a 440-Magnum V-8 and hit 'em hard suspension. Though aimed at "a rugged type of individual," however, Charger ads further noted that the likely buyer was a person "who likes it soft inside." So which was it, ruffian or softy?

Actually, the Charger benefited from a dual personality and qualified on both counts. Vinyl-trimmed bucket seats and posh amenities lured comfort seekers, with a cushion available to position an extra passenger between the buckets. An aggressive exterior with power to match was enough to pull in the performance boys—especially when abetted by a pair of pipes blaring out the back, and brawny red-sidewall rubber hitting the pavement.

Hemi and Magnum engines were only part of the story, after all. Standard Charger fittings included a mild-mannered 318-cid V-8 with an adequate, if uninspiring, 230 horsepower. Next step up: Chrysler's 383, with 290 or 330 bhp. Only by ordering an R/T or checking off the 375-bhp Magnum or 425-bhp Hemi did the Charger turn from pussycat into mean machine.

Copywriters for muscle-car ads evidently had a nasty streak, pushing their products' potential antisocial tendencies with forthright abandon. A Charger's

SPECIFICATIONS

Engines:	all ohv V-8: 318 cid (3.91 × 3.31), 230 bhp; 383 cid (4.25 × 3.38), 290/330 bhp **Charger R/T** 426 cid (4.25 × 3.75), 425 bhp; 440 cid (4.32 × 3.75), 375 bhp
Transmissions:	3-speed manual (318-cid only); optional 4-speed manual and 3-speed TorqueFlite automatic (TorqueFlite standard on R/T)
Suspension, front:	short/long arms, torsion bars, sway bar
Suspension, rear:	live axle, leaf springs
Brakes:	front/rear drums (front discs optional)
Wheelbase (in.):	117.0
Weight (lbs.):	3100-3646
Top speed (mph):	**Hemi** 142-156 **R/T** 113+
0-60 mph (sec):	**Hemi** 4.8 **R/T** 6.0-7.2

Production: 1968 96,108 **1969** 69,142 **1969 Charger R/T** 20,057

Note: 225-cid six was available on 1969 Charger.

Swoopy second-generation Charger debuted for 1968 (opposite page, bottom). The 1969 version (below) gained a split grille while elongated horizontal taillights replaced the pair of twin round lights used in '68. A Charger 500 was introduced in '69 (opposite page, top and middle) with a filled-in fastback roofline and flush grille.

suspension, they reported, "treats an angled grade crossing in the rain with studied insolence," while this "Beautiful Screamer" with an "impertinent flip of the spoiler on the rear deck" contained "440 cubes of mean." Manual-shift fans were encouraged to imagine how the "four-speed box changes cogs with the precision of a sharp ax striking soft pine." In other words, Dodge ads proclaimed exactly what America's sneering adolescents wanted to hear. "American guts" were promised, in a car "shaped like a Mach 2 jet on wheels."

Action matched the aggressive stance, too. A 440-Magnum Charger R/T could reach 60 in 6.5 seconds or less. A Hemi might actually beat the five-second barrier, earning its $604.75 cost for those who appreciated such skills. Front-disc brakes were still a $73 option, as was a tachometer at $48.70. Like some other muscle cars, Charger became a movie star, chased by Steve McQueen in *Bullitt* and playing against Elvis in *Speedway*.

A minor facelift with split full-width grille wasn't the biggest news for 1969. More exciting was the emergence of the Charger name on two special models: the Hemi-powered Charger 500, built for competition; and the bullet-nosed Daytona with its far-above-the-crowd wing stabilizers, aimed at NASCAR racing. A 500 sold for $3860, the Daytona an even four grand. Most ordinary folks settled for a garden-variety Charger, an R/T, or new SE (Special Edition) with "leather-vinyl" front buckets and a sports-type steering wheel.

Take your R/T "to the strip where the men are," the ads suggested, where the Hurst shifter could be used to greatest advantage directing the power produced by either a Magnum or Hemi engine. Stepping downhill in scope, Chargers also came with six-cylinder engines in 1969.

Certainly, the restyled Charger ranked as one of the best-looking mid-size cars of the late '60s: long and low, pleasingly rounded, headlights hidden again behind a simple grille. *Car and Driver* claimed that only the restyled Corvette challenged the Charger in the styling department, even pointing out rear-view similarities between the two.

Shoppers evidently flocked to the second generation in droves, too. Sales streaked to new heights, with 96,108 Chargers hitting the showrooms in 1968 and only 7000 less in '69. For sheer drama even when standing still, however, this notchback hardtop with its semi-fastback roofline, even if NASCAR-inspired, lacked the panache of the initial fastback Charger. But either example ranks as memorable American muscle today.

1968-69
Dodge Coronet R/T
& Super Bee

Mid-size madness afflicted the Dodge lineup for 1967 as the humble Coronet added an R/T (Road/Track) edition with the big 440 Magnum engine. As its name suggests, the new mill displaced a whopping 440 cubic inches—this in a car that was typically thought of as supermarket and vacation transportation. At least it didn't come as an ordinary sedan, but only in hardtop coupe and convertible dress, decorated by dual paint stripes and a hood scoop. Early R/T ads declared that the "rampaging" Magnum "speaks softly, but carries a big kick."

Dodge wasn't about to let Pontiac's GTO and other muscle-car rivals pull ahead in the marketplace, so the R/T package carried on when Coronets earned their 1968 restyling. Ranking among the most attractive intermediates, the new Coronet wore rounded bodies in the popular "Coke-bottle" shape that enhanced its long, low silhouette. Like other members of the Dodge Scat Pack, the R/T came with "bumblebee" stripes wrapped around the tail, unless the buyer specified otherwise.

Standard again was the 440 Magnum V-8 with three-speed TorqueFlite. The 425-bhp Hemi engine and four-speed gearbox were available, too. Brakes were larger than on other Coronets, but front discs remained a $73 option. So did special instruments, including a tachometer, which added $90. Exhaust gases exited through twin pipes, and a special handling suspension was standard. Both the hardtop and convertible wore all-vinyl bucket seats, and came in 16 colors.

"Acceleration is very rapid," declared *Car Life* after its test of an R/T convertible that rushed to 60 in 6.6 seconds, "yet the engine never seems to be laboring. The 440's brute torque makes high revving completely unnecessary."

Apart from a revised split grille and taillights, change for 1969 was minimal. R/T gear included a simulated woodgrain instrument panel, sill and wheel-lip moldings, Rallye suspension with sway bar, F70×14 Red Line wide-tread tires, and Power Bulge hood.

To satisfy shoppers who felt an R/T coupe's $3379 sticker was too high for comfort, Dodge added a budget-priced Super Bee during the 1968 model year. This few-frills, back-to-basics muscle coupe carried a special 335-bhp, 383-cid V-8, serving as Dodge's answer to the hot-selling Plymouth Road Runner. The engine contained various components taken off the 440 Magnum, including cylinder heads and hot camshaft. Instead of bucket seats, for instance, the Super Bee came with a vinyl bench, in an interior more reminiscent of a taxicab than a near-luxury traveler. A four-speed was standard; TorqueFlite the option.

Both a hardtop coupe and pillared coupe made the Super Bee lineup, the latter with flip-open back windows instead of roll-up glass. Super Bee's Rallye instrument panel came out of the Charger. Hemi engines could be ordered.

Something new appeared on Super Bee engines for 1969: a Ramcharger Air Induction System that forced colder, denser outside air through the carburetor, selling for $73 (standard with the Hemi engine). Gathering even greater publicity was the Super Bee "Six Pack" option, consisting of a trio of two-barrel Holley carburetors feeding a 440-cid V-8, all hidden beneath a pinned-down, flat-black fiberglass hood. Priced at $463 above the $3138 hardtop base figure, the Six Pack delivered 390 horsepower, along with a brawny 490 pounds/feet of torque. That was sufficient to permit 0-60 mph acceleration times of 6.3 seconds or so. Strangely enough, an ordinary 383-equipped Bee could handle the job in less time: as little as 5.6 seconds reported by *Car and Driver*.

Nearly all of the 10,849 R/Ts built in 1968 were Magnum-powered; a mere 230 had the Hemi, whose days were numbered. In 1969, fewer than half as many Hemis went under R/T hoods, as production shrunk to 7238. Price was part of the reason, since the Hemi added $604.75 to an R/T's cost. Super Bee figures tell a similar story. Of the 27,846 built for 1969, only 166 had a Hemi installed.

Both the Coronet R/T and Super Bee hung on for one more year. Although overshadowed at the end by Chargers and the winged if seldom-seen Daytonas, the final Coronets proved themselves to be true dual-purpose machines. Serving as subdued family transportation most of the time—just like their Coronet Deluxe and 440 brethren—with the proper drivetrain on tap they were also able to turn into Mr. Hyde with a hard slap at the gas pedal. For both traits, they'll be fondly remembered.

In the late '60s, most manufacturers offered a wide selection of engines in their intermediates, but none went to the extremes of Chrysler Corp. Under "B-Body" hoods could reside anything from an economical 225-cid Slant Six with 145 bhp up to a 440-cid V-8 with 390 bhp; those in a real hurry could even order the fabled 426-cid Hemi with a tire-shredding 425 bhp. Dodge's mid-size "muscle car" was the Coronet R/T (a '68 below; a '69 opposite above), which came standard with a 440 V-8. Joining it in late '68 was the budget-priced Super Bee (opposite below), a stripped model carrying a 383-cid V-8.

SPECIFICATIONS

Engines:	all ohv V-8: **Coronet R/T** 426 cid (4.25 × 3.75), 425 bhp; 440 cid (4.32 × 3.75), 375 bhp **Super Bee** 383 cid (4.25 × 3.38), 335 bhp; 426 cid, 425 bhp; 440 cid, 390 bhp
Transmissions:	4-speed manual or 3-speed TorqueFlite automatic
Suspension, front:	short/long arms, torsion bars, stabilizer bar
Suspension, rear:	live axle, leaf springs
Brakes:	front/rear drums, (front discs optional)
Wheelbase (in.):	117.0
Weight (lbs.):	3440-3721
Top speed (mph):	R/T 123 Super Bee 117-129
0-60 mph (sec):	R/T 6.6 Super Bee 5.6-6.3

Production: 1968 Coronet R/T 10,849 **1969 Coronet R/T** 7238 **1969 Super Bee** 27,846

DODGE

1969
Dodge Charger Daytona

In 1957, the Automobile Manufacturers Association responded to strident calls from the insurance industry and safety lobby to abandon its participation in racing. While there was much disappointment in this wholesale pullout at first, a few years later the AMA's decision didn't look like such a bad idea after all. The Volkswagen revolution and Eisenhower recession had occurred, and everybody was building economy cars—so who needed racing? That attitude lasted until about 1962, by which time the industry had staged a full recovery, and auto companies once again lent their support to racing efforts.

The Dodge Charger Daytona's evolution dates to 1963, when Chrysler decided to overlook the AMA agreement and engage Ford in NASCAR. Chrysler Engineering was asked to design a new 426-cid Hemi V-8, reviving the potent concept that Chrysler had developed in the 1950s. Hemi Plymouths and Dodges blew everybody's doors off at Daytona in 1964, but Ford retaliated with big-bore engines and "factory" racing options, and continued to dominate the Grand National scene.

In 1966, Dodge introduced the Charger fastback, which looked like an aerodynamic NASCAR contender but proved much slower than its shape suggested. Two years later it was redesigned as a handsome coupe, and Dodge fitted competition models with spoilers to glue them to the track. While the '68 was indeed more slippery than its predecessors, it still proved four mph slower than the Ford opposition—and in stock-car racing, one mph is equal to the length of a football field per lap. That sent Dodge back to the drawing board. The Charger Daytona was the result.

While the 1968 Charger did have good aerodynamic properties, it also exhibited a fair degree of rear-end lift. The solution was a tall, adjustable rear-deck stabilizer

SPECIFICATIONS

Engines:	all ohv V-8; 426 cid (4.25 × 3.75), 425 bhp; 440 cid (4.32 × 3.75), 375 bhp
Transmissions:	4-speed manual, 3-speed automatic
Suspension front:	upper and lower control arms, longitudinal torsion bars
Suspension rear:	live axle, leaf springs
Brakes:	front disc/rear drum
Wheelbase (in.):	117.0
Weight (lbs):	approx. 3900
Top speed (mph):	NA
0-60 mph (sec):	NA
Production:	505

Conceived as an aerodynamic weapon for the NASCAR circuit, the Dodge Charger Daytona wore a pointed 18-inch nose, along with a rear spoiler that towered two feet above the trunklid. Rear-facing scoops on the front fenders allowed for tire clearance on racing versions.

made up of twin fins and a horizontal wing. A pointed snout was added for good measure, and the combination proved to increase lap speeds by five mph, giving Dodge a car that could truly challenge the Fords and Mercurys. Dodge planned to build 500 of the "winged warriors," the minimum number necessary to qualify them as "production" vehicles for NASCAR.

Charger Daytonas were built by Creative Industries, the Detroit firm responsible for numerous "specials" over the years. Actual production estimates range between 501 and 507; the official factory source states 505. They could have built more: dealers took about 1200 orders, and Dodge sent hurried telegrams imploring them to persuade their customers to settle for something else. The Charger Daytona sold for about $300 more than the Charger R/T hardtop and lost between $1000 and $1500 per unit, which was unimportant: its purpose was to win races.

Racing cars all received the 426 Hemi with close-ratio four-speed gearbox and Hurst shifter. At Talladega, the Daytona set a new official world's closed-lap speed record at close to 200 mph, but unfortunately the Fords didn't show up to compete and it was a muted victory.

Disappointment turned to embarrassment the following month at Charlotte, North Carolina, where the Daytonas finally did meet the Fords—and were badly beaten. Tire wear was the culprit: Chargers were forced to make brief challenge spurts, then drop back to conserve rubber. According to engineer Larry Rathgeb, the tire problem was never really solved. "Firestone could not, and Goodyear would not, built a tire that could stand up at 200 mph. After five laps you were out of rubber, and that's not good at all."

Salvation finally arrived at the Texas 500 in December, when Bobby Isaac's Daytona firmly beat the Ford entries with a 144.277 mph average. The Daytona went on to win 80 percent of its races in 1969, finishing with 22 Grand National victories, only four fewer than Ford. But Dodge's fling with stock-car racing ended after that year, and Plymouth took up the corporate torch with the similar (and quite successful) Road Runner Superbird.

1961-63
Dual-Ghia L6.4

If you know about the Dual-Ghia L6.4, you're either a rabid Chrysler fan or a collector of automotive minutiae. But don't feel badly if this "other" Dual-Ghia is foreign to you. After all, it mostly *was* foreign, and even rarer than its better-known predecessor.

That car was born in the mid-'50s when Eugene Casaroll, owner of a Detroit trucking firm called Automobile Shippers, quit dabbling in Indianapolis racing to pursue his "dream car." This was basically a production version of the 1954 Dodge Firearrow, one of a series of image-building "idea" exercises penned by Chrysler's Virgil Exner and realized by Italy's famed house of Ghia.

Casaroll secured rights to the Firearrow's four-seat convertible design, then signed Ghia's Giovanni Savonuzzi to engineer it into a practical road machine. Toward the same end, Ghia was contracted to modify styling and build the bodies, which it welded onto shortened Dodge chassis shipped to Turin. Running gear and much minor hardware were liberally borrowed from Chrysler bins, and final assembly was carried out at Casaroll's small Dual Motors facility in suburban Detroit. Nevertheless, the resulting Dual-Ghia was a unique, handcrafted convertible offering high European style and high American performance at a predictably high price: a minimum $7750 in debut '56— a king's ransom at the time.

But this was merely "mad money" to the tycoons, bluebloods, and Hollywood types Casaroll deliberately chose as clients; and no more than 150 each year at that. As a result, the D-G owner's list soon read like an elite *Who's Who*, with "rat packers" Sammy Davis, Jr., Dean Martin, Peter Lawford, and Frank Sinatra conspicuous among them—all of which led columnist Dorothy Kilgallen to quip that a "Rolls-Royce is the status symbol for those who can't get a Dual-Ghia."

Unfortunately, Casaroll couldn't get Hemi V-8s after 1958, Chrysler having phased them out for simpler, cheaper wedgehead engines. Furthermore, the American automaker's planned switch to welded unibody construction for 1960 ended Casaroll's supply of separate chassis. But this was just as well, for Casaroll

Only 26 Dual-Ghias were built between 1961 and 1963, carrying a price tag that read $15,000—nearly four times the price of a Corvette. Opposite page, middle: It may say "Ghia," but the engine was actually from Chrysler, as were the transmission, suspension, and brakes. Opposite page, bottom: Dual-Ghias came loaded with everything from air conditioning to fitted luggage for the leather-lined interior.

SPECIFICATIONS

Engines:	ohv V-8, 383 cid (4.25 × 3.38), 335 bhp
Transmission:	3-speed Chrysler TorqueFlite automatic
Suspension front:	upper and lower A-arms, longitudinal torsion bars, anti-roll bar
Suspension rear:	live axle on semi-elliptic leaf springs
Brakes:	front/rear drums
Wheelbase (in.):	115.0
Weight (lbs):	4000
Top speed (mph):	est. 120
0-60 mph (sec):	est. 9.5
Production:	26

had been taken with a newer Chrysler showpiece, the aptly named Dart retractable hardtop convertible of 1957, and decided it would make a dandy starting point for a new Dual-Ghia.

The result, announced in August 1960, was considerably less radical: a 2+2 notchback coupe mating the original D-G's "big mouth" front-end look with a squarish new tail and an airy greenhouse bearing a huge wraparound rear window. Wheelbase and overall height were unchanged (115 and 52 inches, respectively), but overall length grew seven inches (to 210) and width swelled two inches (to 75). Curb weight stayed around two tons. The chassis was now a drop-center affair fabricated entirely by Ghia, but Chrysler components again prevailed, including torsion-bar front suspension, leaf-sprung live rear axle (pulling rather sprightly 3.23:1 gearing), all-drum "Total Contact" power brakes, and "Full-Time" power steering. Running gear remained Chrysler's, too, but in place of the earlier D-G's 315-cubic-inch Dodge hemi and two-speed PowerFlite automatic were a tuned 383 wedge and far superior three-speed TorqueFlite.

Christened L6.4 (the liter equivalent of 383 cid), the new coupe went on sale in early '61 at a stratospheric $15,000—almost twice the convertible's price—though that included air conditioning, radio, and power everything. Ironically, Casaroll hoped to hold down costs by having Ghia build the L6.4 entirely, Dual Motors becoming merely the U.S. distributor (which is why the marque name was officially Ghia, not Dual-Ghia). He didn't distribute very many. Though the rich, famous, and influential again queued up, only 26 L6.4s were delivered through early 1963, when Casaroll ran out of funds.

The L6.4 was not the performer its predecessor was: slower in the 0-60 test by a good second, and far less wieldy off the straight and narrow. Leon Mandel, after driving one for a 1979 *Motor Trend* retrospective, termed the L6.4 "scary . . . particularly on vividly cambered county 2-laners: it bounces; it judders; it shudders and it dances." He also found it "perilous" to drive on a sunny day: "Inside and out there are vast vistas of chrome that turn the driving compartment into one vast reflector." He might have added that the cockpit was as Italian as any contemporary Ferrari's, swathed in aromatic leather and filled with knobs, switches, and dials.

Today, of course, Gene's creations have nowhere near the status of Enzo's. But as one man's "ultimate car," the L6.4 was no less personal or intriguing. That's reason enough to remember it here, even if it's not completely "American."

1960
Edsel

Edsel jokes were getting tired 10 years ago, and now they are plumb worn out. The Edsel cost Ford Motor Company $350 million, and during a bad year nowadays they can lose that much in a month—sometimes in a week. Furthermore, the Edsel fiasco was the root of Ford's solid success in the '60s, prompting the corporate structure that remains to this day.

When the Edsel bombed, Lincoln, Continental, and Mercury were reunited into one division, leaving Ford with just two U.S. passenger car entities. When we look at the dreadful duplication and confusion among the five GM divisions today, how can we not see the Edsel as a kind of hero? Today Ford is even successfully separating the styling of shared bodies, like the Cougar/Thunderbird and Sable/Taurus, further distancing the image of one from another. While the $350 million loss may not be the cheapest lesson Ford ever received, the Edsel's failure may eventually go down in history as a blessing in disguise.

The car itself was perfectly suited for the times and in several ways quite innovative. Along with its unique vertical grille and narrow horizontal taillights (which one cynic likened to an ingrown toenail), the Edsel featured numerous gadgets. Its "Teletouch" automatic transmission was controlled by pushbuttons recessed in the steering wheel hub; the speedometer was a rotating drum; and almost everything except the rearview mirror could be power assisted.

Announced in a four-model range with 18 different body styles in 1958, the Edsel had been conceived in bountiful 1955, when sales of medium-price cars were booming. By the time the glitzy new entry actually appeared, however, new-car sales were in a slump generally, and the market for vehicles in the Edsel's price range had dropped by about a third. Edsel Division, conceived by Ford as part of a multi-divisional approach mirroring General Motors, had planned to sell 100,000 '58s. The final tally was 63,000.

Now 63,000 is not bad, but it's hardly encouraging for a new car upon which millions had been expended, and factory resources were geared for six-figure production in a couple of years. Retrenchment was fast and furious. In 1959, the line was pared to three models and 10 body styles, while Ford hastily made arrangements to merge Edsel back into Lincoln-Mercury Division and stop building the standard-size Edsel as soon as it was practical. But the name itself was intended to live on: For several months, Ford planned to bestow the Edsel badge on Mercury's new compact. However, the sales fiasco was so great (production of 1959 models was only 45,000) that Mercury dropped this plan and settled instead on "Comet," which had no bad connotations.

By 1960 the Edsel was obviously not long for this world. It shared a body that year with the Ford Galaxie, albeit on a one-inch-longer wheelbase, and incorporated just enough styling alterations to make it slightly different. The upright center grille that had been an Edsel hallmark since introduction was replaced by a horizontal motif, divided in the center, which looked suspiciously like that of the (successful) 1959 Pontiac. Heavy chrome accents were used on the fenders and sides of the body, whose shell was new in 1960 and thus looked reasonably fresh. Two-speed or three-speed automatic transmission, power steering, and air conditioning were options, but the range was trimmed to just two models: the Ranger in five flavors of sedan, hardtop, and convertible; and the Villager wagon with either six- or nine-passenger capacity.

Production figures of 1960 Edsels excite collectors because these are truly rare cars. The Ranger four-door sedan was the only model with over 1000 copies; the rest saw minuscule production. Scarcest of all are the Ranger convertible (76 built) and the nine-passenger Villager wagon (59 units total).

The Edsel was clearly doomed by 1960, when it shared a basic bodyshell with the Ford Galaxie, albeit with unique styling touches. Due to its limited sales volume, some models are extremely rare; only 76 convertibles were built, while Villager wagons totaled just 275. The station wagon shown (opposite page, bottom) was created by grafting Edsel trim onto a Ford two-door Ranch wagon, as all real Villager wagons were four doors.

SPECIFICATIONS

Engines:	ohv I-6, 223 cid (3.62 × 3.50), 145 bhp; ohv V-8, 292 cid (3.75 × 3.30), 185 bhp; 352 cid (4.00 × 3.50), 300 bhp
Transmissions:	3-speed manual; 2 & 3-speed automatic optional
Suspension front:	upper and lower A-arms, coil springs
Suspension rear:	live axle, leaf springs
Brakes:	front/rear drums
Wheelbase (in.):	120.0
Weight (lbs):	3502-4046
Top speed (mph):	NA
0-60 mph (sec):	NA

Production: Ranger 4d htp 135 **4d sdn** 1288 **2d htp** 295 **2d sdn** 777 **cvt** 76 **Villager 9p** 59 **6p** 216

1965-69
Excalibur Series I

Many "replicars" have come and gone since the mid-'60s, so it's fitting that the first and best of the breed would survive the longest. It was, of course, the Excalibur, that splendid creation of noted industrial designer Brooks Stevens.

The first Excaliburs were lightweight race-and-ride roadsters built in 1951 with "vintage-modern" bodywork on the Henry J chassis, but the production Excalibur was born in 1963 at Studebaker, where Stevens had been a consultant the previous four years. Having completed clever, low-cost facelifts on the compact Lark and sporty Hawk coupe, he was asked by company president Sherwood Egbert to come up with some show cars to convince people that moribund Studebaker had a future after all. At first, time permitted only a trio of dolled-up Larks. But for the annual New York Auto Show in April 1964, Stevens wanted something that would really "get people to come to that damn booth." Egbert, sadly, was stricken with cancer by then, but successor Byers Burlingame agreed to go along.

Stevens devised what he called a "contemporary classic," a new car that looked like the supercharged Mercedes SSK he once owned. Badged "Studebaker SS," the dashing cycle-fendered roadster, riding a Lark Daytona convertible chassis with supercharged, 290-horsepower 289 V-8, was completed in just six weeks by Stevens and his sons David and William.

No sooner did it arrive in New York than Studebaker backed out, officials saying it was at odds with their new "common sense" theme. Undeterred, Stevens exhibited the SS on his own, and immediately drew an avalanche of orders. This prompted his sons to form SS Automobiles in August 1965, and within a year they'd built 56 examples of a modified SS bearing the Stevens-registered name Excalibur—and "sword-in-circle" radiator mascot that suggested, but didn't infringe upon, Mercedes' jealously guarded tristar emblem.

Studebaker, meantime, had ceased production, but the Stevens brothers secured 300-bhp 327 V-8s from Chevrolet that gave their lithe, 2100-pound Excalibur exhilarating performance. With standard 3.31:1 rear axle, 0-60 mph took less than five seconds, versus seven for the Studey-powered prototype. And projected top speed was near 160 mph!

Though quite old, the Lark chassis was narrow and thus literally suitable for

SPECIFICATIONS

Engines:	**1965:** Studebaker 289 cid (3.56 × 3.62), 290 bhp; **1966-69:** Chevrolet 327 cid (4.00 × 3.25), 300 bhp
Transmissions:	4-speed manual, 3-speed automatic
Suspension front:	upper and lower A-arms, coil springs
Suspension rear:	live axle on semi-elliptic leaf springs
Brakes:	front discs/rear drums
Wheelbase (in.):	109.0
Weight (lbs):	2100-2650
Top speed (mph):	150+
0-60 mph (sec):	5.0-6.5

Production*: 1965 roadster 56 **1966 roadster** 87 **phaeton** 3 **1967 roadster** 38 **phaeton** 33 **1968 roadster** 37 **phaeton** 20 **1969 roadster** 47 **phaeton** 44

*1965-68 total SSK roadster 168 **"standard" roadster** 59 **phaeton** 89

the Excalibur's slim body. It was also firmly X-braced, though the high power-to-weight ratio demanded considerable reworking for good handling. That task fell to David Stevens, as did numerous others. The vintage-style cowl, for example, forced him to lower pedals and steering column. He also had to change spring rates and caster/camber angles, but the car went as quickly around curves as it did on straights. This chassis continued under all "Series I" Excaliburs. For 1970's revamped "Series II," young Stevens designed a new box-section frame with all-independent suspension.

Uncompromising quality would always set Excaliburs apart from the motley group of "neoclassics" they inspired. Papa Stevens, for example, secured Mercedes' original German supplier for his car's simulated outside exhaust pipes, and chose French-made freestanding headlamps closely resembling the original SSK units.

Early production Excaliburs were bodied in hand-hammered aluminum, but fiberglass was soon substituted for reasons of cost and practicality. Radiators, though, were always cast in aluminum, and the dash was filled with purposeful white-on-black gauges in an engine-turned panel. All this in a hand-built car with sensational performance and secure roadability made the announced $7250 base price simply unbelievable.

Buoyed by their initial success, the Stevens brothers added two models in 1966: a more elaborate roadster with full fenders and running boards, and, very late in the year, a surprisingly roomy four-place Phaeton convertible. Prices inevitably escalated, reaching $10,000 by 1969, but Excaliburs remained remarkable values. Not until 1976 would prices exceed $20,000, and then mostly because of inflation and government mandates, though a progressively upgraded equipment list no doubt added to the total. Standard features by 1969 included air conditioning, heater/defroster, variable-ratio power steering with tilt wheel, power front-disc brakes, radial tires on chrome-plated wire wheels, twin sidemounts, luggage rack, AM/FM stereo, leather seats, air horns, driving lights, rear air shocks, "Positraction" limited-slip differential, and self-shift Turbo Hydra-Matic (the last two from GM, of course).

The Excalibur survived the '70s through Series II and III models that picked up where the Series I left off. Then came larger and slower Series IVs, which piled up big losses in a topsy-turvy market, forcing the Stevens brothers to sell out in the late '80s. New owners tried to keep things going, but the firm slipped into the limbo of bankruptcy in 1991, where it remains at this writing. We hope it won't stay there long.

Above: *Designer Brooks Stevens (standing), along with sons William and David, pose with an early Excalibur. Later models grew bulky, being aimed more at the luxury market, but the Series I (both pages) was a lithe, ferocious performer.*

1960-61
Ford Galaxie
Sunliner & Starliner

You don't see many full-size 1960-61 Fords any more, not even at gatherings of blue-oval boosters. That's strange, because few Fords are more attractive than these, and none before them were more potent. In addition, they were the literal foundation for the "Total Performance" 1962-64 models that most big-Ford fanciers favor, perhaps not appreciating from whence they came.

Ford went all-out for 1960, fielding not only its first compact, the Falcon, but an equally all-new group of "standard" or "full-size" cars. They were the biggest Fords yet. Though wheelbase grew only an inch from '59 (to 119), overall length rose 5.7 inches and width swelled 4.7 to a massive 81.5 inches overall—*too* wide to be legal in some states (though authorities didn't seem to notice).

Matching the more expansive dimensions was new styling that seemed a hasty reply to Chevrolet's "batwing" '59, though lead times made any similarities quite coincidental. The Ford was arguably prettier anyway. Where the '59 look was boxy, "correct," and somewhat fussy, the '60s were sleeker, more rounded, and much cleaner. Glassier, too, with lower beltlines and larger windshields, the latter abetted by straightening out the knee-banging "dogleg" A-pillars of yore. If not the best-looking Big Three standard for 1960, Ford had the advantage of being fresh against a facelifted Chevy and tasteful against a bizarre new Plymouth.

That freshness extended underneath, where a strong new full-perimeter frame replaced the old '50s X-member type. Also, rear leaf springs were repositioned rearward so that only a third, rather than a half, of their length stretched ahead of the axle, which helped reduce cornering roll. New body and driveline mounts enhanced refinement, as did added sound-deadening materials.

The Sunliner convertible remained the glamour leader of a big-Ford line reordered (from the bottom) into Custom 300, Fairlane, Fairlane 500, and Galaxie series, plus parallel station wagon offerings. Joining it in the top-shelf Galaxie group was an airy new two-door hardtop called Starliner (an old Studebaker name) with a racy, gently curved semi-fastback roofline.

But there was more to the Starliner than mere looks. Against other closed

Above and opposite page, middle: *Galaxie Starliner coupe introduced in 1960 wore a thin-pillar semi-fastback roofline that made it more aerodynamic than its square-roof counterparts in the Ford line. Opposite page, top: For 1961, full-size Fords received a complete makeover, the rear end featuring round taillights and small, canted fins. Interiors of the '61 Sunliner convertible (opposite page, bottom) wore two-tone upholstery and a smooth, uncluttered dash.*

SPECIFICATIONS

Engines:	I-6, 223 cid (3.62 × 3.60), 135/145 bhp; ohv V-8, 292 cid (3.75 × 3.30), 175/185 bhp; ohv V-8, 352 cid (4.00 × 3.50), 220/235/300/360 bhp; ohv V-8, 390 cid (4.05 × 3.78), 300/375/401 bhp
Transmissions:	3-speed manual, 3-speed Cruise-O-Matic automatic
Suspension front:	upper and lower A-arms, coil springs
Suspension rear:	live axle on semi-elliptic leaf springs
Brakes:	front/rear drums
Wheelbase (in.):	119.0
Weight (lbs):	3566-3743
Top speed (mph):	95-150
0-60 mph (sec):	7.1-12.0

Production:1960 Sunliner 44,762 **Starliner** 68,461 **1961 Sunliner** 44,614 **Starliner** 29,669

Galaxies with their boxy, Thunderbird-style roofline, it proved far superior aerodynamically on high-speed stock-car tracks. Indeed, racing seemed to be its reason for being. Yet with close to 68,500 sales, the Starliner was also one of 1960's more popular big Fords. As one enthusiast observed, it was "the kind of car you never forget."

As before, 292 and 352 V-8s were Ford's mainstream big-car engines for 1960. But with the Big Three resuming open track competition after three years of a self-imposed "ban," Ford's maximum 300 horses weren't enough. Accordingly, the division unleashed its first high-performance engine since 1957. Arriving midseason as the "Interceptor 360," it was a 352 packing 360 bhp via a huge four-barrel carburetor and 10.6:1 compression. *Motor Life* got hold of an Interceptor-equipped Starliner prototype, and was startled when the 4141-pound car ran 0-60 mph in 7.1 seconds and an honest 150 mph flat out. (By contrast, *Motor Trend*'s 300-bhp/automatic Starliner needed 11.7 seconds 0-60.) Yet all that extra go cost just $150 extra. "Total Performance" had arrived.

After besting arch-rival Chevy by some 20,000 cars for model-year 1960, Ford introduced handsomely facelifted '61 standards with simple concave grilles, recontoured bodysides, and little '57-style "blade" fins atop big round taillamps. Models were basically as before, and all made a notable nod to practicality with longer chassis-lube and oil-change intervals (30,000 and 6000 miles respectively), plus new self-adjusting brakes.

More exciting by far was a newly optional 390-cubic-inch "Thunderbird Special" V-8. Essentially a larger, stronger 352, it delivered 300 standard bhp with single four-barrel carb—same as the previous high-output 352—but far more torque, a bountiful 427 versus 381 pounds/feet. More potent still was the "Thunderbird 390 Super," conservatively rated at 375 bhp and optional for any big '61 Ford save wagons. It was strictly for performance: Power steering, power brakes, and automatic weren't available. At midyear came an even hotter 390 with three two-barrel carbs and extra-high compression, good for a mighty 401 bhp.

The 390s put Ford in the thick of another Detroit "horsepower race" along with Pontiac's 389 V-8 and the new Chevy 409. The Starliner looked to run away with the contest, but was left at the gate because far more buyers preferred square-roof Galaxies. Sales dropped below 30,000, and the Starliner would not return for '62.

But Ford as a whole was going great guns, and even more big-car excitement was just ahead in snazzy bucket-seat Galaxie 500XLs, spearheaded by a young new division chief named Lee Iacocca. That success story is told elsewhere, but let's credit the 1960-61s for making it possible—and as still largely "undiscovered" but eminently worthy collectibles from the peak decade for Detroit performance.

1960
Ford Thunderbird

Lay aside everything you've heard in condemnation of the four-seat Thunderbirds—all that stuff about forsaking the sports car, substituting glitz for function, adding the hated back seat. It is all immaterial because it misses the point: Despite its deviation from the original concept, the first four-seat Thunderbird was simply a masterpiece of design.

In fact, it may well be one of the outstanding American automotive achievements of the decade. Furthermore, it earned this honor without relying upon the technological dead-ends of the era: air suspension, fuel injection, supercharging, retractable hardtops. Though all of these were considered, all were rejected.

Chief Thunderbird body engineer Bob Hennessy claims the "Squarebird" was revolutionary. "Take that car and stick it in front of your house today. It doesn't look at all out of date. When we were working on it, the standard automobile sat maybe 61 inches off the ground—shoulder height. The Squarebird sat 52.5 inches off the ground. To get a low sports-car look, we took 10 inches out of the then-standard car height." The four-seat 'Bird was a huge commercial hit, too, far more successful than the two-seater ever was.

For model year 1960, Ford Styling had proposed a number of revisions to the now-two-year-old Squarebird design. The Thunderbird roofline had been applied to large Fords in 1959, and stylists were concerned that it was losing its originality. But sheet metal changes were not feasible from either a cost or merchandising standpoint, according to Ford Division committee minutes. "Similarly, partial revision to existing surface, i.e., roof, front end, bumpers, etc., did not provide enough visual difference to warrant the required expenditure of funds." The Bird was in its last year of a styling cycle, and it was felt wiser to withhold serious changes until 1961.

The 1960 Thunderbirds were down very slightly in weight but up in price. The base figures were $3755 for the hardtop, $4222 for the convertible. No mechanical changes occurred, and there were only a few styling differences: vertical hashmarks added to rear fenders, "Thunderbird" script on the door projectile, a square-mesh grille with full-width horizontal bars, and six taillights instead of four. There were minor changes to emblems and ornaments, and a standard rectangular outside mirror. Door handles were blended more closely with the upper belt molding, and the door trim was changed to incorporate a built-in armrest. On early models (built through the end of December 1959), there was a smooth belt molding; this was corrugated on cars built in 1960. The '60 model also used a number of stainless-steel components, and two were actually built entirely of stainless steel by one of Ford's suppliers, Allegheny-Ludlum Steel Corporation.

One thoughtful new item did appear, however, in the form of a semi-convertible. For 1960, Thunderbird introduced the first sliding metal sunroof on a postwar American car. It looked good, and it worked well. However, the sunroof was not by any means the first choice of product planners, many of whom wanted a retractable hardtop, like the big Ford Skyliner. But the engineering would have been tremendously complicated owing to the Squarebird's short deck, and even the conventional soft top proved a complicated affair, taking up most of the room under the decklid when lowered. Planners also considered a "roof incorporating flippers," probably indented sections that telescoped back or lifted when the door was opened. This idea was also rejected for reasons of cost and complexity.

Ford's attention to detail was evident in the presence of a roof-mounted chrome railing, which directed wind and noise away from the passenger compartment when the hatch was open. Sunroofs were fitted to 2159 standard hardtops plus 377 with the optional 430-cid engine—fewer than three percent of production.

What were the faults of the Squarebird? Roadability, certainly. It was far from "the kind of handling car it should be," *Motor Trend* wrote in 1960. "Steering is slow and not precise . . . it has no reputation for . . . the dimensional attributes of a compact and yet lacks some of those same characteristics of maneuverability"—a curious assessment from the magazine which two years earlier called it the "Car of the Year."

But the Squarebird was notable for several things, and *Motor Trend* knew it: "What it does have is originality, freshness, and newness of concept. . . . It has, more than any current domestic car, the spirit and quality that made the classic roadsters and tourers of the 1930s such memorable favorites."

SPECIFICATIONS

Engines:	all ohv V-8; 352 cid (4.00 × 3.50), 300 bhp; 430 cid (4.30 × 3.70), 350 bhp
Transmissions:	3-speed manual; overdrive, 3-speed automatic optional
Suspension front:	upper and lower A-arms, coil springs
Suspension rear:	live axle, leaf springs
Brakes:	front/rear drums
Wheelbase (in.):	113.0
Weight (lbs):	3799-3897
Top speed (mph):	NA
0-60 mph (sec):	NA
Production:	cpe 78,447 "goldtop" cpe 2536 cvt 11,860

The first postwar sliding steel sunroof was offered on the 1960 T-Bird, which had otherwise been carried over from 1959 with few changes. Like the Thunderbird in general, interiors were leaning more towards luxury than sport by this time.

1961-63
Ford Falcon Futura

Ford's Falcon was easily the most popular of the Big Three's new 1960 compacts because it was closest to what buyers wanted: simpler and more reliable than Chevrolet's air-cooled rear-engine Corvair, cheaper and less gimmicky than Chrysler's Valiant. But humble cars seldom remain so, and by 1968 the Falcon had evolved into a junior intermediate—and a rather boring one at that. As such, it lost much of its original appeal, which helps explain why the 1961-63 Futuras and Futura Sprints are now widely regarded as the best Falcons: sportier than the original '60s, but just as clean and lithe, and blessed with a sterling V-8 for '63.

The Futura bowed about a year after Chevy's Corvair Monza uncovered a huge new market for low-cost cars with "European" features. Offered only as a two-door sedan, it followed Monza in having vinyl-covered bucket-type front seats, but split them with a chrome-covered glovebox à la Thunderbird. Full carpeting and narrow-band whitewalls were also included—as was the trusty 144-cubic-inch Falcon six. But 85 horsepower wasn't nearly enough for a car with even mildly sporting pretensions, and the optional 101-bhp 170 six wasn't much help. Standard column-shift three-speed manual and optional Fordomatic were on hand as per other Falcons, but there was no four-on-the-floor. Still, Futura sales were creditable despite a late, midyear introduction.

The basic package returned for 1962, when all Falcons received bright new "electric shaver" grilles. Within a few months, Ford issued "The Lively Ones," the first in an annual squadron of midyear models to boost spring sales. Falcon's contribution was T-Bird-style rooflines for two- and four-door sedans, including Futura, which could be further dressed up with an optional vinyl roof covering. But while Ford focused on show, competitors were offering more go—notably Corvair's new Monza Spyder and Oldsmobile's F-85 Cutlass Jetfire, both with sprightly turbocharged engines. Futura sales dropped by more than half.

Ford caught up for 1963, giving all Falcons a nicer-looking new convex grille and expanding Futura into a separate series. Offerings consisted of two- and four-door sedans, plus a sharp new convertible with standard power top, front

SPECIFICATIONS

Engines:	ohv I-6, 144.3 (3.50 × 2.50), 85 bhp; ohv I-6, 170 cid (3.50 × 2.94), 101 bhp; ohv V-8, 260 cid (3.80 × 2.87), 174 bhp (optional 1963 Sprint only)
Transmission:	3/4-speed manual, 2-speed Fordomatic automatic
Suspension front:	upper and lower A-arms, coil springs
Suspension rear:	live axle on semi-elliptic leaf springs
Brakes:	front/rear drums
Wheelbase (in.):	109.5
Weight (lbs):	2322-2645
Top speed (mph):	90-110+
0-60 mph (sec):	12.0-18.0

Production:**1961 2d sdn** 44,470 **1962 2d sdn** 17,011 **1963 2d sdn** 27,018 **4d sdn** 31,736 **htp cpe** 28,496 **Sprint htp cpe** 10,479 **cvt** 31,192 **Sprint cvt** 4,602

bench seat, and the larger six. Prices were still Falcon-affordable: $2236 for the basic two-door Futura, $2470 for the ragtop.

Then came another group of midyear "Lively Ones" starring a pretty "slantback" Futura hardtop plus even sportier Futura Sprint convertible and hardtop. Buckets, 6000-rpm tachometer, simulated wood-rim steering wheel, wire wheel covers, chrome engine and rocker trim, heavy-duty suspension and rear axle, free-flow muffler and air cleaner, and four-speed floorshift manual transmission were all standard on Sprints, which cost only some $130 more than their regular Futura counterparts: $2320 for the hardtop, $2600 for the convertible.

And there was more: a 164-bhp "Challenger V-8," the high-revving, 260-cid "thinwall" unit introduced the previous year with the new mid-size Fairlane. Optionally available for any '63 Falcon, the V-8 transformed a dowdy grocery-getter into a budget bomb with 0-60 times of just under 12 seconds. Falcon was now a step ahead of Valiant and the orthodox, year-old Chevy II, neither of which had anything so potent.

The V-8 was a natural for the Sprint, making it as fleet-footed as its name. *Car Life* called the combination "La Petite Sport," praising a high power-to-weight ratio (21 lbs/bhp) and the easy way the engine could exceed its 5000-rpm redline despite a "choking" two-barrel carburetor. The V-8, said *CL*, was "completely devoid of fussiness, and exhibits a surprising amount of torque from rather ridiculous rpm levels. [It's] much happier in Falcon surroundings than it ever seemed to be in the Fairlane."

Ford knew the V-8 Sprint had the makings of a rally winner, and hired the Holman & Moody shops of stock-car racing fame to modify three hardtops for the 1963 Monte Carlo Rally. Though a Saab was the outright winner, one Sprint captured all the special stages—a Monte first—and another won the big-engine class.

An optional 200-bhp 289 V-8 made the '64 Sprints even livelier, but the package was shortly rendered redundant by the wildly successful Mustang, a purpose-designed sporty compact. Blockier, more contrived Falcon styling didn't help, and the Sprint vanished after 1965. The Futura name hung on until decade's end, but merely on "luxury" Falcons that weren't all that plush.

V-8 Sprints, ragtops especially, are now far and away the collector's Falcons of choice. Six-cylinder Sprints come next, followed distantly by 1961-63 Futura two-doors. Happily, all are still just as affordable as they were when new. You can't say that about every American car of the '60s, great or otherwise.

Introduced in 1961, Futura was to the Falcon what Monza was to the Corvair: a sporty, "dressed-up" version of an otherwise plain economy car. The '62 model (above) carried on with nothing more than a 101-bhp six under the hood. But in 1963 (opposite page and this page, below), Ford brought out a convertible version, offered bucket seats and a four-speed transmission, and blessed the Falcon line with an optional 260-cid V-8, though little else changed. Futura interiors were quite sporty—for a Falcon.

1961-63
Ford Thunderbird

The early '60s were perhaps the Thunderbird's finest hour. There was nothing radical about the third generation design that began in 1961; the radical ideas had been developed with the previous 1958-60 series. Rather, the 1961-63 T-Birds were soundly designed, well engineered, and beautifully styled.

Two designs were considered, one by Elwood Engel and another by Bill Boyer, heading two separate styling teams. Engel's chiseled, squared-off shape was ultimately chosen for the 1961 Lincoln Continental, while Boyer's aircraft-oriented body with its big round "flowerpot" taillights got the nod for the T-Bird. "We wanted to keep it very youthful, and that meant aircraft and missilelike shapes," Boyer recalled. But the new 'Bird and Continental still had a lot in common. Both featured highly integrated bumper/grille combinations; there was similarity in the windshield and side glass; both cars had unit bodies; and they were built side-by-side in the Wixom, Michigan, plant that had also built the 1958-60 Thunderbirds. Both had a new "dual-unitized" structure in which separate front and rear sections were welded together at the cowl. Because these structures were dimensionally similar on both cars, great cost savings were realized.

Coupled to the dual-unit body was a new chassis featuring what Ford called "controlled wheel recession"—rubber bushings allowing fore/aft as well as up/down wheel movement. Suspensions were revised and the power steering ratio reduced, requiring only 3.5 turns lock-to-lock. Brakes were power assisted with vastly increased lining area. Standard engine was a 390, bored and stroked from the Ford 352, which provided a significant increase in torque: 427 pounds/feet at 2800 rpm, up from 381 in 1960. The typical '61 T-Bird would do 0-60 in about 10.5 seconds and 115 mph flat out.

Interior designer Art Querfeld probably spent more time on the 1961 Thunderbird than any single model in his nearly 40-year tenure with Ford. "I wanted to emphasize and delineate the positions of the driver and front seat passenger," Querfeld said, "and I conceived of two individual compartments separated by a prominent console." The console swept forward, where it curved left and right, meeting the doors and continuing around the sides. Querfeld actually eliminated the traditional glove box door because it would have introduced seams in his gracefully curved paneling.

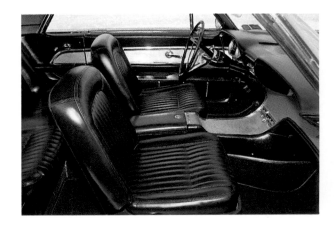

Opposite page, top: *A radical styling departure from previous-generation T-Birds, the 1961s featured a spearlike profile with flowing lines.* Above: *Interior was designed around a prominent center console that split the cabin into two cockpits. Styling had changed only in detail when the '63s bowed (below and opposite page, bottom), adopting front fender creaselines and some added chrome trim.*

SPECIFICATIONS

Engine:	ohv V-8, 390 cid (4.05 × 3.78), 300-340 bhp
Transmission:	3-speed Cruise-O-Matic automatic
Suspension, front:	upper and lower A-arms, coil springs
Suspension, rear:	live axle, leaf springs
Brakes:	front/rear drums
Wheelbase (in.):	113.0
Weight (lbs.):	3958-4471
Top speed (mph):	115-120
0-60 (sec):	8.5-10.5

Production: 1961 cpe 62,535 **cvt** 10,516 **1962 cpe** 69,554 **cvt** 7030 **sp rdst** 1427 **1963 cpe** 42,806 **Landau** 14,139 **cvt** 5913 **sp rdst** 455

(A small glove box was placed in the center console.) Also notable was the Swing-Away steering wheel, an invention of Ford's Stuart Fry: the steering column swung along a curved track fitted behind the dash, with a flexible coupling connecting it to the steering linkage.

The '61 was a smash hit. By the time a special gold model paced the 50th Anniversary Indy "500" in May, sales had already reached 50,000 for the model year. Ultimately, Ford sold 73,051, of which 10,516 were convertibles, and joyfully expanded the line with two new models in 1962.

Most important among the '62s was the Sports Roadster, a special convertible with Kelsey-Hayes wire wheels and a fiberglass tonneau which covered the back seats and formed headrests for the front seats. It wasn't intensely practical—there was no place to put it if you wanted to remove it, and there was really only one front-seat position that properly mated the seat to the headrests—but the Sports Roadster had glamour and allure, and has since become a prized collector's item. A second new model was the Landau, a hardtop with a padded vinyl roof and dummy landau bars—an attempt to upgrade the T-Bird's luxury image. New features common to all 1962 models included a revised grille, different side trim, combination tail/stop/parking lights, a hand-controlled parking brake, standard Swing-Away steering wheel, and other minor interior adjustments. Aside from an aluminized muffler, larger master cylinder, and more sound insulation, there were few engineering changes, but an optional "M-Series" 340-bhp engine with three two-barrel carburetors was offered for $242 extra. The M Series would do 0-60 in 8.5 seconds and had a top speed of 120 mph. Most 340 engines went into Sports Roadsters: 120 in 1962, 37 in 1963.

After another successful year (over 78,000), Ford stood almost pat with the '63s. Styling changes involved a molded creaseline on the front fender and door, new rear fender script, and a vertical-bar grille. Inside, the '63 had door panel courtesy lights and a new AM/FM pushbutton radio. The 1963 Landau could be ordered with a black, white, blue, or brown top, and had simulated walnut trim on the interior and steering wheel. Prices kept sales of convertibles (5913 units) and Sports Roadsters (455) low. This was the last year the Roadster would appear as a distinct model.

In January, Ford ran off 2000 Limited Edition Landaus, which premiered in Monaco and were known as the "Princess Grace" models. They featured white-on-white paint and trim with a rose-colored vinyl top, white steering wheel, simulated rosewood interior trim, landau bars set in a white background, and knock-off style wire wheel covers. This now highly collectible Bird cost $200 more than the standard Landau.

FORD

1962-64
Ford Galaxie 500XL

When charismatic Lee Iacocca replaced the conservative Robert McNamara as Ford's general manager, he brought a far different set of priorities to the job. Up to this time, sportiness wasn't part of Ford's big-car picture. Such a notion served Thunderbirds nicely, but not full-size hardtops and sedans.

Now was the time, Iacocca figured, to take aim at the emerging youth market. And what did young guys want? Fast cars with sporty physiques, of course.

A glance at the facelifted full-size Galaxie lineup provided the springboard to a new phase at Ford. Because Iacocca also favored midyear debuts, the XL Victoria hardtop coupe and Sunliner convertible arrived as a subseries of the Galaxie 500 in mid-1962, along with sporty bucket-seat editions of the compact Falcon and intermediate Fairlane. That XL suffix stood for "extra lively" or, in the case of convertibles, "extra luxury" as well. Though not the most sizzling seller at the time, the 500XL went on virtually to *define* "Total Performance," Ford's upcoming sales theme.

Taking the cleaned-up Galaxie body with its quad headlights and round taillights (tucked above semicircular bumper cutouts), neatly decorated by a single wide bodyside molding, Ford simply added a few identifiers: an XL badge on the fuel-filler flap, parallelogram emblems on rear fenders, and crests on sail panels. Rear fender skirts were optional, but added to the allure. Mylar-trimmed, deep-pleated bucket seats flanking a center console caught the eye inside. Colors? Galaxie customers could choose from 13, plus 21 two-tones.

Powertrains weren't the central focus at first, since the standard setup was a 170-bhp, 292-cid V-8 with Cruise-O-Matic. Greater goodies entered via the option list. A 352-cid V-8 headed the selection, followed by a 300-bhp 390. Then came Ford's NASCAR-aimed 406-cid V-8, able to whip up an easy 385 or 405 horsepower with either four-barrel carburetion or three deuces.

Motor Trend shot an ordinary Galaxie sedan with the 406 engine off to 60 mph in 7.1 seconds, estimating a 140-mph top speed. Rapid-transit prospects for the fancier 500XL looked bright, especially with one of its top mills coupled to a Borg-Warner four-speed, and an available 8000-rpm tachometer counting the revs. Not only would Ford be offering a broad range of XL engine/gear combinations; its high-performance department was busy developing extras for specialists in quarter-mile acceleration runs.

Cheap, the XLs were not. At $3108, the hardtop cost $434 more than a six-cylinder Galaxie 500. Nevertheless, 13,183 convertibles hit the showrooms, and more than twice as many hardtops.

Reskinning of the same basic body gave the 1963 "Super Torque" Galaxies new lower sheetmetal and a leaner look, headed by a concave, tighter-mesh grille. A hardtop sedan joined the original two body styles, but the base engine temporarily shrank to 260-cid size, backed by the two-speed Fordomatic. A 289-cid V-8 and three-speed Cruise-O-Matic replaced it during the year. At the other end of the spectrum, the 406 engine got a quick rebore to 427-cid displacement, boosting output to 410/425 bhp.

Additional drama arrived at midyear in the form of a sleek Sports two-door hardtop with sloped thin-pillar slantback roofline. Suspension modifications for '63 also improved the XL's ride, helping to move nearly 95,000 cars in the four body styles. Options included a swingaway steering column, simulated wire wheel covers, vinyl roof, and AM/FM radio.

Yet another cosmetic touch-up came for 1964, with a switch to a flat-faced horizontal-bar grille and addition of lower-body sculpturing. Formal-look rooflines faded away, while four-speeds were now built by Ford itself. *Motor Trend* whipped a 500XL hardtop sedan with 300-bhp engine to 60 in an uninspiring 9.3 seconds with Cruise-O-Matic. A twin-carb 427 with four-speed shaved nearly two seconds off that mark, but cost $462 extra (plus $109 for the second carburetor). Tom McCahill of *Mechanix Illustrated* reported that his 390-equipped hardtop took the corners "like a snake in a rat hole."

Galaxie XLs stuck around through 1970, enjoying several strong years, but sales generally suffered from the growing popularity of mid-size muscle. Yet along with Chevrolet's Impala Super Sport, they'd demonstrated that powerful engines and big bodies can blend into a tasty recipe for the sport-minded.

Sporty Galaxie 500XL debuted in 1962 (opposite page, top), the convertible shown being equipped with the mighty 406-cid V-8 offering 385 or 405 bhp. For 1963, the 500XL received only a mild facelift, though a Sports thin-pillar slantback roofline was added at midyear (opposite page, bottom), as was a 427-cid version of Ford's big V-8 that provided up to 425 bhp. Restyle for the '64s was more dramatic (below), with sculptured sides and revised front- and rear-end treatments.

SPECIFICATIONS

Engines:	all ohv V-8: **1962** 292 cid (3.75 × 3.30), 170 bhp; 352 cid (4.00 × 3.50), 220 bhp; 390 cid (4.05 × 3.78), 300 bhp; 406 cid (4.13 × 3.78), 385/405 bhp **1963** 260 cid (3.80 × 2.87), 164 bhp (early); 289 cid (4.00 × 2.87), 195 bhp (midyear); 352 cid, 220 bhp; 390 cid, 300 bhp; 406 cid, 385/405 bhp; 427 cid (4.23 × 3.78), 410/425 bhp **1964** 289 cid, 195 bhp; 352 cid, 250 bhp; 390 cid, 300 bhp; 427 cid, 410/425 bhp
Transmissions:	3-speed Cruise-O-Matic; optional 4-speed manual
Suspension, front:	upper and lower A-arms, coil springs, anti-roll bar
Suspension, rear:	live axle, leaf springs
Brakes:	front/rear drums
Wheelbase (in.):	119.0
Weight (lbs.):	3622-3877
Top speed (mph):	108-140
0-60 mph (sec):	6.5-9.3

Production: **1962** Victoria htp cpe 28,412 Sunliner cvt 13,183 **1963** htp cpe 29,713 Spt htp cpe 33,870 htp sdn 12,596 cvt 18,551 **1964** htp cpe 58,306 htp sdn 14,661 cvt 15,169

1963-65
Ford Falcon
Futura Sprint

Few would have thought of the first Falcons, debuting for the 1960 model year, as cars that excite. Their mission was practical transportation, and some even proclaimed them as modern successors to the everlasting Model A Ford. Others took a dimmer view, branding Falcons as prime examples of the short-lived, disposable automobile.

Appearance of the Futura two-door by 1962, with bucket seats no less, sparked just a twinge of interest among the sporty set. But only a twinge. After all, Falcons were powered by a minimalist 144-cid six: easy to service, reliable enough, but anemic when hitting the pedal, especially when equipped with two-speed Fordomatic. Upgrading to the bigger 170-cid six with its 101 horsepower didn't deliver a vast improvement. Falcons rode pleasantly and were surprisingly roomy inside—but rarely delivered thrills.

Then came 1963, and two big changes: arrival of a pretty little Falcon Futura convertible, accompanied by installation of a V-8 engine in the Sprint series added at midyear. A Sprint hardtop coupe also became available, which wore the rounded Falcon body quite well, with its restyled horizontal-bar grille.

First of the V-8s was a "Challenger" small-block of 260-cid displacement, cranking out 164 horsepower. Not until late in 1964 did a bigger 289 arrive, jacking output up to 200 bhp. Stuffing in a V-8 gave Falcons a much-needed performance boost, but without losing much of the fuel economy for which they'd become famous.

Sprints had special trim (including a simulated hood scoop), bucket seats alongside a console, and full instrumentation, including a 6000-rpm tachometer mounted atop the dashboard. Leatherlike vinyl trim came in five color choices, while simulated wire wheel covers and a sports-type steering wheel rounded out the package. A floor-shifted four-speed proved more pleasing than Falcon's customary column-shift three-speed.

Car and Driver ran an early V-8 Sprint through its paces, ambling off to 60 in a comparatively leisurely 12.1 seconds. A quarter-mile dash (figuratively speaking) took 18 seconds, with the Sprint edging up to 73 mph. *Motor Trend* was quicker, making the 60-mph trip in 10.9 seconds. In muscle-car terms, there was nothing to get excited about here; but for a Falcon, this was mighty quick travelin'.

Road-testers also had a crack at the Sprints that had taken the top two honors in their class at the 2500-mile Monte Carlo rally. No other cars in that class even finished the event. With its V-8 boosted to a delicious 260 horsepower via 10:1 compression and four-barrel carburetion—among other stimulants—this special Rally edition squeezed the 0-60 time down to an eye-opening 7.5 seconds.

A total of 15,081 Sprints were built in their opening season, 4602 of them convertibles. That was just a small fraction of the total output of 328,399 Falcons in 1963, but gave shoppers a broader range of possibilities from which to select. Cobra engine performance kits for the 260-cid Falcon, inspired by Ford-powered Cobras, were available through Ford dealers to satisfy owners who might enjoy tuning their Sprints to reach as far as 225 horsepower or so.

Falcons adopted a much different personality for 1964 with their all-new bodies. Wedge-look bodysides with twin tapered creaselines replaced the original chubby-cheeked roundness, giving the whole car a more leaning-forward stance. The flatter, slightly angled grille displayed a looser crosshatch pattern. Inside the Sprint was a racing-style three-spoke steering wheel. Only a handful of 289-cid V-8s went into '64 Falcons (late in the year), but their 36 extra horsepower gave the compact an even greater performance jolt than the initial V-8.

A more potent (105-bhp) six went into '65 Falcons, which could also get a larger (200-cid) six and three-speed Cruise-O-Matic. All V-8s were 289-cid size, but the Sprint variant was fading fast. Futuras could have the V-8 engine, and sold reasonably well, but Ford brochures neglected to mention the Sprint at all. Only 3106 came off the line this time.

Lee Iacocca merits First Prize for turning the pedestrian Falcon into a sprightly Sprint. After 1965, the Falcon name continued but on a completely different, larger car, kin to the Fairlane. Convertibles were out. Falcon's legacy reached in other directions, however, making a mark on the Mustangs and Comets of the 1960s, and even the Maverick of the following decade.

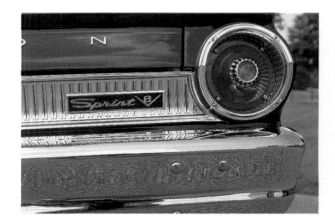

Sprint took the Futura idea one step further in 1963, adding a few more sporting touches. The '64s (both pages) gained squarer, more chiseled styling, and late in the year, a 289-cid V-8 with 200 bhp supplanted the 164-bhp 260 V-8. The 289 was standard on '65 Sprints, making for a fairly quick package; yet only 3106 were sold, and the sporty Sprint was allowed to fade away.

SPECIFICATIONS

Engines:	all ohv V-8: **1963-64** 260 cid (3.80 × 2.87), 164 bhp **1965** 289 cid (4.00 × 2.87), 200 bhp
Transmissions:	3-speed manual; optional 4-speed manual, 2-speed Fordomatic or 3-speed Cruise-O-Matic (1965)
Suspension, front:	lower A-arms, coil springs, stabilizing struts, anti-roll bar
Suspension, rear:	live axle, leaf springs
Brakes:	front/rear drums
Wheelbase (in.):	109.5
Weight (lbs.):	2308-3008
Top speed (mph):	**V-8** 105-107
0-60 mph (sec):	**V-8** 10.9-12.1

Production: 1963 htp cpe 10,479 **cvt** 4602 **1964 htp cpe** 13,830 **cvt** 4278 **1965 htp cpe** 2806 **cvt** 300

1964
Ford Fairlane Thunderbolt

Unlike most of the cars spotlighted in these pages, Ford's Thunderbolt wasn't ready for the street. Only a handful of '60s fans have so much as seen a Thunderbolt in action, much less roared down a quarter-mile drag strip in one. More than a few enthusiasts haven't even heard of this rarely spotted Ford, offered for just one year. That's because a Thunderbolt was about as far removed from a highway machine as anyone could get in the beginning of the performance era.

T-bolts were for dragging; that's all, nothing more. And they were created for professional race drivers whose only goal was to get to the end of a quarter-mile strip as fast as humanly possible.

One way to get there quicker has always been to take a lightweight car and drop in a beefy engine. Ford's Thunderbolt stretched that concept almost to its limit. Galaxies were going great around the NASCAR ovals, their considerable weight being offset by decent aerodynamics (for the time) and powered by the brutish High Riser 427-cid V-8. On the drag strips, though, Galaxies simply had too much heft to haul down the line.

With its 115.5-inch wheelbase, a Fairlane 500 measured 3.5 inches shorter than a full-size Galaxie—and weighed some 700 pounds less. Throw in a full collection of weight-cutting ideas, and the result could be promising indeed.

A few drag racers, in fact, were already running experimental Fairlanes. At Dearborn, the corporate folks didn't object to the idea of another winning Ford. This was the age of Iacocca, after all, and motorsports were a major part of his program. An initial batch of cars was ordered from the Dearborn Steel Tubing Company (near Ford headquarters), followed by two more groups delivered later; yet the total came to only a hundred Thunderbolts, most of them painted Wimbledon White. No wonder they're so little known.

Stuffing that 427 into position wasn't easy, demanding an extensive reworking

Standard Fairlanes were rather timid performers in 1964; the Thunderbolt was anything but. Interiors were stripped of all frills, including carpeting and armrests. Beneath the domed fiberglass hood lurked a 427-cid V-8 rated at 425 bhp, though it probably put out more. Doors and front fenders were also fiberglass (as was the front bumper on early models), and inner headlights were replaced with scoops that routed air to the carburetors. Surprisingly, exteriors boasted fancy Fairlane 500 trim.

SPECIFICATIONS

Engines:	ohv V-8, 427 cid (4.23 × 3.78), 425+ bhp
Transmissions:	4-speed manual or 3-speed automatic
Suspension, front:	shortened upper A-arms, coil springs
Suspension, rear:	live axle, leaf springs, traction bars
Brakes:	front/rear drums
Wheelbase (in.):	115.5
Weight (lbs.):	3225
Top speed (mph):	120-126 (at end of quarter-mile)
0-60 mph (sec):	4.5 (est)
Production:	100

of the front suspension, and refabrication of major components. Cutting weight was the order of the day, starting with the use of fiberglass for the car's pinned-down bubble-topped hood, as well as doors and front fenders. Early T-Bolts wore fiberglass front bumpers, but aluminum went into later cars in response to a ruling by the National Hot Rod Association. Plexiglas filled rear and side window openings, but the windshield remained stock.

Brutal and basic are perhaps the two words that best describe a Thunderbolt. Nonessentials were summarily dismissed: Thunderbolts contained no mirrors, sun visors, armrests, jack, lug wrench—nothing that didn't contribute to its ability to blast through a quarter-mile distance.

Twin screens replaced the Fairlane's inner headlights, shooting great gulps of air to the carbs through huge flexible ducts. Apart from that change, the front end looked fairly ordinary. So did the bodyside, which kept its full-length Fairlane trim strip. Except for the massive hood bubble and lack of hubcaps, in fact, a quick glance revealed little about what lurked within.

Underneath, the 427 breathed through twin Holley four-barrel carbs and exhausted via equal-length headers. A 12.7:1 compression ratio contributed to the engine's official 425-bhp rating, but contemporary analysts estimated that it actually put out a hundred or so more horses.

As *Hot Rod* explained, a Thunderbolt was "not suitable for driving to and from the strip, let alone on the street." Warranties? Forget it. Every customer had to sign a waiver absolving Ford of any responsibility for either repairs or potential injuries. Buy a T-Bolt, and you're on your own.

Price for all this performance was $3780 for a Thunderbolt with Borg-Warner four-speed, or an extra hundred if it carried the frequently installed three-speed automatic, adapted from Lincoln's transmission. Regular Fairlanes, let's recall, started at $2194. A few lucky folks got a T-Bolt for a buck, reports Thunderbolt expert Bob Trevarrow, because they qualified as favored customers.

Was it worth the cost? We're talking ETs (elapsed times) in the mid-11 second range here, with a T-Bolt ending its quarter-mile leap at 120 mph or more. Gas Ronda took the 1964 NHRA Winternationals prize by making the trip in 11.6 seconds, hitting 124.38 mph. For those who revel in such goings-on, those are figures to make the mind dance with joy. At the same time, Thunderbolts set a sterling pace for Ford's "Total Performance" theme.

1964-66
Ford Thunderbird

The fourth generation 1964-66 Thunderbirds were not far removed from the third generation, retaining the same basic understructure and unit-body inner stampings while wheelbase increased fractionally to 113.2 inches. But a complete reskinning vastly altered them on the surface. "There's a more powerful look which the stylists obtained by lengthening the hood and shortening the roof lines," said *Car Life*. "And there's a cleaner, stronger rear, achieved with two of the biggest tail/turn/stop lamps ever seen on an automobile." The turn signals of the '64 were intended to be sequential, but Ford ran into trouble with certain state regulations and was forced to wait a year while applying for the necessary permissions.

In detail, the '64 retained a family resemblance to the '63 but was obviously new. The pointed profile was still evident, but from front or rear it was completely altered. The quad headlamps were moved to the extreme edge of the fenders, where they cut into the face of the car in canted oval cutouts. The rear end was the best design element, set off by two oblong taillights surrounded by protective bumpers. A lower pan, painted body color, contained the backup lights. The decklid retained the "twin-pontoon" theme of earlier models. Under it was a new "deep well" trunk, which gave much more luggage space, carrying the spare tire well forward. The 1964 roofline retained the formal air of the past, but, taking advantage of a low-pressure area behind the backlight, now featured Silent-Flo, the first windows-closed flow-through ventilation system on an American car. With a console lever, the driver could actuate a vacuum servo that opened a vent under the rear window. This helped blast fresh air through the car. Flow-through ventilation had been introduced by Mercedes on its 1954 300SL gullwing coupe, and Mercury had used the meat-ax approach to create it with its retractable backlights in 1957, but the Thunderbird's was an elegant, functional design, and was soon widely imitated.

Designers had created more room in the 1964 T-Bird, but it probably didn't matter. The typical Thunderbirder was a front-seat dweller. Nestled in a big vinyl bucket, restrained by a seatbelt extending from a retractable reel built into the seat edge, and surrounded by levers, buttons, dials, and wheels, the driver was confronted with all the gimmicks at Dearborn's command. It was an experience *Car Life* described as "begadgeted and bedazzling.... It should keep boys of all ages occupied." Ford ads repeated the slogan, "Flight plan cleared—proceed to Thunderbird."

SPECIFICATIONS

Engine:	all ohv V-8, 390 cid (4.05 × 3.78), 300/350 bhp; (4.13 × 3.98) 345 bhp
Transmission:	3-speed Cruise-O-Matic automatic
Suspension, front:	upper and lower A-arms, coil springs
Suspension, rear:	live axle, leaf springs
Brakes:	front/rear drums
Wheelbase (in.):	113.2
Weight (lbs.):	4359-4588
Top speed (mph):	115-120
0-60 (sec):	9.0-10.5

Production: 1964 cpe 60,552 **Landau** 22,715 **cvt** 9198 **1965 cpe** 42,652 **Landau SE** 4500 **cvt** 6846 **1966 cpe** 13,389 **Twn Htp cpe** 15,633 **Landau** 33,105 **cvt** 5049

Ford had wanted to use sequential rear turn signals on the redesigned '64 T-Birds (below), but feared federal regulations would prohibit them. Clearance was finally obtained and the unique feature was added to the '65s (opposite page, bottom), which were otherwise little changed in appearance.

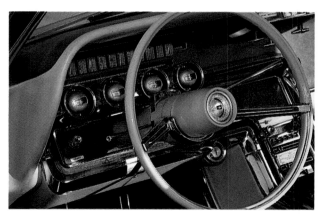

The drivetrain was unchanged from 1963, but the M-series (340 bhp) engine was eliminated, along with the previous Sports Roadster model. Sales were terrific, exceeding 90,000, the best in T-Bird history.

In styling, the '65 naturally resembled the '64. The grille was busier with its six new vertical bars bisecting the thin horizontal bars of 1964; the '65 also had dummy side louvers and new "turbo style" wheel covers. The drivetrain was unchanged and the 300-bhp 390 engine remained the 'Bird's sole powerplant. A fourth model, the Limited Edition Special Landau, was added to the line in March 1965. Finished in Ember-Glo metallic, it had a parchment-colored vinyl top with matching carpets and upholstery. The owner's name was engraved on a numbered plate on the console, and the wheel discs were color-keyed. Simulated woodgrain interior embellishments were done in a material somewhat richer than the standard Landau's. Yet the Special Landau cost only $50 more than the standard, which was a good deal if you happened to like Ember-Glo metallic.

Shoveling 'em out the door, Ford Division sold close to 75,000 1965 Thunderbirds—not as good as '64, but still the pace to beat in the personal-luxury car market. Despite growing competition from the Olds Toronado and Buick Riviera, sales at nearly 70,000 remained excellent for the 1966 model, which in some ways was the nicest of its generation.

The '66 line included the usual hardtop, convertible, and "Town Landau," plus a new "Town Hardtop," using the plain metal roof style *sans* padded vinyl or dummy landau bars, and selling for $100 less than the Landau. Both Town models had a "Safety-Convenience" panel mounted in the central forward roof, including a seatbelt reminder light; all four models were available with a new stereo tape deck. Good news for performance-minded buyers was a new optional 428 V-8 which offered a rousing 345 bhp for only $64 extra. The 428 shaved 1.5 seconds off the 0-60 time and gave the 'Bird a genuine 120 mph capability.

The late John R. Bond summed up the pros and cons of these Thunderbirds quite adequately in 1965: "[It offers] more symbolism than stature. Only the blessedly ignorant view it as anything more than a luxury-class car for those who want to present a dashing sort of image, who worry about spreading girth and stiffening arteries, and who couldn't care less about taste." Even when viewed in that light, however, the Thunderbird must be admired. It is extremely well done for its purpose. Its roofline, bucket seats, and console have inspired dozens of lesser imitations, which, as the saying goes, is the sincerest form of flattery.

Top: In 1966, the last year of this styling cycle, the T-Bird gained a redesigned grille and taillights, along with a bigger engine option; a 428-cid V-8 rated at 345 bhp. A popular accessory during this period was the Swing-Away steering wheel (above), which swung about 10 inches to the right to ease entry and exit.

1965-66
Ford Mustang

It doesn't invite much argument to say that the Mustang was the most important car of the '60s. The initial 1965 model (there was never a "1964½" as many believe) sold a staggering 680,989 copies and changed forever young America's attitude toward Detroit cars, which was just what the Mustang's patron and creator, Lee Iacocca, had hoped to achieve.

Iacocca, the wizard sales ace who rose from obscurity to a vice presidency and the head of Ford Division within five years after joining Ford, had observed the gap left by the long-departed two-seat Thunderbird. He was sure that a youthful, sporty, inexpensive car—but with four seats—which was peppy and snazzy looking and started at under $2500 would be a powerful new product. Iacocca formed a committee to study the idea and a series of prototypes were evolved, culminating in the four-seat, conventionally laid out, 108-inch wheelbase production Mustang. There were three models: a hardtop, convertible, and semi-fastback coupe. A six-cylinder engine was standard, but there were 260-cid and later 289-cid V-8s on the option list, along with just about every other accessory one could imagine—a key ingredient in Mustang's broad appeal to several different market segments.

Careful use of the option book, for example, could result in a basic-transportation Mustang, a thundering drag racer, or a deceptively nimble sporty car. Transmission choices comprised automatic, four-speeds, three-speeds, and overdrive. Handling packages, power steering, disc brakes, air conditioning, tachometers, and clocks were available. A Mustang could be ordered with bench seats instead of the standard buckets, though very few were. For $170, the GT package offered a pleasant assortment of goodies including front-disc brakes, full instrumentation, driving lights, and special identification. A wide variety of interiors was available, along with accent stripes and special moldings for the exterior. Though the entry-level Mustang cost as little as $2372, it wasn't hard to spend $4000-$4500 on one, and that, of course, was when it really made money.

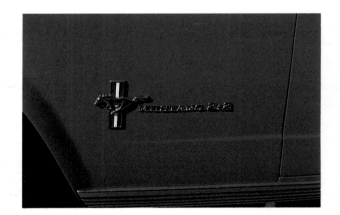

Mustang galloped into the marketplace in mid-1964, and sold over 680,000 copies its first year out. Much of its appeal was due to the fact that it could be tailored to the individual buyer, with numerous performance and luxury options and engines ranging from a thrifty 170-cid six to a powerful 271-bhp 289 V-8. Three body styles were offered: coupe (opposite page, top), convertible (opposite page, bottom), and 2+2 fastback (this page).

Mustang's look was the work of Joe Oros, David Ash, and Gale Halderman of the Ford Division styling studio. The long-hood/short-deck close-coupled appearance was not new—Studebaker had really invented it with the Loewy coupes and Hawks of the '50s—but Mustang exploited it wonderfully well, and it fascinated both the public and the industry well into the early 1970s. For many of those years, it was the basic formula for what soon became known—in honor of Iacocca's brainchild—as the "ponycar."

The styling was so good, in fact, that it was hardly changed at all during the first few years. The 1966s can most easily be distinguished from the '65s by their thin horizontal grille bars replacing the previous year's single thick bar behind the famous galloping horse emblem. The '66 also has small windsplits added to the dummy air scoop on the rear fenders. Inside, the cheap-looking Falcon-based standard instrument panel was replaced by the five-gauge arrangement formerly used in the GT package.

Well before 1966, the smaller Ford 170-cid six and 260 V-8 were dropped from the engine lineup. Six-cylinder models were upgraded from 13- to 14-inch wheels, and engine mounts on all cars were revised to reduce vibration. These two years were also the only time when Mustangs were *not* available with hairy, big-block engines. Still, the small-block 289 was a superb powerplant, offering outputs from the base 200 bhp up to 271, in which guise it was potent indeed. The 289 small-block was a classic design—light, efficient, and powerful. Advanced, thin-wall casting techniques made it the lightest cast-iron V-8 on the market. It featured short-stroke design, full-length water jackets, wedge-shaped combustion chambers, hydraulic lifters, automatic choke, and centrifugal vacuum advance distributor. The High Performance 271 developed .95 bhp per cubic inch and offered 312 pounds/feet of torque at 3400 rpm. Mounted in the light Mustang body, it was more than adequate motivation for this monumental automobile.

Both pages: Mustangs continued virtually unchanged for 1966, though grilles carried a slightly different design, and instrument panels adopted round gauges previously used only in GT editions.

SPECIFICATIONS

Engines:	ohv I-6, 170 cid (3.50 x 2.94), 101 bhp; 200 cid (3.68 x 3.13), 120 bhp; ohv V-8, 260 cid (3.80 x 2.87), 164 bhp; 289 cid (4.00 x 2.87), 200/225/271 bhp
Transmissions:	3-speed manual; 4-speed manual, 3-speed Cruise-O-Matic automatic optional
Suspension front:	lower A-arm, coil springs, stabilizing struts
Suspension rear:	live axle, leaf springs
Brakes:	front/rear drums; front discs optional
Wheelbase (in.)	108.0
Weight (lbs):	2488-2789
Top speed (mph)	V-8: 110-123
0-60 mph (sec):	V-8: 7.6-9.0

Production: 1965 cpe 501,965 **fstbk** 77,079 **cvt** 101,945
1966 cpe 499,751 **fstbk** 35,698 **cvt** 72,119

1966-67
Ford Fairlane
500XL/GT & GT/A

In the eyes of many a car buyer, sportiness and Fairlane hadn't been synonymous terms. Not everyone seized on the fact that Ford's sizzling 271-bhp rendition of the 289-cid V-8 first went under Fairlane hoods. Fewer yet were aware of Fairlane-based Thunderbolt exploits in '64.

An alluring array of handling and performance options soon slipped into the selection sheets, though most shoppers still saw Fairlanes as sensible family transportation. A Fairlane sedan was more attractive than some, mannerly on the road—but basically an oversize Falcon.

Perceptions changed for 1966 with the appearance of the stylish 500XL and the performance-oriented GT. Each boosted Fairlane's image as a car worthy of notice.

Mid-size Fords earned a new body that year, keeping the former 116-inch wheelbase. The boxy profile was history. Clean, freshly sculpted lines and a minimum of trim gave Fairlanes a sleek, well-tailored look, highlighted by curved side glass. Protruding stacked quad headlights injected a leaping-forward attitude, with tall vertical rectangular taillights, upswept quarter panels, and low-profile 14-inch tires adding to the illusion of speed. Two-door hardtops displayed a sweeping semi-fastback roofline.

Topping the line, the 500XL hardtop coupe and convertible gave occupants buckets alongside a console, plus bucket-style rear seats. Four powerplant choices ranged from a basic 120-bhp six to a pair of big-block 390 V-8s. Most stuck to the middle ground: a 289-cid V-8 with 200 capable horsepower. For a few dollars more, XLs could be dolled up with a vinyl roof, accent striping, and wood-tone steering wheel.

Racier yet, the GT took a Thunderbird Special hop-up of the 390 as standard equipment, its 335 bhp promising to "twist the tail of *any* tiger." In addition to such internal goodies as a high-lift cam and big Holley four-barrel carb, the 390 was dressed in chrome. GTs wore bold triple racing stripes (low on the body), nonfunctional hood vents that displayed engine displacement, a rear-deck emblem, and special black-out crossbar-style grille.

A three-speed gearbox was standard, but many opted for a four-speed at $183, or SportShift Cruise-O-Matic at $215. Selecting automatic transformed a GT into a GT/A, yet this transmission still allowed manual shifting through the gears. A tachometer cost extra.

Tightened handling was part of the Gran Touring theme, so stiffer springs and a thicker front stabilizer were installed. Firestone 7.75×14 whitewalls were rated for 125 mph. Optional cast steel wheels cost $93.

This was the first year for a Fairlane convertible. In GT trim, it listed for $3068 ($225 more than the hardtop), with power top optional. Although popular on their own, XL and GT editions amounted to one-fifth of total Fairlane output.

Engine selections shifted for 1967, as GTs adopted a standard small-block Challenger 289-cid V-8. This time, a two-barrel 390 added $74 to the price; the four-barrel, $150. Ford's top big-block lost 15 bhp due to installation of a Thermactor emissions system.

Body changes were minimal. The GT's black-out grille was now a single eight-segment aluminum unit, and backup lights split the taillights into two sections. Decorative hood "power domes" contained integral turn-signal indicators. On the mechanical side, power front-disc brakes were GT standards, as were F70×14 Wide-Oval tires. Shiftable automatics adopted the SelectShift name, with a T-bar lever on the console.

Interior changes included a new padded steering wheel hub and windshield pillars, plus a lane-change position on the turn-signal lever. Accent paint striping was available in black, red, or white; optional hardtop vinyl roofs came in black or white. Standard on the XL, a console cost extra inside a GT. Music lovers could get a Stereo-Sonic tape system using 70-minute cartridges.

All well and good, but could big-block Fairlanes move out as promised? *Motor Trend* provided the answer to that question when their early 335-bhp GT/A shot to 60 in a mere 6.8 seconds, and ran the quarter in 15.2 (reaching 92 mph).

Yet several dozen impatient types, dissatisfied with the 390's potential, managed to acquire a Fairlane with the famed "side oiler" 427-cid V-8, which promised an eye-opening 410 or 425 horsepower. Strangely, this engine was only offered in base, 500, and 500XL models, not the GT. But even without the muscle of a 427, Fairlane GTs helped establish Ford's role in the burgeoning "supercar" race of the late 1960s, quickly evolving into the Torino and Cobra.

Ford's mid-size Fairlane received new styling and more power for 1966, the latter taking the form of a 390-cid V-8 with up to 335 bhp, which was the standard engine for the GT and GT/A (above and opposite page, top). The '67s were nearly identical, though GTs and GT/As now came standard with a 289-cid V-8, which is the engine fitted to this '67 500XL (opposite page, bottom).

SPECIFICATIONS

Engines:	**1966 500XL** ohv I-6, 200 cid (3.68 × 3.13), 120 bhp; ohv V-8, 289 cid (4.00 × 2.87), 200 bhp; 390 cid (4.05 × 3.78), 265/275/315 bhp **1966 GT & GT/A** 390 cid, 335 bhp **1967 500XL** 200 cid, 120 bhp; 289 cid, 200 bhp; 390 cid, 270/315 bhp **1967 GT & GT/A** 289 cid, 200 bhp; 390 cid, 270/320 bhp
Transmissions:	3-speed manual; optional 4-speed manual and 3-speed Cruise-O-Matic
Suspension, front:	upper A-arms, strut-stabilized lower arms, coil springs (anti-sway bar on GT & GT/A, and all 1967 models)
Suspension, rear:	live axle, leaf springs
Brakes:	front/rear drums (front discs optional on 1966 GT, standard on 1967 GT)
Wheelbase (in.):	116.0
Weight (lbs.):	2955-3607
Top speed (mph):	**V8-289** 108 **GT/A 390** 125
0-60 mph (sec):	**V8-289** 10.6 **GT/A 390** 6.8-8.1

Production: 1966 XL htp cpe 23,942 **XL cvt** 4560 **GT htp cpe** 33,015 **GT cvt** 4327 **1967 XL htp cpe** 14,871 **XL cvt** 1943 **GT htp cpe** 18,670 **GT cvt** 2117

FORD

1967-68
Ford Mustang

With Chevrolet's Camaro and Pontiac's Firebird in the running, and Plymouth's Barracuda redesigned, the Mustang faced tougher competition in 1967. One way Ford met it was with the biggest engine in town, the Thunderbird 390, optional for the first time on Mustangs. This was 40 more cubes than the largest expected Camaro engine—though Chevrolet soon brought forth the competitive Camaro 396. The Mustang 390, with its 320 bhp, would do 0-60 in 7.5 seconds, the standing quarter mile in 15.5 seconds at 95 mph, and had a top speed close to 120 mph. But with nearly 60 percent of its weight over the front wheels, it understeered with merry abandon. Standard F70×14 Firestone Wide-Oval tires helped reduce the understeer somewhat, but almost anybody who drove a 390 said the 289 Mustang was a far-better-handling car. Experts recommended that customers ordering 390s get the competition handling package: stiffer springs and front stabilizer bar, Koni shocks, limited-slip differential, quick steering, and 15-inch wheels. Also offered on High Performance 289s, this option improved handling at the expense of ride.

Besides the new engine option, many other features were added to the 1967 Mustang. All models were restyled from the beltline down. Fastbacks received a sweeping new roofline which blended cleanly into the rear deck and lost the angular look of 1965-66. Tail panels were now concave, the front end was longer, and the grille was wider. Engineers also paid attention to noise and vibration complaints by using rubber bushings at suspension attachment points. A two-inch wider track, though adopted mainly to make room for the 390 engine, provided important gains in roadability.

Against their competition, the 1967 Mustangs compared quite favorably. Mustangs were generally lighter and more economical on fuel than the major rivals, and offered a wider selection of V-8 engines. But competition hurt, and sales for the model year were down about 25 percent from 1966. Much of the loss was suffered by the best-selling hardtop. The convertible and fastback seemed to have a more or less permanent market, and the latter's slick new styling gave it 70,000 customers in 1967. Overall, at 472,121 sales, Ford could hardly be anything but pleased: after all, the

*Though still based on the original Mustang body, the '67s
(opposite page, top) boasted different front and rear styling,
which was carried over to '68 (above) with very few changes.
Opposite page, middle and bottom: Coupes maintained the
previous model's squared-off roofline, but fastbacks (1968s shown)
received a more gradually sloping roof that helped double sales of
that version.*

SPECIFICATIONS

Engines:	ohv I-6, 200 cid (3.68 × 3.13), 120 bhp; ohv V-8, 289 cid (4.00 × 2.87), 200/225/271 bhp; 302 cid (4.00 × 3.00), 230 bhp; 2390 cid (4.05 × 3.78), 320/325 bhp; 427 cid (4.23 × 3.78), 390 bhp
Transmissions:	3-speed manual; 4-speed manual, 3-speed Cruise-O-Matic automatic optional
Suspension front:	lower A-arm, coil springs, stabilizing struts
Suspension rear:	live axle, leaf springs
Brakes:	front/rear drums; front discs optional
Wheelbase (in.):	108.0
Weight (lbs):	2568-2745
Top speed (mph):	approx. 120
0-60 mph (sec):	7.5 (390 cid)

Production: 1967 cpe 356,271 **fstbk** 71,042 **cvt** 44,808
1968 cpe 249,447 **fstbk** 42,581 **cvt** 25,376

Mustang was now in its third year and still pretty much unchanged from the original.

Ford probably waited one year too long, because sales took a nosedive in 1968. On paper the losses were difficult to explain: car sales were up overall, including Ford Division. And the '68s offered the widest selection of engines and options to date. The answer was continued competition from GM and Chrysler, joined now by the American Motors Javelin, and a rise in Mustang prices. There was also competition from other Ford products: the Mercury Cougar of course, but also the Ford Torino, an intermediate fastback that rivaled Mustang's version of that body style. Furthermore, the number of American troops in Viet Nam had peaked, and this was putting a severe crimp into the Mustang's youthful market.

Since a facelift had been performed in 1967, the '68s were little changed. New rear quarter panels had the trademark simulated air scoops just ahead of the rear wheels, but these were integrated with the side sculpture for the first time. Creaselines ran back from the upper front fender around the fender scoop and forward again into the lower part of the door. On GT models the sculpting was accented with tape striping, which gave the cars a look of forward motion. The grille was deeply inset, with an inner bright ring around the galloping horse emblem. On GTs, driving lamps were contained within the grille opening.

Some engines were detuned to meet new federal emission standards, but the change was thus far insignificant. The middle performance engine was now the 302, a considerably altered small-block producing 230 bhp. As before, it was a tractable, economical compromise between the basic V-8 and the high performance engines, adding only about $200 to the cost of the car. The top engine in 1968 (at a whopping $755 extra) was the huge 427 with 10.9:1 compression and 390 bhp, and curiously available only with automatic. While 427s could leap to 60 in six seconds, they were skittish beasts to drive, and mostly purchased by racers.

At over 300,000 units for 1968, Mustang sales were fine by any other standard than Mustang's. But the heady pace of 1965 could hardly be sustained once the initial market was satisfied, and 300,000 units of anything is still pretty good news to a Detroit manufacturer. By now, too, the Mustang was firmly enshrined in the hearts of Americans, and judging by the numbers held by collectors today, perceptions are still overwhelmingly positive.

1967-69
Ford Thunderbird

Thunderbird fortunes for 1967-69 rested on a new fifth generation design that departed abruptly from past practices. Gone was the convertible; arrived was a four-door sedan, which sold much better, but was somehow not in the expected T-Bird image. Gone were styling hallmarks like fender skirts and quarter vents. Size was up—wheelbases were 115 to 117 inches. Most prices, remarkably, stayed below $5000 base.

This was the most changed Thunderbird since 1958—a compromise, as longtime T-Bird stylist Bill Boyer said, between David Ash's Corporate Projects Studio and his own Thunderbird Studio. "My studio essentially did the roof, backlight, and rear half of this car. Dave was responsible for the front end. The rear end of Dave's car was a strong wedge shape, the first real attempt to do a wedge. But that ultimately got watered down, and we had a hybrid." Ash's Ferrari-like front end, with its hidden headlamps and full-width grille supported by a strong, thin-section bumper, was an impressive frontispiece. The headlights were mounted on the back of dummy grille panels that rotated into place when turned on. The 1967-69 Thunderbirds were the first examples of the marque to offer this feature.

"The four-door just sort of happened," Bill Boyer continued. "In the studio we did a rendering in black cherry with a black vinyl roof, a four-door with center-opening doors and a 'sail' on the rear door where it hinged to the body. [Ford general manager] Iacocca saw that and just about flipped. 'Let's get that four-door nailed down,' he said. "The four-door Landau was a very difficult car to handle. The door opening just followed the landau bar down, but to retain the theme of formality we needed to hold on to the formal roofline. It did quite well in sales." (The four-door accounted for 25,000 units in its first year, about twice as many as any convertible model.)

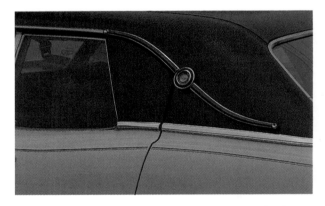

The most significant conceptual change on these Thunderbirds was the switch back to separate body and frame construction, dictated by cost and a desire to reduce the price of bodywork. Rigidity lost by dropping the unit body was replaced by stiffening ribs, sheetmetal crossmembers, and a full-length tunnel stamped into the floor pan. All 14 body mounts were located ahead of or behind the passenger compartment, to reduce noise and vibration within.

For 1967, the 'Bird continued to offer the 390 V-8 as standard and the 428 as an option. A new twist was SelectShift Cruise-O-Matic, which had a selector pattern that encouraged holding the lower gears like a manual shift—but mounted in the wrong place; on the steering column. A throwback to 1958 was the '67's new coil spring rear suspension with trailing arms, designed to improve the very supple Thunderbird ride.

Not only were Thunderbirds restyled for 1967, but a new four-door joined the line to replace the slow-selling convertible—one more indication that the T-Bird was leaning more and more towards the luxury market. A 390-cid V-8 with 315 bhp (opposite page, top) was standard in '67 and '68, but a 360-bhp 429 became the standard (and only) engine in '69. The 1968 four-door model shown was representative of the series, as few styling alterations were made to these 'Birds.

SPECIFICATIONS

Engines:	all ohv V-8; 390 cid (4.00 × 3.78), 315 bhp; 428 cid (4.13 × 3.98), 345 bhp; 429 cid (4.36 × 3.59), 360 bhp
Transmission:	3-speed Cruise-O-Matic automatic
Suspension front:	upper and lower A-arms, coil springs
Suspension rear:	live axle, trailing arms, coil springs
Brakes:	front disc/rear drum
Wheelbase (in.):	2d 114.7 4d 117.2
Weight (lbs):	4248-4460
Top speed (mph):	115-120
0-60 mph (sec):	9.0-10.5

Production: 1967 cpe 15,567 **Landau cpe** 37,422 **Landau sdn** 24,967 **1968 cpe** 9977 **Landau cpe** 33,029 **Landau sdn** 21,925 **1969 cpe** 5913 **Landau cpe** 27,664 **Landau sdn** 15,695

For 1968 Ford Division advertised "Thunder for sale: 2 doors or 4." Aiming for higher sales through greater seating capacity, they made the bench front seat standard and listed six separate models: hardtop, and two- and four-door Landaus, all with either bench or bucket seats. Buckets outsold benches on the two-door models but benches were the rule on four-doors. Federal requirements now meant the '68s had front side-marker lights and rear side-reflectors, squeeze-type interior door handles, and an energy absorbing steering column. Styling changes were minor—a larger mesh grille, narrow body-sill moldings, and a change in badging. Standard engine was still the 390, but a new 429 with 360 bhp was optional. This big-block had been designed with the government's new emission standards in mind.

Sales in 1968 were well off 1967's pace, and sales for 1969 were the worst since 1958. The Thunderbird, many said, was becoming too generalized, too much like every other car on the road, and it lost its market leadership in the personal-car field to the Pontiac Grand Prix and Buick Riviera. The Grand Prix had been outsold 2-to-1 by Thunderbird in 1968, but in 1969 it better than reversed this performance; it cost $1000 less and perhaps was not in the same class, but even the archrival Buick Riviera outsold the T-Bird in 1969, and that was unheard of.

On 1969 Landaus, Ford closed in the rear roof quarters, creating one of the all-time great blind spots. Among other 1969 changes were mag-type wheel covers and a new grille composed of small horizontal louvers. The most interesting new option (Landaus only) was an electric all-metal sunroof, controlled by a small dashboard button. Inside was the familiar dashboard of 1967-68. A posh interior option was "Brougham" cloth and vinyl upholstery.

Handling was vastly improved on two-door models through changes in suspension settings. Yet with its great weight (4500 pounds) and sound deadening, the two-door Landau continued to provide a comfortable, quiet ride. The sole engine offered in 1969 was the 429 V-8, probably influenced by Buick's 430, whose performance the T-Bird matched. But there were many rivals in the personal-luxury field Thunderbird had invented, and Ford's top car would face tough sledding in the '70s.

1968-69
Ford Torino GT

The name was new, but beneath the surface the Torinos of '68 were basically updates of the Fairlane 500XL—with one big exception: the dramatic Torino GT fastback with its l-o-n-g sloping roof and severely slanted back window. Ford soon named this striking shape SportsRoof, which delivered a far different feeling—and stronger identity—than the ordinary notchback hardtop. Yet Ford was a little late entering the full-fastback foray; Dodge's comparably profiled Charger was already two years old, and even that was occasionally mocked as a copy of the Rambler Marlin.

Torinos were part of the Fairlane series, serving as the plushest of the mid-size models. This year's restyling produced a stronger tie to big Fords, highlighted by a five-inch-longer greenhouse. Despite the dramatic look of the SportsRoof, the long-hood, short-deck notchback silhouette was quickly gaining converts throughout the industry.

Ventless side glass didn't please everyone, but admittedly cleaned up the side view. Torinos wore rectangular matte-gray grilles, dramatically set back from the fender tips. GT touches included tapered accent striping and styled steel wheels, which held Wide-Oval whitewalls. Deep-pleated bucket seats and a console cost extra.

Fastbacks wore a series of five short trim strips on the vast C-pillar, just to the rear of the upswept-curved window. A tinted backlight was standard. A mesh-patterned grille sat behind a floating center bar with "GT" emblem. Rectangular taillights resided in a scooped-out deck panel, with round GT insignia at the center of a slim chrome strip.

Base Torino engine was a 115-bhp six. The trio of GTs—notchback hardtop, fastback, and convertible—started with a new 210-bhp, 302-cid V-8 (though Ford's early catalog claimed the old 289 as standard power). Foremost among the step-ups was the 390 V-8, offered in 265- and 325-bhp flavors with either two- or four-barrel carburetion. Dubbed "Thunderbird Special GT," the latter ran with 10.5:1 compression and included dual exhausts, adding $158 to the price.

Torino nameplate was affixed to dressy versions of the Fairlane starting in 1968, and performance versions added the GT moniker. Though also available in notchback coupe and convertible body styles, the new SportsRoof fastback drew more attention (opposite page, top). Also in '68, a Torino was chosen to pace the Indy "500" (opposite page, lower left). The '69s were little changed in appearance (below and opposite page, lower right), though GTs gained a hood scoop that was functional when the Ram-Air option was ordered.

SPECIFICATIONS

Engines:	all ohv V-8: **1968** 302 cid (4.00 × 3.00), 210/230 bhp; 390 cid (4.05 × 3.78), 265/325 bhp; 427 cid (4.23 × 3.78), 390 bhp; 428 cid (4.13 × 3.98), 335 bhp **1969** 302 cid, 220 bhp; 351 cid (4.00 × 3.50), 250/290 bhp; 390 cid, 320 bhp; 428 cid, 335 bhp
Transmissions:	3-speed manual; 4-speed manual and 3-speed SelectShift Cruise-O-Matic optional
Suspension, front:	upper arms, strut-stabilized lower arms, coil springs
Suspension, rear:	live axle, leaf springs
Brakes:	front/rear drums (front discs optional)
Wheelbase (in.):	116.0
Weight (lbs.):	3173-3356
Top speed (mph):	V8-302 109 V8-390 115+
0-60 mph (sec):	V8-390 7.2 V8-428 6.0

Production: **1968** htp cpe 23,939 fstbk cpe 74,135 cvt 5310 **1969** htp cpe 17,951 fstbk cpe 61,319 cvt 2552

An all-synchro three-speed still was standard (heavy-duty version extra), but the optional floor-shift four-speed and SelectShift Cruise-O-Matic tempted plenty of shoppers. When a console was ordered, automatics came with a T-bar shift lever.

Ah, but those twin big-block 390s were just the beginning. Ford had an even better idea: nothing less than a bigger-block 427, churning up 390 horsepower, described by *Car and Driver* as the "racing-bred engine." Not exactly bargain-basement at $623, this was a streetable version of the mill that had endured Le Mans and Grand National races. At midyear, yet another high-performance choice entered the roster: the new Cobra Jet 428, offering 335 bhp for a more modest ($306) charge.

A Torino GT fastback listed for $2747, just $37 more than an ordinary Torino hardtop. Only the convertible edged over the $3000 mark, though checking a few of those tempting options could shoot the total a lot higher. A new SelectAire air conditioner was available for comfort; a 6000-rpm tachometer on the dashboard and front-disc brakes for performance.

"Born to move, wheel, swing, streak, impress, dazzle. . . ." The Fairlane/Torino sales catalog promised that much and more for 1969, including a "sizzling" Ram-Air option for the big 428-cid V-8 that was "not for the timid soul."

Standard engine again was the 302, with twin "Windsor" 351s rounding out the selection. Wide-tread belted tires on competition-styled steel wheels and special bodyside striping marked the GT, which included a bigger clutch and competition suspension when equipped with the 428. Whether fed by Ram-Air or the ordinary induction system, the 390 put out an advertised 335 horsepower and could blast a GT to 60 in close to six seconds. The top 428 cost an extra $421 and demanded either a four-speed or automatic.

Torino appearance didn't change much for '69. GTs had a hood scoop as well as a unique plastic grille with a horizontal bar ahead of a tight mesh pattern, above the "GT" badge. This year's SportsRoof fastback wore a tapering C stripe along the sides. Color-keyed racing mirrors and exhaust extensions were optional.

Regular Torinos had a new 250-cid six, but in these heady years of American muscle, that wasn't headline news. Although sales slipped in 1969, Torino GTs still found plenty of avid customers, especially in fastback form. It's a safe bet that most of them turned to Torino for a chance to hit the pedal now and again, lured into the showroom by the promise of 390- or 428-cid exhilaration.

1969
Ford Mustang Grande
& Mach 1

Mach 1 package debuting for 1969 would run through 1978, though later models lost the original's performance edge. Standard engine was a 351 (above) with 250 or an optional 290 bhp; also on the option list was the Cobra-Jet 428 with 335 bhp (this page, bottom), which could be ordered with a functional "shaker" hood scoop. Grande version of the Mustang (below and opposite page) was aimed at the luxury end of the market, yet could be ordered with anything from a 200-cid six to the 428 Cobra-Jet.

Not only did Ford's popular "ponycar" get a major restyling in 1969, it added a selection of memorable models: five in all, plus a pair of "Bosses" later on. Throw in the selection of seven engines, and Mustang offered enough choices to satisfy every styling and performance appetite.

In just about every dimension, the revamped Mustang looked a little plumper, a mite exaggerated. Quad headlights continued to define its personality, with the outer pair positioned in a recessed niche—far removed from mates within the grille opening. Windows lost their vent glass. Even dashboards were more dramatic.

Not everyone agreed that each change followed the correct course. Back panels stuck closest to the original Mustang theme, albeit with flattened tri-section lenses. Otherwise, the car's proportions seemed a bit distorted, due largely to the expanded overhang out front.

Nevertheless, the year brought new monikers destined to enter the performance-car lexicon. The Mach 1, billed as the "wild newcomer," borrowed its name from a futuristic 1967 show car, the designation signifying the speed of sound (about 750 mph). With a handle like that, a car just had to travel with virtual supersonic haste—which it did, at least when the available Cobra Jet 428-cid V-8 lay under the hood.

Motor Trend proved as much when their testers flashed an early Mach 1 with 335-bhp Cobra Jet to 60 in just 5.7 seconds, completing the quarter-mile in 14.3 seconds at a flat 100 mph. This, by the way, was accomplished with a three-speed automatic, the Mach 1 taking advantage of the 428's prodigious 440 pounds/feet of torque.

Not wholly impressed, the magazine complained that the "sum is far short of its parts" and performance didn't match the car's unabashedly aggressive demeanor. Gripes aside, they ranked this Mustang the "toughest one yet."

Available with or without Ram-Air, the Cobra Jet was one of five Mach 1 engines on the selection sheet. Choose Ram-Air, and a "shaker" hood scoop replaced the customary simulated opening. Base engine was Ford's "zesty" 351-cid

V-8, with two- or four-barrel carburetion, and in between: a 390-cid engine. All but the 351 displayed quad-tipped dual exhausts. Big-blocks came with a four-speed or available SelectShift Cruise-O-Matic. Oddly, a tachometer cost extra.

Mach 1's long fastback profile rolled past tiny swing-out quarter windows, ending with a gracefully curved integral spoiler. Dual reflective stripes decorated the spoiler and quarter-panel extension; two-tone striping adorned bodysides. Other differences from the garden-variety SportsRoof fastback included a special grille, black honeycomb rear applique, and a racy dome airscoop atop the hood's matte-black center section. Neither fastback retained Mustang's former pillar-mounted air extractor.

Every Mach 1 carried GT-style equipment including E70 Wide-Oval belted whitewalls on styled chrome wheels, competition springs and shocks, and quick-fill gas cap. Racing mirrors faced both the driver and passenger. High-back buckets were trimmed in vinyl, and the driver handled a three-spoke wood-rimmed steering wheel. Teak woodtone decorated both the dash and the door panels. Low-gloss hood/cowl paint eased eyestrain when the going got tough, and pin-type latches held down the hood.

Grande was a Mustang of far different hue, aimed at another target. Focused more on luxuriant ride than hot motion, the Grande could have any Mustang engine, starting with the 200- or 250-cid six, on up through any of half a dozen V-8s (all the way to the Cobra Jet). Decorated by narrow two-tone stripes, racing mirrors, and wire-style wheel covers, Grandes had a manual three-speed or optional SelectShift, with T-bar gearshift lever. Black and white vinyl roofs were available. Passengers reveled in knitted vinyl and hopsack cloth bucket seats, while vinyl-trimmed door panels wore teaktoned accent appliques. Woodtone also highlighted the dashboard. More than twice the usual amount of insulation helped soak up noise and vibrations.

A Mach 1 sold for $3139, while $2866 bought a six-cylinder Grande—this at a time when the base Mustang went for $2635. Ford ads promoted the fact that a modified Mach 1 held 295 USAC land speed records, achieved on the salt flats of Bonneville.

Despite the popularity of the Mach 1 and Grande, total Mustang output (not including Boss versions) slumped to 299,870 for 1969, down from 317,404 the year before and close to twice that total in 1966. Yet without the additional selection, the year might have ended at an even lower point.

Though the Mach 1 and Grande nameplates lasted through the early 1970s, they had a hard time capturing as many customers as in their opening season. However, this was due more to the changing marketplace than to any deficiencies in the cars themselves, for these are prime examples of what Detroit could accomplish when its imagination was given free rein.

SPECIFICATIONS

Engines:	**Grande** ohv I-6, 200 cid (3.68 × 3.13), 115 bhp; 250 cid (3.68 × 3.91), 155 bhp; ohv V-8, 302 cid (4.00 × 3.00), 220 bhp; 351 cid (4.00 × 3.50), 250/290 bhp; 390 cid (4.05 × 3.78), 320 bhp **Mach 1** ohv V-8, 351 cid, 250/290 bhp; 390 cid, 320 bhp; 428 cid (4.13 × 3.98), 335 bhp
Transmissions:	3-speed manual; 4-speed manual and 3-speed SelectShift Cruise-O-Matic optional
Suspension, front:	upper arms, strut-stabilized lower arms, coil springs, link-type stabilizer
Suspension, rear:	live axle, variable-rate leaf springs
Brakes:	front/rear drums (front discs optional)
Wheelbase (in.):	108.0
Weight (lbs.):	2873-3175
Top speed (mph):	**Mach 1** 115
0-60 mph (sec):	**Grande V8-351** 8.0 **Mach 1 V8-428** 5.5-5.7
Production:	**Grande** 22,182 **Mach 1** 72,458

Note: A small number of Mach 1 Mustangs were special-ordered with a 427-cid engine.

173

1969 Ford Mustang Boss 302 & 429

As if five all-new Mustangs weren't enough when the 1969 model year began, Ford had two additional ideas in mind. The twin "Bosses," each introduced later, proved to be some of the most remarkable Mustangs of the "ponycar's" entire life span.

Had Henry Ford II not hired Semon E. "Bunkie" Knudsen away from General Motors early in 1968, to become company president, the whole "Boss" episode might never have occurred. Knudsen felt that a super-hot small-block soon would be needed to compete against Chevrolet's Camaro Z-28. A street version of the racing Mustang that had torn up Trans-Am courses sounded like just the ticket.

Besides that, Ford had come up with a 429-cid V-8 that it needed to homologate for NASCAR competition. Now wouldn't *that* make a nice trophy under a few hundred roadgoing Mustang hoods? Two cars—two engines—two different personalities.

In addition to his contribution toward this year's new SportsRoof fastback body, stylist Larry Shinoda—hired by Ford along with Knudsen—earns credit for the "Boss" name. The big Boss came first, in mid-January, wearing a monstrous Ram-Air hood scoop and front spoiler, with chubby F60×15 Goodyear Polyglas tires pounding the pavement. Kin to the 429-cid V-8 aimed at NASCAR, the "semi-hemi" engine was built for toughness, with four-bolt mains and a forged steel crankshaft. A 735-cfm Holley four-barrel straddled the high-riser manifold. Cylinder heads were aluminum, with cast magnesium covers.

Some early engines had hydraulic lifters, until solid tappets became standard. Even Ford admitted that the 375-bhp official rating was understated. Torque output was listed at 450 pounds/feet. Whatever the actual figures, a Boss 429 could accelerate to 60 mph in as little as 5.3 seconds (or as slowly as 7.2), running the quarter in just over 14 and hitting 102 mph.

This page: *Like some other high-performance Fords of the day, the Boss 302 engine was accused of producing more than its rated 290 bhp—which it almost certainly did. Handling was exemplary for the day, something that couldn't be said about its big brother, the Boss 429 (opposite page), which carried a heavy big-block engine under the hood. Huge 429 required sheetmetal and suspension alterations to make it fit, and the added heft made the Boss 429 rather front-heavy.*

SPECIFICATIONS

Engines:	ohv V-8 **Boss 302** 302 cid (4.00 × 3.00), 290 bhp **Boss 429** 429 cid (4.36 × 3.59), 360/375 bhp
Transmission:	4-speed manual
Suspension, front:	upper arms, strut-stabilized lower arms, coil springs, anti-sway bar
Suspension, rear:	live axle, leaf springs, anti-sway bar (429)
Brakes:	front discs/rear drums
Wheelbase (in.):	108.0
Weight (lbs.):	3210+
Top speed (mph):	**Boss 302** 118-133 **Boss 429** 115-130+
0-60 mph (sec):	**Boss 302** 6.5-8.1 **Boss 429** 5.3-7.2
Production:	**Boss 302** 1934 **Boss 429** 858

Note: Some sources claim Boss 429 production was only 852 units in 1969.

Extensive metalwork was required to squeeze in the bulky 429. Kar Kraft of Brighton, Michigan, did the custom work, which included widening spring towers, installing shorter upper control arms, and lowering the suspension. Staggered shocks and a "clamp-on" stabilizer bar were installed at the rear. Eschewing flashiness, Boss 429s wore no striping but carried a black spoiler and grille.

Mandatory options (heavy-duty four-speed, 3.91:1 locking axle, manual-disc brakes) jacked up the Boss's $3498 base price by another $1300. No more than 858 went on sale, making it one of the rarest Mustangs of the lot.

Ford built the Boss 302 on its own, without outside help but following a Kar Kraft prototype, sending the result to showrooms in March 1969. *Car and Driver* called it "easily the best Mustang yet . . . the best handling Ford to ever come out of Dearborn." *Road & Track* later described a Boss 302 as "delightfully sporting when driven hard."

Priced at a more modest $3588 (nearly $1000 higher than a base Mustang), the Boss 302 wore a deeper front "chin" spoiler than its big-block counterpart and could be ordered with an adjustable wing rear spoiler for $19. High-back bucket seats added $84. Distinctive rear-window louvers ($128), hinged at the top, helped give the smaller Boss a look all its own.

Despite the advertised figure of 290 horsepower, the 302-cid small-block V-8 undoubtedly delivered a whole lot more. Estimates ranged as high as 400 bhp. Running on 10.5:1 compression, the engine carried Cleveland heads and 2.23-inch intake valves, an aluminum high-riser manifold with 780-cfm Holley four-barrel carburetor, and aluminum rocker covers. Low-restriction headers fed large-diameter dual exhausts.

Ford's wide-ratio four-speed went into early 302s, with a high-capacity 10.4-inch clutch—eventually augmented by a Hurst shifter. Suspension tweaks included stiffer springs and staggered rear shocks. Specially flared wheel openings were needed to accommodate the fat Goodyear F60×15 Polyglas rubber, which rode seven-inch Magnum 500 wheels. The "Daytona" rear axle incorporated a standard 3.50:1 ratio, but could also get a 3.91:1 or 4.30:1 cog.

Matte black paint highlighted the hood, rear deck, and outer headlight area. Bodyside striping included a "Boss 302" designation on the leading edge.

Although the factory claimed a 0-60 time of 6.0 seconds, actual Boss 302 tests proved a mite slower: 6.5 seconds and up. Quarter-mile times went into the mid-14s, with speeds in the upper 90s. Only 1934 were built in 1969.

Both Bosses continued into 1970, when 6318 Boss 302s and about 498 of the 429s were produced. The 302 was billed as "Son of Trans-Am," even though—as fortune dictated—Chevrolet's Camaro had emerged victoricus in Trans-Am racing.

1969
Ford Cobra &
Talladega

One for the street . . . one for the street by way of the track. That's one way to describe and differentiate the two special Fairlane/Torino-based coupes that blasted onto the Ford scene for 1969, enjoying a brief but inspiring stay.

Cobra was Ford's budget-price, minimal-trim supercar, named for Carroll Shelby's Ford-powered sports cars. Produced in SportsRoof (fastback) and notchback body styles, Cobras all carried a 428-cid V-8, "conservatively" rated at 335 bhp (according to Ford), first used in the Mercury Cyclone.

Ram-Air induction, at $133 extra, consisted of a fiberglass hood scoop with special air cleaner assembly. At nearly full throttle, cold air stormed directly into the carburetor's throat, bypassing the filter element. With that brand of power, Ford insisted, a "Cobra Jet belts out enough torque to leave two black lines right to the horizon."

Standard fittings included a four-speed manual gearbox, Wide-Oval F70×14 tires, black grille, and exposed competition-style hood tie-down pins. A beefed-up suspension consisting of stiffened springs, large-diameter front stabilizer bar, and high-damping shocks was aimed at providing minimum body roll and maximum directional stability.

Cobra's long fastback profile, with upswept quarter windows and severely slanted backlight, was accented by three trim strips at the vast rear pillar. Split square taillamps brought up the rear, with dual exhausts exiting below the bumper.

Interiors were no less austere than the bodies, containing a plain bench seat and four-dial dashboard. Priced only a few dollars higher than a Torino Squire station wagon, a Cobra hardtop started at $3164; the fastback, $25 more. Options included power front-disc brakes at $65, a 6000-rpm tachometer for $48, and SelectShift Cruise-O-Matic at $37. Even bucket seats and a console cost extra ($121 and $54, respectively).

"Power to spare, yet well-behaved in city traffic," declared the Ford brochure,

Cobra was offered in fastback or notchback form (opposite page) carrying rather plain trim, but came standard with a 428 Cobra-Jet rated at 335 bhp, making it one of Ford's budget muscle cars. This page: Talladega, with its fastback roofline and grafted-on snout, was aimed at providing an aerodynamic shape for NASCAR racing.

SPECIFICATIONS

Engines:	ohv V-8, 428 cid (4.13 × 3.98), 335 bhp
Transmissions:	**Cobra** 4-speed manual; 3-speed SelectShift Cruise-O-Matic optional **Talladega** SelectShift Cruise-O-Matic
Suspension, front:	short/long arms, coil springs, anti-roll bar
Suspension, rear:	live axle, leaf springs
Brakes:	**Cobra** front/rear drums (front discs optional) **Talladega** front discs/rear drums
Wheelbase (in.):	116.0
Weight (lbs.):	**Cobra** 3354-3525 **Talladega** 3537
Top speed (mph):	125-129
0-60 mph (sec):	5.6-7.3

Production: Cobra htp cpe NA **fstbk htp cpe** NA **Talladega** cpe 754

a Cobra "uncoils for action on command." Maybe so, though one magazine was "disappointed" by a Cobra's 7.2-second 0-60 time, and 15-second (98.3 mph) quarter-mile. However, most thought it the tightest, best built, and quietest running of that year's supercar crop.

Other trials yielded quicker times. *Car and Driver* sent its Cobra to 60 in a mere 5.6 seconds, and cracked the quarter in 14 at 100.6 mph. *Car Life*, on the other hand, took 7.3 seconds to hit 60 mph, and 14.9 for the quarter (topping 95 mph).

Motor Trend hit 60 in 6.3 seconds with a Cobra four-speed, running the quarter in 14.5 (at 100 mph). "When the Ram Air cuts in," they exclaimed, "the car really puts you back in the seat." On the down side, the Cobra's suspension "can be hairy in hard corners" and gas mileage worked out to nine mpg or less.

Ford pushed Cobras "for folks who don't want anyone stepping on their tails." While "great in competition" and "recommended to cure dull driving," a Cobra was nonetheless described as "gentle on a Sunday drive."

Ford's traditional rivalry with Chrysler wasn't limited to battles at the showroom, but extended onto the stock-car ovals. In order to enter NASCAR Grand National races as a "production" vehicle, Ford had to build 500 streetable examples. Thus arose the Talladega (often called Torino Talladega), named for a new speedway in Alabama.

At the start of 1969, Ford closed its Atlanta plant for two weeks to focus on this special model, which started life as a base SportsRoof. Enhanced aerodynamics were the key, led by a streamlined front end and flush-fit grille that stretched the body to 206 inches. Among the many alterations, Ford had to re-roll the rocker panels to develop the lower body needed for racing, which required modification of the front fenders to match. Aero extensions were welded to each front fender, whose leading edges mated with the grille.

Beneath the flat-black hood, NASCAR racers would get a Tunnel-Port 427-cid V-8. Talladegas sold to the general public carried the 428 Cobra Jet mill, with Cruise-O-Matic and a 3.25:1 Traction-Lok axle. Staggered rear shocks were part of the Talladega's competition handling suspension.

Only three colors were sprayed: Royal Maroon, Presidential Blue, and Wimbledon White—with one exception. A single bright yellow preproduction example was built for president Knudsen. Inside was nothing special: a black-upholstered bench seat, ordinary column gearshift, standard instruments.

By the time Ford was finished, 754 street Talladegas had been built, including prototypes. It would not return for a second season, making this "one-year wonder" a rare find today.

1960-63
Imperial

Virgil Exner's heroically finned Imperials of the early '60s were the kind of cars that cause modern stylists to grimace, but every stylist on salary was turning out exactly this type of car back in 1957 when these Imperials began to be designed. They were perfectly valid at that time, and if sales petered out fast it was because the fickle public abandoned its interest in tailfins around 1960—just when all the tailfinned cars designed at the height of the craze were beginning to come off the production lines. Too bad for Imperial!

Chrysler had set up Imperial as a make in its own right in 1955, and it had a tremendous year in 1957 when it displaced Lincoln as number two in the luxury market. But sales tapered off after that, and during the early '60s, 10,000-12,000 units was typical Imperial production. The cars always rode Chrysler's largest standard wheelbase, but unlike its other 1960 products, retained separate body-on-frame construction. This allowed greater insulation between body and frame, necessary in those days to achieve the level of smoothness and silence luxury-car buyers demanded. In 1960, there was but one engine, the wedgehead V-8 as used in 1959, with 350 bhp and 10:1 compression.

Three standard 1960 models were offered: Custom, Crown, and LeBaron, about $600 apart in base price. Custom-built Crown Imperial limousines, which had been around since the days when Imperials were models of Chrysler, were still available on a special 149.5-inch wheelbase. Styling was a 1959 facelift, with a new grille and a "wrapover" bright metal roof panel extending all the way to the windshield.

Comfort was the Imperial's ace feature in 1960. Comfort was indeed *always* the ace feature. The new, high-back driver's seat padded in thick foam rubber, the adjustable spot-air conditioning, the six-way power seat with single rotary knob control, Auto-Pilot cruise control, and automatic headlamp dimmer, all bespoke Imperial's determination not to let the driver do anything a machine or a motor could do for him. Crown upholstery was nylon and vinyl, wool, or leather; wool broadcloth was used for LeBarons.

The 1961s were altered considerably, though they retained the 1960 shell. Fins were now the most blatant ever to appear on an Imperial, and perhaps any other Chrysler product, accompanied by Exner's new styling gimmick: freestanding headlamps pocketed in the curve of the front fenders. At the back were freestanding taillamps, suspended from the towering fins like yo-yos. The idea was to invoke a theme from the Classic era, a practice in which Exner had proved talented and imaginative earlier, but in this case it just seemed weird. The headlamp feature survived through 1963, but the back end became more orthodox during 1962 and 1963. Custom, Crown, and LeBaron models were again offered, but the four-door pillared sedans were eliminated.

Before Exner left Chrysler in 1962, he had planned a new, truncated Imperial for that year, a companion for his downsized 1962 Dodges and Plymouths. This didn't reach production, which was a good thing. The actual 1962 Imperial was an improved version of the '61. The tailfins were shorn to mere nubs of what they'd been; new, elongated bullet taillights were still freestanding, but blended in better. Sales predictably improved—who was it that said "no one ever lost money underestimating the taste of the American public?" Dealers moved nearly 7000 examples of the bread-and-butter Crown four-door hardtop, the best single model performance enjoyed by Imperial since halcyon 1957.

Imperial settled for another mild and good facelift in 1963. This included a new grille composed of elongated rectangles, a crisp new squared-off roofline, and a squarer rear deck. The designer responsible for much of this was Elwood Engel, who had been hired to replace Virgil Exner as chief of Chrysler design in mid-1961. The lineup of models was unchanged: two- and four-door hardtops in the Custom and Crown Series, a Crown convertible, and LeBaron four-door. The Crown Imperial, briefly dropped in 1962, returned for a run of 13 units. Sales were on par with 1963, management left the model year happy, and Elwood Engel prepared to show his all-new and completely redesigned 1964 models.

Below and opposite page, top: *Imperial entered the '60s with a facelifted '59 carrying huge fins and a "smiling" grille. The '61s gained freestanding headlights (which were carried through to 1963), and taillights suspended below the tips of the tailfins (this page, bottom). By 1963 (opposite page, bottom), fins were trimmed to mere nubs, and a fake spare tire adorned the trunklid.*

SPECIFICATIONS

Engines:	ohv V-8, 413 cid (4.18 × 3.75), 340/350 bhp
Transmission:	3-speed automatic
Suspension front:	upper and lower control arms, longitudinal torsion bars
Suspension rear:	live axle, leaf springs
Brakes:	front/rear drums
Wheelbase (in.):	129.0 limo 149.5
Weight (lbs):	4655-5960
Top speed (mph):	NA
0-60 mph (sec):	NA

Production: 1960 Custom cpe 1498 **sdn** 2335 **htp sdn** 3953 **Crown cpe** 1504 **sdn** 1594 **htp sdn** 4510 **cvt** 618 **LeBaron sdn** 692 **htp sdn** 999 **limo** 16 **1961 Custom cpe** 880 **htp sdn** 4129 **Crown cpe** 1007 **htp sdn** 4769 **cvt** 429 **LeBaron htp sdn** 1026 **limo** 9 **1962 Custom cpe** 826 **htp sdn** 3787 **Crown cpe** 1010 **htp sdn** 6911 **cvt** 554 **LeBaron htp sdn** 1449 **1963 Custom cpe** 749 **htp sdn** 3264 **Crown cpe** 1067 **htp sdn** 6960 **cvt** 531 **LeBaron htp sdn** 1537 **limo** 13

1964-66
Imperial

In the first half of the '60s, Chrysler dispensed with design and engineering heroics in favor of careful market planning, unified "committee control" at the top, more conservative styling, and vast—sometimes rash—expansion. To his credit, president Lynn Townsend had smoothed the turbulent waters of the Tex Colbert/Bill Newberg administrations, and began concentrating on the business of making money. If a trend away from Chrysler's innovation and independence during the '50s could be seen in all this, no one was complaining. After all, Chrysler was giving the public what it wanted.

The 1964 Imperials were the first models designed by someone other than Virgil Exner since Imperial had become a separate make in 1955. The "someone" was Elwood Engel, who had come over from Ford to replace Exner in 1961, and who had begun to influence surface styling of Chrysler products as early as 1963.

Engel drastically revised the 1964 Imperial line. The old silhouette was now eliminated below the beltline, as well as above (the transformation had begun with a different roofline in 1963). The car was squared off, very much like the Lincoln Continental with which Engel had been closely associated. Like the Continental, its fenderline was traced in brightwork and there were lots of square corners. A divided grille was adopted, and Exner's freestanding headlamps summarily dropped. The rear deck was revised, not quite eliminating Exner's spare tire outline. The Custom Imperial line was canceled, leaving the Crown as the base model and the LeBaron the most expensive. Also dropped as unnecessary was the "Southampton" designation for pillarless models—all Imperials were hardtops, except the convertible. The Crown Imperial limousine built by Ghia in Italy was available with either six or four side windows, and continued on the special 149 1/2-inch wheelbase.

Imperial had an excellent year with over 23,000 '64s built, 65 percent better than

SPECIFICATIONS

Engines:	all ohv V-8; **1964-65** 413 cid (4.18 × 3.75), 340 bhp; **1966** 440 cid (4.32 × 3.75), 350 bhp
Transmission:	3-speed automatic
Suspension front:	upper and lower control arms, longitudinal torsion bars
Suspension rear:	live axle, leaf springs
Brakes:	front/rear drums
Wheelbase (in.):	129.0 **limo** 149.5
Weight (lbs):	4950-6100
Top speed (mph):	NA
0-60 mph (sec):	NA

Production: 1964 Crown cpe 5233 **htp sdn** 14,181 **cvt** 922 **LeBaron htp sdn** 2949 **limo** 10 **1965 Crown cpe** 3974 **htp sdn** 11,628 **cvt** 633 **LeBaron htp sdn** 2164 **limo** 10 **1966 Crown cpe** 2373 **htp sdn** 8977 **cvt** 514 **LeBaron htp sdn** 1878

Below and opposite page, bottom: New straight-edged styling for '64 resulted in a clean, stately look. The '65s gained a one-piece grille with covers over the headlights (opposite page, top) but were otherwise little changed. Opposite page, middle: Comfort was the name of the game, and even rear-seat passengers sat in the lap of luxury (note assist handles, reading lamps, and grab handles on the back of the front seat).

1963 and the second best year on record. Under Engel, a Lincolnesque design philosophy had emerged: the luxury car, Engel said, should not suffer the indignity of a comprehensive annual restyle. Like Mercedes (and Elwood's own Continentals) Imperial design now merely evolved; it did not change significantly from one year to the next.

The only major change for 1965 was a new grille with glass-enclosed quad headlamps. At the New York Automobile Show, Imperial displayed the exotic LeBaron D'Or show car, which used gold striping and embellishments, and was painted a special Royal Essence Laurel Gold. Prices rose a couple hundred dollars and the model lineup was unchanged.

Ghia of Turin stopped building Crown Imperial limousines in 1965, though 10 were constructed in Spain for 1966, using grilles and rear decks from that model. Starting in 1967, Imperial arranged to have the limousine built domestically. Production during 1964-66 was only 10 units per year.

Again in 1966, an evolutionary approach produced a line of Crowns and LeBarons that closely resembled the design of the 1964-65s. The changes did make 1966 one of the most beautiful Imperials, and probably the cleanest and most understated of them all. The split grille of past models was replaced by an oblong unit that framed multiple rectangles. The rear deck was smoothed off, finally eliminating the ungainly looking bird emblem and tire cover outline. Wheelbase and overall length were unchanged. The previous 413-cid V-8 was replaced by Chrysler's new 440, which was rated at 350 bhp, 10 more than 1964-65.

The 1966 Imperial was the last with a separate body and frame, and thus marked the end of the Imperial's different construction method compared to other Chrysler products. After 1966, Imperials would share the Chrysler unit body, and gradually they became more and more like a luxury version of the Chrysler. To management's disappointment, Imperial had never really established itself as a separate make, and most people still referred to it as a "Chrysler Imperial." This image problem made it difficult to rival Lincoln, let alone Cadillac. Production tailed downward, with only about 18,000 1965s built and fewer than 14,000 of the lovely '66s. Convertibles were extremely low volume cars, the figures being 922, 633, and 514 for 1964 through 1966, respectively.

1967-68
Imperial

Ostensibly, the reason for Imperial's abandonment of the separate body and frame was technological. By 1967, Chrysler argued, methods of insulation and soundproofing had become so advanced as to make the use of a separate body unnecessary. Vast technical improvements had indeed occurred, allowing computerized stress testing of the unit body/chassis before its construction. As a bonus, the unibody also reduced average weight by 100 pounds or so. The 1967 Imperial, the company said, was if anything quieter and smoother than the 1966.

Another compelling reason for the change in construction technique was overhead: it was certainly cheaper to build unit-body Imperials with a Chrysler inner shell, albeit on a slightly longer wheelbase.

As a result of this basic change, the 1967 models were all-new and completely restyled. A new grille with a prominent nameplate was accompanied by sharp front fenders that housed the parking lights. Headlamps remained integrated with the grille. There were vertical rear bumpers and horizontal "character lines" along the bodysides. The wheelbase came down two inches to 127.

Sales did pick up, exceeding 17,000 in 1967 and 15,000 in 1968. Prices also rose, Crown hardtops exceeding $6000 base for the first time. To compensate, Imperial reinstated the Crown four-door pillared sedan, which started at around $5400. Convertibles remained, but just barely: production was only 577 for 1967 and 474 for 1968, the last year for the Imperial soft top.

Imperial's continued inability to dent the Cadillac/Lincoln market share caused management to rethink their approach and make a far-reaching decision. For 1969 and beyond, Imperial would share exterior sheetmetal with Chrysler. The '68s,

Above: *Imperial abandoned body-on-frame construction for 1967, joining other Chrysler products in using a unibody assembly. Styling maintained the straight-edge look, but was completely different from the previous year. The '68s were little changed (below and opposite page), though the grille now wrapped around the front fenders to enclose the side-marker lamps.*

meanwhile, were only slightly changed from 1967. Features included a new grille that extended around the front end to enclose the parking and cornering lights, dual moldings on the lower bodysides, and rear side-marker lights (now required by law). Narrow paint stripes were applied along the beltline on all models. The 440 V-8 remained standard, with a dual exhaust/twin snorkel option that boosted output from 350 to 360 bhp.

Road tests of Imperials in this period point out some of their problems compared to their chief competitors. Typically, an Imperial had better seating and more maneuverability than a Lincoln or a Cadillac, but lacked the opposition's level of quality control (long a Lincoln hallmark and lately being emphasized by Cadillac). Imperials were also slower: a *Motor Trend* comparison test of a LeBaron with a Coupe DeVille and a Continental gave 9- or 10-second 0-60 times for the Cadillac and Lincoln, against 12.4 seconds for the Imperial, which was also considerably slower in the standing start quarter-mile and the 50-70 passing test. Imperials got slightly better gas mileage than the Cadillac, but were inferior to the Lincoln in this respect.

Motor Trend criticized all these characteristics, along with the Imperial's styling and brakes, but there was also a long list of things they *did* like: individual lighters in each door, slanted power toggle switches on door armrests, rear compartment reading lights, time delay ignition light, seating comfort and ride, stereo system, lift-up door handles, individually operated power front seats, and thermostat air temperature control. The LeBaron defied a fad by using antiqued bronze inlays across the dashboard and doors instead of wood veneer. Imperial, the editors said, had the best dashboard layout, with a wide padded top that allowed the dash to be recessed underneath. "Because of this arrangement, toggle switches are used and are much more convenient than sliding handles or padded knobs."

In 1967-68, a new Imperial limousine was offered, built by Stageway Coaches of Fort Smith, Arkansas, a supplier of airport limos. Twelve of these LeBaron limousines (the Crown Imperial name was dropped) were built on an enormous 163-inch wheelbase, and justifiably advertised as the largest luxury cars in the world. Unlike Ghia Crowns, Stageway limos had an extra window and panel between the front and rear doors. Prices ranged between $12,000 and $15,000 depending on equipment.

SPECIFICATIONS

Engines:	ohv V-8, 440 cid (4.32 × 3.75), 350/360 bhp
Transmission:	3-speed automatic
Suspension front:	upper and lower control arms, longitudinal torsion bars
Suspension rear:	live axle, leaf springs
Brakes:	front disc/rear drum
Wheelbase (in.):	127.0 limo 163.0
Weight (lbs):	4660-6300
Top speed (mph):	NA
0-60 mph (sec):	12.4

Production: 1967 sdn 2193 **cvt** 577 **Crown cpe** 3235 **htp sdn** 9415 **LeBaron htp sdn** 2194 **limo** 6 **1968 Crown cpe** 2656 **sdn** 1887 **htp sdn** 8492 **cvt** 474 **LeBaron htp sdn** 1852 **limo** 6

1969 Imperial

Chrysler's flagship always seemed to sell best when it was imitating its Big Three rivals. Take 1957, when Virgil Exner's finny, low-slung creations "out-Cadillac'd" Cadillac to give Imperial what would be its all-time best production run: some 36,600 cars.

Its second best model-year tally was the 23,300 of 1964, the year Imperial became more like a Lincoln. That was hardly surprising, because Elwood Engel had designed the template '61 Lincoln before coming to Chrysler as Exner's replacement.

For 1967, Imperial took another tack, becoming neither Cadillac nor Lincoln but . . . a Chrysler. Of course, that's precisely what it had been before becoming a make in its own right for 1955. And for 1969, at least, it didn't hurt. In fact, Imperial gained some 7000 units in model-year production over '68—and with fewer models to boot—ending near the '64 level at just over 22,000.

The tipoff to the '67 Imperial's "more Chrysler" design was as close as the spec chart. Body-on-frame construction, exclusive to Imperial within the corporate camp since 1960, was abandoned for the unitized C-body structure of that year's redesigned Chryslers, senior Dodges, and Plymouth Furys. However, you didn't need to be James Bond to spot shared elements like side window lines and windshield/A-pillar angles.

The similarities increased for '69, when Chrysler again fully redesigned its big cars. All bore fulsome new "fuselage styling," an advertising term used only by Chrysler, though it was equally apt for the others. Imperials still rode the longest wheelbase, the 127-inch span adopted for '67. That remained three inches longer than Chrysler's, and, as before, it was all ahead of the cowl, where extra inches are relatively cheap and easy to add even on a unibody car. Returning as Imperial's one and only engine was the big-block 440-cubic-inch wedgehead introduced for '66, still rated at 350 horsepower and teamed, as ever, with Highland Park's matchless TorqueFlite automatic transmission.

Of course, you could get all that in Chrysler's other full-size '69s, so Imperial distinctions came down to equipment—full-house as usual—and styling, which was pretty good: burly, handsome, and distinct from what Caddy and Lincoln were offering. Though a Chrysler connection was clearer than ever, the Imperial, appropriately, was a touch more formal and massive-looking. More massive it was, too. Overall length was up five inches to a sizeable 229.7, and the newly ballooned bodysides made the cars look at least that much wider, though they weren't. Nor were they heavier, though they looked that, too. In fact, the '69s were about 100 pounds lighter than the '68s.

What few styling differences there were from Chrysler existed mainly up front, where Lincoln-like vertical parking lamps flanked a full-width eggcrate grille with hidden headlights. The last was a first for Imperial, though the '69 Chrysler 300 claimed it, too. Big rear bumpers with integral taillamps were a longtime Imperial trademark, but the '69 affair was slimmer and pleasingly simple. As before, large chrome caps slithered up to brace the trunklid opening as the mother of all bumper guards.

Model choices were reshuffled. The Crown convertible departed, leaving a four-door sedan, identically priced hardtop sedan, and hardtop coupe. The uplevel LeBaron four-door hardtop gained a companion two-door for the first time. Though still badged as a series, LeBaron was now technically an option package, still with standard vinyl roof and nicer interior trim but no more small, "formal" rear window.

Making Imperials even more like Chryslers allowed further price cuts for '69, and in some cases they were drastic. The Crown hardtop coupe was $270 cheaper than its '68 counterpart, while the top-line four-door LeBaron was $800 less than the year before—which may explain why LeBarons outsold comparable Crowns for the first time.

The '69 Imperial was smooth, hushed, and fairly quick and nimble for a luxury biggie. It was also the last Imperial to sell in really respectable numbers, though volume remained a fraction of Cadillac's and even Lincoln's. Production promptly dropped by half on the little-changed 1970-71s, recovered to the mid-teens for 1972-74, then plunged to 8800 for '75. By then, Imperial was just an upmarket Chrysler New Yorker, which it became in name as well as fact when the marque was canceled the following year.

Imperial has since been twice revived, first as a mid-size "bustleback" coupe for 1981-83, then as another New Yorker spinoff for 1990. But neither was very popular. Unlike Cadillac, Chrysler has apparently yet to learn that cloning only multiplies models, not necessarily sales.

Imperial for '69 wore a Chrysler body stretched three inches forward of the cowl, but distinctive front and rear ends helped hide the fact that it was basically just a bigger Chrysler. Hidden-headlight grille was a first for Imperial, though it shared the concept with that year's Chrysler 300.

SPECIFICATIONS

Engines:	ohv V-8; 440 cid (4.32 × 3.75), 350 bhp
Transmission:	3-speed TorqueFlite automatic
Suspension front:	upper and lower A-arms, longitudinal torsion bars, anti-roll bar
Suspension rear:	live axle, semi-elliptic leaf springs
Brakes:	front discs/rear drums
Wheelbase (in.):	127.0
Weight (lbs):	4555-4710
Top speed (mph):	est. 110
0-60 mph (sec):	est. 10.0

Production: Crown htp cpe 224 **htp sdn** 823 **4d sdn** 1,617 **LeBaron htp cpe** 4,592 **htp sdn** 14,821

1961-63
Lincoln Continental

The revolutionary 1961 Continental was one of the finest Lincolns ever built and probably cost more to conceive, design, develop, and manufacture than any previous model in Lincoln history. That the effort was worth it is proven by production figures, which doubled from 1960, and went on to top 30,000 for the look-alike years of 1962-63. The public was responding to a classic and beautiful design combined with superb engineering—one of the most satisfying Lincolns since the Continental Mark II.

The chiseled, sculptured styling was the work of seven Ford designers, who received the annual award of the Industrial Design Institute in June 1961: Eugene Bordinat, Don DeLaRossa, Elwood Engel, Gale Halderman, John Najjar, Robert Thomas, and George Walker. The IDI, which rarely gives prizes to car stylists, called their product an "outstanding contribution of simplicity and design elegance."

Although the Lincoln Continental looked unique, it shared tooling around the cowl with the equally new 1961 Ford Thunderbird—indeed the original design, nicknamed the "Engelbird," had been slated for the T-Bird, until Ford decided that its formal look was better applied to Lincoln. Jointly tooling two relatively low production cars saved a lot of money; yet the Continental and T-bird did not look like twins. The Continental was a big four-door sedan or convertible on a 123-inch wheelbase, while the T-Bird was a two-door on a wheelbase 10 inches shorter.

Styling of the 1961-63 models involved a smooth-lined body surface set off with bright metal fender strips that ran uninterrupted from front to rear, plus a conservative grille composed of horizontal and vertical elements. The fenderline emphasis made all four fenders easily visible from behind the wheel, which helped

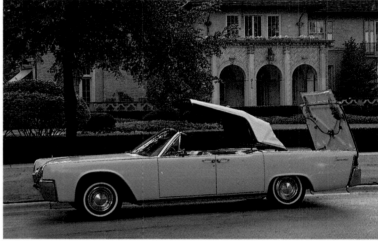

Opposite page: The '61 Lincoln replaced the gaudy sculpturing of the earlier generation with straight-edged styling that was literally award-winning. All '61-'63 Lincolns had four doors, the rears opening "suicide" style—including those on the unique convertible. Lincoln insisted that it would avoid "change for the sake of change," and true to its word, the '62s (This page, top and right) and '63s (above) differed little from the '61s.

SPECIFICATIONS

Engines:	ohv V-8, 430 cid (4.30 × 3.70), 300/320 bhp
Transmission:	3-speed Turbo Drive automatic
Suspension front:	upper and lower control arms, coil springs
Suspension rear:	live axle, leaf springs
Brakes:	front/rear drums
Wheelbase (in.):	123.0
Weight (lbs):	4927-5370
Top speed (mph):	115
0-60 mph (sec):	11.0

Production: 1961 sdn 22,303 **cvt** 2857 **1962 sdn** 27,849 **cvt** 3212 **1963 sdn** 28,095 **cvt** 3138

maneuverability. In front view, the windows sloped inward toward the roof for the greatest angle of "tumblehome" yet seen on a large American luxury car, and marked one of the first uses of curved side glass in regular production.

The Continental four-door convertible, offered from the beginning, was the first "convertible sedan" since Kaiser-Frazer's abortive 1951 Frazer Manhattan. Unlike the Frazer's, the side glass and window frames slid completely out of sight. So did the convertible top—with the help of 11 complicated relays connecting a maze of mechanical and hydraulic linkages.

Aside from styling, these Lincolns were renowned for construction quality, thanks mainly to Harold MacDonald, chief engineer of Ford's Car and Truck Group. MacDonald fostered no startling innovations, but instead refined existing techniques. He adopted the most rigid unit body and chassis ever mass-produced, the best sound insulation and shock damping in existence, extremely close machining tolerances for all mechanical components, an unprecedented number of long-life service components, a completely sealed electrical system, and superior rust and corrosion protection.

Continentals also received the most thorough product testing yet applied by Detroit. Each engine was tested on a dynamometer at 3500 rpm (equal to about 98 mph) for three hours. Then it was torn down for inspection and reassembled. Every automatic transmission was tested for 30 minutes before installation. Each finished car was road tested for 12 miles and had to pass inspection in nearly 200 individual categories. Next, black light was used to visualize a fluorescent dye in the cars' lubricants as a check for oil leaks. As proof of the Continental's invulnerability, Lincoln offered a two-year, 24,000-mile warranty, then unprecedented.

Public response was immediate and satisfying, putting Lincoln ahead of Imperial for keeps in 1961. Styling changes in 1962-63 were minimal, since Lincoln had declared its intention to make improvements only for function. The '62 had a cleaner grille with higher-mounted headlamps and a smoother front bumper. The '63 had a square-textured grille, a restyled back panel, and increased trunk space.

1964-65
Lincoln Continental

Lincoln went from strength to strength in the '60s, model-year production bounding from around 25,000 to a new all-time high of near 56,000. The foundation for this success was the all-new 1961 Lincoln Continental. Easily one of the decade's styling landmarks, it was instantly acclaimed so by no less than the prestigious Industrial Design Institute. So good was its basic design that only careful annual refinements would be needed to carry it well past decade's end.

The '61s and the little-changed 1962-63 Continentals had taken a fair chunk of business from Cadillac (even more from Imperial). Additional conquest sales were behind the significant changes made for 1964—enough to qualify the cars as second-generation versions of the original design.

Lincoln-Mercury had promised the timeless '61 styling wouldn't change for the sake of change, and they kept their word for '64. Thin-pillar four-door sedan and America's only convertible sedan returned, both with center-opening doors as before, plus a mildly revised grille with five vertical bars, a deeper and newly lipped trunklid, slightly sharpened sedan rear side windows—and flat instead of curved door glass. The last was suggested by Ford styling chief Gene Bordinat as a cost-cutting measure, but Bob Thomas, a member of the '61 design team, was horrified. "The car was just not designed for flat glass," he said later. "It didn't look right."

Less obvious, perhaps, was a wheelbase stretched three inches, to 126, and overall length that now measured 216 inches. Thankfully, these gains had little effect on weight, and even this longer Continental was still shorter than a '64 Cadillac or Imperial.

Even better, the extra rear overhang added some trunk space and made room for a lower-profile convertible top, while the flat side glass, debated though it was, added 5.4 inches to overall shoulder room. The longer wheelbase showed up in extra rear leg room, which was much needed, and also brought three-inch-longer rear doors that improved entry/exit. A front seat moved two inches forward added more space in back. To compensate for the resulting loss of room up front, the previous "twin-cowl" dash gave way to a trimmer full-width design, matched by a shorter steering column.

The '64s benefited from several new standard features, including a low-fuel warning light, vertically adjustable steering column, auxiliary map light, automatic parking-brake release, and inch-larger (15-inch) wheels providing better brake cooling. Chassis specs were otherwise unchanged save the expected recalibrating of springs and shocks. The driveline was also untouched, Lincoln's big 430 V-8 returning with 320 horsepower and again mating with Twin-Range Turbo-Drive automatic transmission.

That the Continental would evolve in so measured a way was by now an article of faith among buyers, particularly those who had crossed over to Lincoln after being turned off by Cadillac's constant revisions. Keeping the faith convinced some 4000 more to join the ranks for '64, though Cadillac sales were also up—but not nearly as much. The sales gulf between these rivals was still huge, thanks to Cadillac's broader lineup and bigger dealer network, but it was smaller than it had been for quite awhile.

Continental's considered evolution continued for 1965, when Lincoln bucked tradition by not raising prices so much as a dollar despite adding front-disc brakes to an already lengthy list of standard equipment. Styling updates were as mild as ever: just a new horizontal-bar grille with prominent center bulge, wraparound parking/turn signal lamps visible from most every angle, and back panels without the customary metal appliqués echoing grille texture. A vinyl roof covering was a new sedan option ($105) and proved quite popular. Air conditioning, which now reached a 90-percent installation rate, was the only other major extra ($505) save individual power front seats ($281).

As it had every year since 1961, Lincoln volume increased for '65, ending just above 40,000, over 3000 more than in model-year '64. The sedan accounted for most of the gain; the convertible was still selling at a 3000-3400 annual clip.

Lincoln had every reason to be satisfied with this performance—but, of course, it wasn't. Seeking still-higher sales, Lincoln was readying even bigger and better Continentals for 1966.

The 1964 Continental (opposite page, top) looked very much like the '63, though wheelbase was stretched by three inches. The most radical styling changes since the car debuted in 1961 were seen on the '65s (below and opposite page, bottom right). A flat grille with protruding center section replaced the convex grille of previous models, while the rear end lost the simulated grille panel between the taillights. Opposite page, bottom left: Longer wheelbase added rear seat room, while flat dash made the front seem more spacious.

SPECIFICATIONS

Engines:	ohv V-8, 430 cid (4.30 × 3.70), 320 bhp
Transmission:	3-speed automatic
Suspension front:	upper and lower A-arms, coil springs
Suspension rear:	live axle, coil springs
Brakes:	front/rear drums **1965:** front disc/rear drums
Wheelbase (in.):	126.0
Weight (lbs):	5055-5475
Top speed (mph):	110
0-60 mph (sec):	10.0

Production:1964 htp sdn 32,969 **cvt sdn** 3,328 **1965 htp sdn** 36,824 **cvt sdn** 3,356

1966-67
Lincoln Continental

Most of Detroit had a good 1966, almost as lucrative as banner '65. Lincoln, however, had a veritable bonanza, scoring record production of nearly 55,000 units. But there was no mystery to it, for the heavily revised 1966 Continental offered not only handsome new looks but more model choices and more power, all for less money.

Though unchanged in wheelbase, the '66 Lincolns arrived with all-new bodyshells measuring four inches longer overall. Curved side glass returned for the first time since 1963, matched by conservatively upswept rear fenderlines and "faster" windshield and rear-window angles. Elwood Engel's straight-edged front fenders and chrome-edged beltlines were retained, but the hood/grille assembly became a bulged "power dome," and bumpers were more massive. Parking lights returned to the front bumpers, designers not anticipating the federally required side-marker lamps for '68 (when fendertip parking lights returned). Taillights received the same treatment.

Inside, a new deeply hooded "pedestal" control center jutted out firmly from an otherwise slim dashboard to cradle the steering wheel, which was now a two-spoke design available with optional seven-stage tilt adjustment. In a retrograde step, warning lights replaced all gauges save fuel and speedometer. An angled panel held audio and climate controls combining knobs, pushbuttons, and radio-type displays.

Continental continued for '66 as a thin-pillar sedan and unique four-door convertible, but a two-door hardtop was restored to the Lincoln line for the first time since 1960. One can only guess why it took so long to revive that perennially popular type.

Continentals were restyled for 1966, and though they rode the same 126-inch wheelbase, overall length increased by four inches. A coupe was reinstated to the line (above), having been absent since 1961. Four-door sedan (below) continued to be the top seller, while the unique four-door convertible (opposite page) remained in the line but accounted for less than six percent of total production.

Cadillac had come within an inch of matching Lincoln in the "displacement race" two years before. Continental's 430-cubic-inch V-8 was accordingly bored and stroked to a massive 462 cid to again become Detroit's biggest (though Cadillac would top it for '68). The result was 20 extra horsepower—340 in all—and a monumental 485 pounds/feet of torque. Unfortunately, it weighed an equally monumental 750 pounds, but it was Lincoln's most powerful (and last) pre-emissions V-8. Features included redesigned cylinder heads and intake manifold, and water passages around the exhaust valves and plugs nearly twice as large as before.

Though capable of far more power had it been required, the 462 was purposely understressed (it made only 0.73 bhp per cubic inch), designed for smooth, quiet cruising above all—as witnessed by a long-striding final drive ratio of only 2.80:1. Even with that, though, few '66s returned better than 10 miles per gallon, so a newly enlarged gas tank was welcome if not essential.

Of course, the 462's payoff was sprightlier performance: 0-60 was now available in as little as 10 seconds. Top speed improved, too, the hardtop able to reach 125 mph by dint of being the lightest model—if you can call 5000 pounds "light," though curb weights were actually just five-10 pounds more than on the '65s. Complementing the big new engine was a more efficient automatic transmission: Ford's new high-capacity C-6 three-speed unit. Other mechanical refinements included a stronger rear axle, double-cardan joints for both ends of the driveshaft, and longer rear springs for a smoother ride.

At $5750, the new hardtop coupe was the cheapest Lincoln in years. That's probably why it generated an impressive 15,766 sales, about half the sedan total but five times convertible volume. Four-door prices were actually cut some $400, but you now paid extra for previously standard six-way power seat, power door locks and vent windows, AM radio, and whitewall tires. New options for '66 included signal-seeking AM/FM radio, AM radio with 8-track tape player, and automatic temperature control.

For 1967, Lincoln fell back to its pre-'65 selling pace, mainly because it had little new to offer against a redesigned Cadillac. Mechanicals and models were the same, and you had to look twice to discern any styling change (one being the deletion of the Lincoln badge forward of the wheelwell). Forced-air "Fresh Flow" ventilation was a noteworthy new standard for all models. The interesting four-door convertible was in its final year, ever unprofitable (it had never sold more than 3500 annually) despite a long stand as the "ultimate Lincoln." Its '67 volume was the lowest ever: just 2276 units.

SPECIFICATIONS

Engines:	ohv V-8, 462 cid (4.30 × 3.70), 340 bhp
Transmissions:	3-speed automatic
Suspension front:	upper and lower A-arms, coil springs
Suspension rear:	live axle, coil springs
Brakes:	front/rear drums
Wheelbase (in.):	126.0
Weight (lbs):	4985-5505
Top speed (mph):	120+
0-60 mph (sec):	10.0-11.5

Production: 1966 4d sdn 35,809 **cvt sdn** 3,180 **htp cpe** 15,766 **1967 4d sdn** 33,331 **cvt sdn** 2,276 **htp cpe** 11,060

Few visual changes occurred for 1967, the most noticeable being the deletion of the Lincoln badge at the leading edge of the front fender. The four-door convertible (below) would be in its last season, having never sold more than 3500 units a year. Coupes continued to make up a sizeable portion of overall production, but Lincoln sales in general were down significantly from '66.

1968-69
Lincoln Continental

America's sole four-door '60s convertible didn't make it to the first year of federal safety standards, not so much because it was any less safe than closed Continentals, just less saleable. Besides, Lincoln had concocted something very saleable for 1968: a reborn Continental Mark, which garnered over twice as many model-year orders as Lincoln's last '67 convertible, despite an abbreviated six-month selling season.

But that was only 17 percent of total 1968 Lincoln volume that rose fractionally from model-year '67—a record 46,904. Though the new Mark III would leap beyond 23,000 sales for '69, Lincoln's lifeblood, as ever, was the Continental sedan, which for '68 was nearly two-thirds of its business.

That sedan and its hardtop running mate still evidenced much of the award-winning 1961 styling that had so captivated buyers. But there was no escaping Washington mandates, which were plenty evident for '68. For example, parking lamps and taillights were again mounted in the fendertips to meet the new requirement for illuminated side markers. Another rule banning exterior features injurious to pedestrians brought a temporary end to the Continental's traditional star hood ornament, which moved down to just above the grille. (Spring-loading would later bring it back.) The Feds should have objected to the hardtop's new ultra-wide C-pillars, but there was no statute prohibiting big obstructions to driver vision. How odd the workings of the bureaucratic mind.

More safety-think appeared inside, the '68 Continentals gaining recessed door handles, front seatbelts, and padded steering-wheel hub as required no-cost items. Shiny glare-producing materials were also newly barred, and Continental complied with flat-finish or low-gloss surfaces. Not required, but welcome, was a more readable black-face instrument cluster, though instruments were still confined to just speedometer and fuel gauge. Pseudo-walnut dash appliqués and leather-wrapped door pulls combined for a somewhat warmer ambience.

Above and opposite middle and top: *Continentals gained wrap-around front turn signals and rear taillights in '68 to comply with the federal regulation regarding side-marker lamps. Coupes received even wider C-pillars that looked more formal, but made for huge blind spots to the rear.* Opposite page, bottom: *For 1969, the grille was raised slightly over the center section and taillight elements were rearranged, but there were few other changes.*

SPECIFICATIONS

Engines:	ohv V-8, 460 cid (4.36 × 3.75), 365 bhp
Transmissions:	3-speed automatic
Suspension front:	upper and lower A-arms, coil springs
Suspension rear:	live axle, coil springs
Brakes:	front/rear drums
Wheelbase (in.):	126.0
Weight (lbs):	4883-5005
Top speed (mph):	NA
0-60 mph (sec):	NA

Production: 1968 htp cpe 9,415 **4d sdn** 29,719 **1969 htp cpe** 9,032 **4d sdn** 29,258

A more fundamental mandated change, this one for cleaner air, was found under '68 Continental hoods. It was an all-new 460-cubic-inch V-8, the larger of two Ford Motor Company "385-series" engines (Thunderbird's 429 was the other) designed specifically for emission controls. Despite reduced bore and stroke from the previous 462, the 460 produced 15 more horsepower and, surprisingly, equal extra torque. Offered only with four-barrel carb and high 10.5:1 compression, it featured large canted valves with ultra-clean porting, Chevy-style stud-mounted rocker arms, and precision-cast "shallow-block" crankcase.

As ever, Continentals came only with three-speed automatic transmission, the new-for-'67 C-6 unit that Lincoln called Multi-Drive. Other equipment was pretty much carryover too, but AM/FM stereo radio, front headrests, and warm-air rear-window defogger were new extra-cost items.

The senior Continentals virtually duplicated their '68 sales performance for 1969. Per established policy, design alterations were few. The main one was a square, vee'd eggcrate grille (with each "crate" carrying multiple tiny squares) surmounted by a restored block-letter "Continental" nameplate. New bumpers bumped up overall length 3.2 inches to 224.2 inches, but weight was little affected. Among various detail changes were reworked interior trim panels, new pushbutton climate controls, the usual color/trim shuffles, "dual-stream" windshield-washer nozzles and, per government order, a dual-circuit brake system with failure warning light (which Lincoln might have thought of itself).

More significant for future sales was a new "Town Car" interior option for the sedan. Inspired by some recent, like-named Lincoln show cars, this comprised "unique, super-puff leather-and-vinyl seats and door panels, luxury woodtone front seatback and door trim inserts, extra plush carpeting, and special napped nylon headlining."

Thanks mainly to the Mark III, Lincoln set another production record for '69: a smashing 61,000-plus. On the other hand, Cadillac was doing four times that volume. But Lincoln would continue its upward trend through most of the '70s by adhering to the basic design and product philosophy responsible for its spectacular resurgence in the '60s. Which only goes to show that following tradition literally pays sometimes—or, as the latterday maxim says, "If it ain't broke, don't fix it."

1968-69 Lincoln Continental Mark III

Despite all the stuff you hear about bean-counters and hard-boiled corporate managers with no sense of history, there is more reverence for the past in the car industry than most fields of endeavor. Time and again, more often to their ultimate loss than gain, car companies have tried to recreate modern versions of classics. The LaSalle (ultimately appearing as the 1963 Buick Riviera), the several generations of postwar Imperials, "trunkback" Cadillac Sevilles of 1980-86, and today's Buick Roadmaster are recent examples. One classic that repeatedly influenced modern counterparts is the first Lincoln Continental, spawned by Edsel Ford in 1940 and produced through 1948. Eight years later, responding to repeated urgings from dealers, customers, and their own management, Ford Motor Company produced a Mark II Continental—a splendid car in many ways, but one that cost Ford about three or four dollars for every dollar it made. Twelve years after that came the Continental Mark III, designed in its predecessors' image as a personal luxury car of the highest refinement, but with a difference: this one was designed to make money. And it did.

The Mark III was the new product most closely linked to Henry Ford II, grandson of the founder, who had run the company with considerable flair since 1945. Just as his brother William Clay Ford had influenced the 1956 Mark II, Henry II insured that the Mark III would be a reflection of his own personal taste. (In naming it the Mark III, product planners incidentally ignored the Continental Mark III-IV-V built during 1958-60, which were big, ornate vehicles not in keeping with the older Continental tradition.)

The Mark III entered the product-planning stage in late 1965. From the beginning, the goal was clear: a personal-luxury car with a long hood and short deck, like the early Continentals. Styling was supervised by design chief Eugene Bordinat.

SPECIFICATIONS

Engines:	ohv V-8, 460 cid (4.36 × 3.85), 365 bhp
Transmission:	3-speed automatic
Suspension front:	upper and lower A-arms, coil springs
Suspension rear:	live axle, trailing arms, coil springs
Brakes:	front disc/rear drum
Wheelbase (in.):	117.2
Weight (lbs):	4739-4762
Top speed (mph):	NA
0-60 mph (sec):	NA
Production:	**1968** 7770 **1969** 23,088

Lincoln joined (or perhaps we should say rejoined) the personal-luxury market in mid-1968 with the Continental Mark III. Intended to convey a kinship to the classic Mark II of 1956-57 (rather than the overblown Mark III, IV, and V of 1958-60), the '68 version was intended for large-scale production, as opposed to the Mark IIs, of which only 1769 were built. Little changed for '69 (both pages), when the Mark III sold over 23,000 copies in its first full year.

Hermann Brunn, namesake of the great coachbuilder and a member of Bordinat's staff, was largely responsible for the interior. Brunn designed large, comfortable bucket seats and a wood-grained dashboard with accessible controls. Henry Ford II selected the final shape from a number of designs submitted by company stylists in early 1966.

The Mark III was ready by April 1968. Because of its late introduction, only a few thousand were built that year, but there was no question that it was fit for the market: more than 23,000 were sold at a tidy $7000-$8000 in 1969. The price, if quite high, was also quite reasonable: the Mark II had cost $10,000 in 1956, equivalent to $20,000 in 1968, or about three times the Mark III's cost in real dollars. This shows how carefully Ford planners had placed the Mark III as a profitmaker. With Cadillac's rival Eldorado at about the same price, it also explains what competitor Lincoln was shooting at.

The Mark III rode a 117.2-inch wheelbase, some nine inches shorter than the Mark II's, but the same length as the Eldorado. Although the front-wheel-drive Eldo was more advanced technologically, the Continental had more magic in its name. In sales, it virtually matched the Eldorado during its four-year life span, and never trailed by more than 2000 units a year. This was a significant achievement, because Lincoln's total production was never more than a fraction of Cadillac's, and its dealer base was smaller.

Powered by a 460-cid V-8 with 10.5:1 compression, the Mark III was one of the industry's most powerful cars. It was also good looking, with one of the longest hoods (more than six feet). Buyers had a wide choice of luxury interiors and could choose from 26 exterior colors including four special "Moondust" metallic paints. The 1969 model cost more but carried few changes. Standard features on all Mark IIIs included Select-Shift Turbo-Drive automatic, power brakes (discs front, drums rear), concealed headlamps, ventless side glass, power seats and windows, flow-through ventilation, and 150 pounds of sound-deadening insulation.

With the Mark III, Lincoln finally established the personal luxury car as a permanent member of its line, and acquired a second distinct model in addition to its traditional sedans.

197

1960
Mercury

Mercury models of the late 1950s could make a sensitive soul shriek in horror. Recalled today as veritable icons of their time, the big boats were laden with chrome, sharply sculptured angles, and windshields curved so severely as to defy the imagination—everything, in short, that signified excess.

Sure, sales slipped in 1958—the year of what many consider the most excessive Merc of all, and a rough year for the industry. Yes, fewer yet were sold in 1959, when Mercs displayed a slightly less cluttered look—but added even more inches. Nevertheless, thousands of Americans took these overstuffed Mercs to heart and eagerly brought them home; just as thousands of others were overjoyed to acquire the latest Edsel.

What looks hideous in retrospect, of course, didn't seem half bad at the time—at least in the minds of many a middle-class motorist. And today, plenty of collectors covet the most glaring examples of American overstyling. Mercury wasn't alone in catering to questionable tastes, to be sure; plenty of makes were comparably baroque. Depending on one's taste, Mercury was either the best or the worst example of the lot. If nothing else, they were unique, with an undeniable identity.

Overall, the '60 facelift was an improvement, with less chrome decoration and rounded lines softening the former sharp edges, even though the basic shapes and rooflines remained. Slim, vertical taillights encased within upright bumper pods replaced the huge triangular lenses of '59, and though vestigial fins were discernible above, it made for a more subtle attitude. Quad headlights moved down into the new concave grille, giving the front end a less immense and blocklike stance. Both windshields and backlights again displayed startling compound curves.

Continuing on a 126-inch wheelbase, these were mighty big cars, offered on three levels. Montereys carried a 312-cid V-8 (383-cid optional), while the more costly Montclair and upscale Park Lane stuck with their Lincoln-derived 430-cid V-8, reduced to 310 bhp from its former 345, via reduced compression. Cutting back on power came as a surprise after the Fifties horsepower race, but was

SPECIFICATIONS

Engines:	all ohv V-8; 312 cid (3.80 × 3.44), 205 bhp; 383 cid (4.30 × 3.30), 280 bhp; 430 cid (4.30 × 3.70), 310 bhp
Transmissions:	3-speed manual; overdrive, 3-speed Merc-O-Matic (standard on Montclair), and Multi-Drive Merc-O-Matic (standard on Park Lane) optional
Suspension, front:	upper and lower A-arms, coil springs, link-type stabilizer
Suspension, rear:	live axle, leaf springs
Brakes:	front/rear drums
Wheelbase (in.):	126.0
Weight (lbs.):	3901-4558
Top speed (mph):	**V8-430** 110-115
0-60 mph (sec):	**V8-430** 12.0-13.1

Production: Monterey Cruiser 4d htp 9536 **4d sdn** 49,594 **Cruiser 2d htp** 15,790 **2d sdn** 21,557 **cvt** 6062 **Montclair Cruiser** 4d htp 5548 **4d sdn** 8510 **Cruiser 2d htp** 5756 **Park Lane Cruiser** 4d htp 5788 **Cruiser 2d htp** 2974 **cvt** 1525 **Commuter** 4d wgn 14,949 **Colony Park** 4d wgn 7411

triggered by the severe recession of 1958.

Also for economy, 2.71:1 and 2.91:1 axles were available with the 383- or 430-cid engine. Still, with 460 pounds/feet of torque on tap, the 430 V-8 remained a mighty machine. No one need have feared, in any case: before long, bhp figures would be rising again.

Park Lanes displayed the most brightwork, including rocker panel moldings that extended through fender skirts and across the quarter panels to meet the vast taillight housing. A sharp creaseline above the rocker panel reached over the front wheel. Five trim pieces ahead of rear wheel openings identified the Park Lane; three such strips went on Montclairs; none on Monterey.

A column-shift three-speed was standard on Monterey; Montclairs came with Merc-O-Matic, with Park Lanes adding Multi-Drive to the automatic. Mercury's ladder frame had bowed box-girder side rails, with convertibles adding X-type center reinforcement.

Convertibles were offered in the Monterey and Park Lane lines, while Commuter and Colony Park station wagons (the latter sided in woodgrain) formed a series of their own. Prices ranged from $2631 for a Monterey two-door sedan to $4018 for the luscious Park Lane ragtop. A diverse color selection included 15 Super Enamel monochrome hues and 35 two-tone combinations. Options ranged from power steering at $106 and a four-way power seat for $76.50, to air conditioning at $471. Lesser-ranked Mercs could step up to Multi-Drive Merc-O-Matic (with dual drive ranges) in exchange for extra dollars.

Substantial size translates to ample weight, and Mercury was no exception. A Park Lane convertible tipped the scales at 4500 pounds; the Colony Park wagon added a few more.

Even with all that heft to haul, performance wasn't too bad. *Motor Trend* evaluated a Montclair with the 310-bhp, 430-cid V-8 and optional Multi-Drive Merc-O-Matic. Taking off in D-1 Range yielded a 0-60 time of 12 seconds flat, while the quarter-mile demanded 17.7 seconds at 76 mph. Using D-2 range took an extra 1.1 seconds to hit 60 mph, and the quarter-mile lasted 18.6 seconds (75 mph).

Reaching the 154,000 mark, full-size Mercury production was up a few thousand from 1959. As it would turn out, however, this was to be the last Mercury with a distinct identity. Starting in 1961, Mercury would shrink to a 120-inch wheelbase and amount to little more than a restyled, posher, and more costly Ford—just as it continues to be today.

This Monterey convertible is representative of Mercury's entry-level car for 1960, which carried less chrome trim than high-line models. It would be the last Mercury to ride the longer, 126-inch wheelbase, as later models shrunk to a 120-inch span and looked more like their Ford counterparts.

1962-63
Mercury S-55

Right from its birth in 1939, Ford Motor Company's "in-between" car established a performance reputation to match its name. Mercury maintained that image into the early '50s with speedy, good-handling cars that competed well in events like the famed Mexican Road Race—but also the Mobilgas Economy Runs. The make then lost its way for a few years, blowing up into costly, begadgeted "Big M" cruisers that moved well enough on straights but didn't like curves at all. Aggravated by 1958's flash recession, Mercury finished the decade with model-year production below 150,000, less than half its 300,000-unit record of 1955.

But Mercury would revert to saner cars in the '60s while reasserting its performance image. First came a sensible compact, the Comet, based on Ford's new-for-'60 Falcon, followed by trimmer, simpler, and cheaper 1961 "standards" based on the contemporary full-size Ford. Production returned to the 300,000 level, helped by an improving market that was showing strong interest in sporty cars like Chevrolet's bucket-seat Corvair Monza and Impala SS.

Having tested the sporty-car waters with the '61 Comet S-22, Mercury jumped in with both feet for '62. The S-22 returned along with a similar S-33 edition of the new mid-size Meteor, a clone of Ford's Fairlane. But the pride of the sports department was a pair of big bucket-seat Mercs called S-55.

More properly, we should call it the Monterey Custom S-55, as the new convertible and hardtop coupe were officially sub-models in Mercury's upper-level '62 big-car line. They were also "half-year" models, arriving simultaneously with the Ford Galaxie 500XLs they essentially duplicated.

Though still on Ford's 1960 full-size platform, the '62 Monterey, Monterey Custom, and Station Wagon lines wore a slightly busier version of Mercury's '61 big-car styling. Overall, they probably came off better then than they do now, but "forgettable" is about the worst you could say of them.

The S-55s were far more memorable. Where '62 Montereys came with a lowly 223-cubic-inch six and Customs a 170-horsepower 292 V-8, S-55s packed a brawny 390 "Marauder" V-8, new the previous season, with two-barrel carb and 300 horses. An optional four-barrel carb boosted that to 330. But there was still more, for also arriving with the S-55s (and Ford XLs) was a pair of limited-production Marauder 406s. Both were basically bored-out and beefed-up 390s boasting wilder camshafts, mechanical instead of hydraulic lifters, high 10.9:1 compression, low-restriction air cleaner, tuned headers, and dual exhausts. The "ordinary" four-barrel version, offered mainly to qualify for stock-car racing, pumped out 385 horses and a tremendous 444 pounds/feet of torque. For drag strip duty, there was a triple two-barrel 406 rated at 405 bhp—almost the magic "1 h.p. per cu. in." and the most power Mercury had ever offered.

But sporty fast-road work, not winning track performance, was the S-55's main mission. As a result, most of the '62s left the factory with one of the 390s and standard three-speed Multi-Drive automatic (Cruise-O-Matic at Ford), though four-speed manual was a no-cost, if seldom ordered, option. Besides, the 406s were expensive ($321 for the "NASCAR" mill, $406 for the "drag" engine).

Then again, the S-55 was hardly budget-priced itself, as it carried a sticker nearly $520 over comparable Customs. But at least it offered a fair amount of equipment to offset its cost: slim-back front bucket seats, a shiny center shift console with glove box, all-vinyl trim, special tri-color wheel covers and "S-Fifty-Five" exterior i.d., heavy-duty suspension and brakes, and meatier 7.10×15 tires. But price was evidently a problem, because S-55 sales stopped at just under 4100. Pontiac, meanwhile, moved over 30,000 of its plush new '62 Grand Prix hardtops.

Nevertheless, the S-55 returned for '63. Though the basic package was unchanged, the 406 options were joined by a pair of new 427s: four-barrel 410-bhp and twin-four-barrel 425-bhp. Mercury's '63 styling was all new and quite distinctive, especially the reverse-slant "Breezeway" roof with drop-down rear window on the S-55 hardtop coupe. But there was also a four-door hardtop S-55 in addition to the convertible, and at midseason there appeared a handsome "slantback" hardtop coupe called Marauder, offered in both Custom and S-55 form (covered separately in this book). The added models meant a slightly broader price range, and this plus a full sales year boosted S-55 production to 8764—better, but still far behind other big sporty models.

With such modest popularity, It's hardly surprising that the S-55 disappeared from Mercury's 25th Anniversary big-car line. However, its essential features survived in a "Sports Package" option for the top-line 1964 Park Lane convertible and Marauder two- and four-door hardtops. But the S-55 would return, a somewhat sorry story told a little further on.

Opposite page, top: S-55 became Mercury's "sporty" big car in 1962, and though it carried a standard 300-bhp 390-cid V-8, up to 405 bhp was available from an optional 406. Only coupe and convertible versions were offered, and exterior identification consisted of special wheel covers and discreet "S-Fifty-Five" badges. For 1963, the S-55 line expanded to include a semi-fastback two-door and a four-door hardtop, the latter joining the coupe (opposite page, bottom) in adopting the reverse-slant Breezeway roofline. Subtle identification was used outside, but the S-55 was most noted for its sporty buckets-and-console interior (below) and newly optional 427 V-8 with up to 425 bhp.

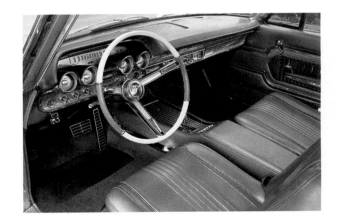

SPECIFICATIONS

Engines:	all ohv V-8; 390 cid (4.05 × 3.78), 300/330 bhp; 406 cid (4.13 × 3.78), 385/405 bhp; 427 cid (4.23 × 3.78) 410/425 bhp (1963 only)
Transmissions:	4-speed manual, 3-speed automatic
Suspension front:	upper and lower A-arms, coil springs
Suspension rear:	live axle on semi-elliptic leaf springs
Brakes:	front/rear drums
Wheelbase (in.):	120.0
Weight (lbs):	3800-4050
Top speed (mph):	110-120
0-60 mph (sec):	7.7-9.5

Production: 1962 htp cpe 2,772 **cvt** 1,315 **1963 fstbk htp cpe** 2,319 **"Breezeway" htp cpe** 3,863 **"Breezeway" htp sdn** 1,203 **cvt** 1,379

1963-64
Mercury Marauder

Mercury first used the Marauder moniker to denote its brawniest engines in the late '50s, but the name wasn't applied to a car until 1963. It's a handle that probably wouldn't be considered today: the safety lobby would surely condemn it as fostering reckless driving, while Mercury marketers would likely veto it as not reflecting the typical buyer's lifestyle. But Mercury was on the prowl even in those pre-Cougar days, and Marauder was perfect for what it was trying to accomplish.

The company's apparent goal was to recapture a performance image more or less abandoned after 1956. Significantly, that was the last year Mercury won a major stock-car race until 1963, when Parnelli Jones drove a new Marauder fastback to victory, launching a string of Mercury triumphs in NASCAR that would run well into the '70s.

And racing—or rather improved aerodynamics for higher top speed—was the main reason behind the Marauder and its new-for-'63 Ford cousin, the Galaxie 500 Sports Hardtop. After several years of a self-imposed truce, the Big Three had resumed open track warfare, and Dearborn's blocky period rooflines were a decided disadvantage in long-distance events on newer high-speed supertracks like Daytona.

Taking a cue from their own 1960-61 Ford Starliner, Dearborn designers sliced the old boxy superstructure from their big hardtop body, raked the windshield to lower overall height about 1.5 inches, then applied a new roofline sloped more gradually to the rear deck. The result wasn't quite as smooth or slick as the Starliner, but it made a big difference on the track. Better still, it looked racy, yet somehow "formal" enough to appeal to Mercury's usual clientele.

Compared to Ford's prosaic Sports Hardtop handle, Marauder seemed a more appropriate title for this slicked-down hardtop coupe. Mercury must have thought so, too, for it nailed bold name script onto its cars' front fenders. However, there was no mistaking the fastback Marauder with its "lesser kin," as other models wore the "Breezeway" roof, a fling with the retractable, reverse-slant rear window first seen on 1958-60 Continental Marks.

Though undoubtedly conceived after the fact, Marauder's semi-fastback roof

Marauder, with its semi-fastback roofline, could be ordered "plain" or in S-55 trim for 1963. S-55 was dropped for 1964, when Marauders came in two body styles (coupe and hardtop sedan) with three levels of trim—six models in all. The Montclair Marauder (below and opposite page) was the mid-line series. Standard engine was a 390 V-8 with 250 bhp, though four-barrel versions (above) offered up to 330 bhp.

mated handsomely with the big '63 Merc's reskinned lower body, marked by an attractive full-width concave grille, Lincolnesque chrome-edged beltline, and a reshaped tail with triple lamp clusters. Like its sister division, Mercury initially fielded a bench-seat Marauder, in the Monterey Custom line, and a buckets-and-console version, in sporty S-55 trim. Sales were respectable for a half-year model at just under 7300, though Ford did far better with over 135,000 Sports Hardtop Galaxies.

In partial observance of its 25th Anniversary, Mercury in 1964 returned to its four-series big-car model group of the late '50s, with price-leader Monterey, midrange Montclair, and posh Park Lane, plus a parallel Station Wagon line. Marauders multiplied to six, with a hardtop coupe and new hardtop sedan in each series. Styling was elegantly evolved from '63, with a redesigned front end being the biggest change. S-55s took a vacation, but a new Sports Package option made two-door Park Lanes, including the Marauder, into something similar. Any '64 Marauder could be a real rocket, as engine options expanded to include new big-block 427s with 410 or 425 horsepower. But, of course, these were mainly for racing. For most Mercury buyers, the smooth, durable 390, still offering from 250 up to 330 horses, was more than adequate.

Racing Marauders began asserting themselves in '64, winning five NASCAR and seven USAC events. But again, the slantback Fords did better still, both on the track (30 victories in NASCAR alone) and in the showroom. The Ford garnered nearly 73,000 sales compared to less than 34,000 for Marauder. Of course, the Mercs cost more than the Fords, though not a lot, but Marauders still cost no more than comparable Breezeways.

Though long overshadowed by contemporary big Fords, the full-size 1963-64 Mercurys exhibit similar sterling qualities (no surprise, as all used the same basic platform). Chief among these are robust construction, superb ride, competent handling, and strong, silent V-8 performance. Even a mild 390-cid Marauder could pull 0-60 mph in eight-nine seconds; the 427 could lower that to near seven seconds—thrilling even today. A pity these cars don't get the collector recognition they deserve, but it is often thus with Mercurys versus Fords.

The Marauder story pretty much ends with 1964 and for two obvious reasons. Sporty full-size cars were fast giving way to mid-size muscle on street and track alike, and the all-new big '65 Mercs abruptly retreated from overt performance toward a luxury orientation "in the Lincoln Continental tradition." After a token presence on '65 Montclair and Park Lane hardtops, the Marauder name was again confined to Mercury engine compartments.

SPECIFICATIONS

Engines:	all ohv V-8; **1963-64** 390 (4.05 × 3.78), 250/300/330 bhp (1963), 250/266/300/330 bhp (1964); **1963** 406 (4.13 × 3.78), 385/405 bhp; **1964** 427 (4.23 × 3.78), 410/425 bhp
Transmissions:	3/4-speed manual, 3-speed manual w/overdrive Dual-Range Merc-O-Matic automatic
Suspension front:	upper and lower A-arms, coil spring
Suspension rear:	live axle on semi-elliptic leaf springs
Brakes:	front/rear drums
Wheelbase (in.):	120.0
Weight (lbs):	3887-4056
Top speed (mph):	110-125+
0-60 mph (sec):	7.0-9.5

Production: 1963 Monterey Custom htp cpe 7,298 **S-55** htp cpe 2,319 **1964 Monterey** htp cpe 8,760 **Monterey** htp sdn 8,655 **Montclair** htp cpe 6,459 **Montclair** htp sdn 8,655 **Park Lane** htp cpe 1,052 **Park Lane** htp sdn 4,505

1964-65
Mercury Comet Cyclone

After plopping a small-block V-8 into the last of the first-generation Comets, Mercury was ready to turn toward some real muscle—and hoping to wind up with a rock-solid reputation for machines that could move.

Four different series were found in the Comet lineup for 1964, but only one came with the enlarged 289-cid V-8 as standard fare. That was the Cyclone two-door hardtop, which paved the way for the transformation of the practical but anemic Comet-based line into one of the hottest performance names of the decade.

Breathing through a four-barrel carburetor, the 289 whipped up 210 horsepower and 300 pounds/feet of torque. Both three- and four-speed gearboxes continued (the latter supplied by Warner Gear), but Multi-Drive Merc-O-Matic replaced the former two-speed automatic on the option list. Little by little, performance was getting the nod from Mercury engineers. Other Comets, including the new Caliente series, came with six-cylinder power or the carryover 260-cid V-8; or could be ordered with the 289.

The short-lived Meteor was gone, a victim of sales that never got off the ground. Thus, Comets would have to serve as both compact and mid-size elements in the Mercury line. Styling changes included a switch to 14-inch tires and a wider stance, along with enough body modifications to produce a new personality. Quad headlights rested horizontally in a mesh grille, and remnants of tailfins remained out back, while bodysides displayed prominent, tapered creaselines, not unlike those of the restyled Falcon.

Car Life appreciated the removal of spears and flashes from the Comet body, and though the editors didn't care for the new fender cutout moldings, they nonetheless stated that the restyle "represents a pinnacle of restraint for [Lincoln-Mercury] stylists." Wheel covers were designed to look like bare wheels, with holes for chromed lug nuts.

Not exactly a hot seller off the line, the early Cyclone went for $2655. Only 7454 were produced in that first year. *Car Life* described the early Cyclone as a "spirited sprinting machine which should certainly appeal to that 'youth market' so avidly

This page: *Comets began living up to their name in 1964 when the Cyclone version was introduced, carrying a standard 225-bhp 289 V-8. Little separated them appearance-wise from standard Comets except for their "chrome" wheels—which were actually chrome wheel covers. Opposite page: A restyle bringing vertical headlights and horizontal taillights marked the '65s, and Cyclones gained twin hood scoops to differentiate them from regular Comets.*

SPECIFICATIONS

Engines:	ohv V-8, 289 cid (4.00 × 2.87) **1964** 210 bhp **1965** 225 bhp
Transmissions:	3-speed manual; 4-speed manual and 3-speed Multi-Drive Merc-O-Matic optional
Suspension, front:	upper arms, strut-stabilized lower arms, coil springs
Suspension, rear:	live axle, leaf springs
Brakes:	front/rear drums
Wheelbase (in.):	114.0
Weight (lbs.):	2860-2994
Top speed (mph):	103-109
0-60 mph (sec):	8.8-11.8
Production:	**1964** htp cpe 7454 **1965** htp cpe 12,347

sought after by all the manufacturers."

Modest cleanup of the bodysides gave the next Cyclone a neater look, helped by vertically stacked headlights and a wide, uncluttered rectangular grille of horizontal bars. Mercury called it an "enthusiast's dream car in every detail," which proved closer to the mark than most such claims.

A console separated the bucket seats, which held upholstery of pleated crinkle-grain vinyl and faced a woodtone three-spoke steering wheel. Special chrome-plated wheel covers wore bright lug nuts. Cyclone's standard 289-cid V-8 earned a boost to 225 bhp and 305 pounds/feet of torque, running with a four-barrel carburetor and 10:1 compression. Other Comet models used a two-barrel version, rated at 200 horsepower.

Options included a black or white vinyl roof; a performance handling package with more responsive steering, modified shocks and higher-rate springs; and a "Rally-Pac" gauge cluster that put a vacuum gauge and elapsed-time clock atop the dashboard, along with the tachometer. An engine dress-up kit was standard gear, brightening the rocker covers, air cleaner, dipstick, and radiator cap. Checkered flag insignias went on rear fenders. All told, Cyclones were starting to *look* like performance cars—just as they added the goodies to behave like one.

Motor Trend got a 9.7-second 0-60 time from its 210-bhp Cyclone hardtop with four-speed in 1964. A quarter-mile dash took 16.2 seconds, reaching 80 mph. The next year, with an additional 15 horses waiting, the 0-60 figure dropped to 8.8 seconds. Other road testers weren't quite so quick, taking as long as 11.8 seconds to 60 with the 210-bhp edition. While these were hardly muscle-car figures, the Cyclone's time was soon to come.

Production rose sharply in Cyclone's second season, reaching 12,347 units. Though a laudable performance—and a harbinger of things to come—it was still barely a blip in Mercury's total output.

Like the SC/Rambler, for one, early Cyclones ranked as "sleepers" in the muscle car arena, barely noticed behind the GTOs, Hemis, and Super Sports that were grabbing all the applause. Yet Comets and Cyclones were proving their mettle on many battlefields. Four basically stock Cyclones powered by 271-bhp 289s went to Daytona and drove 100,000 miles, averaging over 105 mph. Meanwhile, a team of Comets ran the rigorous East African Safari. Fewer than 20,000 Cyclones had left the assembly lines in two years, but the name already was established and another generation was on its way.

1966-67
Mercury Cyclone GT

A different breed of Comet—and of performance-packed Cyclone—entered the Mercury lineup for 1966. Because Ford and Mercury models were now so closely related, a body change at Ford invariably affected Mercury's side of the street, too. But since its introduction in 1960, Mercury's Comet was always somewhat larger than the Ford Falcon on which it was based, though smaller than the intermediate Ford Fairlane introduced in 1962. By 1966, however, it was apparently decided that the expense of producing three different "small" bodys wasn't justified, so FoMoCo followed GM's lead by "cloning" its intermediates, moving the Comet up to share the newly redesigned Fairlane's 116-inch wheelbase.

Four Comet subseries comprised the new lineup: budget-priced (and shorter) 202, plus a Capri, Caliente, and Cyclone, the last three stretching to 203 inches in length. Wheelbases measured 116 inches on all, up from 114.

As in its prior incarnation under the Comet Cyclone banner, the bigger (maybe even better) new Cyclone came in just two body styles—hardtop coupe and convertible—in either base or GT form. The latter got only one engine choice: a 335-bhp, 390-cid V-8 with four-barrel carburetor and dual exhausts. Sound familiar? Fairlane GTs used the same engine. Mercury ads promised that their GT "delivers go that can shove you right back into your bucket seat."

Suspensions earned an upgrade, but obviously the big change was in the body. All Cyclones wore vertically stacked quad headlights recessed into separate round housings, dual pinstripes, and a twin-section grille.

Dramatic lower-body race striping between the wheel openings, a checkered-flag front-fender insignia, and a pair of flat hood scoops (which led nowhere) were part of the GT package. Though similar in shape to the regular Comet/Cyclone grille, the GT version had its own pattern of horizontal bars, plus a tiny checkerboard segment on one end. Two thin full-length stripes ran along the

SPECIFICATIONS

Engines:	ohv V-8, 390 cid (4.05 × 3.78) **1966** 335 bhp **1967** 320 bhp
Transmissions:	3-speed manual; 4-speed manual and 3-speed Sport Shift Merc-O-Matic optional
Suspension, front:	upper arms, strut-stabilized lower arms, coil springs, anti-sway bar
Suspension, rear:	live axle, leaf springs
Brakes:	front/rear drums (front discs optional in **1966**, standard in **1967**)
Wheelbase (in.):	116.0
Weight (lbs.):	3075-3595
Top speed (mph):	123
0-60 mph (sec):	6.6

Production: 1966 GT htp cpe 13,812 **GT cvt** 2158 **1967 GT htp cpe** 3419 **GT cvt** 378

Note: A few Cyclone GTs might have been equipped with 427-cid V-8s, producing 410/425 bhp.

Smoother styling graced the 1966 Cyclone, and the '67s (both pages) bore few changes, though the taillights went from horizontal to vertical. A 390 V-8 was the standard (and only) engine both years, and though production of the '66s reached nearly 16,000, fewer than 4000 '67s were sold.

upper fender line. Not everyone realized it, but the GT's hood was made of fiberglass.

GTs also included an engine dress-up kit, 7.75 × 14 whitewalls on heavy-duty 5.5-inch wheels, 3.25:1 axle ratio, and console-mounted gearshift lever. The heavy-duty suspension used a large-diameter front stabilizer bar. Bucket seats were upholstered with pleated vinyl, available in solid colors or two-tone mixtures. The driver faced a sports-style two-spoke steering wheel, a raised group of instruments, and black matte dashboard.

Either a four-speed manual or Sport Shift Merc-O-Matic could replace the standard three-speed. Sport Shift permitted manual control of 1-2-3 shift points, or easy cruising in Drive range.

Since the loss of the Meteor after 1963, Mercury had no mid-size model at all; so the enlarged Comet-derived series appealed to a fresh set of customers. GTs outsold regular Cyclones by almost 2-to-1, with 15,970 reaching the showrooms. Even so, the cheaper Comets scored higher, led by the low-budget 202 series with nearly 64,000 coming off the line.

Little more than cosmetic changes marked the '67 models, which wore a single-section, horizontal-bar grille with center insignia. Taillights and rear-end decorations also enjoyed a freshening. Engine modifications dropped the 390-cid V-8 down to 320 horsepower. The regular 289-cid Cyclone V-8 remained at 200 bhp.

Lower-body rally striping again helped identify the Cyclone GT, as did its black-out grille. GT extras didn't change much, including a twin-scoop hood, bright engine components, Wide-Oval whitewalls, stiffened suspension, and power front-disc brakes.

By 1967, the Comet name was officially used only on basic 202 sedans. This was not a good year for Cyclone sales—or for that matter, any Comet-derived models. GT production dropped sharply, down to only 3797 in all and a mere 378 ragtops. Even fewer ordinary Cyclones left the plant.

After a strong start, Mercury's performance mid-size seemed to be faltering, unable to catch hold like its Fairlane cousin. Service as Pace Car for the 1966 Indy "500" (with Benson Ford at the helm) and an award from *Super Stock* magazine as "performance car of the year" weren't helping at the showroom. Disappointed they had to be, but the folks at Mercury weren't ready to quit just yet, as the next generation of intermediates would demonstrate.

1967-68
Mercury Cougar

Today, the Mercury Cougar is an alternate Thunderbird, but it started life as an upmarket Mustang. It was designed to compete with the likes of the Pontiac Firebird, offering a standard V-8 and other equipment not found on the base Mustang for a few hundred extra dollars. Considering that Mustang had been taking huge gobs of the "ponycar" market for two years before the first Cougar arrived, and taking into account Lincoln-Mercury Division's smaller dealer base, it was a huge success. Sales totaled over 150,000 copies in its first year and more than 110,000 in its second. It was very much in the typical "ponycar" image, almost always fitted with bucket seats and center console. (Although bench seat Cougars were available, only about 7400 were produced in 1967.)

The original Cougars were pretty cars, identified by a Remington shaver grille and hidden headlights. Sequential turn signals had been a Cougar feature from the first models. Few changes were made to the '68s, which can be identified by their Federally mandated side-marker lights. Cougar put the finishing touches on a determined reversal of Mercury's image, which by 1967 was one of performance as well as luxury. By the end of the '60s, Mercury had successfully reassumed the hot-car image it had enjoyed in the late '40s and early '50s.

There were three Cougar models in 1967, all two-door hardtop coupes: base, GT, and XR7. The GT was a performance package, consisting of the jumbo 390-cid V-8, Wide-Oval whitewall tires, low back-pressure exhausts, power front-disc brakes,

SPECIFICATIONS

Engines: all ohv V-8; 289 cid (4.00 × 2.87), 195-225 bhp; 302 cid (4.00 × 3.00), 210-240 bhp; 390 cid (4.05 × 3.78), 265-325 bhp; 427 cid (4.23 × 3.78), 390 bhp; 428 cid (4.13 × 3.98), 335 bhp

Transmissions:	3/4 speed manual; 3-speed automatic optional
Suspension front:	upper and lower A-arms, coil springs
Suspension rear:	live axle, leaf springs
Brakes:	front/rear drums; front discs optional
Wheelbase (in.):	111.0
Weight (lbs):	2988-3174
Top speed (mph):	NA
0-60 mph (sec):	NA

Production: 1967 cpe 116,260 **GT** 7412 **XR7** 27,221 **1968 cpe** 81,014 **XR7** 32,712

Conceived as an upmarket Mustang, the Cougar debuted in 1967 (above) to rave reviews. Like the Mustang, it featured a host of options, one of the more unusual (and thankfully rare) being a "mod" paisley vinyl roof (this column, top). Few changes were made for '68, the most notable visual clue being the addition of side-marker lights. The top model was again the XR7 (this page, right), and the GT became an option package that was joined by a GT-E version (opposite page and this page, middle) that added a 427 V-8 and automatic transmission.

special trim, and stiffer suspension; a limited-slip rear axle was also available.

The best of the '67s was the XR7, which had a rich interior of leather upholstery and comprehensive instrumentation set into a simulated walnut dashboard. Standard equipment on XR7s included a four-speed manual gearbox, which was optional in the standard models. Merc-O-Matic Select Shift automatic transmission was available on all Cougars, and there was a 225-bhp version of the standard 289 V-8 (but not, as in Mustang's case, a 271-bhp 289). Since Cougars were better equipped than Mustangs to start with, they had a much shorter list of options. The main ones were air conditioning, power brakes-steering-windows-seats, two-tone paint, and vinyl top.

For 1968, the GT was not listed as a separate model but remained available, still with the 390 V-8. One rung higher was the new GT-E with even more power: the 427 cubic inch V-8 and automatic transmission standard, combined with twin hood scoops, styled steel wheels, quadruple trumpet exhausts, modified grille and taillights, silver gray trim on the lower body, stiff suspension, and wide-tread radial tires. At midyear, Mercury offered the CJ 428 V-8 rated at 335 bhp, and a stronger 302 with 240 bhp.

An impressive 1967 Cougar racing team of Dan Gurney, Parnelli Jones, Peter Revson, and Ed Leslie was fielded under tuning specialist Bud Moore. Simultaneously, Mercury announced a "Group Two" package: a pair of four-barrel carbs on a solid-lifter 289 V-8, supposedly producing 341 bhp. Mercury also tossed in heavy-duty suspension and quick-ratio steering. But there is no substitute for cubic inches, and the Cougars were outperformed by the 302 Camaros and lighter Mustangs. Mercury abandoned its Trans-Am effort after this one season, though continued racing in NASCAR's new Grand Touring series for sporty compacts, run mainly on oval tracks. Tiny Lund won the title in 1968, driving one of the ex-Trans-Am Bud Moore cars.

1968-69
Mercury Cyclone GT

Once again following the lead of Ford, the Mercury boys turned their sinking Cyclone into a Torino clone. Sure enough, sales just about doubled. Unfortunately, the 1967 total had sunk so low that even twice that figure wasn't likely to induce euphoria.

Most of the attention went to the rakish, long-profiled fastback with its vast rear quarter reaching back in a straight line from the roof. Bodyside striping stretched from headlight to tail, kicking up at the quarter window to accent the illusion of endless length on the GT edition. Another stripe flowed between GT wheel openings, helping to spotlight its graceful contours.

Though less dramatic, the formal-roof notchback hardtop—also offered in base and Cyclone trim—displayed a pleasing shape. Evidently, however, it was not pleasing enough, as it would fade away after '68. Both versions gave the impression of added size, but wheelbases were unchanged at 116 inches. The notchback's increase wasn't entirely illusory; it measured three inches longer than the fastback. Either GT model started at $2936, nearly a hundred bucks less than a '67 GT hardtop.

Beneath the hood of both base and GT Cyclones sat a 302-cid V-8, delivering 210 horsepower and driving a three-speed manual gearbox. Checking the option list brought a more potent 302 (230 bhp), or a Marauder 390 carrying four-barrel carburetion and 10.5:1 compression—along with a muscular 325 bhp. Settling for a 390 with two-barrel and 9.5:1 compression meant only 265 horses. Any of those mills could be ordered with Select-Shift Merc-O-Matic or a four-speed manual box.

Topping the list was a 427-cid V-8, detuned to a still-sizable 390 horsepower. Also available in the Cougar GT-E, the 427 came only with Merc-O-Matic and included heavy-duty cooling. By the time the model year got rolling, Mercury announced deletion of the 427 as a Cyclone option. No problem. Availability of the Cobra Jet 428 with its 335-bhp purring away was almost as good.

The restyled 1968 Cyclone GTs carried over into 1969 (below) with few changes, though the GT became an option package, replaced by the CJ as Cyclone's performance model. A NASCAR-inspired Cyclone Spoiler was offered in two flavors for 1969; a blue-on-white "Dan Gurney Special" (above), and a red-on-white "Cale Yarborough Special" (opposite page).

GT bucket seats were upholstered in Comfort-Weave vinyl, able to "breathe." Higher-rate springs and shocks, and large-diameter stabilizer, were part of the performance/handling GT package. Turbine-style wheel covers further augmented the image of ready-to-roll muscle. So did the down-to-basics black-out grille perched behind a trio of simple horizontal bars.

A few dollars more bought a tachometer to check out the action. More yet: an AM radio with Stereo-Sonic tape, or a Whisper-Aire conditioner. Styled steel wheels could be ordered for $96, but wire wheel covers quickly left the option list.

Among other changes for 1969, the GT was demoted from an official Cyclone model to a mere appearance option group, while the dramatic fastback came in base and CJ trim.

Closely related to Ford's performance-packed Cobra, the CJ measured two inches longer. CJs wore a black-out version of the revised Cyclone grille, with protruding center segment and a slim silvertone center bar. But the real goodies lay behind that grille: a standard 428-cid V-8, its 335 horses eager to blast a CJ off the mark with the greatest of ease. Ordering Ram-Air induction for $138.60 added a hood scoop to gulp in the fresh, cold air demanded by the four-barrel carburetor, plus a set of hood lock pins. A four-speed was standard; Select-Shift optional. Both a tachometer and bucket seats cost extra.

Did performance match the CJ's assertive stance? Definitely! *Car and Driver* needed only 5.5 seconds to hit 60 mph, and just 13.9 seconds to slam through the quarter-mile. Even in 1969, that was traveling.

This is not to say, however, that its predecessor was any slouch. A year earlier, *Motor Trend* took just 6.1 seconds to dash to 60 with its automatic-equipped Cyclone, also running the quarter in 13.9 seconds.

Cyclones performed well not only at the drag strips, but around NASCAR ovals as well: notably the 1968 Daytona 500, won by Cale Yarborough at an average 143.25 mph. No matter how hard Mercury tried, though, customers weren't exactly beating down the doors for a chance at a Cyclone. Production would rise in 1970, but sink to an even drearier mark in '71, the final season for these quick but overlooked remnants of American muscle.

Rarest of all is the Cyclone Spoiler II, which must be mentioned before leaving the Cyclone series in the dust. Only 519 were built, for NASCAR homologation, wearing flat front ends like the Talladegas that did similar duty for Ford.

SPECIFICATIONS

Engines:	all ohv V-8; **1968 GT** 302 cid (4.00 × 3.00), 210/230 bhp; 390 cid (4.05 × 3.78), 265/325 bhp; 427 cid (4.23 × 3.78), 390 bhp; 428 cid (4.13 × 3.98), 335 bhp **1969 Cyclone** 302 cid, 220 bhp; 351 cid (4.00 × 3.50), 250/290 bhp; 390 cid, 320 bhp; 428 cid, 335 bhp **1969 CJ** 428 cid, 335 bhp
Transmissions:	3-speed manual; 4-speed manual and 3-speed Select-Shift Merc-O-Matic optional
Suspension, front:	upper A-arms, strut-stabilized lower arms, coil springs, anti-sway bar
Suspension, rear:	live axle, leaf springs
Brakes:	front/rear drums (front discs optional)
Wheelbase (in.):	116.0
Weight (lbs.):	3273-3634
Top speed (mph):	**GT (V8-302)** 112 **CJ 428** 116
0-60 mph (sec):	**CJ 428** 5.5-6.1

Production: 1968 GT fstbk htp cpe 6105 **GT htp cpe** 334 **1969 fbk htp cpe** 5882 **CJ fstbk htp cpe** 3261

Note: An additional 519 Cyclone Spoiler coupes were produced in 1969, for NASCAR racing homologation.

1969
Mercury Cougar

After two years and over a quarter-million well-deserved sales, Mercury's luxury "ponycar" returned with more and less of everything. Models and powerteams proliferated, and there was even a gesture to the quarter-mile crowd, but something was lost that had set earlier Cougars apart from the "ponycar" herd. Perhaps not coincidentally, sales were lost, too.

The big news for '69 was the first-ever Cougar convertible, joining the familiar hardtop coupe in base and uplevel XR7 trim.

Styling was fully revised and still recognizably Cougar, but more derivative, particularly the Buick-like sweepspear bodyside character line and a full-width horizontal grille (still hiding the headlamps) that somehow lacked the character of the previous split frontispiece.

Wheelbase was unchanged, but overall length stretched 3.5 inches (to 193.8), width swelled by no less than three inches (to 74.2), and height came down half an inch (to 51.3). The increases, of course, reflected a change in basic body/chassis structure shared with Ford's '69 Mustangs, which were larger, too. At least Cougar prices weren't appreciably higher: up only $100 or so from comparable '68s. Predictably, the XR7 ragtop was the costliest '69 at around $3500 base, though options could easily boost that to near five grand.

Once again, Cougar ended a model year with a different engine roster than it started with. Unlike Mustang, Cougar still didn't bother with sixes, so a small-block V-8 continued as base power. For '69, however, this was Dearborn's new emissions-friendlier 351 engine, a stroked version of the previous 289, delivering 250 bhp with standard two-barrel carb, or 290 with four-barrel. Next up was the four-barrel big-block 390, restored to its 1967 rating of 320 bhp. Topping the list was a new 428 big-block called "Cobra Jet," replacing the previous year's "dirtier" 427 option and available with or without Ram Air induction. Both 428s were conservatively rated at 335 bhp to placate insurance companies, though the Ram Air setup surely packed more. A functional scoop and racing-style lockpins adorned Ram Air hoods, while all

Both pages: *The Eliminator was Cougar's version of the Mustang Mach 1, coming standard with a 290-bhp 351-cid V-8. Top engine option for '69 was a 428 with 335 bhp (above).*

428s came with heavy-duty radiator, uprated handling suspension, and E70 fiberglass-belted tires. Transmission choices were more or less dictated by engine. The CJ, for example, required the four-speed manual or heavy-duty three-speed SelectShift automatic.

The 290-bhp 351 was standard for a new package model called Eliminator, the Cougar counterpart to the '69 Mustang Mach 1. Ostensibly a separate model inspired by "Dyno" Don Nicholson's record-setting Cougar funny car, it was less elaborate than the high-dollar GT-E it replaced. To get one, you first specified a base hardtop with a $130 "Eliminator Equipment Package." This comprised high-back front bucket seats, special instrumentation, front air dam, decklid spoiler, styled steel wheels, black-finish grille, hood scoop, "performance" axle ratio, and bodyside tape stripes. Then on the order form you checked off the $70 "Eliminator Decor Group" composed of black rocker moldings, "Rim-Blow" steering wheel, custom door trim, rear-seat armrest, door-mounted courtesy lamps, and padded interior moldings. From there you could exercise free reign with other extras in the Cougar catalog. A bit complicated? Yes, but only typical of the '60s.

Additional performance excitement arrived at mid-model year in the form of a high-winding 302 small-block offered as a four-barrel "street" engine and in racing tune with dual quads. The latter was the Trans-Am powerplant from the racing Mustang Boss 302, a name also worn by Cougars so equipped. Both versions carried the same 290-bhp rating, again understated so as not to cause ulcers among underwriters. Very late in the year came a street version of Ford's big-block 429 NASCAR engine with a nominal 370 bhp, though installations were few, if any.

Cougars of any kind were fewer in '69, model-year production falling by about 10,000 to just over 100,000 units. The similar '70s would attract only some 72,000 sales, less than half those of the debut '67 Cougars. The reason, at least in retrospect, is clear: Performance cars of all stripes were on the wane, and "ponycar" demand was withering fastest of all.

But considering what Cougar became in the '70s—a Thunderbird-style luxury cruiser—the '69s look mighty appealing. *Motor Trend* timed a 351 XR7 at 8.1 seconds 0-60 and 15.8 seconds at 86 mph in the standing quarter-mile. And *Road Test* magazine's Boss 302 Eliminator, though a bit lacking in low-end torque, ran the quarter in 14.84 seconds at 96.16 mph—virtual muscle-car stuff.

So if not the best Cougars, the '69s are at the least "ponycars" in the winning mold of the original 1967-68 Cougars. And that counts for something, especially now.

SPECIFICATIONS

Engines:	all ohv V-8; 302 cid (4.00 × 3.00), 290 bhp; 351 cid (4.00 × 3.50), 250/290 bhp; 390 cid (4.05 × 3.78), 320 bhp; 428 cid (4.13 × 3.98), 335 bhp;
Transmissions:	3/4-speed manual, 3-speed automatic
Suspension front:	upper and lower A-arms, coil springs, anti-roll bar
Suspension rear:	live axle, semi-elliptic leaf springs
Brakes:	front/rear drums; optional front discs
Wheelbase (in.):	111.0
Weight (lbs):	3219-3343
Top speed (mph):	115-120
0-60 mph (sec):	7.6-9.0

Production: htp cpe 66,331 **cvt** 5,796 **XR7 htp cpe** 23,918 **XR7 cvt** 4,024

While the XR7 and performance models are most sought-after today, the majority of Cougars sold were base models (below). Biggest news in the Cougar lineup for 1969 was the addition of a convertible, offered in base and dressier XR7 trim (opposite page), though the latter saw only 4024 copies.

1969
Mercury Marauder

Though sales had long since tapered off, perhaps it was tradition that kept big '60s performance cars around right through decade's end. Mercury maintained a token presence in this limited market through 1967 with various S-55s, and many thought those large, "sporty" Mercurys would be the last of their breed. Two years later, however, the Big M released another big bruiser, this one reinvoking the hallowed Marauder name.

It was, to say the least, poorly timed. Not only had the performance action long since shifted to the mid-size ranks, but soaring insurance rates and more government-mandated safety and emissions standards promised to sap all Detroit performance cars, regardless of size. The reborn Marauder was thus doomed to fail.

As a car, though, this Marauder succeeded. Essentially it was a "Mercuryized" version of Ford's fully redesigned '69 XL, with an identical wheelbase that was three inches shorter than on other big Mercs. L-M didn't bother with a convertible like Ford, contenting itself with a hardtop coupe in base and pricier X-100 trim. Mercury's top-shelf Marquis donated a hidden-headlamp "power dome" front, while a "flying buttress" roofline with upright "tunneled" backlight were shared with the Ford. X-100s sported styled wheels and rear fender skirts (both optional on the base model) plus matte-black "sports tone" rear-deck finish. The latter could be deleted for credit or by ordering the extra-cost vinyl roof.

Marauder was billed as having "the prowling instincts of Cougar, the elegance of Continental." At 79.5 inches wide and a minimum of two tons, it was hardly "ponycar"-lithe, but it was definitely Lincoln-lush. Base Marauders boasted deep-pile carpeting, simulated burl-walnut accents, and cloth/vinyl upholstery fit for a sofa—which aptly described the standard front bench seat. X-100s offered additional woodgraining, "Rim-Blow" steering wheel, and three seat/trim packages: leather/vinyl front bench with dual center armrests; a split "Twin Comfort" bench with optional reclining right backrest; and all-vinyl or optional leather trim with front buckets and a center console mounting a horseshoe-shaped transmission selector.

Most Marauders were equipped with SelectShift automatic, though a three-speed manual was standard. Engine choices numbered four V-8s. X-100s carried Dearborn's big new 429 with four-barrel carb, 10.5:1 compression, a conservative 360-horsepower rating, and a massive 480 pounds/feet of torque. This was optional for base Marauders, which came with Ford's workhorse two-barrel 390, good for 265 bhp on 9.5:1 compression. There was also a pair of two-barrel base-model options: a high-compression 280-bhp "390P" and a 320-bhp 429.

Performance naturally depended on equipment. Despite a loping 2.80:1 rear axle, the X-100 was capable of about eight seconds 0-60 mph, standing quarter-miles of just under 16 seconds at 86-88 mph, and upwards of 125 mph flat out. Mileage was predictably piggish—*Motor Trend*'s X-100 returned only 10.8 mpg—making the big 24-gallon fuel tank more necessity than luxury. Heavy-duty Autolite shocks were standard, and X-100s rolled on wide-tread fiberglass-belted tires, but press-on types ordered the cheap ($31.10) "competition suspension," which *Car and Driver* said provided "very reassuring" shock control. Still, understeer and body roll were prominent regardless of chassis tuning, but the ride was typical Mercury, thanks in part to a new perimeter frame with four torque boxes.

All this plus abundant front-seat room, decent rear-cabin space, and cavernous 18 cubic-foot trunk made the Marauder a perfect long-haul mile-eater. But so were other big Mercs, and price competition was fierce. Though Marauder starting prices were attractively low at $3368 for the base version and $4091 for the X-100, delivered prices broke $5000 with air and other popular options—only $1000 or so below the likes of Ford Thunderbird, Buick Riviera, and Olds Toronado. Pontiac, meantime, had a smaller, more nimble new Grand Prix starting at just under $3900. Buyers voted with their wallets and Marauder lost: under 15,000 model-year sales—barely three percent of total Mercury volume—versus over 112,000 Grand Prixs.

The Marauder returned for 1970, little changed except for sales, which dropped by more than half (to 6043 total, including a mere 2646 X-100s). Sumo-size sporty cars had by then outlived their usefulness at Mercury and elsewhere, and the Marauder—despite its appeal—would not be back, nor even missed.

Below: *Marauder X-100 was distinguished by fancier trim and a matte-black rear deck, though the latter was deleted when the optional vinyl roof was ordered (opposite page). Standard on X-100s was a 360-bhp 429, which was optional on the base Marauder.*

SPECIFICATIONS

Engines:	all ohv V-8; 390 cid (4.05 × 3.78), 265/280 bhp; 429 cid, (4.36 × 3.59), 320/360 bhp
Transmissions:	3-speed manual, SelectShift 3-speed automatic
Suspension front:	upper and lower A-arms, coil springs, anti-roll bar
Suspension rear:	4-link live axle, coil springs
Brakes:	front/rear drums; front discs optional
Wheelbase (in.):	121.0
Weight (lbs):	4045-4200
Top speed (mph):	125
0-60 mph (sec):	8.0
Production:	htp cpe 9031 X100 htp cpe 5635

1960
Oldsmobile

"Every view is refreshingly new," boasted the sales brochure for the restyled Rocket Oldsmobiles. Sounds like typical advertising hype; but this time, at least, it was basically true. Essentially reskinned below the belt, the first big Olds of the '60s closely followed the enlarged "Linear Look" of the prior year, but had a more subdued and dignified demeanor than the dreamboats it replaced.

Each pair of headlights sat closer together, separated only by a narrow insignia. That left space for a wider grille made up of 24 bright blocks arranged in three rows. The hood's leading edge contained a wide scoop-styled nameplate, mating with the pronounced bodyside crease that ran around front fenders to stretch all the way back to the protruding horizontal taillamps.

A lower bodyside trim strip ran alongside another creaseline, tapering down behind the rear wheel opening, which itself displayed a graceful tapering-off. Twin creases decorated the decklid, and round backup lights were built into the massive, arched bumper.

Promotional drawings exaggerated the broad expanse of the back end, but the artist needn't have bothered. The decklid was plenty wide enough in real life.

So, did all these styling touches add up to the "fresh, balanced, enchanting symmetry" promised in the brochure? Well, maybe that's reaching a tad too far. Gaudiness wasn't exactly gone. The compound-curve windshield remained. So did the Holiday hardtop sedan with its flat-top roof extending beyond a radically wrapped back window. Let's be satisfied by admitting that the latest Olds was a substantial improvement over 1959, and vastly cleaner than the chrome-riddled '58.

Oldsmobile customers liked their comforts. "Quadri-balanced Ride" was claimed to emanate from the wide-stance chassis. Vibra-Tuned body mounting at points of minimum vibration, insisted the copywriters, would insulate passengers from road noise and harshness. Convenience options ran the gamut from Guide-Matic that dimmed the headlights automatically, to a four- or six-way power seat and power decklid release. If flipping the vent glass open and shut sounded just too, too taxing, powered ventipanes were available. Three-seat Fiesta station wagons came with a power window lift that dropped the glass into the tailgate.

Model names and body styles were similar to 1959, with two-door hardtops known as SceniCoupes, four-door hardtops named Holiday, and four-door sedans continuing the Celebrity nameplate. At the base of the price scale, the Dynamic 88 carried a 371-cid (240-bhp) V-8, running on regular gas with its Econ-O-Way carburetion. Both the mid-level Super 88 and posh Ninety-Eight used the 394-cid Premium Rocket Engine with its Multi-Jet carburetion and 9.75:1 compression, producing 315 bhp.

Both "88" series rode a 123-inch wheelbase, while Ninety-Eight wheels measured 126.3 inches between centers and the car stretched nearly 221 inches overall. That kind of bulk translated to some sizable poundage: All Oldsmobiles hit the scales at over two tons. Road-testing revealed the inevitable result. *Motor Trend* tried a Dynamic 88 SceniCoupe, and found its 0-60 time to be an uninspiring 12.7 seconds, with the quarter-mile mark coming up in 18.3 seconds at 75 mph. Not too swift, especially when compared to the rousing Olds 88 coupes of a decade earlier, which had combined the then-new overhead-valve V-8 with lightweight bodies to achieve some striking acceleration figures.

Air suspensions faded into the sunset, with few regrets over their demise. Some owners liked them, but on the whole, air springing had proven to be trouble.

Oldsmobile's promise of "American-size, six-passenger room" was fulfilled with ease. The Holiday SceniCoupe's interior had Jeweltone leather bolsters, and front-seat passengers faced a Twin-Cove instrument panel, with a glove box shaped like the driver's gauge panel.

Oldsmobile offered a lot of car for a few dollars more than comparable Buicks. Budget buy was the Dynamic two-door sedan at $2835. Most costly: a Ninety-Eight convertible with a $4362 price tag. No surprise there.

Both critics and customers had liked the 1959 Olds, buying close to 383,000 copies. This time, total output slid to 347,141, causing Oldsmobile to drop a notch behind Dodge in the industry rankings, to seventh spot. Considering that Olds had ranked fourth not long before, that wasn't good news. A big job lay ahead for the next generation of Oldsmobiles, which would turn to a revived performance image to complement the traditional Olds reputation for easy motoring.

Like other full-size GM cars of 1960, Oldsmobiles carried facelifted '59 styling. Top-line Ninety-Eights rode a 126.3-inch wheelbase, while Dynamic 88s and Super 88s were shorter at 123.0. However, the "small" Super 88 (both pages) was powered by the larger Oldsmobile's engine (a 315-bhp 394 V-8), making it the hot rod of the group. Flashy two-tone interior carried bucket seats and plenty of chrome trim.

SPECIFICATIONS

Engines:	all ohv V-8; **Dynamic 88** 371.1 cid (4.00 × 3.69), 240/260 bhp **Super 88 and 98** 394 cid (4.13 × 3.69), 315 bhp
Transmissions:	**88 and Super 88** 3-speed manual; Jetaway Hydra-Matic optional **98** Jetaway Hydra-Matic
Suspension, front:	upper and lower A-arms, coil springs, stabilizer bar
Suspension, rear:	live axle, leaf springs
Brakes:	front/rear drums
Wheelbase (in.):	**88** 123.0 **98** 126.3
Weight (lbs.):	4026-4506
Top speed (mph):	**Dynamic 88** 100
0-60 mph (sec):	**Dynamic 88** 12.7

Production: Dynamic 88 2d sdn 13,545 **Celebrity 4d sdn** 76,377 **SceniCoupe 2d htp** 29,368 **Holiday 4d htp** 43,761 **cvt** 12,271 **Fiesta 4d wgn** 14,542 **Super 88 Celebrity 4d sdn** 35,094 **SceniCoupe 2d htp** 16,464 **Holiday 4d htp** 33,285 **cvt** 5830 **Fiesta 4d wgn** 7240 **98 Celebrity 4d sdn** 17,188 **SceniCoupe 2d htp** 7635 **Holiday 4d htp** 27,257 **cvt** 7284

1961-64
Oldsmobile Starfire

Under Bill Mitchell, who took over as head of General Motors styling in 1958, all GM cars quickly abandoned jukebox design for a clean, extruded look. However, Mitchell took care—which today's GM does not—to keep divisional design separate and, to some extent, competitive. Oldsmobile developed a unique look, and with it a limited edition using the discarded Starfire name, which originally stemmed from a jet fighter aircraft.

GM in those days was lightning-quick to react to the market. When the Corvair Monza more or less accidentally uncovered an untapped demand for bucket-seat sporty models, GM was out with similar packages division-wide (except for Cadillac) within the year. Compared to a restyle or facelift, of course, the job here was easy: take a production body like the Oldsmobile Dynamic 88, throw in "buckets" (contoured individual seats, really) and a center console housing a tachometer, add distinctive exterior trim, and print more sales pads.

In 1961, the Starfire came as a convertible only, with a special engine, deluxe interior, and a host of standard luxuries, identified by its broad band of bodyside stainless steel—a fetish of Mitchell, and also his predecessor, Harley Earl. Starfires had all the Dynamic 88 equipment—courtesy lights, two-speed wipers, etc.—plus their own special goodies: power seats upholstered in leather, console with tach and shifter, a rear seat speaker nestled between the rear seatbacks, and a resonant dual exhaust system. A hardtop was added in 1962 and would become the only body style four years later, since convertible sales tapered off rapidly. In 1967, the Starfire was displaced by the Toronado as Olds' personal luxury car.

In its debut season, the Starfire was offered only as a convertible (opposite page, top and lower left), though a hardtop joined the line for 1962 (this page and opposite page, lower right). Exteriors featured special trim including wide, stainless-steel bands running the length of the body, while interiors boasted lavish trappings.

The early Starfires can easily be told apart. Broad stainless steel body paneling marks the 1961 and '62 models, the latter interrupted by louvers on the forward door. The panel became narrower in 1963 and disappeared in 1964, when Starfires were marked by a "trident" in chrome just behind the front wheel arches. That was the end of the really distinctive Starfires, as the later models were little different from run-of-the-mill Oldsmobiles.

Performance was exceptional in 1961 with the 325 bhp, 394-cid Oldsmobile V-8, in what was essentially the bodyshell of the baseline Dynamic 88. It gradually became quite ordinary as the years passed and the big Olds became heavier, though it never lost the expansive, 123-inch wheelbase. Most Starfires were fitted with all power options and, of course, Hydra-Matic transmission. They were big, deluxe road cruisers, comfortable and easy to drive, but thirsty and relatively ponderous handlers. "What the Starfire misses most," wrote *Motor Trend*, "is a distinctive exterior, such as the Thunderbird has. This is unfortunate, because the Oldsmobile is a superior car in many respects, and with a more individualistic appearance overall, it might very well have turned out to be sensational." To make it *that* different would have taken more magic than even Bill Mitchell had, given the time limitations—and of course General Motors already *was* working on a more individualistic car: the Buick Riviera, introduced two years later.

Conceptually, the Starfire was quite similar to the Riviera, but with its conventional body it would never be as exclusive. This is reflected today by the lower values assigned Starfire hardtops compared to Rivieras (though Starfire convertibles are worth more). They appeal to dyed-in-the-wool Oldsmobile collectors who know enough to be discerning. They will never possess the prestige and desirability of a Riviera, but they remain among the most coveted big postwar Oldsmobiles—especially the scarce convertible models. Production of ragtops never exceeded 7600 (in the first year), and by 1964 was down to only 2410. Hardtops, on the other hand, were almost commonplace, with a high of 34,839 in 1962.

SPECIFICATIONS

Engines:	ohv V-8, 394 cid (4.13 × 3.69), 325-345 bhp
Transmission:	3-speed automatic
Suspension front:	upper and lower A-arms, coil springs
Suspension rear:	live axle, trailing arms, coil springs
Brakes:	front/rear drums
Wheelbase (in.):	123.0
Weight (lbs):	4167-4334
Top speed (mph):	115-120
0-60 mph (sec):	9.0-11.0

Production: 1961 7600 **1962 cpe** 34,839 **cvt** 7149 **1963 cpe** 21,148 **cvt** 4401 **1964 cpe** 13,753 **cvt** 2410

Opposite page: *A wide stainless-steel band continued to adorn Starfire bodysides in 1963, though it dropped to a rocker-panel molding for '64 (below). By this time, however, sales were dwindling, as the Starfire was being overshadowed by rivals—some of which were from other GM divisions.*

1962-63
Oldsmobile F-85 Jetfire

Anyone picking up a brochure for the newest Olds at the New York Automobile Show might have wondered what the fuss was about. "There's something extra under this hood," the headline stated. "There's nothing like it on the road today."

What was this new marvel? A turbocharger, of all things. Though no big deal today, an exhaust-gas-driven turbo was something new and radical in '62.

This was a special sort of turbo, too, with fluid injection. Only by injecting a mixture of distilled water and methyl alcohol into the fuel/air charge could the combustion chamber be cooled properly—mandatory in view of the engine's high (10.25:1) compression ratio. Without fluid injection, Oldsmobile insisted, high-temperature, high-pressure operation would have been impossible with available fuels, and carbon buildup might have grown nasty. The turbo rotated at up to 90,000 rpm, boosting power by nearly 40 percent in Oldsmobile's estimation.

Ad copywriters had a field day coming up with terminology to hype the turbo. Sales catalogs explained how the new Turbo-Rocket engine mixes "the extra wallop of an exhaust-powered turbocharger [with] the extra efficiency of fluid injection." With a turbo shoving fuel and air into the carburetor, the aluminum V-8 was able to blast out "one hustling horsepower for every cubic inch of displacement." Jetfire's small aluminum V-8 squeezed out 215 horses from 215 cubic inches, all stuffed into a handsome hardtop with bucket seats and compartmented console "made for the man who thrives on high adventure." In short, the turbo packed 60 more horsepower than the ordinary 215-cid V-8 installed in F-85s, and 30 more than the "Power-Pack" hop-up. Who could resist?

Modern turbos come equipped with a boost gauge that demonstrates how much extra "squeeze" is hitting the intake system. Earlier supercharged engines had one, too. Oldsmobile took a different course, installing an elementary gauge on the console. The scale showed red (Power) on the right, green (Economy) on the left.

SPECIFICATIONS

Engine:	ohv V-8, 215 cid (3.50 × 2.80), 215 bhp
Transmissions:	3-speed manual; 4-speed manual and 2-speed Jetaway Hydra-Matic optional
Suspension, front:	upper and lower A-arms, coil springs, stabilizer bar
Suspension, rear:	4-link live axle, coil springs
Brakes:	front/rear drums
Wheelbase (in.):	112.0
Weight (lbs.):	2739-2774
Top speed (mph):	103-107
0-60 mph (sec):	8.5-10.2

Production: 1962 2d htp cpe 3765 1963 2d htp cpe 5842

Opposite page, bottom: *Like its big brother the Starfire, the '62 Jetfire was a sporty derivative of a standard model—in this case, Oldsmobile's compact F-85, introduced a year earlier. The package would look tempting in a sales brochure even today: a lightweight coupe powered by a turbocharged, small-displacement aluminum V-8 producing 215 bhp. Jetfires were reskinned for '63 (below and opposite page, top), with square taillights and creaseless bodysides.*

That's all—a lack that was noted with disdain by *Motor Trend*.

Otherwise, the interior was regulation compact Olds. Outside, a Jetfire nameplate on the cowl, just below the wide aluminum trim strip that stretched from stem to stern, set the turbo Olds apart from garden-variety F-85s, which were introduced for 1961.

The F-85's wide grille was made up of thin vertical bars, while twin creases decorated the hood. Styling was similar to the Buick and Pontiac versions of the compact body, highlighted by sharp bodyside creases.

Oddly enough, the F-85 evolved from the same platform used by the rear-engine Corvair, which introduced a turbo for its Monza Spyder. Oldsmobile's hit the market a few weeks earlier, at the New York Auto Show in April 1962. Price tag: $3049, versus $2694 for a comparable Cutlass sport coupe.

Dual outlet exhausts and a 3.36:1 axle ratio were Jetfire standards. Although 14-inch wheels were included in the package, 15-inchers could be ordered.

Not everyone was overjoyed by the Jetfire's behavior when hitting the gas hard. Even with 300 pounds/feet of torque at bay, *Motor Trend* was unable to catapult its Jetfire test car with Hydra-Matic to 60 mph in less than 10.2 seconds. That was 2½ seconds quicker than a comparable F-85 sedan with 155 bhp. Even so, the magazine declared that "as a performance package," the Jetfire edition "leaves much to be desired," complaining that engine response virtually stopped dead around 4600 rpm. A trip along the quarter-mile strip lasted 18.7 seconds, touching 80 mph. Brakes and Hydra-Matic earned no kudos, either.

Car Life evaluators were more pleased, able to hit 60 in 8.5 seconds with their automatic-equipped Jetfire.

Oldsmobile literature attempted to pass off its Jetfire—and also the F-85 Cutlass and full-size Starfire—as "sports cars" in 1963. Not quite, though each offered a unique flavor that reached beyond their bench-seat mates. Bodysides lost their creasework, and large square taillamps helped give the F-85 line a more conventional, upright silhouette.

Small Oldsmobiles sold well, but the Jetfire never turned into a hot number. In two years, only 9607 were built. Unreliability was part of the problem. Then too, the larger F-85 generation that arrived for 1964 had more space for its engine, eliminating the need for a small mill with big muscle. Whatever the cause, the American auto industry just wasn't quite ready for the turbo revolution.

1964-65
Oldsmobile F-85
Cutlass 4-4-2

Some great names blast their way into public consciousness immediately. Others take a while to simmer. Oldsmobile's 4-4-2, introduced as an option package for the F-85 series, falls into the latter category. Those "in the know" learned the significance of those three digits early on. Everyone else? Well, after a time they'd start to see more of these specially equipped Oldsmobiles around and begin to wonder.

For their first year of life, the digits had an unambiguous meaning. They stood for a four-barrel carburetor, four-speed (manual) gearbox, and dual exhausts. Available with any F-85 model (except station wagons), the 4-4-2 package delivered goodies intended to delight the rising number of "muscle car" fans—though that term hadn't yet entered full public awareness either. In essence, this was the "police pursuit" package under a new name. "Police needed it," trumpeted early 4-4-2 ads; "Olds built it. . . . Now ready to put more muscle and hustle into *your* everyday performance needs!"

Oldsmobile's formerly compact F-85 series wasn't so little anymore, having switched to mid-size status. Brochures blared that the new version was "Stepped up in size. . . . Stepped up in performance. . . . All new from the nameplate back." An extra 10 inches in length translated to extra room for people's legs, as well as a claimed 30-percent increase in luggage capacity. Additional bulk resulted from lengthening the F-85's wheelbase by three inches, and spreading the tread width by two inches.

Powertrains were new, too. Base F-85s now started with a 225-cid V-6, stepping up to the possibility of a 330-cid V-8 (standard on Cutlass models). A new variable-vane Jetaway automatic was optional. So was a console with tachometer. Bigger 14-inch wheels were installed, along with larger brakes.

Because the 4-4-2 debuted late in the 1964 model year, no mention was made in the sales catalogs. No Econ-O-Way V-6s or anemic V-8s here: only a potent variant of the 330-cid Jetfire Rocket V-8, tuned to 310 horsepower (versus 230-290 bhp on lesser models) and 355 pounds/feet of torque.

As an option package rather than a separate model, 4-4-2 components commonly found their way onto one of the three Cutlass bodies: Holiday hardtop coupe, Sports coupe, or convertible. Each had bucket seats, Red-Line tires, and heavy-duty chassis components for extra stability on the road.

Anyone who didn't think 330 cubic inches were enough had only a short time to wait for 70 more (and 35 extra horses). "Buckle yourself into this bucket, brother," warned one 1965 ad for the 4-4-2, "and you'd better be out for kicks *because that's what you're in for!*" Under this year's hood was a 400-cid V-8 that whipped up 345 bhp and a whopping 440 pounds/feet of torque.

The performance Olds was easier to recognize this time, with a "4-4-2" emblem and special grille. Nevertheless, it was still an option package, available on any F-85 or Cutlass coupe or ragtop body.

Either a close-ratio four-speed or Jetaway automatic could replace the standard three-speed, so the original 4-4-2 definition was lost. Now, the digits stood for 400 cid, four-barrel, and (acoustically tuned) dual exhausts. Front and rear stabilizers helped glue tires to the pavement, while a heavy-duty frame and drivetrain/suspension components kept everything tight.

All F-85/Cutlass models switched to a "dumbbell" shaped grille, from the former rectangular unit. A wide center strip spelled out the Oldsmobile name, with 4-4-2 designation in the corner below. Promotions included a Golf-O-Rama contest with four 4-4-2s as prizes.

"The engine is a sweetheart," declared *Car and Driver*. Their 1965-model 4-4-2 with four-speed roared from zero to 60 mph in 5.5 seconds. Nevertheless, they concluded that Oldsmobile's brand of muscle lacked "the explosive savagery of the GTO." It was "like owning a perfectly virile, aggressive pet tiger, but keeping him on tranquilizers so he won't bite you." A year earlier, *Motor Trend* sent its 310-bhp 4-4-2 hardtop with four-speed to 60 mph in 7.5 seconds, and through the quarter-mile in 15.5 at 90 mph.

Intended as a rival to Pontiac's GTO, and to the other quickly rising stars in the muscle-car marketplace, Oldsmobile claimed that the 4-4-2's price started "lower than any other high-performance car in America designed for everyday driving." *Motor Trend* pinpointed the 4-4-2 as proof "that Detroit can build cars that perform, handle and stop, without sacrificing road comfort." Enthusiasts were beginning to agree that a 4-4-2 for $250 or so above a Cutlass was a deal worth making.

Below and opposite page, top: In debut 1964, the 4-4-2 package included a special 310-bhp version of Oldsmobile's 330-cid V-8, and was optional on any F-85 save the station wagon. Intended as a competitor to Pontiac's wildly successful GTO, the numbers stood for four-speed transmission, four-barrel carb, and dual exhausts. For 1965 (opposite page, bottom), the engine grew to 400-cid and 345 bhp, available with 3- and 4-speed manuals as well as a two-speed automatic.

SPECIFICATIONS

Engines:	all ohv V-8;
	1964 330 cid (3.94 × 3.38), 310 bhp
	1965 400 cid (4.00 × 3.98), 345 bhp

Transmissions:	**1964** 4-speed manual
	1965 3-speed manual;
	optional 4-speed manual and
	2-speed Jetaway Drive

Suspension, front:	upper and lower A-arms,
	coil springs, stabilizer bar

Suspension, rear:	live axle, coil springs
Brakes:	front/rear drums
Wheelbase (in.):	115.0
Weight (lbs.):	2824-3338 (approx.)
Top speed (mph):	**1964** 116 **1965** 110-125
0-60 mph (sec):	**1964** 7.5 **1965** 5.5-7.8
Production:	**1964** 2d htp cpe NA **1965** 2d htp cpe NA

Note: 4-4-2 was an option package on F-85 and Cutlass models; production breakdown not available.

1965-66
Oldsmobile Starfire

The combination of sport and luxury in a full-size Olds wasn't coming on quite so strong anymore. Only 16,163 Starfires had found their way into dealer showrooms in the 1964 model year, down from nearly 42,000 in 1962, its second season on the market. What the company continued to call the "Flagship of Oldsmobile's sports car fleet" was starting to slip down the ladder of success, both in hardtop coupe and open-top form.

Following the path of many an automaker during the '60s, Oldsmobile deduced that a bigger engine was the answer. (Part of the answer, at any rate.) So the '65 Starfire hardtop coupe and convertible carried a potent 425-cid Super Rocket V-8 (achieved by extending the stroke of the prior 394), controlled either by a new T-stick Turbo Hydra-Matic or a floor-shift four-speed. Yes, a manual, shift-for-yourself four-speed: a "first" for the big Oldsmobile, which had virtually been synonymous with Hydra-Matic for a quarter-century. A tachometer installed on the console kept the driver informed, while leather-appointed bucket seats soothed eager passengers.

Curvier—indeed bulkier—bodies graced all full-size Oldsmobiles of 1965, conferring a different personality from their straight-sided predecessors even though the wheelbase didn't change. The difference was greater yet with the tapering roofline that characterized hardtop coupes. Extra bulk also translated to additional room inside—as if the full-size Olds wasn't big enough already.

Starfires were packed with standard gear, including power brakes and steering, a padded instrument panel, electric clock, wheel discs, and windshield washers. Convertibles came with power windows and seats, whitewalls, and an outside mirror. Running on 10.5:1 compression and breathing through a four-barrel carburetor, the massive V-8 was good for 370 horsepower and a muscle-flexing 470 pounds/feet of torque.

A unique Starfire grille consisted of four rectangular segments arranged around a

SPECIFICATIONS

Engines:	ohv V-8, 425 cid (4.13 × 3.98), 370/375 bhp
Transmissions:	3-speed Turbo Hydra-Matic or 4-speed manual
Suspension, front:	upper and lower A-arms, coil springs, stabilizer bar
Suspension, rear:	live axle, coil springs
Brakes:	front/rear drums
Wheelbase (in.):	123.0
Weight (lbs.):	4013-4247
Top speed (mph):	124
0-60 mph (sec):	NA

Production: 1965 2d htp cpe 13,024 **cvt** 2236 **1966 2d htp cpe** 13,019

Both pages: For 1965, Starfires were restyled along with the rest of Oldsmobile's full-size models, and the previous 394 V-8 was replaced by a stroked version with 425-cid and 370 bhp. It would be the last year for the big, sporty convertible version, and Starfire's waning popularity would spell the end of the series after 1966.

crossbar-style center. Wide lower-body trim moldings added more than just a decorator touch: They ended at the rear in functional side exhaust outlets—a trifle reminiscent of the built-in pipes that served several General Motors models, dating back to the '53 Cadillac. Rear ends displayed square taillights and a satin-chrome back panel.

Befitting what was, after all, basically a luxury car, the Starfire could be outfitted with a pleasant collection of extras: Tilt-Away steering wheel, Four-Season air, power windows and ventipanes, Guide-Matic, Signal Seeker radio, and plenty more.

Neither restyling nor extra inches seemed to do the trick. Only 13,024 Starfire hardtops left the plant during 1965, ready to sell for $4138. Convertibles totaled 2236 units, with a $4778 sticker price. This at a time when an Impala Super Sport ragtop started at $3212, and Buick's Wildcat went for $3727.

Only the hardtop coupe returned for the 1966 model year, wearing a restyled grille in the familiar "dumbbell" shape. The V-8 added five horsepower, but the most significant change came from the marketing department, not from engineering. What would be the final full-size Starfires lost a chunk of standard equipment, in exchange for a $574 price cut. Either Strato buckets or a new Strato bench seat went inside; fender vents outside.

Looking back, it's perhaps no surprise that the Starfire name faded away with so little fanfare. With one or two exceptions—led by Chevrolet's Super Sport—the blend of full-size automobile and sporty performance image simply wasn't the route to take in the mid-1960s. Oldsmobile's other performance-oriented full-size model of the time, the Jetstar I, fared a little better at the showrooms in its abbreviated life. But that limited success was partly due to its lower price.

As the Age of Aquarius took hold, big cars had a hard time grabbing the attention of youthful baby boomers. And parents tended to prefer their luxuries uncontaminated by a surplus of sportiness.

Besides that, Oldsmobile's innovative new Toronado—also full-size but with an undeniable front-drive difference—was grabbing all the publicity. As a result, Starfires just slipped away into the history books (though the name was revived a decade later for an undistinguished Olds variant of the little Chevrolet Monza). Nice to look at, pleasant to cruise in, Starfires rank as one of the oft-overlooked minor jewels of the '60s.

1966-67
Oldsmobile 4-4-2

Even though the new front-drive Toronado stole much of the spotlight from Oldsmobile's existing models, the sporty 4-4-2 was catching hold. In its mid-1960s restyle, a "Coke-bottle" profile replaced the straight beltline on all F-85 and Cutlass models, including the 4-4-2 series. Performance fans could have their fun in a choice of five models: the F-85 club coupe and Holiday coupe, and a trio of Cutlasses.

As they'd done since 1963, copywriters promoted the 4-4-2 as one of the company's "sports cars," noting that its "cool good looks [were] equally at home at a sports car rally or on a quiet Sunday ride." Could be, but neither the 4-4-2 nor any brand of American muscle was quite ready to race a pack of Jaguars and Triumphs around a winding course. Straight-off-the-line was where they shined.

Changes were less than drastic under the hood, which carried the 400-cid V-8 introduced a year earlier, churning out 350 frenzied horses (five more than before). Ordinary F-85/Cutlass models had to make do with a maximum of 330 cubic inches.

In addition to feeling the surge of power, 4-4-2 drivers tuned into the alluring rumble of acoustically tuned twin pipes. Only by checking off a few option boxes, though, would the 4-4-2's recessed instrument selection include a tachometer for consultation, or a console with performance gauges installed. Prices ranged from $2604 for a 4-4-2 coupe to the $3118 convertible (about $150 above a plain Cutlass).

This year's "dumbbell" shaped full-width front panel contained a simple grille opening with single horizontal bar. Quad headlights in square housings filled the ends of the space, with a 4-4-2 insignia in the corner.

Transmission choices beyond the standard column-mounted three-speed included a Hurst four-speed stick, floor-shifted three-speed, and two-speed Jetaway Drive. Strato-Bucket seats and Red-Line tires were part of the 4-4-2's temptations, as was a heavy-duty suspension aimed at reducing rear-end "squat."

With an optional Tri-Carb assembly underhood, a 4-4-2 streaked to 60 mph in 7.2 seconds. The quarter-mile demanded 15.2 seconds. Adding $265 to the car's price and 10 digits to its horsepower rating, the trio of two-barrel carbs "brightens performance several magnitudes," according to *Motor Trend*. A 4-4-2 handily won *Car and Driver* magazine's six-car supercar test.

For 1967, Oldsmobile's "Swashbuckler" had a new front-end look that included a louvered hood. The 4-4-2 nameplate resided along the horizontal bar of the narrower grille, with each pair of headlights split by a rectangular park/signal light. Helping send its energy to the ground in the most efficient manner was newly optional three-speed Turbo Hydra-Matic, replacing the former two-speed Jetaway. Naturally, a floor-shifted four-speed also was available to anyone dissatisfied with the three-speed stick.

By American standards, at least, Oldsmobile's "anti-boredom machine" was looking good in the handling department as well as at the drag strip. *Car and Driver* ranked 4-4-2 the "best-handling car of its type we've ever tested," describing the muscular Olds as "a driver's car." As for swiftness, it needed 7.8 seconds to hit 60—with automatic yet—and 15.8 to run the quarter-mile (at 91 mph). *Motor Trend* shot this year's 4-4-2 to 60 in 7.1 seconds, versus 8.7 for an ordinary Cutlass. Quarter-mile time was 15.5 seconds (at 91 mph), besting the Cutlass by a full second.

Options for '67 included a new transistorized ignition, front-disc brakes, and tachometer/engine gauge. Emphasis on safety caused Olds to promote such equipment as the new energy-absorbing steering column and padded instrument panel.

Dealers were able to install a special option late in the 1967 model year. The W-30 cold-air package consisted of two big ducts that surrounded the turn signals, blasting cold air into the air cleaner via flexible hoses. The claimed 360 bhp of a W-30 engine was considered a conservative estimate. *Hot Rod* magazine breezed through the quarter-mile in 14.5 seconds with its automatic-equipped W-30; and 13.9 seconds with a four-speed stick.

Mid-size movers with heavy action on tap were tempting young America—and a few older Americans to boot. Nobody realized that the muscle-car era, begun so recently, had only a few more years to go.

Even if Oldsmobile's tri-digit performance model didn't have a song written about it like Chevy's "409," it was coming on strong enough in the showrooms. Dealers offered a total of 24,833 in 1967. Olds was preparing a new look for its Cutlass series, and the 4-4-2 would again be part of the program.

Like all GM intermediates, the Cutlass acquired a new "Coke bottle" silhouette for 1966 (opposite page, top), and added five bhp to its 400-cid V-8. Only minor styling changes marked the '67s (below and opposite page, bottom) though the late-year addition of a high-performance W-30 package made cars so equipped not only rare, but also very quick.

SPECIFICATIONS

Engines:	ohv V-8, 400 cid (4.00 × 3.98), 350/360 bhp
Transmissions:	3-speed manual; optional 4-speed manual and 2-speed Jetaway (3-speed Turbo Hydra-Matic in **1967**)
Suspension, front:	upper and lower A-arms, coil springs, stabilizer bar
Suspension, rear:	live axle, coil springs, stabilizer bar
Brakes:	front/rear drums (front discs optional in **1967**)
Wheelbase (in.):	115.0
Weight (lbs.):	3454-4047
Top speed (mph):	130
0-60 mph (sec):	6.3-7.8

Production: 1966 2d cpe 1430 **2d htp cpe** 3827 **2d spt cpe** 3937 **Holiday htp cpe** 10,053 **cvt** 2750 **1967 2d spt cpe** 5215 **Holiday htp cpe** 16,514 **cvt** 3104

Note: Production totals by body style are approximate. Total 4-4-2 production was 21,997 in 1966 and 24,833 in 1967.

1966-67
Oldsmobile Toronado

Another example of how strong a role tradition plays in Detroit styling is the Oldsmobile Toronado. It was the first big front-wheel-drive car since the old Cord 810 and 812 of the late '30s—that classic design by Gordon Buehrig, which the 1966 Toronado more than faintly resembled.

There's a lot of Cord in the Toronado besides front-wheel drive: hidden headlamps, big slotted wheels, and the low, wide grille composed of horizontal bars. Toronados will never rival the *value* of Cords, (there were a lot more Toros, for one thing), but it is certain that they will go down as among the most desirable Oldsmobiles ever built. Had there been a convertible model, the early Toro would be one of the most sought-after '60s cars today. As a hardtop, it is still relatively inexpensive to buy a nice example, and it is a terrific value for the money.

Toronado project engineer Andy Watt's goal was to combine traditional American big-car power with outstanding handling and traction. Toronado's 425-cid V-8 was shared with conventional Olds models, but was teamed with a unique automatic transmission that was the key to its operation.

The transmission was essentially in two pieces: the torque converter was mounted behind the engine, while the gearbox was located remotely under the left cylinder bank. They were connected by a chain drive and sprocket, which Olds said was virtually unbreakable, yet flexible. Adopted to lower weight and reduce costs, the system resulted in a very compact engine/drivetrain package and a front/rear weight distribution of 54/46, remarkable for a front-wheel-drive car.

Toronado styling was as sophisticated as its mechanicals. The C-pillars fell gently from the roof, there was no obvious beltline aft of the rear windows, and the roofline flowed downward smoothly into a rakish fastback. The curved fuselage was set off by boldly flared wheel arches. The front and rear ends were clean and wrapped tightly underneath, as were the bodysides.

One of America's great road cars, the Toronado runs effortlessly at 100 mph and can do 135 when pressed, even with the standard axle ratio and automatic transmission. Understeer is present, as in all front-wheel-drive cars, but is well controlled and not excessive. Rear compartment room is restricted and visibility out the rear quarters is not good, nor is gas mileage. For such a revolutionary new design, the early Toronado was remarkably free of bugs. One reason is that it was built on an exclusive, relatively slow-moving assembly line. Toros do chew up tires, but tire technology has improved over the years and modern radials survive better. Doors are ponderous to open and close—a built-in assist arrived in 1967.

The engine/drivetrain was strong, but the combination of Quadrajet carb and high underhood temperatures caused a rash of engine fires. Otherwise, the Toronado was remarkably reliable, and good examples remain so today.

The public responded to the Toronado instantaneously. Over 40,000 were sold in the first model year. This was an initial spurt, and sales in 1967 were significantly less, though the Toronado gradually established itself in buyer confidence, and Oldsmobile would produce up to 50,000 a year during the 1970s.

The company promised to make few changes to Toronados except for function, so the first two years produced almost identical cars, both with big, flared wheel arches connected by lower-body creases. The '67 model lost some of the Cord hallmarks; the horizontal grille and slotted wheels were replaced by a split eggcrate grille and rather plain wheel covers.

Clearly, the early Toronado is one of the great cars of the '60s. It was the outstanding Oldsmobile of that decade—possibly of all time. In its original, clean form of 1966-67, it was distinct and not imitated. Given these considerations, it is extraordinary that prices have not (yet) risen into the stratosphere.

Oldsmobile's Toronado was a landmark car when it was introduced in 1966, being the first big American front-driver since the classic Cords of the 1930s. In fact, the initial version (both pages) carried Cord styling cues such as a horizontal-bar grille, hidden headlights, and slotted wheels.

SPECIFICATIONS

Engines:	ohv V-8, 425 cid (4.13 × 3.98), 385 bhp
Transmission:	3-speed automatic
Suspension front:	upper and lower control arms, torsion bars
Suspension rear:	solid axle, leaf springs
Brakes:	front/rear drums
Wheelbase (in.):	119.0
Weight (lbs):	4310-4366
Top speed (mph):	135
0-60 mph (sec):	8.5
Production:	**1966** 40,963 **1967** 26,454

1968-69
Oldsmobile 4-4-2

Even at a glance, the Cutlass line—including the hot 4-4-2—looked dramatically different for '68. It had a new, smaller stance, with fresh fastback styling on a 112-inch wheelbase (three inches shorter than before), stretching 201.6 inches overall. Three models could have 4-4-2 equipment this time: the Holiday coupe, sports coupe, and convertible. In fact, 4-4-2 was now a series rather than a mere option package.

Front ends of the "Youngmobile for the purist" displayed a fresh appearance, with concealed wipers and a louvered hood. Quad headlights again resided in square housings, the pairs separated by rectangular parking/signal lights. A large "4-4-2" insignia sat at the center of a rather narrow, rectangular crosshatch-patterned grille. Rear sculpturing was also revised. Dual exhausts exited through chrome collars notched into the rear bumper.

Not everyone was getting the performance message from Oldsmobile, as sales weren't exactly going through the roof. A new twist was needed. So Olds pushed harder with its Force-Air Induction System, which had debuted in 1967 on a small number of 4-4-2s. To give the engine an extra jolt, the W-30 Force-Air collected cold air through intakes at the front bumper, cramming it into the carburetor. Coupled with internal engine modifications that included special heads and a high-output cam, Force-Air tacked 10 horsepower onto the usual 350-bhp rating with a four-speed.

Standard Rocket V-8s with Turbo Hydra-Matic yielded only 325 bhp. Farther down the scale, Olds also offered a 290-bhp L65 Turnpike Cruising powerplant this year, with two-barrel carburetion and lower (9:1) compression to run on regular gas. Such a setup obviously guzzled less, but also tended to dilute the 4-4-2's performance image.

Few would have realized it from thumbing through the sales brochures, but this year's series of 400-cid engines differed from the one used in prior 4-4-2s, with

Above: A fastback roofline headed the styling changes for Oldsmobile's intermediates (and therefore, the 4-4-2) in 1968. Though bore/stroke dimensions were revised, the 400-cid V-8 still put out 350 bhp, or a conservative 360 with Force-Air Induction. Headlights were closer together and taillights were vertical for 1969 (below and opposite page), but there were few other changes to Oldsmobile's numeric muscle car.

SPECIFICATIONS

Engines: all ohv V-8; **1968** 400 cid (3.87 × 4.25), 290/325/350/360 bhp
1969 400 cid, 325/350/360 bhp

Transmissions:	3-speed manual; optional 4-speed manual and 3-speed Turbo Hydra-Matic 400
Suspension, front:	upper and lower A-arms, coil springs, stabilizer bar
Suspension, rear:	live axle, coil springs, stabilizer bar
Brakes:	front/rear drums (front discs optional)
Wheelbase (in.):	112.0
Weight (lbs.):	3502-3580
Top speed (mph):	108-122
0-60 mph (sec):	**350-bhp** 6.7-7.0

Production: 1968 2d spt cpe 4282 **Holiday htp cpe** 24,183 **cvt** 5142 **1969 2d spt cpe** 2475 **Holiday htp cpe** 19,587 **cvt** 4295

Note: Production totals include Hurst/Olds models (listed separately in this book).

revised bore/stroke dimensions. A Hurst shifter operated both the wide-ratio and close-ratio four-speed gearboxes, as well as the standard three-speed.

Handling got the customary help via 4-4-2's heavy-duty springs/shocks, front and rear stabilizer bars, and Wide-Oval F70×14 Red-Line rubber. Simulated wire or Super Stock wheels could replace the regulars, and axle ratios up to 4.46:1 could be ordered.

Transistorized ignition was recommended for cars that racked up high mileage. An optional Rally-Pac instrument cluster included a large-dial tachometer, electric clock, speedometer, and engine gauges. Rally Striping was part of the Force-Air package, or could be ordered separately.

CARS magazine named 4-4-2 "Top Performance Car of the Year." And no wonder. *Motor Trend* achieved a 0-60 time of 6.7 seconds with its '68 4-4-2, with the 350-bhp engine. Quarter-mile time was 15.3 seconds, hitting 95 mph.

Front-end restyling for 1969 positioned those vital "4-4-2" numerals in the wide center section of a split black-out grille, setting the stage for the grille style that would be used on Oldsmobiles into the 1990s. The digits were repeated on a big badge at the cowl and on the deck. Headlight pairs were separated by a narrow vertical divider.

Claimed to make "everything else look tame," the 4-4-2 again carried a 350-bhp engine (325 with Turbo Hydra-Matic). The emasculated Turnpike Cruising edition was dropped after a single year's service. Force-Air was back, however. Ordering that W-30 package brought the "largest factory air scoops in the business" (more than 26 square inches), as well as low-restriction dual exhausts and dual hood stripes.

Force-Air Induction could also be ordered on lesser Cutlass and F-85 models, the entire group known as the "W-Machines." Oldsmobile insisted that one of these came "as close as you can get to a blueprinted engine."

With its unique "bi-level" hood and contrasting paint stripes, the final 4-4-2 of the '60s looked just a tad outlandish, but remained a sizzling performer. As the ads explained, owning this slick Olds just might deliver some "escape from the ordinary."

Optional five-hole brushed stainless Custom Sport wheels could add a distinctive touch. And with its alluring option list, including a broad selection of axle ratios, a 4-4-2 could be fitted to travel in accord with anyone's wishes. At $3141 for a Sports Coupe ($3395 for a ragtop), a 4-4-2 wasn't quite bargain-basement, but those dollars bought a healthy helping of excitement from the guys at Olds.

1968-69
Oldsmobile Hurst/Olds

To enthusiasts, Hurst was synonymous with precise gear changes. Hurst Performance Products had been supplying its special brand of slick-action gearshifts to a number of manufacturers—including Oldsmobile—for some time. Anyone who wanted to run through the gears with the greatest of ease simply called upon Hurst for help. Now, Hurst undertook an even closer tie with the hottest "Youngmobile." Result: one of the most remarkable Olds models of them all.

As described by Terry Boyce and Robert Lichty in *Hurst Heritage*, Jack "Doc" Watson first created a one-off for Hurst, based on a 4-4-2 coupe. John Demmer, a Lansing industrialist, saw this prototype of what would become an "executive hot rod," and offered to construct production versions at his own factory.

John Beltz, Oldsmobile's chief engineer, liked the idea, believing it could help boost the company's performance image. Among those working alongside Watson on the project was one Robert Stempel, who later rose through the corporate ranks and now serves as GM's chairman. Watson explained to *Motor Trend* that he "wanted a car that would give all the acceleration you want in the straight, but wouldn't look like a floundering duck in the corners."

Demmer's plant installed 455-cid Toronado engines in the Cutlass bodies, circumventing GM's ban on powerplants larger than 400-cid in mid-size cars. Coded W-45, the 390-bhp engines (producing 500 pounds/feet of torque) carried 4-4-2 heads, Force-Air Induction, and a load of internal modifications. Long flexible tubes shot air through dual snorkels from ducts under the bumper. A less-wild variant with air conditioning also was created.

Except for the very first example, each carried Turbo Hydra-Matic, controlled by Hurst's own Dual-Gate gearshift, which allowed either fully manual or automatic operation.

Base color was Peruvian Silver (as used on the '68 Toronado) with black stripes and panels, plus white pinstriping. Because the production line wasn't ready until April 1968, workers had to rush to get the first group out the door as '68s. One man,

Due to a GM mandate that banned engines over 400-cid in intermediate-size cars, the Hurst/Olds, with its 455-cid Toronado engine, had to be built at a separate facility. All '68s (this page) were quite subtle in appearance, painted silver with black accents and featuring discreet under-bumper front air intakes that routed air to the carb through long hoses. The '69s (opposite page) were somewhat less restrained, carrying huge hood scoops, bolder graphics, and a prominent rear spoiler.

SPECIFICATIONS

Engines:	ohv V-8, 455 cid (4.13 × 4.25), 380/390 bhp
Transmission:	3-speed Turbo Hydra-Matic (Hurst Dual-Gate shifter)
Suspension, front:	upper and lower A-arms, coil springs, stabilizer bar
Suspension, rear:	live axle, coil springs, stabilizer bar
Brakes:	front discs, rear drums
Wheelbase (in.):	112.0
Weight (lbs.):	3870-3885
Top speed (mph):	132
0-60 mph (sec):	5.9-6.7
Production:	1968 515 1969 914

Paul Hatton, did virtually all the pinstriping on that batch of 515 cars. Of the total, only 56 were pillared coupes; all the rest were hardtops. Each wore a black-out grille and large black rear panel. Hurst promised "all the muscle characteristics of the finest super car, but without the objectionable interior noise and choppy ride."

Motor Trend suggested—only half jokingly—that H-O should perhaps stand for "Hairy-Olds." Needless to say, they were impressed with the joint-venture's skills, which included the ability to slam through a quarter-mile in a fraction under 14 seconds, passing 97 mph. The 0-60 jaunt demanded 6.65 seconds. *Hot Rod* magazine ran a 13.9-second quarter-mile, at 103 mph. Jack Watson himself managed 12.97 seconds (108.17 mph) for *Car Craft*, piloting the one and only Hurst/Olds four-speed, equipped with Hooker headers.

On the downside, this kind of "slam 'em into the seat" potential made the Olds coupe a friend to gasoline dealers. Owners couldn't expect much more than 10 mpg—less if the temptation to hit it hard proved irresistible. Then again, even everyday V-8s of '68 weren't too adept at passing gas pumps.

"Snarls softly and carries a big stick." That's how Hurst described the very different '69 version, which lost much of its initial subtlety. This time, each example was painted white with Firefrost Gold striping. Blocky twin hood scoops, described in *Hurst Heritage* as resembling a "rural mail box," actually worked better than under-the-bumper air intakes and eliminated the long tubes. Engine output dropped by 10, to 380 bhp.

A Cessna-inspired airfoil-type rear spoiler sat atop the deck. As many as 914 were built this year, with an engraved dash plaque showing the owner's name. Except for two convertibles, all were Holiday hardtop coupes. *Motor Trend* blasted a '69 to 60 in 5.9 seconds, conquering the quarter-mile in 14 flat (at 101.3 mph). *Road Test* magazine actually was pleased by "an unexpectedly high 10.6 mpg, even with a lot of hard driving."

Hurst/Olds coupes performed their major function particularly well: luring shoppers into showrooms. Target buyers were the newly affluent, luxury-craving yuppies (who existed long before that term was coined) of otherwise strife-torn '68.

Both Oldsmobile and Hurst benefited from the partnership, and each company advertised the product. Not only did the Hurst/Olds coupe continue into the early 1970s, but subsequent versions popped up sporadically, reminding the initiated how much two performance experts working together can achieve.

1968-69
Oldsmobile Toronado

Innovative and handsome the first Toros may have been, but nothing lasts forever. Sales dropped sharply in the second year, so naturally Oldsmobile pondered a restyling—and the prospect of some extra performance. After all, even big-car owners might like to pound the pedal now and again—and feel something happen when they did.

Although similar in basic profile to the original, this restyled Toro had a different front-end look. Bold brightwork surrounded the split rectangular grille, which contained a tight mesh pattern. Hidden headlights returned for another series of seasons, emerging from behind their grilles only as the headlight switch was turned on. Windshield wipers also were concealed. Wraparound turn signal lenses and fender pinstriping rounded out the front-end modifications.

Sad to say, in the minds of most observers, the revamped Toro lacked the clean, uncluttered lines of the original. The brawny combination grille/bumper, in particular, gave the impression of excess girth up front, while the rather plain wheel covers lacked the sportiness of the previous year's slotted wheels.

Oldsmobile's biggest engine ever—455 cid—squeezed out 375 bhp in standard trim, or 400 with Force-Air Induction. With the latter option installed, the V-8 contained a high-output cam and exhausted through twin pipes. Either way, the 455's prodigious low-end torque, reaching a whopping 510 pounds/feet (500 with Force-Air), boosted performance in the lower ranges and cut engine noise at the same time. Turbo Hydra-Matic was the only transmission choice, either shifted at the column or with the assistance of an optional console-mounted floor lever. A 3.08:1 axle drove 8.85 × 15 tires.

As before, Toros were quicker than some expected. *Car and Driver* managed to accelerate to 60 mph in 7.7 seconds, and breeze through the quarter-mile in 15.7 seconds (reaching 89.8 mph). Noting its imperfect handling characteristics off the straightaway, however, testers warned that a Toro was "not for citizens with cardiac conditions," adding that "when you're hurrying through corners, you'd better know

Opposite page: The '68 Toronado featured a redesigned grille and different taillights on an otherwise unchanged body. Engine size increased to 455-cid, with 375 bhp standard, or 400 with Force-Air Induction. For 1969 (below), the body was altered slightly to accommodate a notchback rear end, but otherwise there were few changes.

SPECIFICATIONS

Engines:	ohv V-8, 455 cid (4.13 × 4.25), 375/400 bhp
Transmission:	3-speed Turbo Hydra-Matic
Suspension, front:	upper and lower A-arms, torsion bars, stabilizer bar
Suspension, rear:	solid axle, leaf springs
Brakes:	front/rear drums (front discs optional)
Wheelbase (in.):	119.0
Weight (lbs.):	4316-4374
Top speed (mph):	129-134
0-60 mph (sec):	7.7

Production: 1968 2d htp cpe 3957 Custom htp cpe 22,497 1969 2d htp cpe 3421 Custom htp cpe 25,073

what you're doing." Ordinary driving, on the other hand, "inspires more driver confidence than any American luxury car we can remember."

Promotional material for the "massively male" front-drive Toronado focused on exclusivity, admitting that it wasn't the right car "for every driver on the block." Instead, this "big, burly Olds is for the iconoclast who likes his action with some size to it."

A full load of standard equipment came with the Toro's $4750 base price ($4945 for the Custom model). If that wouldn't suffice, transistorized ignition, radial tires on chrome open-spider wheels, GT pinstriping, vinyl top, and a stereo tape player were some of the available extras. Either individual vinyl buckets (seven colors) with a console or Strato Bench seating could greet the passengers. Flat floorboards showed off the color-matched carpeting.

Extra inches were part of the change for 1969. Additional sheetmetal was tacked onto the back, evidently to try and develop a more conventional notchback profile. Oldsmobile boasted that the expanded Toro was "longer and more luxurious than ever," yet brought "a youthful, sporting vigor to the full-size sporting field."

Powertrains continued without change. Vari-Ratio power steering was standard. Inside, the dashboard displayed a simulated Elm-grain applique. Steering columns contained a new anti-theft lock, as they did on other General Motors vehicles. Drivers in the snowbelt could elect an electrically heated rear window to melt away winter icing.

Not everyone applauded the fact that Oldsmobile veered farther away from the original Toronado's impossible-to-overlook profile. Regardless, as the '70s began, the front-wheel-drive configuration was well established, and Toronados were destined to remain an integral part of the Oldsmobile selection for the next two decades and beyond. They also influenced the advent of front-wheel drive across the size spectrum in the 1980s.

Quite a surprise it must have been for those at GM—and elsewhere in the industry—who'd scoffed at the notion a few years earlier, when Saabs were practically the only front-wheel-drive vehicles on American roads. Oldsmobile had to educate customers to the fact that front-wheel drive heightened a car's traction on slippery surfaces, and to the benefits that arose from having the drive wheels *pull* a car around curves rather than push. Little by little, though, American motorists were catching on.

1960-61
Plymouth Fury

Through 1959, the Fury had been a limited production performance Plymouth. By 1960, the name was too good to squander on such a small market, so "Fury" replaced "Belvedere" as the top-of-the-line model designation, with a four-door sedan and four-door hardtop joining the previous two-door hardtop and convertible. All, of course, used Plymouth's new unibody construction.

The change made good business sense. The styling of the '60 model didn't. It had been conceived in 1957, when tailfins were all the rage, and fin-wise it was as good as the best of them. The problem was that the public had grown tired of tailfins by 1960. Worse, Plymouth sales had been skidding since the 1958 recession. Thus, while Ford and Chevy increased their combined production by about a quarter-million units in 1960, Plymouth barely maintained its 1959 volume level.

Then on the 1961 Plymouths, the fins vanished entirely, replaced by a rounded shape with a swoopy front end that *Motor Trend* once retrospectively compared with "a generation of Japanese sci-fi monsters." The public remained unimpressed, and was now also confused: Plymouth sales dropped by 100,000 and Rambler replaced Plymouth as the number three best-seller.

None of which should suggest that these Furys were bad cars. Compared to their arch rivals, they were as good in most ways and superior in some. Every road tester agreed that they easily outhandled the Chevy Impala and Ford Galaxie, their counterpart top-of-the-line competitors, thanks to their torsion bar front suspension. Plymouth's TorqueFlite automatic was better than Chevy's Turboglide or Ford's Cruise-O-Matic. Fury's unit body was tighter than the separate body/frame rigs of the opposition, and so on. The Fury also had two exclusive options: swivel seats that pivoted when the front doors were opened, and the RCA Victor "Highway Hi-Fi"

Below and opposite page, bottom left: *Plymouth Furys sported huge tailfins for 1960, while most competitors were taming theirs down. The '61s (opposite page, top and right) were much more subdued, the fins being planed down and bent over to shield bullet-style taillights. While this cleaned up the rear view, the new grille was much criticized for its "pinched" design.*

SPECIFICATIONS

Engines:	ohv I-6, 225 cid (3.40 × 4.13), 145 bhp;
	ohv V-8, 318 cid (3.91 × 3.31) 230 bhp;
	361 cid (4.12 × 3.38) 305 bhp;
	383 cid (4.25 × 3.38) 330 bhp
Transmissions:	3-speed manual; 3-speed automatic optional
Suspension front:	upper and lower control arms, longitudinal torsion bars
Suspension rear:	live axle, leaf springs
Brakes:	front/rear drums
Wheelbase (in.):	118.0
Weight (lbs):	3330-3640
Top speed (mph):	120+
0-60 mph (sec):	7.5-17

Production: 1960 cpe 18,079 **cvt** 7080 **sdn** 21,292 **htp sdn** 9036 **1961 cpe** 16,141 **cvt** 6948 **sdn** 22,619 **htp sdn** 8507

record player. But it was styling that sold cars in 1960, and styling, in the public's judgment, was not the Fury's strong point.

The 1960 Fury could be had with a six-cylinder engine, the excellent 225 Slant Six, which gave Plymouth the hottest six in the low-priced field. With 145 bhp and a manual transmission (and aided by Plymouth's relatively light weight), a Fury six could do 0-60 in 17 seconds and still average 20 miles to the gallon. This engine was amenable to much hotter tuning—experimental versions wrung out one bhp per cubic inch at the Chrysler proving ground. But planners never opted for a performance six, and the Fury relied on Plymouth's reliable 318 as its basic V-8.

For all-out performance Plymouth had a bomb: the "Golden Commando 395," which had 361 cubic inches along with a ram manifold and twin four-barrel carbs, delivering 305 bhp and 395 pounds/feet of torque (from which it got its name). New also was the first of Plymouth's now-famous 383 V-8s, packing 330 bhp in similar tune and an impressive 460 pounds/feet of torque. This engine also boasted a one-notch-higher name: "SonoRamic Commando."

It sounds like a video game today, but the SonoRamic Commando could *fly*. Zero to 60 took about 7.5 seconds, nonchalant cruising was possible at over 100 mph, and top speed was over 120.

Despite the apparent radical facelift for 1961, the Fury had merely been reskinned below the beltline—the roof and doors were unchanged, with the styling money spent on fenders, hood, and deck. Plymouth described the result as "a harmony of motion in sleek steel and bright aluminum," and viewed from the side, it didn't look all that bad! Up front there was anything but harmony, with a criss-cross grille puckered between intruding headlamp eyebrows, bending around from front fender creaselines.

Latterday critics haven't really given the '61 Fury a fair shot. All told, it was a major improvement on the '60. It also proved that unit body construction didn't place serious restraints on the ability of designers to create facelifts—a problem that had plagued Nash, Hudson, and American Motors. Unfortunately for Plymouth, styling remained key to sales. To very many people styling means the front end of the car. And from that angle, the Fury really *did* look like the "Insect That Ate Tokyo."

1962-64
Plymouth Sport Fury

The 1962-64 Plymouths weren't nearly as bad as they're usually portrayed. Yes, they could have been built better (Chrysler was still in its "rust period") and the styling certainly didn't suit everyone. But in other respects these cars hold up surprisingly well. In size and balance they're *still* right today, and the long-hood/short-deck proportions were drawn years before we'd ever heard of "ponycars."

But bigger still meant better in early-'60s America, and the market didn't take to "standard" Plymouths (or Dodges) shrunk to near compact size. The result was a well-known sales disaster, Plymouth falling from a tenuous number-three position for 1960 all the way to eighth for '62—its worst placing ever. What's often overlooked is that these same basic cars lifted Plymouth to fourth the very next year (behind amazingly strong Pontiac), though the popular compact Valiant remained a big factor.

Most of what goes for Dodge's 1962-64 standards (covered elsewhere) applies to these Plymouths. Exceptions involve appearance, where Plymouth arguably fared better, and the initial 116-inch wheelbase, which unlike Dodge, Plymouth retained after '62.

Incidentally, those who brand the '62 Plymouth as weird-looking—as many people did at the time—should know that it might have been even weirder. One surviving photo of the "S-series" design program that sired these cars shows a mock-up with virtual 1962 production styling, save a license-plate frame. It "featured" a vestigial trunklid fin offset to the left, echoing the asymmetric theme of Virgil Exner's 1960 "XNR" show car. Intriguingly, another photo shows what appears to be a true full-size Plymouth looking very Pontiac-like and bearing "Super Sport" badges. This suggests that a two-tier lineup, like the Dart/Custom 880 split that Dodge ended up with in '62, had been the original Plymouth plan. A shame it didn't materialize.

What did materialize was a sportier version of the downsized '62 reviving the Sport Fury tag from 1959 (Chevy, of course, owned "Super Sport"). Bowing midyear as a convertible and hardtop coupe, it mainly offered the same features that proved so

This page and opposite page, top: Full-size Plymouths wore revised styling for 1962, and the Sport Fury was still the top-line offering with sporty two-tone interior and flashier exterior trim. Another restyle marked the '63s (opposite page, bottom), bringing straighter lines and a more conventional look.

SPECIFICATIONS

Engines: all ohv V-8; 318 cid (3.91 × 3.31), 230 bhp; 361 cid (4.12 × 3.38), 265/305/310 bhp; 383 cid (4.25 × 3.38), 320/325/330/335 bhp; 413 cid (4.19 × 3.75), 365/380/410 bhp (**1962 only**); 426 cid (4.25 × 3.75), 365/370/375/415/425 bhp (**1963-64**)

Transmissions:	3-speed manual (4-speed in 1964 only); 3-speed TorqueFlite automatic
Suspension front:	upper and lower A-arms, longitudinal torsion bars, anti-roll bar
Suspension rear:	live axle on semi-elliptic leaf springs
Brakes:	front/rear drums
Wheelbase (in.):	116.0
Weight (lbs):	3195-3405
Top speed (mph):	105-120+
0-60 mph (sec):	6.8-9.5

Production: 1962 htp cpe 4,039 **cvt** 1,516 **1963 htp cpe** 11,483 **cvt** 3,836 **1964 htp cpe** 23,695 **cvt** 3,858

Both pages: The '64s were treated to a mild facelift, while coupes wore new V-shaped rear pillars. Sport Furys continued to offer buckets-and-console interior, but gained a fresh dashboard with a row of four round gauges mounted in a brushed-metal panel. Top engine option was a 426-cid "wedgehead" (below) offering from 365 to 425 bhp.

popular on Chevy's Corvair Monza, namely an all-vinyl interior with front bucket seats and center console. Outside, the new twosome was set apart from lesser Furys by black grille accents, special wheel covers, belt molding extension, and a slim bright strip with dummy air vents above the back panel. Unlike lesser models, which came with a Slant Six, Sport Furys carried a standard 361 "Golden Commando" V-8 with 305 bhp. Power options ran through a pair of 383s up to a trio of mighty 413 wedgeheads packing up to 410 bhp with ram-induction manifolding.

Remembering that the '62 Plymouths measured seven inches shorter and up to 400 pounds lighter than the '61s, it's easy to see that Sport Furys could be ferocious performers with one of the bigger V-8s. Part of that weight-savings came from a switch to full unibody construction, without the front subframe of 1960-61, which made for uncommonly tight, solid cars better able to exploit the fine handling of Chrysler's torsion-bar front suspension. No wonder law-enforcement agencies bought so many of these vehicles.

Helped by deftly reskinned standards for '63, Plymouth's model-year production improved from 340,000 to a more heartening 488,500. Quad headlamps came together within a much-simplified grille; "bladed" fenderlines and slab sides gave way to a more conventional, sculptured look; hardtop coupes acquired attractive, Thunderbird-style rooflines; and three extra inches in rear overhang added one cubic foot to trunk space. Special wheel covers and tri-color insignia again identified Sport Furys. Drivetrains were largely as before, but the optional 413s gave way to bored-out 426 wedgeheads with up to 425 bhp.

Another lower-body restyle followed for '64, along with a more conventional dash, and, for hardtops, a distinctive new roofline with vee'd rear pillars and "bubble" backlight. The big mechanical news was a first-time four-on-the-floor option, available with any V-8. *Popular Mechanics* also noted that a 2.5-inch wider rear track "makes for less roll and better handling when taking the curves on a rough road." Testifying to the inherent goodness of its '64s, Plymouth swept that year's Daytona 500 1-2-3, helped by a Hemi V-8 newly revived for competition only—and by a young driver named Richard Petty, future king of the NASCAR world. That convincing victory undoubtedly helped boost Plymouth volume, which rose to nearly 600,000 for the model year, the best since 1957—not bad for a make so down and out just two years before.

This certainly must rank as one of the great sales comebacks of all time. But then, as we said, the cars weren't so bad either.

1963-66
Plymouth Valiant Signet

Plymouth probably wishes it had a car like the Valiant today. Introduced as one of the Big Three's new 1960 compacts, Valiant did good business throughout its long life, which ended in 1976. Without it, Plymouth would have fared far worse than it did in some years, particularly 1962.

That, of course, was the year Plymouth suffered a mighty sales slide with standard cars that looked like Valiants and weren't much larger. But it was also when Plymouth fielded a bucket-seat Valiant hardtop coupe called Signet. Neither Chevy's Corvair Monza, which had uncovered the sporty-compact market, nor Ford's Falcon had anything quite like it, yet model-year sales weren't sensational at some 25,600.

Still, sporty compacts were catching on fast, and the '63 Signet kept pace. It even *set* the pace in some ways. Where Corvair and Falcon again wore facelifts, Valiant styling was all-new—cleaner, though somewhat less distinctive than the year before. Lead times being what they were in those days, it was the work of Virgil Exner and not his replacement, Elwood Engel, who didn't exert serious influence on Chrysler Corporation styling until 1965. Perhaps Exner was hurt by criticism—or slow sales—of his recent efforts, for the '63 Valiant was surprisingly conventional in both form and detail.

Though overall length was up two inches on an unchanged wheelbase, the '63 Valiants looked smaller than previous ones, thanks to more equal hood/deck proportions and rounded instead of sharp contours. Simplicity was a hallmark, from a new dual-headlamp front to a tidy tail with just a hint of fins.

Signet tacked on a "200" suffix, and the familiar hardtop coupe was joined by a nifty new convertible, matching a '62 Corvair offering. The ragtop repeated with a bench seat in the mid-range V200 line, which along with the base V100 series offered two- and four-door sedans and a four-door wagon. Valiant would keep this basic lineup through 1966.

There was no need to change the successful Valiant chassis, so the '63s retained Chrysler's famed torsion-bar front suspension, standard 101-bhp 170-cid Slant Six, optional 145-bhp "Super 225" six, and choice of three-on-the-tree manual or optional pushbutton TorqueFlite automatic. Signets remained the brightest and sportiest Valiants, with additional chrome accents inside and out, plus special wheel covers and all-vinyl bucket-seat interiors. A power top was optional for the convertible in lieu of the standard manual affair.

In all, not very exciting perhaps, but Valiant's main mission was reliable economy transportation, which it delivered. The '63s were priced a few dollars below comparable '62s, and shared in Chrysler's new corporate-wide 5-year/50,000-mile powertrain warranty, an industry first designed to win back buyers put off by the so-so workmanship of recent Highland Park products. This, together with the new styling, boosted Valiant volume by more than two-thirds to over 225,000. Signets accounted for about 18 percent—good but not great even considering some new '63 competition, not the least being Dodge's stylish Dart GT (see entry).

There were two big newsmakers for '64. One was Valiant's first V-8 option, the fine 180-bhp 273 derived from Chrysler's new-generation 318 and also offered for Dart. But from midseason, the 273 was also available in a fastback Valiant derivative, the Barracuda (see entry). Though Signet hardtop sales weren't immediately affected, Barracuda did about two-thirds as well despite its short selling season, a sign of things to come.

Another mild facelift occurred for '65, when the previous year's full-width horizontal-bar grille gave way to a busier three-section treatment. The V-8 was heated up to 235 bhp as a new option, but Valiants offered nothing like the Formula S performance-and-handling package available for Barracuda, which was now separated from the Valiant line and outsold the Signet hardtop by better than 5-to-1. Overall, Signets garnered just eight percent of Valiant's reduced 167,000-unit model-year volume.

A squarish new front with split grille arrived for '66, the last year for the basic '63 Valiant design, and a more formal-looking hardtop roofline could be newly capped with a vinyl top. Signet sales went up a bit, but overall Valiant production was the lowest since 1961: 138,000, versus over a quarter-million just two years before.

Then came conservatively styled all-new '67s that returned Valiant entirely to its original economy-compact role. Wagons went away, hardtops and convertibles became Barracudas, and Signet was merely a better-trimmed pair of sedans above V100s. The name disappeared after 1969, thus ending Valiant's brief fling with sport.

Though the '63 Valiant Signet was built on the same 106-inch wheelbase as the '62, it carried completely new styling that was "boxier" and much more conservative than the previous version. Little changed cosmetically for 1964 (opposite page, bottom), though a newly optional 180-bhp 273 V-8 finally brought performance that matched the Signet's sporty pretensions. The V-8 gained a high-performance version with 55 more bhp for '65, but despite the added performance, sales dropped by two-thirds, and the '66 version (opposite page, top) would prove to be the last of this generation.

SPECIFICATIONS

Engines:	ohv I-6, 170 cid (3.40 × 3.13), 101 bhp; 225 cid (3.40 × 4.13), 145 bhp; ohv V-8, 273 cid (3.63 × 3.31), 180/235 bhp (**1964-66**)
Transmissions:	3-speed manual, 3-speed TorqueFlite automatic
Suspension front:	upper and lower A-arms, longitudinal torsion bars, anti-roll bar
Suspension rear:	live axle on semi-elliptic leaf springs
Brakes:	front/rear drums
Wheelbase (in.):	106.0
Weight (lbs):	2570-2830
Top speed (mph):	90-105
0-60 mph (sec):	10.0-20.0

Production: 1963 htp cpe 30,857 **cvt** 9,154 **1964 htp cpe** 37,736 **cvt** 7,636 **1965 htp cpe** 10,999 **cvt** 2,578 **1966 htp cpe** 13,045 **cvt** 2,507

1965-66
Plymouth Barracuda

Reacting to competitive pressures and buyer demand for sportier compacts, Plymouth tacked a glassy fastback to the Valiant in mid-1964 and called the result the Barracuda—following a contemporary fad for naming cars after ferocious or at least wild animals. The public responded by buying nearly 25,000 of them, so for 1965-66, the Barracuda "glassback" became a separate model, and Plymouth's sales and advertising departments went to work on it. That was the height of the sporty compact era, with a parallel interest in fastback body styles. It followed that a *fastback* sporty-compact would sell like hotcakes, and the Barracuda did, notching 65,000 units for 1965, better than any other Valiant.

The '65 Barracuda had what the old Valiant Signet should have had back in 1962: a 225-cid Slant Six as standard equipment. Thus, even the base 'Cuda would not be embarrassed off the line. And for only a few extra dollars you could opt for the fine 273-cid V-8, developed especially for Valiant applications, which gave 180 bhp in standard tune. But there was yet another layer of performance: the "Formula S" package, including a 235-bhp 273, four-speed gearbox with Hurst shifter, stiff suspension, wide wheels shod with Blue Streak Wide-Oval tires, special striping, and "Formula S" badges. Equipped this way, a Barracuda still cost less than $3400, and at that price it was a bargain.

"Chrysler has come up with a car that's exciting and fun to drive," wrote tester Bob McVay. "It handles like a champ, yet offers a tremendous amount of utility. And they've kept it a quiet, comfortable, pleasant car to drive on extended trips." With optional front-disc brakes and power steering (to get the quicker 3.5 turns lock to lock), McVay thought the Formula S would be just about perfect.

As it was, the car impressed: "With plenty of power on tap, the Barracuda could be drifted through fast bends at will and brought back into a straight line at the driver's discretion by pressing the accelerator. [Yet] the Barracuda's comfortable ride hasn't suffered. We could feel the firmer reaction over washboard roads and deep potholes, but it certainly couldn't be called uncomfortable." Plymouth had worked a minor miracle almost unknown in '60s Detroit: outstanding handling with no sacrifice in ride quality.

The 235-bhp engine combined with a 3.55:1 Sure-Grip differential gave the Barracuda excellent drag strip performance, too. With two people aboard, 0-60 took just eight seconds, and the standing quarter-mile 16 seconds; top speed was 110 mph. "We were impressed," concluded McVay. "The Barracuda offers a wide, wide range of performance with utility. It's roomy and comfortable for five (more so for four), yet its handling is still good, improved if anything by the extra weight. With only two aboard, luggage space is tremendous. Long on performance, handling and utility, it offers the family man a package that should be darn near impossible to resist."

More people were able to resist in 1966, when Barracuda's price was raised and fewer than 40,000 found buyers. This was due more to the fact that the "glassback" design was showing its age than to any demerit in the Barracuda package, which was much the same as in 1965. The '66 could be distinguished by a new grille, with eggcrate sections flanking a body-colored center panel bearing a new emblem—the barracuda fish itself. Pinstriping was added to the beltline and a vinyl top was optional. Standard equipment included full wheel covers, rocker panel moldings, and the usual deluxe Barracuda interior.

How did Barracuda compare to its two main rivals? Considering that the Mustang was purpose-built especially for this market, and that Chevy had vastly improved the Corvair with new styling and a hotter turbocharged model, the 1965-66 Barracuda remained an excellent alternative. It lacked the Corvair's technical sophistication, but would run rings around it; Barracuda also lacked the classic long-hood/short-deck "ponycar" proportions of the Mustang, but handled and rode a lot better and was quicker than any Mustang except the limited-production 271-bhp model. Its weakness was styling: the Barracuda still looked like a Valiant with a fastback. But Plymouth was preparing to take care of that problem the following year.

Opposite page, bottom: *Barracuda became a separate model for '65 after being introduced in late 1964. Though a practical sporty car with good performance (at least when equipped with one of the optional 273-cid V-8s), it faced stiff competition from the phenomenally successful new Mustang, which outsold the Barracuda by about 10-to-1. A revised grille was one of the few changes that marked the '66s (below and opposite page, top), when sales dropped by more than a third.*

SPECIFICATIONS

Engines:	ohv I-6, 225 cid (3.40 × 4.13), 145 bhp; ohv V-8, 273 cid (3.62 × 3.31), 180/235 bhp
Transmissions:	3-speed manual; 4-speed manual, 3-speed automatic optional
Suspension front:	upper and lower control arms, longitudinal torsion bars
Suspension rear:	live axle, leaf springs
Brakes:	front/rear drums; front discs optional
Wheelbase (in.):	106.0
Weight (lbs):	2725
Top speed (mph):	110
0-60 mph (sec):	8.0
Production:	**1965** 64,596 **1966** 38,029

1965-66
Plymouth Sport
Fury & VIP

Plymouth's full-size line was redesigned for 1965 with stacked headlights and straight-edge styling on a longer wheelbase. All carried the Fury name this year, but the flagship of the fleet was again the Sport Fury (above and below), featuring fancier trim, buckets-and console interior, and a standard 318-cid V-8. Little changed for '66, though a luxury VIP edition joined the line (opposite page) to battle the upscale competitors.

Chrysler's breadwinner learned a hard lesson in the early '60s that might be summarized by paraphrasing an old adage: "If you can't beat 'em, *re*join 'em." Plymouth's shrunken 1962 standards were no sales match against full-size Chevys and Fords. Neither was their oddball styling, though that became more orthodox for 1963-64. But by that time, a new team of designers and managers had seen the errors of their predecessor's ways, and had decided to put the mainstream Plymouths back into the mainstream—with a vengeance.

The result was a hugely successful line of "Roaring '65s." Not only was it the broadest lineup in Plymouth history, it featured true full-size cars for the first time in four years. Fittingly, those new big ones were called Fury, a name familiar from recent top-line Plymouths.

Motor Trend described the new order this way: "If corporation executives felt nervous about Plymouth's lost market penetration—if they blamed this loss on the car's looking a little different—they need worry no longer. Their designers have aptly taken up most of the clichés that helped their rivals. . . .

"[T]here's a veritable kaleidoscope of four separate trim combinations (Fury I, II, III, and Sport Fury) . . . plus last year's basic body with a neat new face to fill the intermediate-size (Belvedere) need. . . ."

In size and appearance as well as target market, the reborn big Plymouth was both Chevy Impala and Ford Galaxie. It exactly duplicated their 119-inch wheelbases (121 for Fury wagons), and came within fractions of an inch of their other dimensions. Model choices were similar, too. Fury I and II were available in two- and four-door sedans and four-door wagons. Fury III omitted the two-door but added a hardtop sedan, hardtop coupe, and convertible; the last two repeated as bucket-seat Sport Furys. Styling somehow blended '65 Ford and Chevy. Of course, Elwood Engel and his Highland Park design crew couldn't possibly have seen those cars in advance, yet they came up with stacked quad headlamps, as on Ford's new '65 face, and

Chevy-style back panels with single (I, II) or double (III and Sport Fury) taillamps.

If resolutely inoffensive, the new Furys at least looked good. More importantly, they looked sufficiently different to avoid ruinous sales conflicts with the '65 Chryslers and senior Dodges built on the same new C-body platform. That foundation remained of unibody design, but with a front subframe as in 1960-61 (for easier noise and vibration control), not full-unit construction as on Plymouth's 1962-64 "standards."

Powerplants were the usual corporate array, ranging from 225-cid Slant Six through 318 and "Commando" 383 V-8s up to a big 426 wedge with 365 horses. Three-on-the-tree manual was standard, but Fury buyers generally opted for TorqueFlite automatic, which now lost its hallowed pushbuttons for a conventional column shift. *Motor Trend* mourned the pushbuttons' passing, the result of a marketing study. "We've never talked to anyone who's driven with buttons who'd care to go back to the column-mounted lever. Floor-mounted, yes—but column, no! At least the TorqueFlite hasn't been changed. It's still the most positive shifting of any automatic on the market."

As in every year since '62, the Sport Fury was Plymouth's flashy flagship, with standard 318 V-8 and buckets-and-console cabin. But the '65s sold better than any Sport Fury before. The $3209 convertible, the year's priciest Plymouth, almost doubled in sales over '64, while the $2960 hardtop increased 160 percent to become the fifth best-selling Fury model. Symbolizing these winning ways, a ragtop Sport Fury paced the 1965 Indy "500," the first Plymouth so honored.

Plymouth scored another first for '65: record model-year production of over 720,000 units. Significantly, the Fury line generated almost half of that total. Plymouth's 1966 model-year sales were lower, volume easing to just under 684,000 as the industry took a breather after super-hot '65.

Furys received a minor facelift for '66, with a slightly fussier split-theme grille and back panel. Changes were otherwise few, but front/rear seatbelts, padded dash, and "safety" inside door handles appeared at Washington's insistence, and a new wedgehead 440 V-8 replaced the 426 as the top power option, (though it had the same rated power). The ragtop Sport Fury remained top-of-the-line in price, but the prestige Plymouths were the new Fury VIP hardtop coupe and sedan. Aimed squarely at the previous year's new Chevy Caprice and Ford LTD, they came with woodgrain dash trim and bodyside moldings, cloth or tufted-vinyl upholstery, and swiveling rear reading lamps. Sales weren't great—Caprice attracted something like 25 times more—but sufficient enough that the VIP would hang around a few years, though not as long as the Sport Fury.

SPECIFICATIONS

Engines:	all ohv V-8; 318 cid (3.91 × 3.31), 230 bhp; 383 cid (4.25 × 3.38), 270/325/330 bhp; 426 cid (4.25 × 3.75), 365 bhp (**1965 only**); 440 cid (4.32 × 3.75), 365 bhp
Transmissions:	3/4-speed manual, 3-speed TorqueFlite automatic
Suspension front:	upper and lower A-arms, longitudinal torsion bars
Suspension rear:	live axle on semi-elliptic leaf springs
Brakes:	front/rear drums
Wheelbase (in.):	119.0
Weight (lbs):	3715-3780
Top speed (mph):	105-120
0-60 mph (sec):	8.5-10.5

Production: 1965 Sport Fury htp cpe 38,348 **cvt** 6,272 **1966 Sport Fury htp cpe** 32,523 **cvt** 3,418 **VIP** NA

251

1965-67
Plymouth Belvedere
Satellite & GTX

The 1965 Belvedere was a new application of that time-honored Plymouth model name, now applied to a full line of intermediates, distinct from the new full-size Fury also introduced that year. There were three distinct series: the Belvedere I, with sedans, a wagon, and a light Super Stock hardtop; the Belvedere II, which added a hardtop and convertible; and the Satellite, a luxury model available only as a hardtop or convertible.

Dimensionally similar to the smaller 1964 Plymouth, the Belvedere had Fury-like styling. But because muscle-car action centered on intermediates, it received most of Plymouth's performance options. One of these was the 426 Hemi V-8, replacing the previous 426 wedge as the racer's choice. Offered as an option only on the light Super Stock, the mighty Hemi developed 425 bhp, 60 more than the wedge version.

It provided terrific performance: 120 mph top speed and 0-60 in eight seconds or less. Not cheap at $4671 base price, the Super Stock was frankly designed for racing. It looked like a potential champion, but NASCAR disallowed the Hemi Belvedere, and Chrysler withdrew from competition in protest. A late-season change of heart by NASCAR brought it back, but Plymouth tallied only four wins in the short time remaining. Nor was the Belvedere Hemi welcome in drag racing: the National Hot Rod Association ruled that Plymouth's Super Stock drag racers were too light, preventing them from running cars with fiberglass hoods and fenders.

For 1966, the Belvedere/Satellite received new sheet metal, resulting in a crisp, lithe body that was truly elegant. When equipped with the smaller V-8s of 273, 318, and 361 cid, they were the best all-around Plymouths in the line. Their crisp, chiseled styling was retained for 1967 with few changes.

Plymouth's 1965 intermediates wore a facelift of the '64 editions, carrying many of the styling cues of the upscale Furys. Added as the top-line offering was the Satellite (both pages), which came standard with a 273-cid V-8.

Also for 1966, the incredible 425 bhp Hemi was made available as an option on the Belvedere II and Satellite. The result was the electrifying "Street Hemi," equipped as standard with a heavy-duty suspension and oversize brakes. It was first offered with a four-speed gearbox, later with optional TorqueFlite automatic. In the light Belvedere package, the Street Hemi could be simultaneously a docile boulevard tourer and a demon at the stop light. With the right tires and axle ratio, and correctly tuned, it was one of the quickest production cars available. Right off the floor it was ready for drag-race competition in A/Stock or AA/Stock classes, and along with Dodge's Coronet it was allowed to run on NASCAR's shorter circuits—with predictable results. David Pearson won the '66 NASCAR championship with a Coronet; Richard Petty won in '67 with a Belvedere. These were the major breakups of Ford's otherwise tight stranglehold on NASCAR between 1965 and 1970.

In 1967, the Hemi option was offered on the new Belvedere GTX, in addition to a 440 cid wedgehead "Super Commando" V-8 with 375 bhp. The 440 had first been seen in the 1966 Plymouth Fury and other full-size Chrysler products, but didn't become a performance engine until the 1967 model run. Even in this form it was not highly stressed.

In late summer 1966, a few factory-backed racing Belvederes carried the letters "GTX" in stock-car competition. The meaning wasn't clear until the "win-you-over" 1967s were announced, with a Satellite GTX at the top of the line. Offered as a high-performance hardtop or convertible, the GTX looked its part, with a silver and black grille and rear deck panel, simulated hood air intakes, sport striping, and big dual exhausts. The Belvedere I and II lines were continued with the same models, and a stripped Belvedere wagon was introduced with a base price of only $2579. This proved to be more of a price leader than a serious seller: only 5477 were built, and the model was withdrawn in 1968.

Plymouth's racing victories are so numerous as to preclude mention here, but Richard Petty's NASCAR performance is worthy of note. He scored a record 27 triumphs (out of Plymouth's season total of 31), including 10 straight wins, on his way to his second Grand National driving championship. Both the 27 and 10 figures are records that still stand today.

Opposite page: Chrysler's famous 426 Hemi was offered in only a handful of "drag-strip specials" during 1965, but was made a regular Satellite option in '66. Cars so equipped wore small "426 Hemi" badges on their lower front fenders, but otherwise gave little warning of what lay within. Below: The first Satellite GTX arrived in 1967 wearing sporty trim and dual hood scoops, taking over as Plymouth's top-of-the-line intermediate. Available engines included the 425-bhp 426 Hemi and a new 440-cid "wedgehead" V-8 with 375-bhp.

SPECIFICATIONS

Engines:	all ohv V-8; 273 cid (3.62 × 3.31), 180/235 bhp; 318 cid (3.91 × 2.31), 230 bhp; 361 cid (4.12 × 3.38) 265 bhp; 383 cid (4.25 × 3.38), 270-330 bhp; 426 cid (4.25 × 3.75), 425 bhp; 440 cid (4.32 × 3.75), 375 bhp
Transmissions:	3-speed manual; 4-speed manual, 3-speed automatic optional
Suspension front:	upper and lower control arms, longitudinal torsion bars
Suspension rear:	live axle, leaf springs
Brakes:	front/rear drums; front discs optional
Wheelbase (in.):	116.0
Weight (lbs):	3050-3335
Top speed (mph):	120
0-60 mph (sec):	6.6

Production: 1965 Satellite cpe 23,341 **cvt** 1860 **1966 Satellite cpe** 35,399 **cvt** 2759 **1967 Satellite/GTX cpe** 30,328 **cvt** 2050

1967-69
Plymouth Barracuda

Ten years after Chrysler dramatically captured the styling initiative from GM with Virgil Exner's "Forward Look," the '67 Barracuda almost repeated the feat—but Chrysler itself was modest. One designer frankly acknowledged GM's leadership when he said the Barracuda followed "GM's flowing styling"—referring to the techniques rather than any outright copying. "Stylists attend the same schools, live and work in similar environments, and are influenced by one another's work."

Of course, that kind of thinking has spawned recent generations of Buicks that look like Oldsmobiles, and Eldorados that look like Toronados. The Barracuda may have followed a set technique—smooth, flowing curves blended to form a palatable whole—yet it was distinct, not easily confused with a Mustang or Camaro.

As in the past, the new Barracuda shared the Valiant understructure, but the skins were entirely different. The wheelbase was lengthened by two inches, the overall length by five, and a sleek hardtop and convertible joined the fastback. Engineering features remained the same: torsion-bar front suspension, leaf-springs out back, unit body/chassis. Wheel size increased to 14 inches for better load capacity, and several mandated safety features, such as a collapsible steering column and dual braking system were added. Plymouth also placed the Barracuda in more competitive price territory: the hardtop started at only $2449, the convertible around $2775—exactly in line with Mustang.

It was darn good marketing, and it paid off: production of '67s totaled more than 60,000, 4228 of which were convertibles, the rest about evenly split between coupes and fastbacks. The latter represented a much larger proportion of the total than did the Mustang fastback, suggesting the appeal of the handsome new Barracuda design to customers.

The new design brought more underhood room for a big-block engine, and Plymouth wasted little time in making a 280-bhp version of the 383 V-8 an option. This could be combined with the familiar Formula S package.

Due to its success, the Barracuda was not drastically changed until 1970. A vertical-bar grille appeared for 1968, a checkered grille and redesigned taillights in 1969.

Federal smog regulations were now in place, and Plymouth was altering its engines to meet the emissions mandates. For 1968, the 273 was replaced as Barracuda's base V-8 by the "detoxed" 318. A small-block 340 V-8, created by virtue of a bore increase to the 318, became an option. This was good for 275 bhp with its four-barrel carburetor and 10.5:1 compression. The big-block 383 returned, now with 300 bhp. Plymouth also issued a limited number of Hemi-powered Barracudas for quarter-mile action, mostly for the factory team of Ronnie Sox and Buddy Martin. Like other Plymouth "drag specials" of the early to mid-1960s, these Hemis were lightened considerably, possessing only the barest of necessities to be street-legal.

In 1969, the third and final year for this body style, a new performance option was introduced, appropriately dubbed the 'Cuda. At first, it came only with the 275 bhp 340 or an upgraded 383 with 330 bhp. Later came a whopping 440 engine, rated at 375 bhp. Information on the existence of Hemi-engined 'Cudas in 1969 is sketchy, with conflicting information on how many, if any, were built.

However, the Barracudas most people bought were powered not by Hemis or 383s or 440s, but rather 273s, 318s, and 340s. The best ones had four-speeds and the tight Formula S suspension, and the most flexible back axle ratio—3.23:1, not one of the stump-pulling lower ratios. With this setup, the typical Barracuda was as good or better off the line than a Triumph TR4 or an Austin-Healey, and could equal either one of them around a hairpin without embarrassment. The 'Cuda basically understeered, but could be made to oversteer with a judicious poke at the throttle, and would drift around a turn in the classic sports car fashion with as much grace as an English import. The stiff suspension "did tend to show its teeth on poor surfaces," one road tester admitted, "but it's something we would be loathe to pass up if we were buying a Barracuda, because we feel its benefits far outweigh its drawbacks." One of its benefits was embarrassing sports cars.

Barracudas received new styling for 1967, when notchback coupe (opposite page, top) and convertible body styles joined the existing fastback. Few changes were evident for '68 (below) though the base V-8 grew from 273 to 318 cid. Opposite page, bottom: The little-changed '69s were the last of this generation, and despite being the most popular model, the fastback body style (this page, bottom) would not be offered for the 1970s.

SPECIFICATIONS

Engines:	ohv I-6, 225 cid (3.40 × 4.13), 145 bhp; ohv V-8, 273 cid (3.62 × 3.31), 180-235 bhp; 318 cid (3.91 × 3.31), 230 bhp; 340 cid (4.04 × 3.31), 275 bhp; 383 cid (4.25 × 3.38), 280-330 bhp; 440 cid (4.32 × 3.75), 375 bhp
Transmissions:	3-speed manual; 4-speed manual, 3-speed automatic optional
Suspension front:	upper and lower control arms, longitudinal torsion bars
Suspension rear:	live axle, leaf springs
Brakes:	front/rear drums; front discs optional
Wheelbase (in.):	108.0
Weight (lbs):	2793-2940
Top speed (mph):	118
0-60 mph (sec):	5.6

Production: 1967 cpe 28,196 **cvt** 4228 **fstbk** 30,110 **1968 cpe** 19,997 **cvt** 2840 **fstbk** 22,575 **1969 cpe** 12,757 **cvt** 1442 **fstbk** 17,788

1967-68
Plymouth Sport
Fury & VIP

Having crawled up from the depths of '62 to new sales heights in three short years, Chrysler's bread-and-butter brand pulled out all the stops for 1967.."Plymouth is out to win you over," said the ads, and they didn't lie. Barracuda was beautifully recast as a true "ponycar" competitor for Ford's Mustang, the compact Valiant was just as handsomely transformed, and even the intermediate Belvederes, still basically 1962 underneath, were spruced up in both style and power.

The same applied to the pride of the Plymouth pack, the big Fury, which became even bigger for '67. Though wheelbases and basic structure were 1965-66 holdovers, a complete reskin upped overall length 3.3 to 7.5 inches, and more sculptured lower-body styling made the cars look even longer than that. They also looked broader of beam, thanks partly to flared-out front fendertops and expansive new horizontal taillamps, but overall width was, in fact, an inch or so slimmer. Observing a popular Detroit trend, rear fenders were slightly upswept just ahead of the wheel openings.

VIP returned from its 1966 debut as the finest Fury, still with hardtop coupe and sedan styles. Right alongside them, at near identical prices, were the bucket-seat Sport Fury convertible and a *pair* of two-door hardtops, as Plymouth now offered a choice of hardtop coupe rooflines: a conventional notchback (duplicated in bench-seat Fury III trim) with tapered C-pillars, and a new "Fast Top" style with the same profile but big triangulated quarters that made magnificent obstructions for parking and lane-changing. Though it looked racier, the Fast Top was the style chosen for the luxury VIP, perhaps because those huge C-pillars conferred a tad more "formality"; they certainly better displayed the optional vinyl roof coverings.

Both Fast Tops as well as the VIP hardtop sedan carried louvers beneath their backlights for an exclusive new flow-through ventilation system. This was claimed capable of completely changing interior air four times a minute at 60 mph, but proved far less efficient than that. It would be abandoned after this one year.

As before, VIPs boasted luxury interiors to rival Chrysler's or Imperial's, with special pleated upholstery, pseudo-wood accents on doors and dash, fold-down center rear armrest, and similar trappings. Outside were broad full-length swathes of brushed aluminum above the rocker panels, plus special wheel covers, beltline pinstriping, and a full complement of bright "reveal" moldings. The last were also applied to Sport Furys, which continued with their usual tri-color insignia and all-vinyl interior with front bucket seats and center shift console.

Unlike other Furys, which came with a Slant Six, VIP and Sport Fury retained Chrysler's mainstay 318 V-8 as standard equipment. The engine itself, however, was now completely different, sharing a more compact new "thinwall" design with the 273 Valiant/Barracuda small-block. Power options ran through the customary pair of 383s and on to the big-block 440 (new for '66), which was now a tuned "Super Commando" with 10 extra horses, 375 in all. Options expanded with first-time availability of power front-disc brakes and front headrests and shoulder belts, while standard features now included energy-absorbing steering column and padded dash. That dash was glitzier than ever: awash with thumbwheels and toggle switches and lit up at night with little "spotlamps" beaming down from above.

Fury II and III remained the best-selling big Plymouths by far for '67, but the line-leaders didn't fare badly in a slightly soft year for Plymouth and the industry as a whole. Comparisons are difficult, but at nearly 19,000 units, VIP posted a sizeable gain on half-year '66, while Sport Fury fell only a little short of its previous year's volume at just over 31,500.

Plymouth ran fourth in industry production for 1968, the position it had held since '63, but built 110,000 more cars to finish near three-quarters of a million— a new record. Nodding to Sonny and Cher, ads promised "The Win-You-Over Beat Goes On," but Furys basically sung '67 themes with minor variations: a tasteful facelift, new Federally required safety items like side-marker lights, and engines recalibrated for lower emissions, also per government decree. Dimensions were unchanged. Sport Fury and VIP sales remained healthy but began showing signs of anemia, sliding to 26,000 and 17,500, respectively. As it would turn out, 1967-68 would be Plymouth's last really strong years, at least in sales. But that doesn't mean that the company quit making exciting products, some of which are showcased in the next few pages.

Opposite page, bottom: *Restyled '67 Sport Fury retained vertical headlight/horizontal taillight theme of the previous model, yet looked markedly different. New this year was a two-door "Fast Top" model with huge, triangular-shaped C-pillars. The '68s* (opposite page, top) *were changed only in detail.*

SPECIFICATIONS

Engines:	all ohv V-8; 318 cid (3.91 × 3.31), 230 bhp; 383 cid (4.25 × 3.38), 270/325 bhp (**1967**) 290/330 bhp (**1968**); 440 cid (4.32 × 3.75), 375 bhp
Transmissions:	3/4-speed manual, 3-speed TorqueFlite automatic
Suspension front:	upper and lower A-arms, longitudinal torsion bars
Suspension rear:	live axle on semi-elliptic leaf springs
Brakes:	front/rear drums (front discs optional)
Wheelbase (in.):	119.0
Weight (lbs):	3630-3710
Top speed (mph):	105-120
0-60 mph (sec):	8.5-10.0

Production: 1967 Sport Fury Fast Top/notchback htp cpe 28,448 **cvt** 3,133 **VIP Fast Top htp cpe** 7,912 **htp sdn** 10,830 **1968 Sport Fury notchback htp cpe** 6,642 **Fast Top htp cpe** 17,073 **cvt** 2,489 **VIP Fast Top htp cpe** 6,768 **htp sdn** 10,745

1968-69
Plymouth Sport
Satellite & GTX

It's amazing what steady cultivating can do. In 1962, Plymouth's crop of downsized "standard" cars was like unwanted surplus. Yet with a few interim changes, their descendants of six years later sold over a quarter-million copies.

Progressively nicer styling helped, but a more important factor was the 1965 return of a true full-size Plymouth, the 119-inch-wheelbase Fury. This allowed the existing 116-inch models (wagons: 117) to compete exclusively in the mid-size field, which they successfully did as workaday Belvedere I and II models and a bucket-seat twosome called Satellite.

For 1966, Plymouth lit every street racer's fire by making the famed 426-cid Hemi V-8 a regular production option for its mid-size cars, thus increasing their dominance of the nation's quarter-mile action. The following year, this iron fist was wrapped in a velvet glove called Belvedere GTX, a lush buckets-and-console convertible and hardtop coupe packing a standard 375-bhp wedgehead 440. All that remained was to fix styling that was looking literally and figuratively square against the latest from GM and Ford.

Chrysler did just that for 1968 with a fully redesigned B-body for Belvedere/ Satellite/GTX and Dodge's Coronet/Charger. Plymouth greatly expanded offerings into what it called "The Mid-Size 5." A stripped Belvedere pillared coupe, four-door sedan, and wagon started things off, then repeated with a two-door hardtop and convertible as a "family" Satellite series (replacing Belvedere II). Next up were a new Sport Satellite convertible, hardtop coupe, and four-door wagon with still-better trim, though not necessarily the best performance. That was reserved for the potent GTX duo and a new no-frills muscle coupe, the whimsically named Road Runner, which is a story in itself.

All '68 Plymouth intermediates wore smoother, more rounded styling with modestly humped rear fenders, simple grilles, subtle bodyside creases, more radically tucked rockers, and broad rear decks with wedgy taillamps. Unfortunately, even this

Plymouth's redesigned intermediates wore a "Coke bottle" profile and bulging bodysides for 1968. The Sport Satellite (opposite page, top) came standard with a 318-cid V-8, while its "muscle-bound" brother, the GTX (above and opposite page, bottom), started out with a 375-bhp 440. Optional on the GTX was the fearsome 426 Street Hemi (opposite page, middle), conservatively rated at 425 bhp.

SPECIFICATIONS

Engines:	all ohv V-8; **Satellite:** 318 cid (3.91 × 3.31), 230 bhp; 383 cid (4.25 × 3.38), 290/330 bhp; **GTX:** 440 cid (4.32 × 3.75), 375 bhp; 426 cid (4.25 × 3.75), 425 bhp
Transmissions:	3/4-speed manual, 3-speed TorqueFlite automatic
Suspension front:	upper and lower A-arms, longitudinal torsion bars (anti-roll bar on GTX)
Suspension rear:	live axle on semi-elliptic leaf springs
Brakes:	front/rear drums; optional front discs
Wheelbase (in.):	116.0
Weight (lbs):	3155-3685
Top speed (mph):	105-140+
0-60 mph (sec):	6.3-10.5

Production: 1968 Sport Satellite htp cpe 21,014 **cvt** 1,523 **wgn** NA **GTX htp cpe** 17,914 **cvt** 1,026 **1969 Sport Satellite htp cpe** 15,807 **cvt** 818 **4d sdn** 5,837 **wgn** 6,372 **GTX htp cpe** 14,902 **cvt** 700

slicker B-body proved to be less aerodynamic than the new ultra-smooth '68 Ford Torino/Mercury Cyclone fastbacks, which ran faster around stock-car supertracks and into the Winner's Circle more often. But MoPar still ruled the drags, with the likes of Ronnie Sox and Buddy Martin adding to Chrysler's vast collection of Super Stock trophies.

Naturally, Plymouth's broad intermediate lineup spanned an equally broad engine lineup: everything in the Chrysler cupboard from 225 Slant Six to the amazing Street Hemi—still jokingly rated at 425 horses—and the GTX's standard 375-bhp "Super Commando" 440. Sport Satellites started with a mild 230-bhp 318 and ended with optional 383 V-8s packing 300 or 330 bhp. All rode a typical Chrysler chassis with acclaimed torsion-bar front suspension and available power front-disc brakes. Most '68 "Bs" carried extra-cost TorqueFlite automatic in lieu of manual three-speed, but GTXs included TorqueFlite and offered four-on-the-floor as a no-cost alternative.

As before, GTXs also included stiffer suspension and heavy-duty rear axle with "Sure-Grip" limited-slip differential. Identifying the '68s outside were special striping, bold GTX nameplates, and a "performance" hood with twin outward-facing dummy air intakes (shared with Road Runner). Featured inside were front buckets, console, and pseudo-wood trim.

Though Plymouth still lagged far behind Chevy and Ford in sales, its 1968 total of nearly 750,000 was a gratifying gain of some 111,000 over 1967. Significantly, intermediates accounted for about a third. Satellite was the volume leader by far, but non-wagon Sport Satellites managed around 22,500 and the two GTXs close to 19,000.

Predictably, the '69s changed mainly in trim and appearance details, but speed freaks delighted in a monster 440 with three two-barrel carburetors. It was dubbed, naturally enough, "440 6-bbl." Allegedly making 390 bhp (and probably far more), it was a new option for the Road Runner, as was a functional "Air Grabber" hood and five special Performance Axle Packages. But the GTX got only the last; worse, its center console now cost extra. Though performance remained formidable—under 6.5 seconds 0-60 with the Hemi and automatic, a half-second more with the 440—the GTX was being shoved out of the spotlight by the cheaper "Beep Beep" car. Sales accordingly withered to 15,000, while Road Runner soared beyond 84,000. Sport Satellite improved, too, a new four-door sedan boosting '69 volume to near 29,000.

The once-inspiring GTX would vanish two years later, while Sport Satellite, not all that special anyway, would simply be lost in a crowd of faceless family intermediates. Sad to say, Plymouth let its carefully cultivated garden of the '60s become a weed patch in the '70s. You know the rest.

261

1968-69 Plymouth Road Runner

"No more can we say that species Geococcyx Californianus is a long-tailed ground cuckoo that runs with great swiftness and inhabits only open regions of southwestern North America. It now claims as its habitat the entire nation, through all of whose parts it continues to run with even greater swiftness and increasing profusion." Thus said *Motor Trend* on the occasion of naming their 1968 "Car of the Year," the Plymouth Road Runner. Why choose such a specialty car? The editors gave several reasons: the concept of a low-price two-door sedan body combined with a strong but docile-running engine; the firm suspension and good brakes; clean and simple styling. "If you insist on spending more money you can order a fancier interior, a hardtop, or [starting in 1969] a convertible model, a racing-type Hemi 426 engine and a wide variety of options; but the basic concept of simplicity and low price is what makes it a winner."

If this is the age of nostalgia, try to think of a better nostalgia-jerker than a car that does 0-60 in six or seven seconds, winds out to 120 mph or more, and costs $2896. That's what you paid (plus delivery and prep) to own the taxicab-basic 1968 Road Runner coupe, powered by 335 horses of Super Commando 383 V-8, and equipped with four-speed tranny, heavy-duty suspension, and a funny horn that went "beep-beep" like the cartoon character. The only thing not included was a coyote to make a fool of—but there were plenty of Ford Fairlanes and Chevy Novas around to do that to.

The Road Runner was a marketing ploy to get young kids into Plymouths for a small piece of change, and make them devotees by providing more performance than any Chevy or Ford you could buy for the same money. The interior was stark, and only Road Runner decals graced the unadorned exterior. Both hardtop and pillared coupes were offered, but the latter was cheaper by almost $150, and sold twice as many copies. (Road Runner buyers evidently being quite budget minded.) If you had

SPECIFICATIONS

Engines:	all ohv V-8; 383 cid (4.25 × 3.38), 335 bhp; 426 cid (4.25 × 3.75), 425 bhp; 440 cid (4.32 × 3.75), 375/390 bhp
Transmissions:	4-speed manual, 3-speed automatic optional
Suspension front:	upper and lower control arms, longitudinal torsion bars
Suspension rear:	live axle, leaf springs
Brakes:	front disc/rear drum
Wheelbase (in.):	116.0
Weight (lbs):	3440-3790
Top speed (mph):	104-120+
0-60 mph (sec):	5.5-7.3

Production: 1968 cpe 29,240 **htp cpe** 15,359 **1969 cpe** 33,743 **htp cpe** 48,549 **cvt** 2128

This page, top: *Introduced in 1968, the first Road Runners were stark machines, virtually devoid of exterior trim—save for small decals of the famous cartoon character. Additional trim and a broader list of optional equipment allowed for dressier Road Runners in '69* (opposite page)*, when a convertible also joined the line* (below)*. Standard both years was a 335-bhp 383* (above).

$800 extra, you could opt for the Hemi engine itself. On street or track, the Hemi was dynamite. "It is probably the fastest production sedan made today, and the engine is much different from when it first hit the street in '65—refined," wrote Eric Dahlquist. "Also, surprisingly, even with the extra weight up front, the car has only a bit more oversteer and actually stopped shorter from 60 mph than either of the 383s. This is a direct function of a pair of additional half leafs in the right rear spring that damped out wheel hop braking the 383s showed." (Dahlquist managed 0-60 in 5.5 seconds and the quarter-mile in 13.5 seconds at 105.38 mph with a Hemi Road Runner equipped with the low 4.10:1 rear axle ratio.)

Budget-conscious performance buyers loved the Road Runner. About 45,000 of the '68 models found homes, two and one-half times the number of Satellite GTXs. But Ford dominated the NASCAR tracks, especially the super-speedways, with its fastback Torino. Ford won 20 Grand Nationals, while Plymouth was forced to take second place with only 16.

The Road Runner convertible of 1969 had a slightly more luxurious interior, but otherwise the second year models were little changed. The Super Commando 440 got 15 more advertised horsepower with a midyear option of three two-barrel carburetors (a first for Plymouth) mounted on an Edelbrock intake manifold. Called the "440-6bbl.," it came with a fiberglass hood with a built-in scoop. Road Runners were now at the peak of their popularity, with sales topping 84,000, but it was a different story on the track. Star Plymouth driver Richard Petty had gone over to Ford for the 1969 campaign, complaining about Plymouth's inferior aerodynamics and the need for development work on the Hemi.

There was never any question, Eric Dahlquist wrote, that the Hemi Road Runner would work, "because the Hemi has always worked; it would have made a Gold Cupper out of the Merrimack. But the original 383, even with the high-performance 440 heads, needed just a shade more for the boys, like lower axle radios and cold-air induction and a Hurst shifter. It was not long ago that management would have had to cool such options, letting Pontiac or somebody zoom off with the fruits of the idea, but no more. That, too, is why the Road Runner will keep selling. Once you get an owner's loyalty, a young hard-to-convince owner, he'll stick for as long as you produce." He was right, too: only stricter emissions standards caused the Road Runner to lose sales in the early '70s, and in 1974 with only 170 net horsepower, it still appealed to 12,000 buyers.

1969
Plymouth
Sport Fury & VIP

Nineteen sixty-nine was a big year for big cars, with brand-new designs from each of the traditional "Low-Price Three." But where Chevy and Ford retained familiar styling cues, Fury invited people to "Look What Plymouth's Up To Now" with the most dramatic overhaul of the bunch.

On paper at least, the '69 Furys were exactly the sort of family cruisers the market seemed to want. Shared with that year's new C-body Chryslers and senior Dodges was what Highland Park termed "fuselage styling," the fulsome, rounded look pioneered in spectacular fashion by the slick '68 Dodge Charger. Blown up to full-size scale, it was more lardy than lithe—and less practical, with raised beltlines noticeably reducing glass area and thus outward vision. But Fury was at least clean and much smoother than before, with just enough knife-edged formality in front and rear fenderlines to appease more conservative types.

Without question the new models looked bulkier, and those looks were not deceiving. Wheelbase increased one inch from 1965-68 to match the 120-inch span of Fury's redesigned competitors (save 122 for wagons, still in the separate Suburban line created for '68). Overall length grew 1.5 inches to a massive 214.5, and width spread nearly two inches to a girthy 79.6. But despite appearances—and long-held myth—curb weights were only a few pounds higher model-for-model. The ragtop Sport Fury, for example, weighed just 19 pounds more than its '68 counterpart, the posh VIP hardtop sedan a mere eight pounds more.

There were no big technical changes for '69, so Fury still diverged from its rivals with unit construction (instead of body-on-frame), Chrysler's famed torsion-bar front suspension (versus coil springs), and a familiar lineup of reliable Highland Park engines ranging from the thrifty 225 Slant Six to a burly big-block 440 V-8. A few styling features did have functional ramifications, however. Wipers, for instance, were now concealed GM-style by a rear hood lip, which seemed a good idea until they became *really* concealed by snow packed into their recess. Front-door ventwings vanished from air-conditioned hardtop coupes, controversial at the time because they increased wind noise. Also on hand were 15-inch wheels and tires (previously 14s), which didn't quite fill out the newly ballooned bodysides, but did allow for larger, more efficient brakes. A new and little-known '69 Fury option grouped a two-barrel 383 V-8 with cruise control, power front-disc brakes, long-legged 2.76:1 axle ratio, undercoating, and headlamps-on warning lamp. Plymouth called this the "Turnpike Cruising Package." (One wonders whether they checked that name with Mercury.)

Sport Fury and VIP again headed the big-Plymouth line for '69. VIP expanded from two to three models with the addition of a "formal" hardtop coupe bearing a more upright rear window and wide rear quarters. The old "Fast Top" was superseded as the sporty hardtop by a new style with narrower, more raked C-posts. As before, Sport Fury offered Plymouth's poshest, priciest convertible (at $3502). The aforementioned VIP four-door hardtop remained the costliest non-wagon closed Fury ($3433).

Unfortunately for Plymouth dealers, the high-profit VIP and Sport Fury generated fewer sales for a second straight year. Production of the "Very Important Plymouths" dropped nearly 4000 units to just under 14,000, while the big bucket-seaters lost over 8300 to close at about 18,000. Both still trailed Big Three competitors by substantial margins. Chevy's Impala SS was now an option package and no longer significant, but Caprice outdrew VIP by over 9-to-1—and Ford bested Plymouth by 16-to-1 with its luxurious LTDs. Sport Fury was no better match for Ford's sporty XL, which sold four times as many copies. Adding to the misery, Plymouth as a whole ran a weaker fourth in 1969, while Ford was a stronger second to industry-leading Chevrolet.

In short, Plymouth was selling fewer top-line big cars than either of its archrivals—or third-place Pontiac for that matter—which suggested that the market didn't equate Plymouths with "luxury" the way it did certain Fords and Chevys. More's the pity, too, for this would contribute to Plymouth's steady sales decline in the '70s.

Indeed, VIPs didn't survive past '69, replaced by bench-seat Sport Furys and, ultimately, "Gran" models. Sport Fury lasted only through 1971, with just a husky, 440-powered GT hardtop coupe to continue the performance tradition—one of Detroit's last muscle-bound biggies. In all, a sorry end for what had been Plymouth's best.

"Fuselage styling" appeared throughout Chrysler's line for '69, bringing a fuller, huskier look to the new models. Most, in fact, were larger, including Plymouth's Fury, which rode a wheelbase one inch longer than before. Sport Fury (opposite page) and VIP still led the line, though their popularity was waning. While VIP was aimed at the luxury market, Sport Fury still tried to appeal to those interested in a full-size sports machine by featuring standard buckets-and-console interior (below) and V-8 power.

SPECIFICATIONS

Engines:	all ohv V-8; 318 cid (3.91 × 3.31), 230 bhp; 383 cid (4.25 × 3.38), 290/330 bhp; 440 cid (4.32 × 3.75), 375 bhp
Transmissions:	3/4-speed manual, 3-speed TorqueFlite automatic
Suspension front:	upper and lower A-arms, longitudinal torsion bars, anti-roll bar
Suspension rear:	live axle on semi-elliptic leaf springs
Brakes:	front/rear drums; front discs optional
Wheelbase (in.):	120.0
Weight (lbs):	3583-3729
Top speed (mph):	110-125
0-60 mph (sec):	8.0-10.0

Production: Sport Fury htp cpe 14,120 **cvt** 1,579 **formal htp cpe** 2,169 **VIP htp cpe** 4,740 **formal htp cpe** 1,059 **htp sdn** 7,962

265

1960
Pontiac

Pontiac was one of Detroit's biggest success stories in the '60s, as it would be again in the 1980s. The reason was the same in both decades: enthusiast-oriented leaders who emphasized performance and style. In the '60s, Pontiac consistently outsold every medium-price rival by keeping the public captivated. By 1962, the division had vaulted from midpack in industry sales to a solid number-three, where it would remain through 1970.

The story begins with 1959's all-new "Wide Track" Pontiacs, arguably the cleanest, most roadable cars in that year's Detroit crop. Besides its biggest V-8 ever, the "Trophy" 389, Pontiac prospered with new low-price Catalina models that found immediate favor with value- and performance-conscious buyers.

For 1960, the division presented a tasteful facelift announced by a vee'd horizontal-bar grille. Though this "Air Foil" treatment was attractive, '59s' split-theme grille was already something of a trademark, and it would return for good after this one-year absence. Also featured were recontoured bodysides and twin-tube taillamps (evolved from '59's "twin-fin" fenders).

Bonneville remained the premium Pontiac, offering hardtop Sport Coupe, Vista hardtop sedan, convertible, and four-door Safari wagon in the $3250-$3500 range. All rode a princely 124-inch wheelbase (as for '59) and boasted such royal touches as padded dash and rich vinyl/fabric upholstery. The ragtop came with leather inside and offered extra-cost front bucket seats, Pontiac being well ahead of most other makes with that feature.

One step below was the well-known Star Chief, restricted to pillared and pillarless four-doors plus two-door Sport Sedan, all on the Bonneville chassis with prices in the $2900-$3100 territory. A further step down in size, but not price, was a new Ventura twosome of pillarless coupe and sedan on a 122-inch wheelbase. These were essentially Catalinas dressed up with full wheel covers, snazzy triple-tone (!) "Morrokide" vinyl upholstery, custom steering wheel, and extra interior brightwork.

But the low-price Catalinas remained the best-sellers by far. The 1960 catalog again showed sedans and hardtops with two and four doors, convertible, and Safaris seating six or nine. Prices started at $2631 for the pillared two-door and finished at $3207 for the nine-passenger wagon.

Engines were 1959 carryovers but still superb, the 389 being the fourth enlargement in as many years of Pontiac's modern overhead-valve 1955 V-8. Horsepower depended on transmission. Standard three-speed column-shift manual netted 281 bhp on Bonnevilles and 245 elsewhere; extra-cost Hydra-Matic made those numbers 303 and 283. The differences stemmed from lower compression with manual shift (8.6:1 versus 10.25:1) and Bonneville's standard four-barrel carbs (versus two-barrels). A 215-bhp engine continued as a no-charge alternative for the economy-conscious, while leadfoots flocked to the Tri-Power option with triple two-barrel carbs, 10.75:1 compression and 333 bhp.

Speaking of options, Pontiac offered more than most 1960 cars, the "customizing with the order form" tactic that proved so popular in this decade. Major factory items included air conditioning, "Magi-Cruise" speed control, "Safe-T-Track" limited-slip differential, pull-out "Sportable" transistor radio, tinted glass, and power brakes, windows, and front seat. Heater/defroster cost extra, too, though that was common in 1960. Lesser extras included remote-control outside mirror, spotlight, and seatbelts (yes, even way back then). One option delighted performance fans: a special-order four-speed manual transmission, though not many were installed this year.

Pontiac's "Wide Track" chassis still delivered some of Detroit's best handling, but larger-diameter suspension bushings, revised mounts for rear control arms, and new nylon-sleeve shocks with improved fluid made an already smooth ride even smoother. Other technical updates included a more efficient twin-reservoir water pump and permanent factory-filled antifreeze.

Like the '59s, these Pontiacs were great road cars, but the hot setup was obviously one of the lightest Catalinas, namely the two-door sedan, with Tri-Power and Hydra-Matic or maybe that four-speed. Though Pontiac had not yet lit its fires on the nation's drag strips, it hardly wanted for muscle in 1960.

Nor did it lack for sales. Model-year volume rose to over 396,000, up nearly 14,000 on much-improved '59, good for fifth in the industry. Star Chief, with its "old folks" image, was the slow mover, pulling in a bit less than 44,000 customers. Ventura did well with 56,277 orders, and Bonneville managed over 85,000, impressive for a top-liner. But as we said, Catalina remained the people's choice, racking up nearly 211,000, better than half the total.

Pontiac's 1960 line boasted styling that was a facelift of the new-for-'59 design, and all carried 389-cid V-8s with outputs ranging from 215-bhp up to a triple-carb version with 333. Bonneville (opposite page) remained the top-line offering, but the most popular model was the Catalina, which accounted for more than half of all sales (below). Example shown wears the optional (and rare) eight-lug aluminum wheels.

SPECIFICATIONS

Engines:	all ohv V-8, 389 cid (4.06 × 3.75); 215 bhp ("economy" option), 245/283 bhp (manual/automatic models exc Bonneville), 281/303 bhp (manual/automatic Bonneville), 333 ("Tri Power" option)
Transmissions:	3/4-speed manual, 4-speed Hydra-Matic automatic
Suspension front:	upper and lower A-arms, coil springs
Suspension rear:	4-link live axle, coil springs
Brakes:	front/rear drums
Wheelbase (in.):	122.0 (Catalina/Ventura/Bonneville Safari), 124.0 (Star Chief/other Bonneville)
Weight (lbs):	3835-4365
Top speed (mph):	105-125
0-60 mph (sec):	8.0-10.0

Production: Catalina 2d Sport Sedan 25,504 **4d sdn** 72,650 **Sport htp cpe** 27,496 **Vista htp sdn** 32,710 **cvt** 17,712 **Safari 4d wagon 6P** 21,253 **Safari 4d wgn 9P** 14,149 **Ventura Sport htp cpe** 27,577 **Vista htp sdn** 28,700 **Star Chief 2d Sport Sedan** 5,797 **4d sdn** 23,038 **Vista htp sdn** 14,856 **Bonneville Sport htp cpe** 24,015 **Vista htp sdn** 39,037 **cvt** 17,062 **Custom Safari 4d wgn 9P** 5,163

1961
Pontiac

Pontiac had a busy year in 1961. Besides an innovative new compact, the Tempest (see entry), the "Wide Track" team fielded completely redesigned standard models that must be among the few '60s Ponchos yet to be discovered by today's collectors.

The '61s deserve recognition, for they epitomized everything that made Pontiac great in this decade. Start with styling: as neat and clean as the pacesetting 1959 look, yet wrought on slightly trimmer dimensions. William L. Mitchell had been General Motors design chief for three years when the '61s bowed, and they were definitely his "thing" (as were other big GM cars that year). In fact, Pontiac arguably had the best looks in the corporation's wholly redesigned big-car fleet.

You can judge for yourself from the accompanying photos, but suffice it to say that the big '61 Pontiac was an adroit blend of soft curves and hard edges (announced by a revived split-theme '59-type grille) that belied a welcome withdrawal from the "bigger-is-better" mentality of the '50s. As before, low-end Catalina and step-up Ventura models shared the GM A-body platform with full-size Chevrolets, but were trimmed an inch between wheel centers (to 119), 2.5 inches in beam, one inch in height, and a whopping four inches in overall length. Similar reductions were seen in the senior Star Chief and top-line Bonneville series, again sharing a corporate B-body with Olds and Buick (and unchanged 123-inch wheelbase). Curb weights reflected the modest downsizing, dropping by 175-185 pounds over counterpart 1960 models. One incidental change was a less-wide "Wide Track," front and rear axles narrowing by 1.5 inches.

Model choices decreased by one, the slow-selling Star Chief line losing its two-door sedan. For '61, all two- and four-door sedans retained the lipped rear roofline and wrapped backlight familiar since '59, hardtop sedans—still tagged "Vista"—acquired a more conventional superstructure, and two-door hardtops—again called Sport Coupes—wore elegant thin-section rooflines with tall, slightly wrapped backlights.

Engine choices increased from six to 10, but all were again based on the winning 389 Trophy V-8. Mainstay horsepower ranged from 215 to 303, with outputs varied

Pontiacs lost pounds and inches for 1961, so while engine choices remained about the same, the cars were quicker than previous editions. A particularly potent combination was the top 389 "Tri-Power" V-8 with three two-barrel carbs and 348 bhp (opposite page, top) in a light-weight Catalina or sportier Ventura (this page). Top-of-the-line remained the Bonneville (opposite page, right and lower left), riding a 123-inch wheelbase shared with the Star Chief, versus 119 for the Catalina, Ventura, and Safari wagon.

SPECIFICATIONS

Engines:	all ohv V-8; 389 cid (4.06 × 3.75), 215-363 bhp; 421 cid (4.09 × 4.00), 373 bhp (limited-production option for Catalina "drag special")
Transmissions:	3/4-speed manual, 3/4-speed Hydra-Matic automatic
Suspension front:	upper and lower A-arms, coil springs
Suspension rear:	4-link live axle, coil springs
Brakes:	front/rear drums
Wheelbase (in.):	119.0 Catalina/Ventura/ Bonneville Safari 123.0 Star Chief/other Bonneville
Weight (lbs):	3650-4185
Top speed (mph):	110-125+
0-60 mph (sec):	8.5-10.5

Production: Catalina 2d Sport sdn 9,846 **htp Sport cpe** 14,524 **Vista htp sdn** 17,589 **cvt** 12,379 **4d sdn** 38,638 **4d Safari wgn, 6P** 12,595 **4d Safari wgn, 9P** 7,783 **Ventura htp Sport cpe** 13,297 **Vista htp sdn** 13,912 **Star Chief 4d sdn** 16,024 **Vista htp sdn** 13,557 **Bonneville htp Sport cpe** 16,906 **Vista htp sdn** 30,830 **cvt** 18,264 **4d Custom Safari wgn** 3,323

according to series, transmission, carburetion, and optional equipment. Topping this burly heap were four Tri-Power engines offering 318 to 363 bhp. The last came in a new "Super Duty" unit with unique block, heads, and chamfered cylinder bores. Late in the year, Pontiac moved into the big leagues with a 389 bored-and-stroked to 421 cid. Rated at 373 horses with twin four-barrel carbs, this was a limited production mill intended mainly for drag racing, and was thus typically installed in light Catalina two-doors.

On that subject, Pontiac had been competing—and winning—almost everywhere for some five years. It took the '59 Pikes Peak hillclimb, then in 1959-60 captured Top Eliminator honors in NHRA and six NASCAR Grand Nationals. The streak continued in '61. Fireball Roberts, Joe Weatherly, Junior Johnson, Jack Smith, and David Pearson claimed 21 of 52 scheduled Grand Nationals between them, and 1960 Ponchos took nine more.

Division chief Semon E. "Bunkie" Knudsen was responsible for all this, and he'd watched it pay off in potent cars with a potent image that translated directly into fast sales growth. Even so, Pontiac production paused for '61, declining some 56,000 from 1960 despite the new Tempest. But that would be a temporary aberration. Indeed, Pontiac moved from fourth to third for 1962 with well over half-a-million cars—a stunning achievement like few others in postwar Detroit history. Bunkie had turned a staid "old man's car" into a flashy hot-seller in a remarkably short time, and from 1962 to decade's end, Pontiac wouldn't look back.

The big '62 Pontiacs weren't greatly changed, though styling was softened some and hardtop coupes sported a new roofline (shared with sister GM models) that simulated a convertible's top-up appearance (down to suggestive "ribs" above smaller rear windows). The year's major announcement was the lush Grand Prix two-door hardtop (see entry), Pontiac's push on the personal-luxury trail blazed by Ford's Thunderbird, which displaced Ventura from the lineup. All other models returned. Catalinas (and GP) inched out to a 120-inch wheelbase, but all wagons remained at 119. Though drivetrains remained numerous—and confusing— differences from '61 were slight. Depending on model and engine, buyers could still choose between three- or four-speed manual transmissions, three- or four-speed Hydra-Matics, and seven different axle ratios. Base prices rose about $100, but spanned an attractive $2700-$3600 range. Pontiac added to its trophy case in '62 winning 10 NASCAR events and lowest stock-class ET at the NHRA Winternationals.

Pontiac was definitely on the warpath whether that be street, strip, speedway, or showroom. And this was only the beginning.

1961-63
Pontiac Tempest

Exotic engineering alone seldom sells cars, and often works against sales in terms of price and reliability. Take Pontiac's first-generation Tempest. Though daringly innovative for a Detroit car, let alone a small, relatively inexpensive one, Tempest was consistently outsold by its conventional Buick Special and Olds F-85 sisters through 1963. Not until it became conventional did sales—and profits—become significant.

Introduced for 1961, Tempest, F-85, and Special were General Motors' "second-wave" compacts after Chevrolet's new air-cooled rear-engine 1960 Corvair. Designed as "Project X-100," they used a modified version of the Corvair's unitized Y-body platform with four-inch-longer, 112-inch wheelbase, plus front-mounted water-cooled powerplants.

From there, Tempest diverged greatly. Where Special/F-85 carried a new lightweight 215-cubic-inch aluminum V-8 of 155 horsepower, Tempest employed the first four-cylinder engine in postwar GM history. Essentially Pontiac's 389 V-8 sliced in half, this 195-cid "Indy 4" produced 110 bhp on 8.6:1 compression with a one-barrel carburetor. An optional four-barrel carb delivered 120 bhp, also with standard three-speed manual. Ordering the $172 two-speed "Tempestorque" automatic (a modified Corvair Powerglide) made the figures 120 and 130. A high-compression (10.25:1) 155-bhp version was available with either transmission, as was the Special/F-85 V-8 ($216), which weighed some 180 pounds *less* than the all-iron four.

More radical still was Tempest's exclusive "rope drive" with rear transaxle (combined transmission/differential) and independent swing-axle suspension. Essentially a long bar bent slightly beneath the floor, this thin but lightly stressed propshaft spun within a steel tube, was mounted on bearings, and was permanently lubricated. Its slight sag reduced floor-hump height in front, but not in back. However, it eliminated the need for universal joints and allowed softer engine mounts for better noise isolation. It also made the Tempest less nose-heavy than the Special and F-85.

Though common among imports, the Tempest's swing-axle rear suspension had been seen only on Corvair among domestic cars. Unfortunately, it worked little better on the Pontiac despite the efforts of division chief engineer John Z. DeLorean.

Tempest debuted as a rather radical car in 1961, being a compact with a rear-mounted transmission, all-independent suspension, and a choice of aluminum V-8 or GM's first postwar four-cylinder engine (both mounted in front). The '62s (above and below) were little changed, but the '63s (opposite page) received a complete makeover with smoother bodysides and fresh front and rear styling.

SPECIFICATIONS

Engines: ohv I-4, 194.5 cid (4.06 × 3.75), 110/115/120/
140/155/166; ohv V-8, 215 cid (3.50 × 2.80),
155/185 bhp (**1961-62**); ohv V-8,
326 (3.72 × 3.75), 260 bhp (**1963 only**)

Transmissions:	3-speed manual, 4-speed manual (1963 only), 2-speed automatic (in rear transaxle)
Suspension front:	upper and lower A-arms, coil springs
Suspension rear:	swing axles, coil springs
Brakes:	front/rear drums
Wheelbase (in.):	112.0
Weight (lbs):	2785-3035
Top speed (mph):	95-115
0-60 mph (sec):	9.5-15.0

Production: 1961 spt cpe 14,887 **4d sdn** 62,639 **4d wgn**
23,257 **1962 spt cpe** 51,981 **cpe** 15,473 **4d sdn** 37,430 **cvt**
20,635 **4d wgn** 17,674 **1963 cpe** 13,307 **Deluxe spt cpe**
13,157 **4d sdn** 28,221 **4d wgn** 10,135 **Deluxe cvt** 5,012
LeMans spt cpe 45,701 **LeMans cvt** 15,957

Actually, the Tempest handled pretty well *if* you knew what to expect. But in 1961, most Americans didn't know how to cope with swing-axle oversteer, especially in slippery corners. The same held for Corvair, of course, but Ralph Nader never accused the Tempest of being "unsafe at any speed." And in fairness, the front-engine layout and its resulting better weight balance made Tempests more forgiving *in extremis* than early Corvairs—though not a lot.

One buff magazine termed Tempest "a prototype of the American car for the Sixties." But no U.S. producer ever copied its unusual driveline, and Detroit-built fours wouldn't be common until the 1980s. Tempest was also costly to build for a low-price car, despite rear-end components borrowed from Corvair. As another observer said of DeLorean and his equally ambitious compact, "It is a wonder they let him do it."

But Pontiac did—then maybe wished they hadn't. While Special sold about 145,000 copies for '61 and F-85 117,000, Tempest drew only about 100,000 orders. With that, division planners rightly concluded that buyers didn't care about "advanced" engineering, and began planning a larger, completely orthodox Tempest for 1964.

The '61 Tempests bowed as standard- and Custom-trim four-door sedans and Safari wagons. A pillared coupe arrived midseason in bench- and sportier bucket-seat form, the latter christened LeMans. Deluxe and LeMans convertibles were added for '62 and proved quite popular, prompting a separate LeMans series for '63. The clean styling, courtesy of division chief designer Jack Humbert, didn't change much through '63. A twin-oval grille marked the '61s, a full-width three-section affair the '62s, a revived split grille and squarer body lines the '63s. Prices didn't change much either, with most models in the $2200-$2500 range.

Performance *did* change, however. For '62, the hottest four boasted 166 bhp via reshaped intake runners, while the V-8 went to 185 bhp via high-compression heads. A new manual four-speed option maximized the newfound muscle. For 1963, the aluminum V-8 option was replaced by a cast-iron 326, essentially a debored 389, good for 260 bhp and one very hot compact. Where a four-cylinder Tempest needed a yawning 15 seconds to reach 60 mph, the 326 made it in 9.5 seconds and topped out at 115 mph.

Just as nice for Pontiac, the more profitable LeMans took an increasing share of Tempest sales. The 1962 total of just over 143,000 slipped below 132,000 for '63, but some 46 percent of the latter went to LeMans.

Pontiac listened when buyers talked, a big factor in its great '60s success. As a result, the division wasted little time prepping an even more exciting Tempest for 1964: the now-immortal GTO.

1962-64
Pontiac Grand Prix

If the 1963 Grand Prix testified to the design brilliance of General Motors styling chief Bill Mitchell, the original '62 model testified to the marketing brilliance of Semon E. "Bunkie" Knudsen. The Grand Prix was, in fact, Knudsen's parting gift after six years as division general manager during which Pontiac rose from sixth in industry sales to a strong fourth and finally third for '62—a stellar achievement for a medium-price make.

In creating the Grand Prix, Bunkie took his cue from the high success of Ford's post-1957 four-seat Thunderbirds. The idea was simplicity itself: a Catalina hardtop coupe with unique styling touches and a T-Bird-type buckets-and-console interior. Interestingly, the new model was conceived for the Ventura nameplate, and it effectively replaced that slow-selling Catalina-based series. But Grand Prix was an inspired choice, with its heroic images of Formula 1 competition—and, of course, its literal French meaning, "great prize."

Differences from the parent Catalina were quite modest: slightly revised grille; dummy back-panel grillework; the Catalina's optional front bucket seats as standard; and a shiny center console with tachometer, gauge package, and monochrome color scheme inside and out. But the whole was far greater than the sum of these parts. As *Motor Trend* stated: "Style-wise and price-wise [the Grand Prix] competes directly with the Thunderbird. Performance-wise, it's in a class by itself."

True enough. There were no fewer than five versions of Pontiac's superb Trophy 389 V-8, from a 230-horsepower economy special to a high-compression Tri-Power job (three two-barrel carburetors) with a hefty 348 bhp. Speaking of heft, less weight and more available power gave the GP a decided performance edge on the Thunderbird. *MT* reported 0-60 mph taking a brief eight seconds. Three-speed manual shift was standard, but most GPs were ordered with "Roto" Hydra-Matic, a new three-speed torque-converter automatic shared with Catalina, priced at $231. For the same money,

Opposite page: *The first Grand Prix was essentially a dressed-up Catalina hardtop coupe with buckets-and-console interior, but the result was quite striking and it sold well. The '63 version (above) bore new styling adopted for all of Pontiac's full-size line, and sold even better. Performance was a big part of Grand Prix's allure: The '62s came with a 389 V-8 with up to 348 bhp; by 1964, the top power option was a potent 421 with 370 bhp.*

SPECIFICATIONS

Engines:	all ohv V-8; 389 cid (4.06 × 3.75); 230/303/318/333/348 bhp (**1962**), 230/303/313 bhp (**1963**), 230/303/ 306/330 bhp (**1964**); 421 cid (4.09 × 4.00), 353/370 bhp (**1963**), 320/350/370 bhp (**1964**)
Transmissions:	3/4-speed manual, 3-speed Hydra-Matic
Suspension front:	upper and lower A-arms, coil springs
Suspension rear:	4-link live axle, coil springs
Brakes:	front/rear drums
Wheelbase (in.):	120.0
Weight (lbs):	3835-3930
Top speed (mph):	105-125+
0-60 mph (sec):	6.6-10.0
Production:	**1962** 30,195 **1963** 72,959 **1964** 63,810

confirmed leadfoots could specify four-speed manual floorshift, as well as seven different axle ratios.

For all that, the '62 Grand Prix was a so-so seller. It wasn't that cheap at nearly $3600, and it cost little less than a T-Bird when optioned to match. GP did best Oldsmobile's comparably priced Starfire, but trailed Thunderbird by 2-to-1.

The '63 sold much better, thanks to peerless styling. Like other big Pontiacs, the GP wore slightly curvier contours enhanced by newly stacked quad headlamps, clean bodysides devoid of sculpturing, straight A-pillars and—the crowning touch—an exclusive razor-edge roofline with concave backlight (replacing the previous pseudo-convertible treatment). Despite a mere 1.3-inch gain in overall length, the effect was a larger, "more important" Grand Prix, and it turned heads everywhere.

The impression of extra bulk wasn't just visual, for Pontiac's 1963 "Wide Track" chassis boasted 2.9-inch wider tracks (64 inches total). But curb weight was hardly affected, and power was more plentiful, the two most potent 389s replaced by a pair of new 421s (a size first seen in '61) with 353 bhp (four-barrel) and 370 bhp (Tri-Power). Though they cost a towering $400 each, the 421s delivered equally towering performance. *MT* timed its 370-bhp job at just 6.6 seconds 0-60. Then again, even the lowly 303-bhp 389 could run that sprint in under 10 seconds.

Of course, no car is perfect and neither was the '63 GP. Suspension remained a bit soft, the Hydra-Matic was still plagued by excess slippage, the console-mounted vacuum gauge (replacing the '62 tach) was so hard to see as to be virtually useless, and a new "Cordova" vinyl roof covering was a questionable use of $86.08. But heavy-duty suspension was optional, too, along with Pontiac's handsome multi-spoke aluminum wheels ($122.13), and the performance and styling were all anyone could want. As a result, nearly 250 percent more buyers wanted Grand Prix in '63, a high-water mark that wouldn't be duplicated for another six years.

But this winning design wouldn't last long. The '64 was basically the '63 with a modest facelift and minor mechanical upgrades. After that, all full-size Pontiacs swelled to hippy, heroic new proportions. Not until 1969 would Grand Prix again offer the sort of manageable sports-luxury it had in the beginning—which explains why the 1962-64 models are now so coveted as collector cars. They were, and are, some of Pontiac's best.

1964-67
Pontiac Catalina 2+2

By 1964, a new age of high performance had dawned in America, marked not so much by a horsepower race as by a sophisticated balance between power, handling, and efficient design. Chrome and tailfins were out, bucket seats, mag-style wheels, center consoles, and floor shifters were in—and just about everybody had them. Pontiac, which had reentered the performance market under general manager "Bunkie" Knudsen, had been in the forefront of this movement since the Bonneville in 1957. With the Catalina 2+2, Pontiac achieved a combination of power, road-holding, and fine styling superior to any other big Pontiac, and most of the competition's models besides.

The 2+2 package was first offered as a $291 option on Catalina hardtops and convertibles in 1964. This money bought a potent 389 V-8 with 267-283 bhp, bucket seats, center console with vacuum gauge, special Morrokide interior, and unique exterior badges. Both a four-speed and Hydra-Matic transmission were available. The package was a trial balloon in 1964, and only 7998 Catalinas were so equipped.

A year later Pontiac applied the huge 421 V-8 as standard in the 2+2 package, with fender louvers and special hood/deck badges to identify it. Also included in the basic option was a three-speed Hurst floor shift, heavy duty shocks and springs, a 3.42:1 performance rear axle, chrome engine parts, full wheel discs, and fender pinstriping, details that raised the price of the package to $419 for coupes or $397 for convertibles. Adding a four-speed transmission, the "Custom Gauge Cluster" with comprehensive needle instruments, and power brakes/windows/antenna brought the cost up to

This page, bottom left: The first 2+2 was an option package for the Catalina that boasted bucket seats, console, special interior trim, and subtle exterior badges. Below: In 1965, all full-size Pontiacs received curvy new styling, and the 2+2 package now included a 421-cid V-8 in place of the previous 389. For 1966, the 2+2 became a separate model bearing a mild facelift (opposite page). The 2+2 reverted back to a Catalina option package for 1967 (this page, bottom right), gaining a new face and standard 428-cid V-8.

SPECIFICATIONS

Engines:	all ohv V-8; 389 cid (4.06 × 3.75), 267/283 bhp; 421 cid (4.09 × 4.00), 338-376 bhp; 428 cid (4.12 × 4.00), 360/376
Transmissions:	3-speed manual; 4-speed manual, 3-speed automatic optional
Suspension front:	upper and lower A-arms, coil springs
Suspension rear:	live axle, trailing arms, coil springs
Brakes:	front/rear drums; front discs optional
Wheelbase (in.):	120.0 (1964); 121 (1965-67)
Weight (lbs):	3695-4030
Top speed (mph):	115
0-60 mph (sec):	7.2-8.1
Production:	1964 7998 1965-67 19,672

about $4000 for the hardtop. The '65s had increased in size and weight, but the 2+2's potent drivetrain nevertheless provided terrific performance. With the optional Tri-Power 421 High Output engine and four-speed gearbox, a 2+2 could routinely reach 95 mph in the standing-start quarter-mile.

Bob McVay tried a 2+2 hardtop for *Motor Trend*, which gave Pontiac a blanket "Car of the Year" award in 1965. "Docile as a kitten in town, our 338-bhp charger turned wild when we put our foot down," McVay wrote, using the Royal Plural. "Our" foot gave 0-60 in eight seconds flat. "Equally impressive was the car's excellent passing acceleration and lugging ability in fourth gear, with 459 pounds/feet of torque available at 2800 rpm. . . . This combination of a large-capacity engine in a relatively light body should prove an excellent tow car for the weekend racer or traveler. [But] as with any performance automobile, gas mileage wasn't anything to shout about. . . . The 2+2 is one of those rare machines that asks to be driven fast and well. A good driver can get a lot out of a car like this—a lot of satisfaction and enjoyment in addition to performance."

Few changes occurred in 1966, except that the 2+2 was listed as an individual model, again as a hardtop or convertible. The identifying louvers were now moved to the rear fenders, and a Pontiac shifter replaced the Hurst unit. In 1967 the 2+2 was a Catalina package again, priced as usual around $400, but the base engine was now a 428 with a single four-barrel carburetor. The option included Deluxe wheel discs and steering wheel, Decor moldings, bucket seats, the three-speed, dual exhausts, and a heavy-duty stabilizer bar. A 428 HO engine remained available, but was not offered with Tri-Power.

According to John Gunnell's *Pontiac Buyer's Guide*, only 19,672 Catalinas had the 2+2 option from 1965 through 1967, and a breakdown of coupes vs. convertibles is not available. "The 1965s are the most highly sought after," Gunnell wrote, "even though they had the largest production." He goes on to call the 2+2 "Pontiac's top full-size collector car of this era."

1964-65 Pontiac GTO

The Pontiac GTO was one of those great ideas that was bound to happen. That it happened at Pontiac speaks volumes about the division's marketing savvy in the '60s, as well as its ability to satisfy the public.

Pontiac's new-for-'61 Tempest compact had satisfied enthusiasts seeking technical sophistication, but not the vast majority of buyers who valued smooth, effortless performance and reliable simplicity. That began changing for 1963, when Tempest offered a new 260-horsepower 326 V-8 option, a debored version of Pontiac's then-legendary 389. But adman Jim Wangers wanted even more, and fate played right into his hands with a Tempest bulked up to mid-size proportions for 1964.

It appeared with taut, geometric lines on a new corporate A-body platform shared with Chevrolet's new Chevelle, Oldsmobile's F-85/Cutlass, and Buick's Special/Skylark. Unit construction was abandoned for body-on-frame, a conventional driveline ousted the radical "rope drive" and rear transaxle, wheelbase was stretched three inches to 115, rear swing axles gave way to a solid axle with full-coil suspension, and there were bigger new bodies with extra underhood space for bigger engines. With help from division chief engineer John DeLorean and Pontiac general manager "Pete" Estes, Wangers got his "muscle car." But a General Motors policy prohibited such antics, so they had to package it as an option (at just under $300) for the '64 Tempest LeMans coupe, convertible, and two-door hardtop.

Wangers liked to race cars, so he knew his hot rod had to have more than just a big engine. He thus specified three-speed manual transmission with floorshift, quick steering, heavy-duty suspension, upgraded tires, dual exhausts, and racy touches like a simulated engine-turned metal dash applique. To top it off, Wangers brazenly borrowed "GTO" from a recent Ferrari. The initials denoted *Gran Turismo Omologato*, Italian for a racing-approved production grand touring car.

Sports-car purists took umbrage at that, but the GTO proved worthy of its name in decisive fashion. For one thing, performance was red hot. Special camshaft and lifters, cylinder heads from the potent 421 "H.O." engine, and a big four-barrel Carter carb delivered 325 standard horses; optional Tri-Power carburetion boosted that to 348. With the latter, a GTO could do 0-60 mph in as little as 6.5 seconds, over 130 mph all out, and standing quarter-miles of less than 15 seconds at nearly 100 mph. Then too, Pontiac's GTO was no less a road machine than Ferrari's GTO. In a bold comparison test, *Car and Driver* said a "good" Pontiac would trim the Ferrari in a drag race and lose on a road course. But "with the addition of NASCAR road racing suspension, the Pontiac will take the measure of any Ferrari other than prototype racing cars.... The Ferrari costs $20,000. With every conceivable option on a GTO, it would be difficult to spend more than $3800. That's a bargain."

On that subject, most GTOs ended up being "built" from the sales catalog, partly because Pontiac offered so many goodies. To the basic package one could add heavy-duty three-speed manual or a four-speed gearbox (also with floorshift and Hurst linkage), two-speed Hydra-Matic, metallic brake linings, heavy-duty radiator, limited-slip differential, vinyl top, center console, radio, air conditioning, power steering/brakes/windows, whitewall or red-stripe tires, even side-exit exhaust splitters. Then all you needed was a lead foot and lots of gas.

Pontiac may have been the only one surprised by GTO sales, which proved as hot as the car itself. Against only 5000 initially projected, the division moved over 32,000 for '64—a tremendous success.

With American youth fully overcome by "muscle-car mania," the GTO stood basically pat for '65. Even so, it shared in that year's sharp Tempest facelift, announced by a wider-appearing front end with newly stacked quad headlamps. Options were mostly as before, but standard power was uprated to 335 via revised cylinder heads, and the Tri-Power option (still a bargain at $116) was boosted to 360 via a wilder camshaft.

Sales increased, too—by over 100 percent—despite the advent of the Olds 4-4-2 and Chevy's Chevelle SS396. Even more competition was imminent, but the GTO would see still higher volume in later years.

For many enthusiasts, the 1964-65 GTO remains the only muscle car that matters: the first, if not the best ever built. All GTOs have since become collector's items, but none more than these; indeed, there have never been enough to go around. But that's the way it is with great ideas—and "instant legends."

This page, upper two and opposite page, top: Undoubtedly one of the most influential cars of the decade, the '64 GTO was actually an option package for the Tempest LeMans. A 1965 facelift brought vertical headlights and a full-width taillight (this page, bottom two and opposite page, bottom), while both the standard and optional engines gained a few horsepower.

SPECIFICATIONS

Engines:	all ohv V-8; 389 cid (4.06 × 3.75), 325/348 bhp (**1964**), 335/360 bhp (**1965**)
Transmissions:	3/4-speed manual, 2-speed Hydra-Matic
Suspension front:	upper and lower A-arms, coil springs
Suspension rear:	4-link live axle, coil springs
Brakes:	front/rear drums
Wheelbase (in.):	115.0
Weight (lbs):	3000-3565
Top speed (mph):	130+
0-60 mph (sec):	6.5-7.7

Production: 1964 spt cpe 7,384 htp cpe 18,422 cvt 6,644 1965 spt cpe 8,319 htp cpe 55,722 cvt 11,311

1965-68
Pontiac Grand Prix

After three successful years, Pontiac's Grand Prix entered a four-year sales decline that reflected a general decline in the car itself. Actually, there was nothing wrong with the 1965-68 models that a visit to Weight Watchers wouldn't fix, and if more glitter and gadgets were evident, so was more power that enabled performance to remain respectable. But these GPs were clearly less special than the handsome and balanced 1962-64s, a fact evidently not lost on the public. From a high of 12.4 percent for 1963, Grand Prix skidded to just 4.4 percent of total Pontiac sales by 1966—a record year for the division as a whole. The '68 figure was an equally lackluster 4.6 percent.

This fall in fortunes largely stemmed from two related factors: the advent of mid-size performance cars like Pontiac's own GTO, and a consequent waning interest in sporty big cars like the Grand Prix. Price was not a factor. Despite a bigger, all-new design, the '65 base-priced a dollar *less* than the '64—exactly $3498—and by '68 the sticker was up by less than $200 despite interim inflationary pressures.

Inflated certainly described Pontiac's '65 styling, which contrived to make its wares seem much larger than any dimensional gains suggested. Indeed, GP wheelbase was stretched only an inch, to 121, and just 1.6 inches were added to overall length, though the resulting 214.6 inches were hardly what one would call trim. Curb weight was little affected, too, remaining at just under two tons. Nevertheless, the '65 GP and its cohorts looked like bodybuilders on steroids: bulged and billowed all over the place in the curvy, humped-fender idiom GM hoped to popularize. About all that remained of previous Grand Prixs were the trademark split-theme grille, stacked quad headlamps, discreetly hidden taillamps, and unique roofline with concave rear window.

Happier news awaited underneath. Like GM's other B-body full-size cars that year, the '65 Pontiacs adopted a stronger new full-perimeter chassis that was more resistant to side impact damage than the previous X-member design. Another advancement came as the old never-liked Roto Hydra-Matic transmission gave way to the vastly superior new Turbo Hydra-Matic with enlarged torque converter. Engine choices still comprised a quartet of 389s and a trio of big-block 421s, but

Above and below: *Pontiac's full-size cars took on a bulging new look for 1965, and the Grand Prix followed suit. However, it still maintained its concave rear roofline and distinctive grille and taillight treatments.* Opposite page: *The '66s were little changed save for a mild facelift.*

SPECIFICATIONS

Engines:	all ohv V-8; 389 cid (4.06 × 3.75), 256-338 bhp (**1965-66**); 421 cid (4.09 × 4.00), 338-376 bhp (**1965-66**); 400 cid (4.12 × 3.75), 265/350 bhp (**1967-68**); 428 cid (4.12 × 4.00), 360-390 bhp (**1967-68**)
Transmissions:	4-speed manual, 3-speed Hydra-Matic
Suspension front:	upper and lower A-arms, coil springs
Suspension rear:	4-link live axle, coil springs
Brakes:	front/rear drums
Wheelbase (in.):	121.0
Weight (lbs):	3940-4075
Top speed (mph):	120-125
0-60 mph (sec):	7.7-9.5

Production: 1965 57,881 **1966** 36,757 **1967 htp cpe** 37,125 **cvt** 5,856 **1968** 31,711

Opposite page, top: The '67 Grand Prix boasted the most radical changes of this generation, featuring new side sculpturing and hidden headlights, along with the marque's first—and last— convertible. The facelifted '68s (below and opposite page, bottom) would be the last of the full-size Grand Prixs, scoring fewer sales than any GP since the '62s.

power ratings were up across the board. The standard 389, for instance, gained 22 horsepower for a total of 325, and 421s offered up to 376 with optional Tri-Power carburetion. Helped in no little measure by the new automatic, the base-engine '65 proved quicker than its '63 counterpart by nearly three seconds in the 0-60 dash, according to *Motor Trend*—a 27 percent improvement. Braking suffered, though— by a substantial 44 feet in 60-mph "panic" stops.

Other things suffered, too. A bench seat was standard in lieu of buckets, which now cost extra, and upholstery switched from vinyl to cloth. In short, the GP was turning from sports-luxury to personal-luxury. But Ford's Thunderbird and Buick's Riviera were knocking each other over for king of that hill; GP evidently wasn't seen as a contender. So despite *MT* "Car of the Year" honors to Pontiac—and record division sales—the '65 Grand Prix garnered some 6000 fewer orders than the '64.

The '66 generated less than 60 percent of '64 volume—and the aforementioned 4.4 percent of total Pontiac sales. The main change that year was an attractive, muted facelift of the somewhat exaggerated '65 look.

Sales improved to nearly 43,000 for 1967, when a full lower-body reskin conferred a hulkier look again, dominated by a massive bumper/grille with Grand Prix's first hidden headlamps. Wipers were also hidden, and there was heavy sculpturing around the rear wheels. Federal smog standards were looming, so engine selections were reduced to four: a pair of 400 V-8s and two stroked 428s, all sharing new block and head designs conceived with lower emissions in mind. Power was still plentiful, though, ranging from a 265-bhp "economy" 400 to a 376-bhp 428. But the big '67 news was the first—and last—Grand Prix convertible. Though attractive and eminently desirable, it cost $264 more than the mainstay hardtop coupe, which was not chicken feed then, and fewer than 6000 were called for, only 13.7 percent of GP sales. To no one's surprise, it did not return for '68.

The hardtop did, of course, but yet another lower-body restyle rendered looks debatable. The big bumper/grille was even bigger, side sculpturing more radical, and the rear end became massive and Buick-like. Even Pontiac engineer Bill Collins later called the '68 GP "a disaster. Nobody bought it. It looked like a big fat turkey." Maybe so, but it was not unpalatable to *Car and Driver*: "The performance and roadability . . . are excellent. Only its size and weight keep the Grand Prix from being a Super Car."

But sales were again anything but super—the lowest since debut '62, in fact. A new Grand Prix with more of the original spirit was clearly needed. And that's precisely what Collins and company delivered for 1969.

1966-67
Pontiac GTO

There's something to be said for "second generation" models both as cars and collector's items. Take Pontiac's 1966-67 GTOs. Though more numerous and thus cheaper now than the first 1964-65 models, they offered similar performance and arguably better styling—easily some of Detroit's best in this decade. In short, they were the original "muscle car" made better, which was no small accomplishment.

Appearance received most of the emphasis for 1966. General Motors reskinned all of its A-body intermediates that year, but none fared better than Pontiac's Tempest/LeMans line, the work of longtime division design chief Jack Humbert. Though wheelbase and other dimensions were virtually unchanged from 1965, the '66s managed to look longer, lower, and wider. Contributing elements included more flowing lines with trendy "Coke bottle" upswept rear fenders, a wider-appearing split-theme grille, subtle sculpturing in the rocker-panel area, and, on coupes, a shapely new "tunnelback" roofline with "flying buttress" side panels sloped down and slightly behind a fairly upright rear window.

Reflecting its phenomenal 1964-65 success, the GTO moved from option package to separate-series status, offering convertible, hardtop coupe, and pillared Sport Coupe as before. All were identified by unique slatted taillamps, grille-mounted parking lamps resembling European driving lights, shapely twin-nostril dummy hood scoop, and those all-important GTO badges.

That scoop became functional when you ordered the new Ram Air engine option. Introduced in early 1965 as a dealer-installed package, this gave the Tri-Power 389 the benefit of cold-air induction. Though rated horsepower was the same as for non-Ram versions (360), the package probably made its effects known more on the street than on the dyno. Also returning with few changes was GTO's standard 335-bhp four-barrel unit.

Authors Jan Norbye and Jim Dunne note in *Pontiac: The Postwar Years* that the '66 "hood scoop was positioned so that it could pick up only boundary-layer air. However, it did admit cool air, thus assuring higher volumetric efficiency. The air cleaner was combined with a plenum chamber that covered the carburetor air horns, and was sealed against the closed hood (and hot underhood air) by thick gaskets made of foam rubber."

Pontiac option lists in the '60s seemed to grow longer every year; GTO's was no exception. Besides Ram Air, your '66 could be ordered with a new reclining front passenger seat and contoured plastic inner fender liners (typically rendered in red). Still on hand were full Rally Gauge Cluster, aluminum front brake drums, AM/FM radio, and four-on-the-floor with choice of close- and wide-ratio gearsets. Prices were up only $50-$100 from '65, so a well-optioned GTO still cost under $5000— a tremendous bargain. Not surprisingly, Pontiac couldn't build 'em fast enough. In fact, 1966 would prove the GTO's all-time best model year with nearly 97,000 units, this despite growing muscle competition from most every quarter.

Thankfully, GTO's handsome '66 styling changed only in detail for 1967. Engine availability, however, changed somewhat more. Gone was the nifty Tri-Power setup, the 389 gaining a larger bore to compensate for the loss. The resulting 400 cid V-8 was offered in four versions: 335 bhp standard, 360-bhp H.O. (high output) with and without Ram Air, and—amid howls of protest from GTO lovers—a 255-bhp regular-gas "economy" engine as a no-cost option. Looming Federal safety and emissions standards were responsible for these changes, which took the razor's edge off performance. Although these were still plenty potent Pontiacs, they were definitely "softer" GTOs.

This personality shift was also reflected in things like a smoother (but more efficient) new Turbo Hydra-Matic transmission (replacing the previous two-speeder) and an option list turning from go more to show. Among new '67 items were the now-famous hood-mounted tachometer, 8-track tape player, and cruise control, but also front-disc brakes and more powerful capacitive-discharge ignition system. Federal influence was evident in adoption of a twin-circuit brake system, more interior padding, energy-absorbing steering column, and wider availability of seatbelts and front-seat headrests.

"The Great One," as Pontiac advertised it for '67, still had lots of great history to write. But with production tailing off that year (a first in the model's brief life) by over 15 percent, the GTO would write no more sales records. Of course, rivals were also beginning to feel the pinch, as the muscle car was about to be legislated out of existence. We should be grateful that so many 1966-67 GTOs survive to remind us of the glory days.

Below and opposite page, top: *Restyled GTO for '66 "Coke bottle" profile and tunneled backlight. A facelift marked the '67s* (this page, bottom and opposite page, bottom) *when a 400-cid V-8 replaced the 389, though rated horsepower remained the same.*

SPECIFICATIONS

Engines:	all ohv V-8; 389 cid (4.06 × 3.75), 335/360 bhp (**1966**); 400 cid (4.12 × 3.75), 255/335/360 bhp (**1967**)
Transmissions:	3/4-speed manual, 2/3-speed Hydra-Matic
Suspension front:	upper and lower A-arms, coil springs
Suspension rear:	4-link live axle, coil springs
Brakes:	front/rear drums; optional front discs (**1967 only**)
Wheelbase (in.):	115.0
Weight (lbs):	3425-3555
Top speed (mph):	130+
0-60 mph (sec):	6.6-9.5

Production: 1966 spt cpe 10,363 **htp cpe** 73,785 **cvt** 12,798 **1967 spt cpe** 7,029 **htp cpe** 65,176 **cvt** 9,517

1967-69 Pontiac Firebird

General Motors may be the world's biggest automaker, but it's always had limits. That was true even in the carefree '60s, when GM almost owned the market.

Take Pontiac's new-for-'67 Firebird. Had division chief John DeLorean gotten his way, it would have been a two-seat sports car called Banshee, a low-cost sister to the Chevy Corvette. But GM was hard-pressed to support one sports car, let alone two, and "Banshee" didn't test well with the public. So DeLorean settled for a "Pontiacized" version of Chevy's four-seat Camaro—which was hardly bad.

Camaro stemmed from the "Panther" or "F-car" program that aimed at a direct Ford Mustang-fighter to replace the Corvair Monza as Chevy's mainstream sporty compact. Pontiac was aware of the effort all along, and asked to be cut in once management vetoed DeLorean's two-seater. Firebird was a good name choice, signifying power, beauty, and youth in American Indian mythology and recalling GM's gas-turbine experimentals of the late '50s and early '60s.

Pontiac engineer Bill Collins later stated that the '67 Firebird was "just kind of inherited from Chevrolet." The . . . body had all the Chevrolet sheetmetal and all the same exterior hardware except for the grille and taillamps." Even so, those elements—split-theme grille, "slot" taillamps—were distinctly Pontiac, thus differentiating Firebird from Camaro to a surprising degree.

Moreover, Pontiac's pony benefited from some engineering lessons learned too late to affect first-year Camaros, which went on sale some five months before Firebird's February 1967 debut. The most notable were engines set further back for better front/rear weight balance, and standard rear traction bars to minimize axle windup under hard acceleration.

Another distinction involved marketing. Where Camaro achieved four models through options, Firebird arrived with five separate offerings keyed to engines. Each was available in Camaro's convertible and hardtop coupe body styles. The base Firebird carried Pontiac's year-old, 165-bhp 230-cid overhead-cam six. Next came the Sprint, with 215-bhp ohc six, floor shift, and "road hugging" suspension. One step up

SPECIFICATIONS

Engines:	sohc I-6, 230 cid (3.88 × 3.26), 165/215 bhp (**1967 only**); sohc I-6, 250 cid (3.88 × 3.53), 175/215/230 bhp (**1968-69**); ohv V-8, 326 cid (3.72 × 3.75) 250/285 (**1967 only**); 350 cid (3.88 × 3.75), 265/320 bhp (**1968-69**); 400 cid (4.12 × 3.75), 320/325/330/335/340/345 bhp
Transmissions:	3/4-speed manual, 3-speed Hydra-Matic automatic
Suspension front:	upper and lower A-arms, coil springs
Suspension rear:	live axle on semi-elliptic leaf springs
Brakes:	front/rear drums, optional front discs
Wheelbase (in.):	108.0
Weight (lbs):	2955-3350
Top speed (mph):	110-115
0-60 mph (sec):	4.8-10.1

Production: 1967 htp cpe 67,032 **cvt** 15,526 **1968 htp cpe** 90,152 **cvt** 16,960 **1969 htp cpe** 76,059 **cvt** 11,649 (1969 figures include 697 Trans Am models)

Opposite page, and this page, above and top: *More than just a Camaro with Pontiac styling touches, the first Firebird featured Pontiac engines set further back in the frame to more evenly distribute weight. Few appearance changes were made for '68 (this page, two lower right photos), but the six-cylinder and base V-8 grew in both size and power, while a Ram Air II option was added to the top 400-cid V-8.*

was the V-8 Firebird 326, billed as a "family sportster. 250 lively horses on regular gas" (and two-barrel carb). A further notch up was the Firebird H.O., boasting a four-barrel 326 that Pontiac said made it a "285-hp light heavyweight." Topping the line was the Firebird 400 with 325 bhp and available Ram Air induction. Of course, no Firebird wanted for options, which were expected in "ponycars," with plenty for both show and go—everything from extra instruments and front-disc brakes to short axle ratios and full-house power equipment.

With prices starting about $200 upstream of six-cylinder Camaros—$2666 for the base hardtop and $2903 for the convertible—Firebird generated strong 82,000-plus sales despite an abbreviated debut season. Though that was only half Camaro's volume, it pushed combined F-car sales well over the projected quarter-million break-even point to the delight of GM accountants. About two-thirds carried optional power steering and Hydra-Matic Drive, suggesting Firebird competed less with Mustang—or Camaro—and more with Mercury's new '67 Cougar in an emerging "luxury ponycar" field.

The '68s were little-changed visually but much-changed mechanically. The ohc sixes grew to 250 cid, the 326 V-8 became a 350, the H.O. also became a 350 and claimed 35 more horses, the 400 tacked on five bhp, and a new 400 H.O. arrived with 335 bhp. At midyear, Pontiac offered a 400 Ram Air II option, also rated at 335 bhp, 25 below the comparable GTO unit due to a minor carb change.

The big news for '69 was the fire-breathing Trans Am (see entry), but all Firebirds sported new lower-body styling that further disguised their Camaro origins. Notable was a more prominent chrome "bird beak" grille surrounded by trendy body-color Endura plastic *à la* GTO. Unfortunately, the restyle also added somewhat to weight, as well as 2.3 inches in length and 1.3 inches in width. Engines were basically as before except that the Ram Air II gave way to a 345-bhp 400 Ram Air IV option. Sales continued strong, with more than 100,000 units in 1968 and over 87,000 in '69. That was still only a fraction of Camaro's business but roughly even with Cougar's—about what DeLorean had expected.

You don't see that many '60s Firebirds nowadays, not only due to their lower original volume but because enthusiasts long dismissed them as the Camaro-clones they appeared to be. Happily, that's changed, and deservedly so. After all, these Firebirds *were* Pontiacs, not Chevys, and in the '60s that made all the difference.

Firebird's lowest-priced convertible for '68 was priced at $2996 (less than $200 more than a Mustang) and carried Pontiac's unusual 250-cid overhead-cam six with 175 bhp. The sporty Sprint option (below) included a 215-bhp version of that engine along with special trim. The '69s (opposite page) wore new bodyside sculpturing and a redesigned front end with a separate chrome grille, and headlights surrounded by body-color Endura plastic.

1968-69
Pontiac GTO & Judge

Being first is relatively easy; *staying* first isn't. Nobody in '60s Detroit knew that better than Pontiac, especially when it came to muscle cars. After all, Pontiac had created the breed in 1964 with its GTO, which within four short years faced a slew of competitors, all ready to unseat it as king of Muscle Mountain.

Pontiac struck back with a fully redesigned GTO for 1968. In many ways, it was the best yet. The pillared coupe body style was gone, but convertibles and hardtop coupes returned with clean, muscular new styling dominated by bulged bodysides, fast-sloping hardtop roofline, and a big bumper/grille with newly hidden headlamps. The nose was sheathed in body-colored Endura plastic, a material Pontiac had been playing with since 1964, able to ward off low-speed impacts without chipped paint or dented metal. Pontiac demonstrated its value with a TV commercial showing white-coated "testers" gleefully hammering a GTO's nose to no ill effect.

Enhancing this new appearance was the three-inch-shorter, 112-inch wheelbase applied to all '68 GM intermediate two-doors (four-doors spanned 116 inches). A strong new full-perimeter frame enhanced rigidity and even handling, though it contributed to curb weights some 75 pounds higher than '67. Engines were evolved from the previous roster of 400-cid V-8s. First came a 350-bhp base unit, followed by a 360-bhp H.O. option. To the latter could be added new Ram Air II induction, basically the previous Ram Air I setup with two functional hood air intakes, as on the '64 GTO, instead of one. Later that year, a special tunnel-port engine with revised intake manifold became available, rated at 366 bhp. Last—and least—was a two-barrel "economy" V-8, continued from '67, making 265 bhp on regular gas. Fewer than 3300 of the nearly 88,000 GTOs built for '68 were so equipped.

That grand total was 10 percent better than GTO's 1967 volume, and the new styling was surely a factor. And as might be expected, the GTO was still a fierce performer: *Motor Trend*'s Ram Air II example clocked 6.5 seconds 0-60 and blasted through the standing quarter-mile in 14.45 seconds at 98.2 mph. But that was little better than what the '64 had managed, mainly because the GTO had gained some 500 pounds in the interim. Worse, a MoPar Hemi or 427 Ford Torino could show "The Great One" a clean pair of heels, all else being equal—which, admittedly, it seldom was. Plymouth started a new game in '68, the "budget muscle car," and the surprisingly high sales of its whimsical Road Runner prompted rush replies from rivals for 1969. Pontiac went its own way with "The Judge," a $354 option package for that year's mildly facelifted GTO. The name echoed a bit on the popular "Laugh-In" TV show in which a judicially robed Sammy Davis, Jr., intoned "Here come da judge." It also dovetailed with Pontiac ads portraying GTO as the final arbiter of street performance.

Performance The Judge definitely had, as the package included a new 366-bhp Ram Air III engine. Optional was an equally new 370-bhp Ram Air IV, also available on other GTOs, that used a cold-air box around the carburetors, fed by twin flexible tubes leading from openings in the grille. A late-season (and rarely installed) Ram Air V option reverted to hood intakes, but with driver-controlled flaps. As usual, three-speed manual with Hurst T-handle floorshift was standard, but connected to a 3.55:1 axle; four-speed and Turbo Hydra-Matic were optional, as were 3.90 and 4.33 axle ratios. With just 10.1 lbs/horsepower, The Judge delivered—er, arresting go: 0-60 in just over six seconds, standing quarter-miles of 14-14.5 seconds at 98-105+ mph.

The exterior was just as cop-baiting: psychedelic orange paint, black grille, tri-color bodyside striping, spoked "Rally" wheels, "flower power" name decals, and a five-foot-wide decklid spoiler on three short struts. As on standard GTOs, options included power brakes with front discs, hood-mounted tachometer, and comprehensive Rally instrumentation.

Despite its playful persona and higher standard power, The Judge found few takers. Worse, total GTO sales skidded by over 15,000 for '69. Like every muscle machine, Pontiac's was being slapped with burdensome insurance premiums, plus more Federal safety and emissions rules that threatened to quench its fire—which they ultimately did. Thus would The Judge depart after 1971, followed by the basic '68 GTO design after '72, and (belatedly) the GTO nameplate itself after '74.

Pontiac has yet to revive either Judge or GTO, and we ought to be grateful for that. Great memories should not be diluted by pale latterday namesakes.

Pontiac's famed "Goat" was redesigned for '68 (this page, top and opposite page, top), but engines remained the same as in '67 save for a top 366-bhp addition. "The Judge" (this page, bottom and opposite page, bottom) appeared in '69 as an option package with the 366-bhp V-8, a rear spoiler, and special graphics.

SPECIFICATIONS

Engines:	ohv V-8, 400 cid (4.12 × 3.75), 265/350/360/366/370 bhp
Transmissions:	3/4-speed manual, 3-speed Turbo Hydra-Matic
Suspension front:	upper and lower A-arms, coil springs
Suspension rear:	4-link live axle, coil springs
Brakes:	front/rear drums; optional front discs
Wheelbase (in.):	112.0
Weight (lbs):	3505-3590
Top speed (mph):	130+
0-60 mph (sec):	6.2-9.0

Production: 1968 htp cpe 77,704 **cvt** 9,980 **1969 htp cpe** 64,851 **cvt** 7,436 (incl. 6725 **"Judge" htp cpe** and 108 **"Judge" cvt**)

1969
Pontiac Firebird Trans Am

In the early '80s, Pontiac candidly admitted that Trans Am had become a better-known name than Firebird or even Pontiac. How ironic, then, that the original '69 Trans Am was once slated to be called Sebring or Formula. As it turned out, the former was already locked up by Plymouth (which used it after 1970), and Pontiac had other plans for Formula—which left Trans Am.

That, of course, referred to the Sports Car Club of America racing series for production "ponycars," launched in 1966. Yet as 1969 approached, Pontiac had no engine that met the series' 305-cubic-inch displacement limit, unlike Chevrolet with its 302-cid Camaro Z-28 powerplant. And Pontiac never would. The irony was that the '69 Trans Am never officially raced in the contest for which it was named. Not that it would matter. The Trans Am cast a performance glow over the entire Firebird line that would ensure its future—and indeed, that of lesser Firebirds—right up to the present day.

Pontiac started toying with super-performance Firebirds even before its Camaro-cloned "ponycar" hit the market in February 1967. Those efforts are too numerous to detail here, but two figured directly in the production Trans Am. One was the so-called PFST—"Pontiac Firebird Sprint Turismo"—a European-style package with special high-ability suspension developed by division chassis whiz Herb Adams. The other involved a highly sophisticated small-block version of Pontiac's 326/389 V-8, downsized to 303 cid—to get below the Trans-Am displacement ceiling—and fitted with special tunnel-port heads. A third factor was the styling work toward the 1969 GTO Judge, particularly its wild "floating" rear wing spoiler.

Though development problems and a fast-waning performance market ultimately precluded the would-be racing engine, a special projects committee comprising Adams, chief engineer Bill Collins, product planner Ben Harrison, and adman Jim Wangers hit on the idea of a "Firebird Judge" with a tuned 400 V-8 and PFST-type

SPECIFICATIONS

Engines:	ohv V-8, 400 cid (4.12 × 3.35), 335/345 bhp
Transmissions:	3/4-speed manual, 3-speed Turbo Hydra-Matic
Suspension front:	upper and lower A-arms, coil springs
Suspension rear:	live axle on semi-elliptic leaf springs
Brakes:	front discs/rear drums
Wheelbase (in.):	108.0
Weight (lbs):	approx. 3300
Top speed (mph):	120+
0-60 mph (sec):	approx. 5.0

Production: htp cpe 681 **cvt** 8 (includes 9 Ram Air IV models)

Opposite page, top: The original Trans Am was an option package offered in late 1969 for the Firebird 400. It comprised a sport suspension, body add-ons including forward-mounted hood scoops and a rear spoiler, white paint with blue racing stripes, and the Ram Air III version of the 400-cid V-8 (opposite page, middle). Only 689 Trans Ams were built in 1969, including a mere eight convertibles (below and opposite page, bottom).

chassis tuning. The result bowed at the Chicago Auto Show in early February 1969.

Technically, the Trans Am was a $725 option package available in both hardtop coupe and convertible form. You could have any color as long as it was white, set off by twin blue dorsal racing stripes, Judge-style wing spoiler, dummy twin air exits behind each front wheel, and functional hood scoops sitting much further forward than on Firebird 400s. Those intakes fed a 335-bhp Ram Air III V-8 with big four-barrel carburetor. Also on hand, as planned, were a fortified suspension with one-inch front stabilizer bar, F70×14 white-letter fiberglass-belted tires, 3.55:1 rear axle with limited-slip differential, power front-disc brakes, and variable-ratio power steering. A three-spoke sport steering wheel was included, too, along with heavy-duty three-speed floorshift manual transmission. A four-speed and self-shift Turbo Hydra-Matic were available at extra cost. The one power option was a 400 Ram Air IV with freer-breathing heads that delivered 10 extra horses in exchange for $558.

Not that the basic package was cheap. Figuring in all the "mandatory options" like the front discs, power steering, and special exterior, the Trans Am's actual price was $1163—and that was on top of what a Firebird 400 cost—so the bottom line was close to $4500.

Yet that was hardly outrageous for a limited-edition high performer that enthusiasts roundly applauded. *Hot Rod* magazine, for example, found the T/A surprisingly civilized in "slow driving, hot weather, or tight spaces," judged its "suspension will hang on a lot longer than most drivers will," and turned a standing quarter-mile of 14.1 seconds at 100.78 mph—with automatic! All this, plus the same handsomely facelifted styling and interior gracing all '69 Firebirds.

Actually, the Trans Am did find its way onto the Trans-Am circuit—sort of. Canadian Terry Godsall disguised a '68 Camaro Z-28 as a Firebird and, amazingly, got it past SCCA officials as a "Canadian" model. Yet despite this, and the talents of driver Jerry Titus, Firebirds scored no major wins in 1969.

But again, no matter. The T/A was a success all out of proportion to its modest sales: a mere 689, including just eight convertibles. With the handsome new second generation of 1970, it would go on to much higher volume, ultimately outselling all other Firebirds combined.

All this leaves the rare '69s as unique, one-year-only first editions with high performance and collector prices to match. Those lucky enough to own one possess pearls of great value indeed.

1969
Pontiac Grand Prix

Pontiac was one of the few carmakers in '60s Detroit to appreciate that bigger is not always better and that less can be more. Its lively overhead-cam six was one indication, but so, too, was the trim all-new Grand Prix that bowed for 1969. In many ways, it was the grandest GP in six years.

As noted earlier in this volume, Grand Prix sales had been mostly sliding since 1964, pretty much in unison with increasing girth and glitter. Even some Pontiac people didn't much like the GP by 1968. Not least among them were division general manager John DeLorean, chief engineer Bill Collins, and one Benjamin W. Harrison, the head of special projects at Pontiac Engineering.

It was Harrison who suggested a way to put "sport" back into the sports-luxury Pontiac. General Motors was then planning all-new A-body intermediates for 1968 with full-perimeter frames, fresh styling, and lineups divided along two wheelbases: 116 inches for four-door models, 112 for two-doors. In an April 1967 memo, Harrison proposed putting the new-generation hardtop coupe body on the longer chassis to create a new mid-size Grand Prix. It would be smaller and lighter than its predecessor—rather like a luxury GTO.

On the strength of a hastily prepared clay model by Pontiac stylists Irwin Rybicki and Jack Humbert, DeLorean received approval for this "hybrid" barely four days after receiving Harrison's memo. He then instituted a crash development program to have the model GP ready for an introduction date then barely 18 months away.

Somehow, DeLorean got his car. As Collins later explained in *Pontiac: The Postwar Years*: "In the corporation's way of doing things they only allow you so much tooling a year to work with. So you've got to figure out how . . . can I maximize [its] impact? If you can get the cost down, then you can show [management] that it makes sense to spend more on tooling. That's the way we got the '69 Grand Prix, which had all its own panels."

It had a lot more than that. Internally dubbed "G-body," the '69 GP bowed with a base price of $3866—some $200 less than the '68 figure—plus dashing long-hood/short-deck proportions on a unique 118-inch wheelbase. There were two "Models," J and SJ, designations unabashedly cribbed from the mighty '30s Duesenbergs. Under one of Detroit's longest hoods sat a four-barrel 400-cid V-8 with 350 horsepower, same as in the GTO. Optional for the J and included with the SJ was a 370-bhp version of Pontiac's big 428, with 390 bhp available. Heavy-duty three-speed manual shift was standard, but most '69s got Turbo Hydra-Matic. There was also a manual four-speed option tied to the 428, but it was fitted to only 676 of the 1014 manual-shift cars built for '69.

Inside were the GP's customary buckets and console, only the latter was swept up to meet the instrument panel and curved to face the driver. A forecast of BMW's later "cockpit design," it was called "Command Seat" by Pontiac ad writers, who also extolled standard goodies like Morrokide vinyl upholstery, "Pulse" intermittent wipers, and a radio aerial imbedded in the windshield. Besides the 370-bhp engine, the $316 SJ option added performance axle ratio, more complete Rally gauge cluster, and auto-leveling rear shock absorbers. Also on the options list: leather trim ($200), hood-mount tach, a then-novel electric-wire rear-window defroster ($48), and Cordova vinyl roof.

Ad man and sometime product planner Jim Wangers later termed the '69 Grand Prix "a huge success." That was an understatement: Sales jumped three-fold over admittedly dismal 1968. "It was supported by a popular price," he said, "but it also had a gutsy, high-performance image. . . . [It] now looked like the kind of car Pontiac would build in that idiom." It also went like one. *Motor Trend*, for example, reported 0-60 in 7.7 seconds and a standing quarter-mile of 15.1 seconds at 91 mph—and that was for the base-engine car with automatic!

The '69 GP was a success in two other ways. Though the performance market was already waning, it started a line that's still with us after three subsequent design generations (so far). Second, it prompted the inevitable Chevrolet spinoff, the Monte Carlo, which usually sold even better.

Nevertheless, this is one '60s performance Poncho that should now command museum-high prices, but doesn't—at least not yet. But the way they're being gathered in, it can't be long before this GP moves from "cheap wheels" to primo collectible. That it deserves. It's quite a car.

By 1968, the Grand Prix had become overweight and rather ordinary, which was reflected in poor sales. A trimmer, more exciting Grand Prix debuted in 1969 (both pages), based on a mid-size platform and offering a 350-bhp 400 as standard equipment, while a big 428 with up to 390 bhp was optional. This combination amply fulfilled the promise of a luxury-performance car, and sales skyrocketed.

SPECIFICATIONS

Engines:	all ohv V-8; 400 cid (4.12 × 3.75), 350 bhp; 428 cid (4.12 × 4.00), 370/390 bhp
Transmissions:	3/4-speed manual, 3-speed Turbo Hydra-Matic automatic
Suspension front:	upper and lower A-arms, coil springs, anti-roll bar
Suspension rear:	4-link live axle, coil springs
Brakes:	front discs/rear drums
Wheelbase (in.):	118.0
Weight (lbs):	3715
Top speed (mph):	115-120
0-60 mph (sec):	6.5-7.7
Production:	112,486

1969 Rambler SC/Rambler

The idea of a Rambler with the bargain-basement muscle car character of a Plymouth Road Runner may seem pretty farfetched, but a passable attempt was made by American Motors with the one-year-only SC/Rambler. At a base price under $3000, on par with the Road Runner, AMC offered a 390-cid V-8 with 315 bhp, a close-ratio all-synchromesh four-speed gearbox with Hurst linkage and shifter, and 3.54:1 no-slip differential. Also included were stiff suspension, quick steering, heavy-duty clutch and cooling system, tachometer, dual exhausts with glass-pack mufflers, cold-air induction, and Goodyear Polyglas tires. Added niceties came in the form of chrome hood tie-downs, teardrop rearview mirrors, special exterior paint, woodgrain steering wheel, reclining front bucket seats, and all-vinyl upholstery—all wrapped in the clean, lithe hardtop Rambler Rogue body styled by Dick Teague for the Rambler American. It was quite a buy, and what you bought you took with no alterations. Said an AMC price list: "no other optional equipment items will be included or permitted."

For a generation spawned on econobox Rambler Americans that had once been compared to army ordnance vehicles, Teague's heads-up styling department made sure people would recognize the "Scrambler" as a Rambler with a difference. They painted it red, white, and blue, blacked-out the grille, designed a prominent scoop for the cold-air induction, and equipped the car with Red Line tires on smart mag-style wheels. Hurst had been a partner in its development, so it was jointly announced by Hurst and AMC on February 13, 1969. Drag strip artists Dave Landrith of Hurst and Walt Czarnecki of AMC had much to do with its development.

Production was supposed to be only 500 units, apparently to homologate the SC/Rambler for National Hot Rod Association competition in the F/Stock class. There it would face off against 'Cuda 340s and W-31 Olds 4-4-2s. Rules required only 500, but AMC was hungry enough to build as many as it could sell. Demand caused the final figure to be 1512. There were paint variations and detail changes to items like the hood scoop, but the basic color scheme was a white body with broad red bodyside band outlined in black; a wide blue racing stripe down the roof and deck; another blue stripe on the hood, forming an arrow pointing at the big scoop; and corresponding red/white/blue accents on the gray vinyl interior.

According to marketing vice president R. W. McNealey, "The SC/Rambler is the ideal vehicle for the motorist who wants better-than-average performance and also a car that is uniquely different from 70 million others on the streets today . . . for the motorist who wants a customized car, but has neither the time nor inclination [or the money?] to build it himself." Routine PR stuff, that, but hear another AMC press release: "imagine the looks on faces when you lay down an e.t. in the low 14s at, say, 98 mph . . . right off the showroom floor! And set up for the strip with a little sharp tuning, who knows? You might be turning 12s." This was the AMC that a scant decade before was ridiculing the horsepower race and selling the public on 25 mpg economy. But times had changed.

This dichotomy between the "old" AMC and the new caused many to doubt that the SC/Rambler was really as good as its specifications suggested, but they were wrong. The performance was terrific. *Car Life* ran 0-60 in 6.3 seconds, and confirmed the promise of AMC press releases with a 14.2-second standing quarter-mile. *Car and Driver* praised AMC for creating "a car which makes it in almost all the categories. . . it can run and it can stop. . . . For lack of a better classification, the SC/R is a street rod."

AMC had also suggested the possibility of 12-second quarter-miles. Edrie Marquez's *Amazing AMC Muscle* notes that this too was possible. Dale Young, in an SC/R modified with high-lift cam, Edelbrock manifold with matching Holley carb, modified distributor, and Goodyear racing slicks, made five runs in the 12-second range, the last two being 12.69 seconds at 110.5 mph, and 12.67 at 109.99. A later SC/R, with only $1500 worth of drag modifications, "could turn 12.30s at 112 mph all day long. . . . The Scrambler had permitted the little Rambler American to bow out in a blaze of high performance glory."

Even in the late '60s, the SC/Rambler stood out as one wild ride. Its look screamed "performance," and its mechanicals backed that up. Most came with bold red, white, and blue graphics (opposite page), though about 500 of the 1512 produced had a more subtle paint scheme (this page, top). Only one powertrain was offered: a 315-bhp 390 with four-speed manual and a 3.54:1 rear gear.

SPECIFICATIONS

Engines:	ohv V-8, 390 cid (4.75 × 3.57), 315 bhp
Transmission:	4-speed manual
Suspension front:	upper and lower A-arms, coil springs
Suspension rear:	live axle, leaf springs
Brakes:	front disc/rear drum
Wheelbase (in.):	106.0
Weight (lbs):	3160
Top speed (mph):	108
0-60 mph (sec):	6.3
Production:	1512

1965-66 Shelby GT-350

Carroll Shelby, the Texas chicken farmer who drove for Enzo Ferrari in the '50s, retired from racing for health reasons in 1960. He then became America's most charismatic maker of high-performance specialty cars. Between 1962 and 1970 he built or contributed to such blindingly fast machines as the awesome Cobra 289 and 427, as well as the Sunbeam Tiger and Ford's mid-engine GT40 and Mark IV competition cars. The last took Ford to the performance pinnacle with outright victories in the 24 Hours of Le Mans in 1966-69.

Shelby's most popular project from a sales standpoint was the GT-350, a super-tuned version of the Ford Mustang. It was born of Dearborn's desire to give its new 1965 "ponycar" a solid performance image, and it did precisely that by reigning as national Sports Car Club of America B-production champion for three years in a row (1965-67).

The GT-350 began as a white Mustang 2+2 fastback delivered to Shelby-American's small Venice, California, shop with Ford's "Hi-Performance" 289 V-8 and four-speed manual gearbox options. Shelby applied a "High-Riser" manifold, big four-barrel carb, hot cam, and free-flow exhaust headers, plus trailing arms to locate a rear axle borrowed from Ford's big Galaxie to replace the stock, light-duty Falcon assembly. This brought bigger drum brakes in the rear that Shelby fitted with metallic linings, while Kelsey-Hayes disc brakes were used in front. Also installed were Koni adjustable shocks, quick-ratio steering box, front anti-sway bar, a stout steel-tube underhood brace, and 15-inch cast-aluminum wheels with high-performance Goodyear tires. Finally, the front suspension's forward mounts were relocated for optimum geometry. The result of all this was near-neutral handling instead of the standard Mustang's strong understeer—plus ferocious performance with 306 rated horsepower, versus the factory's 271.

Outside, the Mustang's prancing pony was relocated on the grille, the stock steel hood was replaced by a fiberglass replica with functional scoop, and broad blue racing stripes were applied to rocker panels and atop hood, roof, and trunklid. Inside were racing seatbelts, wood-rim steering wheel, full instrumentation—and no back seat, in order to qualify the GT-350 as a "sports car" under SCCA rules.

But this was just for the street. For the track, Shelby devised a "GT-350R" with special high-power heads, super-duty suspension, racing tires, aluminum transmission case, stripped interior, and a bumperless fiberglass nose with rudimentary air dam and large central air slot. All this reduced curb weight by some 300 pounds. Per his philosophy, Carroll made most of the special racing parts available over-the-counter at selected Ford dealers.

With its race-car dynamic ability and 6.5-second 0-60 acceleration, the street GT-350 drew rave reviews at an initial price of $4547. That was about $2000 above a V-8 Mustang but only $200 more than a Chevy Corvette—and a bargain by any standard. High volume was never a goal, yet Shelby did well to turn out 562 of the '65 models; of these, no more than 30 were R-spec racers.

Despite some subtle softening, the '66 edition was as vivid as the '65. External changes included fixed Plexiglas rear side windows instead of the stock fastback's air-exhaust vents, plus side scoops for rear-brake cooling, Mustang's thin-bar '66 grille, and 14-inch chrome-style or cast-aluminum wheels. After the initial 250 or so units, Shelby expanded color choices to include red, blue, green, and black, all with white stripes. At the same time he added the stock fastback's optional fold-down rear seat, returned the battery to the engine compartment from its former trunk location, reverted to heavy-duty Ford shocks—and offered automatic transmission. But he also listed an optional Paxton centrifugal supercharger that allegedly boosted horsepower beyond 400 and cut 0-60 times to a mere five seconds. Finally, Shelby built a fleet of gold-on-black "GT-350H" models for the Hertz Rent-A-Car company, which leased them at major airports—and soon ceased after finding that many were raced on weekends.

Other GT-350s continued racing and winning in '66, but they were essentially the cars that had competed the previous year, as no '66 R-models were built. However, Shelby did construct six '66 convertibles as gifts—presumably for *very* special friends.

But all good things must come to an end, and Shelby-Mustangs wouldn't be quite the same after 1966. Indeed, post-'67 models became more like regular Mustangs and were even built by Ford, hence the higher status—and prices—of these early models among collectors. But that's only as it should be. Unquestioned thoroughbreds, the 1965-66 GT-350s remain some of the hairiest and most memorable American cars ever built—and always will.

SPECIFICATIONS

Engines:	ohv V-8, 289 cid (4.00 × 2.87), 306 bhp
Transmissions:	4-speed manual, 3-speed SelectShift automatic
Suspension front:	upper and lower A-arms, coil springs
Suspension rear:	live axle on semi-elliptic leaf springs
Brakes:	front discs/rear drums
Wheelbase (in.):	108.0
Weight (lbs):	2800
Top speed (mph):	130+
0-60 mph (sec):	5.0-6.5
Production:	**1965** 562 **1966** 2380

The original Shelby was probably as close to a street-legal racing car as was ever offered by an American company. Standard Mustang fastbacks were fitted at Shelby's factory with high-performance suspension, brake, and engine modifications, while bodies received hood and side scoops along with a special paint treatment. The '66 version (both pages) looked nearly identical to the '65, except that Plexiglas rear-quarter windows replaced the previously used vents.

1967-68
Shelby GT-350 & GT-500

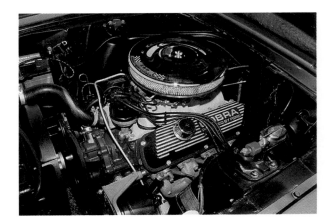

Production Mustangs for 1967 were larger, heavier, and more "styled," which meant that Carroll Shelby's *ne plus ultra* Mustang, the GT-350, would have to change. To keep its weight down and its appearance distinctive, Shelby designers created a custom fiberglass front end to complement the production Mustang's longer bonnet. They also put two high-beam headlamps in the center of the grille opening. (Some later cars have these lamps moved to the outer ends of the grille to comply with state motor vehicle requirements specifying a minimum distance between headlamps.) The 1967 Shelbys had a larger hood scoop and sculptured brake cooling scoops on the sides. Another set of scoops on the rear-quarter roof panels acted as interior air extractors. The rear end received a spoiler and a large bank of taillamps.

As a total design, the 1967 Shelby was stunning. It looked more like a racing car than many all-out racers; there was still nothing like it on American roads.

Certain changes also reflected customer feedback indicating a preference for a more manageable, easier-to-drive car. Power steering and power brakes, for example, became mandatory options. The '67 interior received special appointments not shared with the production Mustang, including a distinctive racing steering wheel, additional gauges, a genuine rollbar, and inertia-reel shoulder harnesses.

In 1967, Ford offered a 390 cid V-8 for its standard Mustang as its top performance engine. In typical Shelby style, Carroll went Ford one better, with a 428 cubic-incher and a new model, the GT-500. It was a popular move, for GT-500s outsold GT-350s by nearly 2-to-1. The GT-350 still carried the Mustang's stock high-performance small-block, but without the previous steel tube exhaust headers.

What Shelby had created by 1967 was a combination of performance and luxury, rather than a car that emphasized performance above everything else. Since carmakers adopted more conservative horsepower ratings in 1967—mainly to keep the insurance companies at bay—the GT-500 was only rated at 355 bhp, although it certainly developed more than that. The GT-350 was rated as before at 306 bhp, which is odd, because without the special headers and straight-through mufflers, its output was likely somewhat lower, probably closer to that of Ford's own 271-bhp high-performance 289. Still optional for the 289 was a $549 Paxton supercharger, which probably increased horsepower to around 400, though no official rating was ever

Mustang put on weight and inches for 1967, and the Shelby followed suit. Due to the added heft and new "mandatory options" like power steering and power brakes, the Shelby was gradually being transformed from a hard-edged racer into a luxury-performance car. The GT-350 (this page) carried on with the 306-bhp 289 V-8, but it was now joined by a GT-500 version (opposite page) boasting a 428 V-8 rated at a conservative 355 bhp.

published. A few GT-500s were special-ordered with a 427 V-8 of 400 bhp. Despite the added muscle, no attempt was made by the factory to race the 1967 models. Altogether, 3225 were built.

By 1968, Carroll Shelby was beginning to tire of the business he'd created. He had won the Manufacturers Championship and had overseen the Ford GT effort, culminating with wins at Le Mans in 1966 and 1967. He had also seen many close friends lose their lives on the race track. Meanwhile, competition had grown and new racing technology made it impossible for most specialists to grasp the many new principles and apply them successfully. Racing, Shelby said, wasn't fun anymore. It was business, and building one's own cars had lost much of its original attraction. Ford was now doing most of the Shelby product planning.

At the end of the 1967 model run, production was moved from Los Angeles to Michigan, where the A.O. Smith Company had contracted to carry out Shelby conversions of Mustangs. The cars were renamed Shelby Cobras (now that the original two-seat Cobra sports car was no longer being built), and Ford handled all promotion and advertising.

With the new name came a new look: A redesigned hood brought the twin air scoops up to its leading edge, while the grille, which now carried rectangular (rather than round) driving lights, became a large, gaping mouth bisected by the slim bumper. In back, sequential turn signals (adapted from the '65 Thunderbird) replaced the previous plain lenses.

Also new was the first Shelby convertible, featuring a built-in rollbar wearing an attractive plastic cover. GT-350s now used Ford's new 302-cid engine, but it had fewer high-performance goodies than the old 289, and put out a comparatively anemic 250 bhp. The Paxton supercharger option was again offered, and Shelby brochures now carried a rating for the blown engine: 335 bhp at 5200 rpm. Luxury features like automatic transmission, air conditioning, tilt steering wheel, tinted glass, and AM/FM stereo dominated the options list, all of which indicated that Shelbys were no longer the hard-core sports machines they once were.

At midyear, the GT-500's 428 engine (rated at 360 bhp for '68) was replaced by a 428 Cobra Jet, which had made a name for itself in drag racing. Although the new CJs wore the high-performance intake manifold and cylinder heads from the mighty 427, advertised horsepower somehow *dropped* to 335—though actual output was undoubtedly higher. Cars with this engine were called GT-500KR ("King of the Road"). Due to a shortage of 428s, a few GT-500s were fitted with 390-cid V-8s (much to the chagrin of their owners), while a few others once again got the 400-bhp 427. As in 1967, the big-block Shelbys were more popular, outselling the GT-350s by 2-to-1. Total 1968 production was 4450 cars, which would prove to be the Shelby's best sales year.

SPECIFICATIONS

Engines:	all ohv V-8:
	1967 GT-350 289 cid (4.00 × 2.87), 306 bhp;
	1968 GT-350 302 cid (4.00 × 3.00), 250/335 bhp;
	1967-68 GT-500 390 cid (4.05 × 3.78), 335 bhp;
	427 cid (4.23 × 3.78), 400 bhp;
	428 cid (4.13 × 3.98), 335-360 bhp
Transmissions:	4-speed manual; 3-speed automatic optional
Suspension front:	upper and lower A-arms, coil springs
Suspension rear:	live axle, leaf springs
Brakes:	front disc/rear drum
Wheelbase (in.):	108.0
Weight (lbs):	2800-3200
Top speed (mph):	120-130
0-60 mph (sec):	6.2 -7.8

Production: 1967 GT-350 1175 **GT-500** 2050 **1968 GT-350 fstbk** 1253 **cvt** 404 **GT-500 fstbk** 1140 **cvt** 402 **GT-500KR fstbk** 933 **cvt** 318

A facelift graced the '68 Shelbys, still offered in GT-350 (opposite page) and GT-500 (above) versions. The GT-350 now carried a 302 V-8 rated at 250 bhp, while the GT-500's 428 was boosted to 360 bhp. At midyear, however, a new 428 Cobra Jet became standard in the GT-500, and cars so equipped were designated GT-500KR.

1969
Shelby GT-350 & GT-500

The 1969 Mustang retained the original 1965 wheelbase, but dimensions were generally increased throughout. Surprisingly, roadability improved too; car for car, a '69 handled better than its predecessor, and the Cobra Jet Mach 1 and Boss 302 were the fastest production Mustangs yet produced.

Tradition demanded that Shelby Mustangs be somewhat faster, but it wasn't going to be easy. By 1969 the Federal government had introduced serious exhaust emission standards and safety requirements. Meanwhile, insurance premiums in the region of $1000 were being quoted for 25-year-old males who drove fast automobiles. The taste of buyers had also changed: luxury was becoming more important than performance. Vietnam, ominously, was siphoning off thousands of young men.

Carroll Shelby saw all these developments and reconsidered his position. Ever the individualist, he had begun in 1965 by building a car he himself wanted to drive—the original GT-350, a hairy, noisy, no-holds-barred American grand tourer for the sporting driver, as opposed to the driving sport. The market for such cars was limited; more buyers wanted luxury, and between 1966 and 1968, the Shelby Mustang had gradually evolved in that direction. Of course, it was still a very potent high-performance grand touring car—but it wasn't like the original.

Neither did Shelby enjoy making decisions in committees where accountants and lawyers usually overruled designers, engineers, and test drivers. Between Ford management and the Federal government, there were more bosses in his hair by 1969 than he'd ever encountered before. Ford, furthermore, was intruding on his turf with cars like the Mach 1 and Boss 302.

Nevertheless, Carroll lent his name to yet another Shelby series, the 1969 GT-350 and GT-500 (the KR suffix was dropped), though they now suffered the indignity of being built alongside regular production Mustangs in Southfield, Michigan. Shelby designers made the heavier, longer, busier production car look considerably more rakish. They extended the hood, fitted another fiberglass front end with a large grille cavity, used fiberglass front fenders to reduce weight, clipped off the tail, and added a spoiler and sequential turn signals. The GT-350 received the new 351 Windsor (Ontario) engine rated at 290 bhp, while the 428 CJ engine continued for the GT-500. A total of 3150 Shelbys were registered as '69s, and convertible versions were scarce: just 194 GT-350s and 335 GT-500 ragtops.

Fuel injection had been considered for '69, but was never adopted. A moonroof and reclining seats were other ideas that never made it into production. While Shelby hadn't cared much one way or the other about the convenience options, he did think that injection or supercharging (the latter having been an option since '66) were important developments that should have been considered. Ford thought otherwise—again.

Who needed it? At the end of 1969, Carroll Shelby called it quits. Production and design had become almost wholly Ford's responsibility anyway, and competition both from within Ford Division and from other makes was terrific. Shelbys weren't being raced much anymore, and the later models weren't his idea of a racing car anyway. Ford Division executive vice president Lee Iacocca agreed to terminate the Shelby program with no penalties or hard words. The association was at an end—at least for awhile.

Since the Shelby's popularity had declined along with its all-out performance character, some 1969s remained unsold at the end of the year and were reserialed as 1970 models. To differentiate them from the '69s, they were fitted with black hood stripes and Boss 302 front spoilers. Only 315 GT-350s and 286 GT-500s were "built" for 1970, after which the once-heralded Shelby Mustang was quietly and unceremoniously laid to rest.

In retrospect, it was good that Carroll Shelby quit when he did. Considering what happened to cars like the Camaro Z-28 and Boss Mustangs as the 1970s wore on, one can only imagine the hollow shell of a car the Shelby GT would have become. Shelby left with all flags flying, renowned for having built some of the finest performance cars of the '60s.

Mustang not only gained a facelift for 1969, but also its own hot versions such as the Mach 1 and Boss 302/429. In addition, federal regulations governing exhaust emissions had begun to be enacted, all of which left little room for Shelby to improve upon Ford's offerings. Lacking the ability to make extensive mechanical changes, '69 Shelbys (both pages) instead leaned more toward visual differentiation, sporting a distinctive fiberglass front end in addition to the usual taillight modifications.

SPECIFICATIONS

Engines:	all ohv V-8;
	GT-350 351 cid (4.00 × 3.50), 290 bhp;
	GT-500 428 cid (4.13 × 3.98), 335 bhp

Transmissions:	4-speed manual;
	3-speed automatic optional

Suspension front:	upper and lower A-arms,
	coil springs

Suspension rear:	live axle, leaf springs

Brakes:	front disc/rear drum

Wheelbase (in.):	108.0

Weight (lbs):	3000-3200

Top speed (mph):	119-121

0-60 mph (sec):	5.5-8.0

Production: GT-350 fstbk 1085 **cvt** 194 **GT-500 fstbk** 1536 **cvt** 335

1960 Studebaker Lark

After 110 years, America's oldest builder of wheeled vehicles fled to Canada in 1963, then ceased building cars altogether three years later. Studebaker's demise was not unexpected. The firm had been through many downturns, rescue attempts, and relapses since the mid-'50s. By the mid-'60s, it was too far gone to save.

The troubles can be traced all the way back to the Great Depression, when Studebaker slipped into receivership. After rebounding strongly with the handsome, low-price 1939 Champion, the company enjoyed record production in the booming late-'40s seller's market by being "first by far with a postwar car." But that was both premature and costly, and Studebaker hung on to the design too long. Its all-new 1953 line, headed by the first of the now-coveted European-style "Loewy coupes," might have turned things around, but was hampered by marketing miscalculations, deteriorating workmanship, and a disintegrating dealer body. A desperate 1954 merger with Packard brought problems of its own. By 1958, increasingly unsalable products and fast-falling public confidence had brought Studebaker to the brink of extinction.

A reprieve came with the compact 1959 Lark, still the basic family Studebaker offered since '53, but shorn of the gross front/rear sheetmetal grafts applied since '55. Perfectly timed for the market's sudden swing to economy, the Lark gave Studebaker its first profit in five years. But the advent of Big Three compacts for 1960 and Studebaker's inability to keep the Lark sufficiently competitive caused sales to slide again. Studebaker had other products in this period, but the Hawk "family sports car" and the later high-performance Avanti were always low-volume sideliners. More comeback schemes followed and failed until financial backers gave up.

Predictably, the 1960 Larks were much like the debut '59s save for minor trim variations and a different grille insert (mesh replacing horizontal bars). Wheelbase remained at 108.5 inches except on wagons, which continued at 113 and again included four-doors (revived from '58) as well as two-doors. Engines were Studebaker's familiar but aging L-head six and ohv V-8. The former, a 169.6-cubic-inch "stroker," gave 90 bhp in Deluxe (meaning "standard") two- and four-door sedans and wagons, as well as the plusher Regal (meaning "deluxe") four-door sedan, hardtop coupe, and four-door wagon. Lark's V-8 (which originated in 1951) displaced 259 cubic inches, making 180 bhp in standard form or 195 with optional four-barrel carb and dual exhausts. Available in the same models as the six for about $280 more, the V-8 was standard for another 1960 newcomer, a pretty Regal convertible. Transmission choices were familiar fare: three-on-the-tree manual, the same with overdrive (with numerically higher rear axle ratio that helped performance, especially with the six), and three-speed self-shift Flight-O-Matic, courtesy of Borg-Warner. Prices were bumped up slightly from '59, but the spread remained highly attractive at $2000-$2700.

So did the cars. The ragtop Regal gave Studebaker an exclusive among 1960 compacts, though only for that year. Studebaker breathlessly extolled it as "the means to enjoy the Lark's marvelous maneuverability and stable agility while reveling in the light of refreshing breezes and warm sunshine."

On the more prosaic side, Lark construction was judged solid for a light, non-unitized car. *Speed Age* magazine found "very little body shake and no rattles or vibration," plus a ride it termed "excellent," thanks to a passenger compartment cradled firmly within the wheelbase (unlike that of the old-fashioned rival Rambler American). Handling was good with the six (badged "VI"), more responsive with the V-8 (labeled "VIII").

The same applied to performance. *Speed Age* timed a 180-bhp V-8 at a decidedly lively 9.9 seconds 0-60. The six was predictably less impressive, *Mechanix Illustrated*'s Tom McCahill reporting 16.8 seconds for the benchmark sprint, but revised carburetion, combustion chamber shape, and axle ratio made the 1960 six quieter and even thriftier. But the V-8 was no guzzler either. In fact, an automatic Lark bested 37 other V-8 cars in the 1959 Mobilgas Economy Run, averaging 22.38 mpg on a drive from Kansas City to Los Angeles.

Yet for all these strengths, the new Big Three competition had the benefit of more dealers and bigger advertising budgets, and they pitted all-new designs against the year-old Studebaker. As a result, Lark lost over 3300 sales from 1959, ending the 1960 model year at 127,715. But this was nothing compared to what lay ahead. Studebaker was again sliding toward oblivion, only this time, there would be nothing to stop it.

Both pages: Studebaker was saved (at least temporarily) by the compact Lark, which debuted in the midst of a recession. As a result, six-cylinder versions (Lark VI) outsold V-8s (Lark VIII), even after the economy turned around and people once again became interested in performance.

SPECIFICATIONS

Engines:	L-6, 169.6 cid (3.00 × 4.00), 90 bhp; ohv V-8, 259.2 cid (3.56 × 3.25), 180/195 bhp
Transmissions:	3-speed manual, manual w/overdrive, 3-speed Flight-O-Matic automatic
Suspension front:	upper and lower A-arms, coil springs
Suspension rear:	live axle on semi-elliptic leaf springs
Brakes:	front/rear drums
Wheelbase (in.):	113.0 wagons, 108.5 others
Weight (lbs):	2588-3183
Top speed (mph):	85-95
0-60 mph (sec):	9.9-17.0
Production:	Lark VI 70,153 Lark VIII 57,562

1960-61
Studebaker Hawk

While the honor of starting the "ponycar" craze has always been awarded to Ford's Mustang, Studebaker fans often claim the Hawk is the rightful originator. Indeed, if the "ponycar" is defined as a close-coupled 2+2 with a long hood and a short deck, a sporty interior, good performance, and a stick shift (preferably a four-speed), then the Studey "backers" surely have a case. The Hawk had all of those except the four-speed in 1960, and the four-speed was optional in 1961.

Like the Mustang, Hawks were powered by a 289-cid V-8, though it was hardly as advanced as Ford's light-weight, thin-wall design. But it must be remembered that Studebaker's 289 stemmed from the original Studebaker 232 V-8 first introduced in 1951. It weighed too much and leaked oil, but gave a Mustang-like combination of performance and economy.

But if Studebaker had a Mustang years before Ford, how come it didn't sell half a million copies? First, Ford's production capacity and dealer network were, by comparison to Studebaker's, gargantuan. Second, Hawks lacked the long list of options, from engines to upholstery, which made the Mustang all things to all people; you couldn't "tailor" a Hawk as a sports, luxury, or economy car the way you could a Mustang.

Finally, Studebaker's antiquated, high-overhead plant generally caused it to build cars priced $500 or so more than GM could have profitably sold them for. The 1960 Hawk was base priced at $2650, close to the "ideal" $2500 laid down by Lee Iacocca for the Mustang. But Iacocca set that figure for 1965, when inflation would have caused the '60 Hawk to sell for $2820. Even in 1960-61, by the time options such as radio, heater, and whitewalls were added, few Hawks were ever sold for less than $3000.

Finally, there's the fact that the public is ever-enchanted with what is "new." The average buyer could see, beneath the Hawk's classic grille and stylish tailfins, a body that had been around since 1953 as the "Loewy coupe." During 1960-61 it wasn't even the hardtop version of that famous shape. Harold Churchill, who stepped in to rescue Studebaker-Packard Corporation with the compact 1959 Lark, reportedly didn't even want to continue the Hawk series, and succeeded in paring it down from the original four models of 1956 to one in 1960-61. (There was a Hawk Six through 1959; after that year these were sold only in export markets.)

Despite its failings, the 1960 Studebaker Hawk remained a successful blend of sporty lines with performance and rugged construction. Still built on the longest wheelbase in the line—Loewy's famous "rubber frame" with its designed-in flex—it had graceful proportions and looked purposeful enough, even with the big, concave tailfins that had been grafted on in 1957. The coupe body with its sturdy B-pillars was a much tighter affair than the hardtop variation, which Studebaker had discarded in 1958. The '60 was also quicker than its immediate predecessor, Studebaker having readopted the 289 V-8 after using the 259 the year before. The 289 had 210 bhp in standard tune and 225 with the optional four-barrel carburetor and dual exhausts. Also available was a heavy-duty manual three-speed gearbox, oversize radiator, bigger clutch, and finned brake drums, all of which improved its roadability. Reclining seats and headrests were offered as well. In sum, the 1960 Hawk was the best one to date—refined, roadable, and quicker than any of its forebears save the supercharged Golden Hawks of 1957-58.

All Studebaker's emphasis was on the Lark, which had done well in the economy field, so Hawk production did not even begin until February 1960. Production for that year was therefore only 3939, yet the 1961 version saw even fewer (3340) copies.

Though it didn't sell any better than the '60, the 1961 Hawk was improved. Outwardly it was little different, but Studebaker's new four-speed floorshift Warner Gear transmission made the Hawk a genuine grand touring car. A 210-bhp four-speed Hawk would do 0-60 in about 11 seconds; the 225 bhp engine lowered this by a second and raised the top speed from 115 to about 120 mph. The '61 also offered contoured, deep-padded vinyl or cloth bucket seats, another step forward.

Studebaker published praise of the Hawk by every connoisseur who bought one, from Lucius Beebe to James Mason (all of whom curiously managed to get one of the first low serial numbers). It was well deserved, but did no good: the public continued to flock to Big Three sporty cars.

Though they look virtually identical at first glace, 1959-61 Hawk coupes are easy to tell apart. The '59s used a red background "eagle" badge; the '60s switched to black and added three small hash marks to the leading edge of the tailfin; the '61s deleted the hash marks and applied a color panel below the fins. All are attractive collector cars today, even if they don't enjoy the (rightful?) status of being the first "ponycar."

Studebaker's Hawk possessed a combination of performance and luxury that should have made it quite popular, but it never was. By 1960 (opposite page) only a pillared coupe was offered, its previous (and better-looking) hardtop coupe stablemate having been dropped in 1958. The '61 (above) was little changed in appearance save for altered side trim below the tailfins, but a four-speed manual joined the option list along with bucket seats to replace the previous bench.

SPECIFICATIONS

Engines:	ohv V-8, 289 cid (3.56 × 3.63), 210/225 bhp
Transmissions:	3-speed manual; 4-speed manual, 3-speed Flight-O-Matic automatic optional
Suspension front:	upper and lower A-arms, coil springs
Suspension rear:	live axle, leaf springs
Brakes:	front/rear drums
Wheelbase (in.):	120.5
Weight (lbs):	3205
Top speed (mph):	115-120
0-60 mph (sec):	10-11
Production:	**1960** 3939 **1961** 3340

1961-63
Studebaker Lark

Nobody likes a loser, which explains why Studebaker died after 1966. As sales dwindled after 1960, so did public confidence, which further depressed sales and meant less money for devising more salesworthy products—the classic downward spiral that had nearly claimed Studebaker in 1956-58. Though the compact '59 Lark temporarily reversed this slide, it didn't generate sufficient profits to fund the all-new family car that Studebaker should have delivered to better compete with Big Three compacts. Ominously, Lark volume fell by more than half for 1961 despite worthy changes to the basic 1959-60 design.

Prime among them was revised outer sheetmetal imparting a slightly squarer look, enhanced by a lowered hood and rear deck, plus quad headlights on V-8 models. Sedans and hardtops also sported flatter rooflines with reshaped rear quarters. Still, all Larks remained unfashionably stubby.

The major mechanical news was a six-cylinder engine reworked with overhead valves. Despite no displacement change from the old side-valver, this "Skybolt Six" delivered over 24 percent more horsepower—112 versus 90—and 6.2 percent more torque, which improved 0-60 performance by some three seconds to around 14 flat. But the Skybolt suffered frequent cracks between valve seats, and warranty claims not only strained Studebaker's cash reserves but further dulled its already tarnished image.

Image was behind the addition of the V-8 Cruiser sedan for '61. Reviving the traditional "luxury Studebaker" idea, it rode the longer 113-inch wagon wheelbase, which gave extra rear leg room to its extra-rich interior. Yet price was a reasonable $2458, making Cruiser the fourth costliest '61 model after the Regal convertible and wagons.

Studebaker got a new president in early '61: the dynamic Sherwood Egbert, recruited from McCulloch Corporation. Soon after taking the helm, Egbert asked Milwaukee-based industrial designer Brooks Stevens to rework both the Lark and the sporty Hawk on a six-month crash basis for 1962. Company styling chief Randall Faurot stepped aside, and Stevens conjured remarkably effective facelifts on a tight $7-million budget. "On the face of it, the job was impossible," Stevens later recalled. "But Sherwood wasn't an automobile man. He didn't know it was impossible."

Delivering his assigned miracle on time, Stevens gave the '62 Larks longer rear quarters that added nine to 13 inches overall, plus round taillights, a Mercedes-like grille (Studebaker had been the North American Mercedes-Benz distributor since 1958), and crisper non-wagon superstructures. Two-door wagons vanished, but there were four new Daytona models: six and V-8 convertible and hardtop offering bucket seats and deluxe trim for about $90 more than equivalent Regals. A Borg-Warner T-10 four-on-the-floor transmission joined the option list and was perfect for Daytona, which was chosen to pace that year's "Indy 500." Despite a 38-day strike, Lark sales rebounded to 93,000—up 40 percent from '61—and Studebaker made a modest $2.56 million. It would be the last profit South Bend ever earned.

Stevens further updated the Lark for 1963, straightening A-pillars, reshaping windshields, thinning window frames, changing rooflines again, substituting a fine-checked grille, and adding a new dash with round gauges and a "vanity" glove box with pop-up mirror. Also new, and very novel, was the "Wagonaire." Offered in Standard, Regal, and Daytona form, it boasted a sliding rear-roof panel that afforded unlimited "head room" for hauling tall loads. Unfortunately, Wagonaires leaked badly even when closed, which explains why fixed-roof companions reappeared during the year. Further expanding the line were six and V-8 sedans in Standard and nicer Custom trim, the latter priced between Regal and Daytona.

But the most surprising '63 development was the midseason arrival of two "Avanti" V-8 options from Studebaker's suave new GT coupe. Based on the proven 289, they comprised a 240-bhp four-barrel R1 and 290-bhp Paxton-supercharged R2, both with special cams and stronger bearings. Combined with both engines was a four-speed manual transmission or heavy-duty automatic, heavy-duty suspension, and new power front-disc brakes. Dubbed "Super Lark," either package made for a flat-out bomb. *Car Life*, testing an automatic R1, clocked 0-60 in 7.8 seconds, the standing quarter-mile in 15.8 seconds at 90 mph, and 123 mph flat-out. An R2 prepped by Andy Granatelli of Paxton Products (then owned by Studebaker) did over 132 mph at Bonneville.

Yet for all this, model-year sales dropped below 75,000, leaving Studebaker ahead of only Lincoln and Imperial in the industry rankings. Egbert, who'd been repeatedly hospitalized, left in November 1963, never to return. (He would die of cancer in 1969.) A month later, new president Byers Burlingame announced the closure of Studebaker's historic South Bend plant after failed last-ditch efforts to obtain financing for future models. Within two years, Studebaker would be gone.

This page, top and opposite page, top: The car that saved Studebaker in 1959-60 received a slight facelift for '61, but the miracle would not be repeated due to increased competition in the compact market from the Big Three. More radical styling changes marked the '62s (this page, middle) which fared a little better, but from this point on, it was all down hill. From 93,000 in '62, production of the near-identical '63s (above and opposite page, bottom) dropped to less than 75,000.

SPECIFICATIONS

Engines:	ohv I-6, 169.6 cid (3.00 × 4.00), 112 bhp; ohv V-8, 259.2 cid (3.56 × 3.25), 180/195 bhp; 289 cid, (3.56 × 3.63), 210/225/240/290 bhp
Transmissions:	3-speed manual, manual w/overdrive, 4-speed manual, 3-speed Flight-O-Matic automatic
Suspension front:	upper and lower A-arms, coil springs
Suspension rear:	live axle on semi-elliptic leaf springs
Brakes:	front/rear drums
Wheelbase (in.):	109.0 2d, 113.0 others
Weight (lbs):	2650-3490
Top speed (mph):	95-123+
0-60 mph (sec):	7.8-14.0

Production: 1961 Lark VI 41,035 **Lark VIII** 25,934 **1962 Lark Six** 54,397 **Lark Eight** 38,607 **1963** 74,201

1962-64
Studebaker Gran
Turismo Hawk

Studebaker's 1962 GT Hawk bore perhaps the most brilliant facelift of the decade. Furthermore, it was created on a pauper's budget by Brooks Stevens Design at the behest of young Sherwood Egbert, the whiz from McCulloch who became president of Studebaker in early 1961 and set about trying to save the company. Unlike Harold Churchill, Egbert liked sports cars; he drove a Mercedes 300SL Gullwing when he wasn't trying a Studebaker. Egbert asked Stevens if he could reskin both the Lark and Hawk with a minuscule $7-million tooling budget—and somehow, Stevens managed to pull it off.

The Lark was improved in the process, but the Hawk was transformed. Shorn of its aging tailfins, fitted with a crisp, T-Bird-like roofline and smooth flanks edged in chrome like the Lincoln Continental, it was remarkably beautiful, and ingeniously cheap to build. For instance, its inset rear window gave it a crisp, unique appearance—but also ducked the expense of tooling a fully wrapped backlight. A "dummy grille" on the rear deck panel was right in style—but it also covered up the old "rib" pattern that had been around since 1956. Bright metal came off the sides, though a stainless steel ribbed rocker panel was placed along the wheelbase.

The front end was also ultra-clean. Stevens specified painted rather than chromed headlamp rims but didn't get them until 1963 (chrome ones were in large supply). He *did* get a more "classic" grille, with a heavy chrome collar giving it a realistic look, though it was a stamped unit instead of die-cast as before. Stevens eliminated the previous chromed hood scoop and grille mesh in the side openings; he wanted, but did not get, new wheel covers to help transform the car's looks, but the old 1961 covers were still around and the company wanted to use them up.

Brooks Stevens said the GT's dash was "a real achievement, with a three-plane instrument panel angling the gauges toward the driver. To the right of the instruments we put in perforated metal, to give the illusion and psychological effect of airiness, and repeated the theme in the door panels. This also hid the radio speaker. None of these features were used by any competitor at the time, though the dash came into vogue later at Ford and GM." The perforated theme was continued in the white vinyl headliner, set off by stainless ribs imitating convertible bows.

Wearing a deft facelift that trimmed the fins from the '56-'61 design, the 1962 GT Hawk (above, below, and opposite page, top) was a luxury sports coupe in the Thunderbird vein, but cost $1000 less. Little changed for '63. The '64s (opposite page, bottom) gained a smooth lower trunklid to replace the fake rear grille used previously, but little else. By this time, sales were down to less than 2000, and the model didn't return for '65.

SPECIFICATIONS

Engines:	ohv V-8, 289 (3.56 × 3.63), 210/225 bhp; **R1** 240 bhp; **R2** 290 bhp;
Transmissions:	3-speed manual; overdrive, 4-speed manual, 3-speed automatic optional
Suspension front:	upper and lower A-arms, coil springs
Suspension rear:	live axle, leaf springs
Brakes:	front/rear drums; front discs optional
Wheelbase (in.):	120.5
Weight (lbs):	3120-3280
Top speed (mph):	105-110+
0-60 mph (sec):	6.7-11
Production:	**1962** 9335 **1963** 4634 **1964** 1767

GT modifications for 1963 were minor. The grille had a checkerboard pattern similar to that of the '63 Lark; side openings were closed up with the fake grilles that Stevens didn't like; round, amber parking lights were installed. Inside, the dash was fully woodgrained, and pleated vinyl seats replaced the poor-wearing ribbed vinyl variety. Suggesting its continental flair, the 1963 GT Hawk had small red, white, and blue tricolor badges on doors and grille; the rear deck overlay was reversed, giving it less the appearance of a rear grille and more the look of a decoration.

Studebaker's South Bend factory closed its doors at the end of 1963, after building only 1767 of the final 1964 GT Hawks. These cars have become quite desirable for their rarity, and their status as the last of a distinguished breed.

The deft changes to the 1964 GT also made it the most sophisticated of the three years. On the outside, Stevens created a landau look with an optional vinyl topping for the forward section of the roof. At the rear he eliminated the deck overlay by finally retooling the age-old decklid, giving it a smooth, less-contrived appearance. The GT gained more glitter: chrome taillight housings, an "S-in-circle" hood ornament and a Hawk emblem for the grille. Inside, the dash went from woodgrain to matte black.

This final GT Hawk received the same good press as its predecessors, and rightly so: it was a good, comfortable, high-speed cruiser with appealing features, a raft of instruments, luxury upholstery, and neat styling. One tester squeezed out 0-60 in 6.7 seconds with a Hawk R2 (the optional Avanti engine), and did 0-90 in under 14. At the same time, this very car was returning up to 16 mpg fuel economy—quite remarkable.

Although Brooks Stevens had proposed an all-new GT Hawk for 1965, Studebaker's departure from South Bend in late 1963 squelched it. Though it could hardly have saved Studebaker no matter how good it was, it surely would have been a memorable car—like its predecessors.

GT seats were buckets with cloth or vinyl inserts; recliners were optional. The 210 bhp 289 was standard, the 225 optional; as in the past, some export Hawks used six-cylinder engines. Other options included Borg-Warner four-speed, overdrive, air conditioning, and power windows/steering/brakes. Typical GTs would do about 105 mph (110 with the 225 engine), and 0-60 in about 11 seconds with the automatic, a hair less with the four-speed.

Unfortunately, this lovely car sold only 9335 units in 1962. Buyers were becoming convinced that Studebaker was not going to survive, and sales resistance multiplied almost as fast as Studebaker dealers jumped ship for other franchises. The 1963 GT Hawk, altered in detail, was on balance a better car, but it sold only 4634 copies including about 1000 in Canada and overseas.

1963-64
Studebaker Avanti

While he had Brooks Stevens working on emergency updates of the Lark and Hawk, Studebaker president Sherwood Egbert called in Raymond Loewy to design a new generation of Studebaker passenger cars. Loewy, who hadn't worked for Studebaker since 1956, jumped in with enthusiasm, promising Egbert a sporting coupe of revolutionary design, from which a complete line of family cars would evolve. Studebaker quit before the family cars were finished, but Loewy did give Egbert one brief shining moment with the memorable Avanti.

Designed in seclusion by Loewy's talented team of Bob Andrews, Tom Kellogg, and John Ebstein, the Avanti (the Italian word for "Forward") was a styling sensation. A coke-bottle waist formed the base for a thin-section roof with a huge rear window and a built-in rollbar. Razor-edged front fenders swept back into the curved rear, then into a jacked-up tail. Loewy threw out the conventional grille, putting an air scoop under a thin front bumper, and an asymmetrical hump in the hood. Inside, ample crash padding was combined with four slim-section vinyl bucket seats and an aircraft-style control panel. The whole package was accepted for production with hardly any changes from Loewy's small scale model.

For reasons of cost and time, Studebaker decided to build the Avanti's body out of fiberglass. It would need a stout platform, so chief engineer Gene Hardig took a beefy Lark convertible frame, shortened and modified it, and fitted anti-sway bars and rear radius rods. The Bendix disc brakes used on the Avanti (as well as some Larks and Hawks) were the first caliper discs in domestic production. The engine was the best V-8 Studebaker had, the faithful 289, which developed 240 bhp in standard ("R1") tune thanks to a ¾ race high-lift cam, dual-breaker distributor, four-barrel carb, and dual exhausts. Andy Granatelli and Paxton also developed a supercharged "R2" with 290 bhp, and a bored-out 304.5-cid version in three higher stages of tune: R3, R4, and R5. Only nine supercharged R3s were built (with a claimed 335 bhp), and the R4 (unsupercharged) and R5 were experimental. The latter had two Paxton superchargers, one for each cylinder bank, magneto ignition, and Bendix fuel injection. It developed an incredible 575 horsepower.

The Avanti had a remarkably slippery shape, even though Loewy had not had time for wind tunnel testing—he just guessed! In late 1962, Granatelli broke 29 Bonneville speed records with an Avanti R3, traveling faster than anyone had before in a stock American car.

Unfortunately, Studebaker failed to deliver Avantis to dealers fast enough to satisfy the initial wave of orders. Unexpected distortion during the fiberglass curing process accounted partly for the delay, forcing the firm to add its own fiberglass body facility. By the time all the bugs were out, most of the customers who'd placed advance orders had given up and bought Corvettes or imports. Fewer than 4600 Avantis were produced during 1963. Production had already ceased by the time Studebaker stopped car production in South Bend in December 1963. Despite slow sales, Studebaker made numerous detail changes to the Avanti beginning as early as July 1962. Officially the car was "not designated by model year, but incorporates changes whenever appropriate." The only determination of dating was the registration date, which designates 809 Avantis as 1964 models. A rule of thumb, though not exactly accurate, is the square-bezel headlamp style, which appeared along with most detail changes in August 1963 for the "1964" models. But Studebaker's first announcement was that these were optional, and some round headlight cars were registered as '64s. Other August alterations included a new grille for the radiator scoop (negating some of Loewy's original thinking), chrome drip moldings above the doors, restyled parking lights, and smooth vinyl upholstery as standard (instead of smooth or perforated at the buyer's option). All Avantis were very fully equipped. The list of standard equipment included a high-output generator, three ashtrays, backup lights, 60 amp/hour battery, chrome engine parts, heater-defroster, clock, center console, internal trunk and hood releases, courtesy and trunk lamps, padded sun visors, tinted glass, and two-speed (later variable-speed) electric windshield wipers.

When Studebaker abandoned the Avanti after 1964, two partners in a Studebaker dealership, Leo Newman and Nathan Altman, purchased the manufacturing rights. They formed the Avanti Motor Corporation (see separate entry) and resumed building the car in an abandoned Studebaker plant, thus reviving one of the decade's great designs.

This page: Fiberglass-bodied '63 Avanti boasted a rakish design and an interior that looks modern even today. The '64s (opposite page) were little changed, though most had square headlight bezels.

SPECIFICATIONS

Engines:	• all ohv V-8;
	1963-64 289 cid (3.56 × 3.63), 240/290 bhp;
	1964 304.5 cid (3.65 × 3.63), 335 bhp

Transmissions:	4-speed manual; 3-speed automatic optional
Suspension front:	upper and lower A-arms, coil springs
Suspension rear:	live axle leaf springs
Brakes:	front disc/rear drum
Wheelbase (in.):	109.0
Weight (lbs):	3140-3195
Top speed (mph):	115-120
0-60 mph (sec):	7.0-8.0
Production:	1963 3834 1964 809

1964-66 Studebaker

Some of the best postwar Studebakers were built in South Bend and Canada for 1964. None sold well because by 1963, virtually everybody was convinced that Studebaker was going out of business, as indeed it did. The Canadian operation declared it was in business to stay, but lacked the long-range research and development teams to contemplate a lengthy life in the automobile business.

Studebaker began the year promoting the availability of Avanti engines in its passenger cars. Since only one non-Avanti with an R3 engine was built (a Commander; nine more were Avantis, one was a GT Hawk), its performance figures are academic; but a road test indicates 0-60 in 7.3 seconds and the standing quarter mile in 15.8 seconds at 90 mph. R2s were sold in greater quantity and were equally impressive. All these high performance specials were dropped after the move to Canada, however.

Brooks Stevens was given little in the way of monetary resources to facelift the 1964 Studebakers, but he used it well. The sedans were all new from the cowl forward, with lower hood and fenders sharply uplifted at the outer edges, a neat trapezoidal grille, and stand-up "S-in-circle" hood ornament. Daytonas and Cruisers had dual headlamps, while cheaper models used single lamps. Stevens made few changes to the rest of the car; the roof he revised again, adding simulated convertible top bows, and at the rear he grafted a pointed panel to the top of the deck, containing arrow-shaped nacelles in its extremities for taillights and backup lights. This section was left plain on inexpensive models, trimmed brightly on Daytonas and Cruisers. Notably, the Lark name was hardly seen. "I convinced management to deemphasize the Lark, which had its own connotations," said Stevens.

With car production centered entirely in Hamilton, Ontario, an abbreviated line of Sixes and Eights made up the 1965 Studebakers—Hawk and Avanti production had ceased. No styling changes were made at all. Continuing a slogan from 1964, Hamilton hailed its '65s as "The Common-Sense Cars [which do not] need yearly

Both pages: *Despite Studebaker's ominous outlook and dwindling sales, the '64 models received a redesigned front end and facelifted rear. Interiors were nicely laid out with round instruments, and higher-line models featured reclining front seatbacks.*

styling changes. The money saved is passed on to you, in added comfort and quality, and in continuing engineering improvements. And, because Studebaker styling won't become obsolete, your car will look new year after year." It didn't become obsolete, all right. It just ended.

Actually there was a considerable difference under the skin. When South Bend quit building cars, it also quit building engines. The Canadian plant, therefore, turned to General Motors. GM duly provided the Chevrolet 194-cid six and 283-cid V-8, renamed the Skybolt Six and Thunderbolt V-8 for the occasion. Both were sound engines, the 283 one of the finest small-block V-8s ever assembled. The Six, at 120 bhp, offered a power increase from the unlamented Studebaker engine it replaced.

The Canadian factory was small—on average, it had built only about 7000 Studebakers a year when it was a subsidiary of the South Bend company. But Hamilton, under the leadership of general manager Gordon Grundy, managed to put out close to 20,000 '65 models, slightly better than half of which went to the United States.

On schedule in the autumn, Grundy released the 1966 Studebakers, last of the breed. They used the same old bodies, but had detail styling changes by a Detroit industrial design firm, Marcks, Hazelquist, Powers Inc. All-new front-end styling included single multi-beam headlamps, and a new grille with four rectangular panels and the old Hawk medallion in the center. Side moldings were repositioned, while a new rear panel carried ventilation extractors built in above the taillights, which were where the backup lights had been in 1965 (the backups were now set down lower). "Refreshaire" was the name given to this flow-through ventilation system, which was quite effective. Split-back reclining front seats and transistor ignition were standard on Daytonas; automatic, power steering, and disc brakes were optional. Daytonas continued to offer vinyl roofs, rear center armrest, padded sun visors, non-glare windshield wiper arms, dual master cylinder, padded instrument panel, two-speed wipers with washers, parking brake warning light, safety door latches, and seatbelts as standard. All models had aluminized rustproofing, which was probably the most refined anti-rust treatment a Studebaker had ever received, and had long needed.

Fewer than 9000 of the 1966 models were built, after which Studebaker production stopped forever—a sad end to America's oldest manufacturer of wheeled vehicles, which began producing covered wagons in 1852, and automobiles in 1902.

SPECIFICATIONS

Engines:	ohv I-6; **1964** 169.6 cid (3.00 × 4.00), 112 bhp; **1965-66** 194 cid (3.56 × 3.25), 120 bhp; ohv V-8; **1964** 259.2 cid (3.56 × 3.25), 180/195 bhp; 289 cid (3.56 × 3.63), 210-290 bhp; **1965-66** 283 cid (3.88 × 3.00), 195 bhp
Transmissions:	3-speed manual; overdrive, 3-speed automatic optional
Suspension front:	upper and lower A-arms, coil springs
Suspension rear:	live axle, leaf springs
Brakes:	front/rear drums; front discs optional
Wheelbase (in.):	2d 109.0 **others** 113.0
Weight (lbs):	2660-3555
Top speed (mph):	NA
0-60 mph (sec):	NA
Production:	**1964** 44,184 **1965** 19,435 **1966** 8947

This page, top and left: The 1965 Studebakers looked virtually identical to the '64s, though they were no longer motivated by Studebaker power. Engines were built at the South Bend, Indiana, factory, so when it closed down, Studebaker turned to Chevrolet for 194-cid sixes and 283-cid V-8s. A facelift marked the '66 models (above and opposite page), which would be Studebaker's last. Fewer than 9000 were built.

INDEX